AMONG FRIENDS

PERSONAL LETTERS OF DEAN ACHESON

AMONG FRIENDS

PERSONAL LETTERS OF
DEAN ACHESON,

Gooderham *(handwritten)*

1893-1971 *(handwritten)*

EDITED BY

David S. McLellan

AND

David C. Acheson

DODD, MEAD & COMPANY
NEW YORK

1   2   3   4   5   6   7   8   9   10

Library of Congress Cataloging in Publication Data

Acheson, Dean Gooderham, 1893-1971.
Among friends.

Includes index.
1. Acheson, Dean Gooderham, 1893-1971.
2. Statesmen—United States—Correspondence.
I. McLellan, David S. II. Acheson, David C.
III. Title.
E748.A15A27   973.918′092′4   79-24127
ISBN 0-396-07721-8

CONTENTS

C.1

FOREWORD

This book is the editors' selection from the letters that Dean Acheson wrote to friends, associates, members of his family, and, in a few cases, to strangers. Those to Felix Frankfurter go back to 1919 when Frankfurter was a professor at The Harvard Law School and Acheson was "secretary," in the parlance of that day, to Louis D. Brandeis, then an Associate Justice of the Supreme Court. Many of these letters were written with a spirit of gaiety and humor, some with somber reflection, all with wit and penetration. The selection includes letters to his former chief, Harry S Truman, which show the deepening of their affinity and mutual respect as they both continued in active political roles after they had left public office.

It is important to say what these letters do *not* purport to be. Those of Acheson's papers that constitute his own records and correspondence from his tours of public service were left by his will to The Harry S Truman Library in Independence, Missouri, so that scholars would have access to them for research into the circumstances surrounding his official acts. The editors have not attempted to work that mine of materials, except for a small quantity of personal correspondence that was found there, since they could not in a reasonable compass of time and space attempt both a compilation of historical papers and a more personal character delineation that is afforded by a strictly private correspondence.

The purpose of these selections is not to tell a story or to "scoop" history, but to bring out the spirit and principles which guided Acheson's outlook upon the people and events in his life. The letters of the early years show him evolving his philosophy and values in response to his exposure to

Holmes and Brandeis, a little later in response to the economic crisis of the 1930s and the New Deal. His development as a lawyer and his wartime service as Assistant Secretary of State are punctuated, if not traced, by letters of the '30s and '40s.

Many of the letters to his family draw upon his keen sense of the comic and bizarre, a quality which helped him to surmount the crises, large and small, of his public and private life.

The letters of the period after 1953 are those of a keen and experienced observer of a succession of political men and events. As critic or counsellor or participant, sometimes as all three, Acheson writes candidly about Eisenhower, Dulles, Stevenson, Kennedy, Johnson, Nixon, and many other figures of the 1953–1971 period. Outspoken as he was in his letters of the 1950s and 1960s, many of the letters for that period, especially to his family and close friends, reflect an inability to take himself too seriously. They reflect zest for life, for the use of the mind, and for the comedy of the human species. They are filled with strategems for avoiding ennui. Above all, they reflect unceasing concern for the life of the republic and the objectives that Acheson sought to defend and sustain.

Some of the letters from Acheson's later life reflect amusement at the criticisms of him for being a "hard-liner" or "cold warrior," amusement because of the reversal of opinion from an earlier day. He waves off the new school of critics with the same sardonic wit with which he dismissed earlier critics such as Joe McCarthy and Robert Taft. Issues about which he felt seriously are argued with powerful force from well-designed philosophic strong points. Letters on lighter matters give full expression to Acheson's belief that life should be lived for what it may hold of fun, and are his own contribution to that end.

The editors' mode of presentation is to minimize explanation and interpolation, and to let Acheson speak for himself. They supply notes only where information essential to understanding is otherwise absent so that to the greatest practicable extent Acheson and the reader are left to themselves. They have corrected obvious misspellings and superficial or typographical errors. Throughout the notes Acheson will be referred to by the initials "DA."

Many of DA's letters were written longhand. The editors have not sought to reproduce DA's hand or to differentiate between longhand and typed material. His longhand letters were often notably informal in syntax, in the style of abbreviation and in terseness of expression, characteristics which will appear in type without further explanation or apology.

The editors wish to acknowledge their gratitude to the many friends of Dean Acheson, and to members of his family, who graciously gave access to his letters to them. The editors are grateful to Miss Barbara Evans, who was most helpful in collecting Acheson's files and resolving archival mysteries, and to the Library of Congress Manuscript Division, The Harry S Truman Library, The John F. Kennedy Library, The Franklin D. Roosevelt Library, and the Yale University Library (Manuscripts and Archives) for their helpful assistance.

DAVID S. MCLELLAN
DAVID C. ACHESON

PART

I

1918–1952

To **FELIX FRANKFURTER**

DA was serving in the Navy at the end of World War I and was preoccupied with plans for his career as a lawyer. He had graduated from The Harvard Law School in 1917 and married, in the same year, Alice Stanley of Detroit, Michigan. In this letter to Felix Frankfurter, a professor at The Harvard Law School, DA adverts to the possibility (which was realized) of becoming "secretary" to Louis D. Brandeis, then Associate Justice on the Supreme Court of the United States. Apparently DA had discussed the matter with Frankfurter whom, with Harold Laski (the British teacher and writer), DA had recently seen.

New York
December 9, 1918

Dear Mr. Frankfurter:

It was very good to see you the other evening if only for a moment. To hear you and Laski again was spring after this dreary Naval winter. But I hope that the end of it is in sight even though not within reach in the words of Mr. Lloyd George's optimistic indefiniteness. We are hoping to be discharged in March at the earliest and in June at the latest. Then comes the situation about which I need your advice. There is no need to tell you the sort of work on which my heart is set. But the great difficulty to me is how to start in order to get into the center of it before my three score are over. There seem to be so many blind alleys.

When you asked me on Friday what I wanted to do I spoke at once of

1

going to Mr. Brandeis. My enthusiasm for that has not abated since its inception. But you know more of the work than I do and whether I am justified in doing it. I cannot look back from the plow once I have really started now and I cannot afford even the unusual association with a great man if after a year it leaves me as comparatively unfit for what I want to do as I am now. This is largely a contradiction in terms and there is probably very little in it. Even though I cannot be Chancellor of the Exchequer at twenty-three, I should hate to be still uttering amiable generalities at sixty. But here, of course, your advice can easily settle the matter.

You do not know how a letter from you would help to clear away the confusion of my thoughts. For one without experience the decision between paths, when the object is any except making money, is the most hopeless prospect to be encountered.

I shall look forward eagerly to hearing from you. As my wife has decided to move to parts unknown after Xmas the above address alone is stable.

Most cordially yours,

To JOHN H. VINCENT

John H. Vincent was one of a coterie of Yale men whom DA knew there and at The Harvard Law School. "W.M.E." was Walker Ellis, a law-school classmate from New Orleans. In this letter DA speculates about law teaching, mentioning the University of Chicago where Vincent's father taught. The reference to "my book" is to DA's manuscript on labor relations and the law, at that time a subject not much developed and highly controversial. "Pound" was Roscoe Pound, an influential professor and dean of The Harvard Law School. "Jane" was DA's first child, born the preceding February. "Laura" (for Lawrason) Riggs was a Roman Catholic cleric who later had a long and distinguished association with Yale. "The Judge" was Associate Justice Louis D. Brandeis. "Arch" was Archibald MacLeish.

Supreme Court of the United States
Washington, D.C.
December 5, 1919

Dear John:

Nolo contendere the accusations which you bring against me. But my failure was not due to lack of appreciation of your letter from the steamer. Procrastination gathers momentum and finally bowls over the stoutest resolution as though it were no more than the fourteenth point.

I am glad that you are taking Jurisprudence. You thought that I was somewhat of a damn fool about it last year—you know that there was some excuse for the leaning toward Poundianism. I wish that we could have a chance to talk over the whole business;—and also the rumors that I hear of your going to New York. You would have been amused here the other day—speaking of Jurisprudence—to have heard the three hour monologue that Justice Holmes gave me. Stan arranged an appointment for me on a good rainy day when the old man was in wonderful form and had nothing to do but blow off steam. I felt like a Hindoo getting his first glimpse of the sacred river when it was in full flood. He began with a full review of the characters of all the men he had ever known on the bench—Peckham, for instance, was a great judge, with just the right proportion of Mephistopholes about him; he approached every question with the major premise of "God damn it." Then he reminisced about Emerson and all his father's gang, and finally launched forth on an exposition of his philosophy. The pearls fell so fast that I could only gather a few and some of the biggest got away. He got off one metaphor which I thought very good. He was talking of man's idea of his place in the universe. "Yes," he said, "we are the leaders of the whole stream of life. We lead it in the same sense that small boys lead a circus parade when they march ahead of it. But if they turn down a side street the parade goes on."

There were lots of things like—"A feeling of responsibility is a confession of weakness." "At the outset of our philosophy we take the supreme act of faith—we conclude that we are not God." "This little artichoke of a life, in which we pull off a leaf of twenty-four hours and find at most one wretched little hour when we are there with both feet." "In literature, history, religion, science, law, philosophy, everything that is over twenty-five years old is dead." (This last is part of his theory of life as a wave which moves without carrying on the particles which make it up.)

Then the next day Laura Riggs came to dinner and afterwards began to discourse on his Catholic "philosophy," the scholastics, whom he thinks are right down the mousehole of truth, and declaring that Kant was muddle-headed. . . . I don't mind people insisting that they have god up their sleeve, but it makes me rather ill when they demand that it must follow that no one else has any sleeves at all. Also any one who says that the admission that you may after all be wrong is the "supreme blasphemy, which negatives the possibility of progress"—really, how can I do more than feed him peanuts of heresy to make him ill or poke him to watch him wiggle.

December 17, 1919

When I began this letter I hoped to conclude it with plans for seeing you at Christmas. But the doctor seems to regard Jane's ambitions to travel as premature and will have none of them. So we stay here and have

Christmas dinner with the Justice. Lawrason's picture of you in glorious isolation in Warren Hastings without even the furniture included in minimum wage computations has greatly stirred my imagination. Pound beating upon such an anvil ought to have done something more than even the best of sparks. It makes me wish very much that I might see you and have a talk about things in general.

December 27, 1919

I shall get this off today though the juristic fabric of the Nation fall in ruins. The period of working day, night and holidays is over for a time,—for which the Lord be praised. I hear that in the New York movies they hissed the Justice for ten minutes after the Prohibition case. However, if there ever was a man who didn't give a damn whether he is approved, applauded, hissed, or cursed, it is the Judge. So everyone is happy.

I have about come to the conclusion that the best thing for me to do with my three score and ten—with luck—is to teach the law and to perform the functions which seem more and more to be connected with that vocation. Last summer Swan at Yale had a talk with me on the subject. He seemed interested but very cautious and, not unreasonably wanted to see Pound, hear from the Justice after he had had a chance to look me over, and find out whether my book was to be published in Moscow. I was to let him know if I still wanted to consider the matter along in the winter and think that I shall do so after a bit. The Judge very delightfully wants me to stay another year, so I have a certain feeling of independence in entering the negotiations. If he wants any recantations I shall pleasantly tell him to go to hell. What do you think of the idea? It is chiefly determined by the Judge's advice.

The other day he had Alice and me to dinner to meet Graham Wallas, who is without doubt one of the world's best. He had a long talk with me after dinner on the possibility of a book along psychological examination of the law—not in the form of "explanation" as the "Psychological Stage" in Sociological jurisprudence but more as a critique. He got me very much interested indeed, gave me a list of books to read as a starter, and sent me off on a long and perhaps doubtful argosy. I am very anxious to do some work in psychology in the summer if I can find the coincidence of a good man, a climate which is possible for the family, and place to live. You ought to be able to answer this.

Further in re teaching:—I have written Dean Bates of Michigan and asked Arch to look into Chicago while he is at home. What are these places like? I mean are they dominated by spark-plug manufacturers and oily Baptists, i.e., is there apt to be a white terror (the last is obviously an unhappy slip, isn't it?) If your father would express himself within the bounds of discretion, I should deem it (that word comes from writing decisions) of great value.

This is a wretched letter, I know. Next time I shall write at home. But be charitable and let me hear from you. Alice and Jane, who is a regular sea-lion, would send love if they knew I was writing you. By the way, do you know whether I have done anything to be ruined with W.M.E.? After a note asking me to write him I did my best, and the result is silence.

As ever,

To FELIX FRANKFURTER

DA stayed a second year with Justice Brandeis. In writing of this decision to Frankfurter, DA reflected a degree of restlessness to become involved in labor work. "Mr. Bates" was Dean Bates of the University of Michigan Law School. William Hard was a friend of DA. The other names occurring in the next two letters were those of various employment contacts which DA was exploring.

January 20, 1920

Dear Mr. Frankfurter:

I have about decided to accept the Justice's invitation to stay with him another year. Yesterday he told me that it was still open and that he would like me to stay if I thought it best. But I do not want to say the final fatal word until I have heard from you, Mr. Bates, and seen Mr. Frederick C. Howe when he returns from New York.

In the first place, have you heard anything from Mr. Walker? I got his address from the Dept. of Labor and sent your letter off a few days after you were here. Mr. William Hard whom I have seen several times to talk over the matter says that plenty of time to become thoroughly acquainted with the field is of the essence in the labor movement. He is rather in favor of my staying with the Justice another year and getting an idea, if possible, who's who and why.

Out of courtesy to Mr. Bates who has been more than kind and interested in my troubles I don't want to finally decide until he has had a chance to comment upon it. I wrote him yesterday and should hear before the week is out. I feel rather selfish taking someone's chance to be with the Justice for a year. It will have to go down on the debit side of my moral transactions to be justified perhaps some time in the future. If you have a moment to spare—which is an assumption wholly unsupported by fact—will you let me know what you think of my staying on another year. It's rather hard on the Justice but it is wonderful for my habit of rather demurring to detail.

Please give my kindest regards to Mrs. Frankfurter. Both Mrs. Hard and my wife have expressed determination that you shall not spirit Mrs. Frankfurter through Washington again without their having joint or several tea with her.

January 22, 1920

Dear Mr. Frankfurter:

I have "bet my soul," as Judge Holmes says that he would have said if he hadn't been in court, on what it would be boasting to call imperfect knowledge. It is blank ignorance. But "when common sense and expediency have found a way it is idle to wander in the by-paths of logic." I am going to stay with the Justice another year.

In the meantime I am trying to get to know people in the Labor Movement, and also get myself in a position to be more useful to them a year from October than I am now. The Rock Island people have already had me in to talk over some of their troubles and draft letters for them to the Secretary of War, and Hard has given me a letter to one Lord of the Mining Division of the A.F. of L., and Louis Waley to some of the Plumb people. Will you let me know if you hear of Mr. Walker coming East so that I may have a chance to remind him that I am in line for a job some day. I shall write Mr. Kerr, tell him the situation and hope that I can keep up some touch with his organization through the next year. On the whole I am rather surprised and encouraged at my budding common sense in staying on. My usual method is to rush enthusiastically into something and then be awfully sick about it. As it is the enlistment period, as you wrote me once, is three score and ten, and with most of the campaigns destined to be trench fighting there is no point wasting energy at this early date.

Thank you for liking the review. I have been told that it is "flippant."

To EARL SANTANGELO

DA wrote to a friend of youth in Middletown, Connecticut, DA's home town, declining an invitation to join the Middletown Post of the American Legion.

Washington, D.C.
January 28, 1920

Mr. Earl Santangelo
145 Main St.
Middletown, Ct.

Dear Earl:

Thank you very much for your letter of January 17th. Only press of work has prevented me from answering it before this.

I am in a rather difficult position. Nothing would suit me better than to belong to an organization which contained not only my friends in Middletown but so great a number of men who distinguished themselves in the war. I should consider it a pleasure and an honor. But unfortunately I am not in sympathy with the purposes and ideals of the American Legion in the whole hearted way in which a member of it should be. And so far as certain practices are concerned which have been committed in its name, I am distinctly opposed to it. So you see it would be highly improper for me to accept the membership which you so kindly offer me.

I am confident that you will receive this in the spirit in which it is meant and believe that I feel the keenest regret in being forced to this conclusion. After all I suppose that we are all working for the same ends, and it should not be a matter for bitterness that we have chosen different methods of approach.

Please remember me to my friends in the Middletown Post and believe me

Most cordially and sincerely yours,

P.S. I am returning the button under separate cover.

To GEORGE PARMLY DAY

Day was head of the Yale University Press, which DA was seeking to interest in publishing a book he had written about industrial labor relations. (The book appears to have remained unpublished.)

[undated]

Mr. George Parmly Day
Woodbridge Hall
New Haven, Conn.

My dear George:
Would the Yale Press be interested in seeing the manuscript of my book on the development of the legal principles governing industrial relations?

The enclosed letters from Dean Pound and the following comment of my own will explain the situation:—

As I told you I spent a half year at Cambridge working along these lines under the Dean, and then from May to October devoted myself to the book. The Dean having inspired it had, of course, the first claim to any value there might be in it. In the fall he, Frankfurter, and Laski read it, were good enough to like it, and the Dean accepted it for the Harvard Studies in Jurisprudence. Then the Harvard Press began to behave as his letters indicate with the result that the volume which should have preceded mine by a year, appearing last fall, is still in the press.

A short time ago I wrote him explaining that an indefinite delay would impair the usefulness of the book, if any, both to its readers and to me, and asking if I might show the manuscript to you. He very kindly consented, offered to write you, etc.

I have not asked him or Frankfurter or Laski to do this. There is no point in having you bombarded with opinions in the nature of puffs.

The book, or more properly monograph, covers about one hundred and forty typewritten pages, including the footnotes. It does not attempt to explain the secret of industrial harmony since its author cannot discover evidence of such an animal. The first part of it is history of the growth of legal concepts; the second, an attempt to indicate their logical development in the work of the War Labor Board. Because it recognizes with the Board that such things as trade unions exist, some idiots will call it radical.

If the Press would care to consider the publication of such a thing I have an unverified stenographer's copy of the manuscript which I could send on to you at once. If it would not, please do not hesitate to say so.

I have enjoyed this year with the Justice so much, and Alice and the baby are so delighted with Washington that we are staying on another year. It is a most seductive manner of life.

To **FELIX FRANKFURTER**

Frankfurter apparently had requested DA's views of Brandeis. "Brother Baker" is Newton D. Baker, Secretary of War, mentioned in connection with his dealings with the labor union at the Rock Island Arsenal.

March 15, 1920

Dear Mr. Frankfurter:

What you ask for is a large order. It is something about which I have wondered ever since I came here and the answer has always eluded me. Sometime when the work eases up a bit I shall put down all my observations for you; now I can only give one suggestion.

The Justice seems to regard a doubtful point as the product of divergent premises based upon imperfect knowledge. Most doubtful points would not be doubtful if all the facts were thoroughly known, not only the facts in regard to the situation also in regard to the law and its making. So he starts off an opinion by about a week of the hardest sort of study of the

situation out of which the case arose. Then he studies the old law, the pro-
ceeding leading up to the new, and the facts of its passage. All this requires
mountains of reports, hearings, investigations, studies, etc., as you, of
course, know.

Sometimes there are other difficulties to be overcome. The most remarkable performance was his reconstruction of the psychological processes of the judge below in a case which came up in a perfect mess. It was
absolutely impossible to tell what the judge thought that his judgment was
to accomplish and therefore, whether it was final so as to give this court
jurisdiction. The Justice discovered that part of the judgment was written
two weeks after the first part, and differed perceptibly from it. So he set to
work to discover what law the judge had been reading in the meantime—
which he did—and from that to work out just what he had attempted to do.

When he finished the whole thing was as clear as day. You could see
that the Judge below was not an idiot as I had not wisely assumed, and it
was obvious that he did not intend to dispose of the case finally.

To me, however, most of these things fall in line with Justice Holmes'
definition of a miracle—"A phenomenon without a phenomenal anteced-
ent." It is not hard to see how he does things after he starts, but the in-
spiration which selects a given method out of all possible methods seems to
me what is called genius for want of a better name. The Justice says that it is
simply the result of hard work and studying the record.

Brother Baker has delivered himself of a letter which would be in the
best caricaturist style of a letter from the Kaiser to the Social Democrats. In
it he tells the men that their advisory functions extend up to and no further
than questions of shop discipline. That he is the Secretary of War and will
decide all questions of policy, such as that of closing or expanding the arse-
nals, without assistance from them; and that harsh criticism of the Ordnance Department from them is uncalled for and needs no reply.

The fact that those harshly criticised have gayly decided to reduce the
working force from 17,000 to 1,500 does not, of course, concern the men
because it is a question of policy and not of shop discipline. If they do not
care for the policy they have the same rights of petitioning Congress as all
other American citizens. The letter was written by the Chief of Ordnance,
but Baker signed it and fortunately so. The men are no longer under any illusion as to what to expect from him and can go ahead with their conference
on solid earth. They are all fairly certain that it means the end of the
chapter.

If you have finished with the file, could you send it off to me? I cannot
forego the pleasure of drafting an answer to the letter and should like to
show from the file that the whole activity of the men from the start has had

to do with policy and that only and with his approval.

The most outstanding fact of this whole business seems to me to be that it is simply another indication of the complete helplessness and powerlessness of labor. The Coal strike, the Steel strike, the Railway fiasco, the Police strike,—all seem to put it beyond doubt that the position of labor is one of contemptuous and absolute subjection. A lot of it comes from their idiocy in being charmed by the glib Democratic Circe during the war. All the Boards and Committees, etc., on which they so prominently and so ineffectively served gave them the idea—not only that political action had some conceivable relation to their troubles—but that they were a power in the State. They are and were about as much of a power as our baby is when she threatens to cry while some one is in for tea. It is better not, of course, but if she wants to make it an issue—!

And still people like Arthur Gleason write articles telling how British labor is getting all it wants through Constitutional agitation—and he is actually imbecilic enough to cite the Coal Commission and the Railway agreement.

Most cordially,

To **GEORGE PARMLY DAY**

Washington, D.C.
April 2, 1920

Mr. George Parmly Day
Yale University Press
New Haven, Conn.

Dear George:

You are very kind to give my manuscript such a genial invitation. I am sending it off to you to-day.

This copy has only been hurriedly corrected, and, particularly in the foot-notes, is full of errors. However, I do not suppose that for your immediate purpose this is a serious matter. I had intended before this was seriously nearing publication to write a foreword warning the reader that this is not an attempt to reconcile labor and capital, so-called, but simply the evolution of principles for the administration of justice to secure the warring interests of the individual and the group under majority control.

These principles would seem to me to be as valid for Russia as for the United States. They necessarily deal with facts as we find them here, but the principles ultimately arise from an attempt to reconcile local conflicts. They also do not attempt to settle all labor disputes because most are not justiciable, any more than the religious wars were justiciable. What they do attempt to do I leave to the manuscript.

Most cordially yours,

To ALICE ACHESON

The excerpt below is from a letter to DA's wife, Alice, who was visiting her parents in Detroit, Michigan. DA writes from the home of a Yale classmate in Greenwich, Connecticut.

June 14, 1920

Yesterday I spent a farewell three hours with Judge Holmes during which he was at his best. At the end of it Mrs. Holmes gave us tea and made me promise to bring you to see her next fall. The Judge was very nice about my article. Some of it he thought was bunk. But my idea of due process as not containing any substantive doctrine but only meaning that you shall not change the presuppositions of whatever rules there are overnight he thought was an original contribution of considerable suggestiveness. I was tickled later to have him quote me to myself as "some fellar whose name I have forgotten said a good thing." He is an old wonder.

To FELIX FRANKFURTER

It is interesting that DA here reflected the view that his talks with the senior partners of Covington & Burling in Washington had come to naught because of Judge Covington's alarm about DA's labor interest. It is not clear how this obstacle was overcome, but it was. DA became associated with that firm later in the same year. "McKenna" in this letter was Associate Justice Joseph McKenna of the Supreme Court.

Washington, D.C.
April 20, 1921

Dear Frankfurter:

Just a line to thank you for the check and to hope that the reports of your illness are exaggerated. I met a law school man yesterday on the golf course who said that you had been laid up for some time and that there was talk of the Dean taking Public Utilities. As the Justice had not said anything about your being ill I was surprised and concerned. This morning, however, the Justice says that it is largely a question of your resting up after the exertions of the Cleveland job. I hope that rest will do it and that you will take it.

I was almost on the edge of settling my problems of next year. Edward Burling asked me to come into his office to work on a Norwegian claim against the U.S. and after talking it over expressed himself as perfectly satisfied to have me work with Frank Walsh also. The final agreement was to have been made on Monday. When I went to his office I found that his partner Judge Covington, late of the D.C. Supreme Court, had been terrified at the thought of my bringing germs into the office and protested vigorously. They wanted me to "keep up my interest in labor but not to do anything active for a year or so until I had had time to think it over." But I told them that I was sick of that sort of thing; and so we parted with vague talk of some arrangement still being possible but knowing that it wasn't. I have still some hope that Frank Walsh will come across with an invitation to join him. He spoke to Norman Hapgood about me on Sunday.

In the meantime I have destroyed another bridge behind me by writing Mr. Whipple that I have given up the idea of coming to Boston and so into his office. His son-in-law wrote a very nice letter of regret saying that they had heard pleasant things about me and had wanted to take me in. So you see if these damn labor skates continue to be so uppish about their legal assistants I shall have a first rate quarrel with them.

The ordinary labor union attorney gets his job, I have discovered, and occupies most of his time by straightening out intra-union rows. He is the smooth article retained by the winning faction.

What did you think of McKenna's panic-stricken utterances of Monday last? If he doesn't stop this business of using the bench as a confessional we are apt to learn something about the judicial process before he gets through. The Schaefer case, the Prohibition case, the Steel Trust case, the Gilbert one and now this, have given us pretty nearly everything except his views on marriage and big league baseball.

I hope that you will be yourself again very soon,

Cordially,

To FELIX FRANKFURTER

Frankfurter must have written slightingly of Associate Justice Mahlon Pitney, of the Supreme Court, and evoked this letter, a staunch defense of Pitney.

Washington, D.C.
April 22, 1921

Dear Frankfurter:

I am sending along the Rent case opinions at once so that you may know the best and the worst. Don't you think that Holmes, J. is in his happiest vein. The years have no more effect upon his mind than machine gun bullets on a tank. I wish some one would point out the rank Bolshevism in McKenna's closing sentence. The idea of having the Constitutionality of legislation depend upon the uncertainties of judicial opinion, he says. The Supremacy of the Courts is all wrong; what we ought to have is the supremacy of some dogma. This dogma must, of course, be above the courts or the legislatures; it must rest upon divine sanction—i.e. force. This is straight from Moscow, if anything ever was. When McKenna begins to distrust the uncertainties of judicial opinion, what is going to become of us.

I think that you rather do Pitney an injustice. He has no trouble coming in on things of this sort; in fact, he is over the hurdle with the best of them. The common idea tends to identify Pitney and Van Devanter, but nothing is more mistaken. Pitney is a splendid lawyer in the strict sense. That is he has not the philosophical attitude of Holmes; he could never say that the life of the law was not logic but experience; but taking the law as he knows it he will accept the traditional method of legal reasoning and the end to which it brings him no matter whether he likes it or not. In the second place he is a Calvinist all the way through. People are responsible for what they do; life is a stern business and a test of character; you can't come to him with any theory that torts are any the less torts because actors are having a poor time in the world. And finally, while he believes in property and contract he believes in government more. The limitations upon it do not appeal to him as much as the positive grants of power and the needs for their exercise.

I think that these observations are fairly well borne out by his opinions—though of course they are very general. Take his Coppage and Kansas and Hitchmand attitude, which is usually all that anyone knows about him. He is perfectly willing that government shall work out the problem of industrial relations and that it should seriously limit rights of private property in doing so. But according to his Presbyterian mind you are not doing that when you tell one side that it is free to organize and strike and picket and throw bricks and generally bust up the other fellow's business. That is not government but the abdication of it. If you tell him that the employers can do just this by the press of the needs of life upon their workmen, he would answer that the law has nothing to do with that, that since Adam life has pressed upon most of mankind, and that the purpose of life is to withstand that pressure and find salvation. Life is hard and rules of law are absolute.

Then, you remember that Pitney was with us on the Prohibition cases, and he was with us in the dissenting opinion in the marine compensation case. The Child Labor case goes against me, though there I think that a logically minded fellow might well have been with the court. On the stock dividend case he was the lawyer interpreting a word as it always had been interpreted in the law; and he was as right as we were. The only person who seemed to me to be pulling his weight in that case was Holmes, J. who said that it wasn't a matter of law but of common sense. On all the late anti-trust cases, including the one which I am sending today, he has been in the minority—the Steel case, the Shoe Machinery, etc.

The Adamson law case, which I forgot to put among the labor cases, fits in with the theory of them without much trouble. It was in his opinion another case of confiscation by force thinly veiled in the forms of legislation.

Pitney is very much of a person, I think, and if only the Court did not have its absurd veto power upon legislation, he would be qualified in every way to be where he is. There is an awful lot in his labor attitude which the labor movement ought to understand and take to heart because it represents the point of view of the part of the population which comes as near as any to making impartial opinion. No matter how peacefully labor pursues its present methods—organization and hold up—it is essentially a lawless procedure from the point of view of those who hold anything of value under the present legal order. It all comes down to the fact that coercion has a very definite substantive meaning. One is coerced, it is true, by the threat of discharge, but it is not the same thing as the strike with a line of pickets around a man's factory and around the factory of those who buy his products preventing operations by threats of injury directly applied to the physical or social well-being of anyone opposing their will. One is an incident to the rules; the other defies all rules, no system can tolerate it not even the Bolsheviks. I am not saying that the labor movement is necessarily on the wrong track; but I do insist that those who direct this policy have no right to complain that courts or outsiders are unsympathetic. It may be that the best way is just to bust the other fellow; but when your method would apply to busting any order which possibly could be conceived you must expect to run afoul of legal tradition.

You touched one of my hobbies when you spoke of Pitney. He represents to me what can be done by law and what cannot. I think that he represents the highest general average that one can hope for on the bench.

Cordially,

To ETHEL SMITH

For the reader who mistakenly believes that the Equal Rights Amendment is a novelty of the 1970s, this letter will be an eye-opener.

September 8, 1921

Miss Ethel Smith
1423 New York Avenue
Washington, D.C.

My dear Miss Smith:

You ask for my views on the proposed Amendment to the Constitution of the United States—"Neither political or legal disabilities or inequalities on account of sex or marriage shall exist in the United States."

Its object, so far as it relates to *legal* disabilities and inequalities, is, I presume, the commendable one of removing the old common law limitations upon the legal capacity of married women, where they still exist, and securing for married women the same rules as for men in matters of inheritance, divorce, and the guardianship of children. But the method—a vague and general limitation upon the power of State Legislations and Congress—shows a dangerous ignorance of our experience with constitutional limitations.

In the equally vague phrases of the 14th Amendment the courts have found a guarantee of a supposed equality among men which, under the name of liberty of contract, has nullified much of our social legislation. For historical reasons women escaped the burdens of this theoretical equality, and for twenty years there has been steady progress in legislation to protect them from untrammeled exploitation. All this, to my mind, is now threatened by this sweeping prohibition of unnamed inequalities and disabilities. If experience furnishes any guide this will be taken by the courts to mean that the protection which women have received through legislation, since it is a restriction of their liberty of contract, is no longer possible and that this new-won equality guarantees to women all the intolerable and antisocial conditions which their brothers in industry now enjoy.

Surely by this time we should have learned that in removing anachronisms from the law we must name them, book and page, and not furnish to the courts undefined powers for nullifying legislation.

Very truly yours,

To ALICE ACHESON

Alice Acheson had escaped the Washington heat in South Ashfield, Massachusetts. This bit of whimsy is excerpted from a letter giving her the home front news.

Washington, D.C.
July 18, 1923

Dearest Al:

. . .

The two stoves are beginning to loom gigantically above my life. They seem to have grown into the places where the men left them—one under the porch, the other in the middle of the new dining room—and to be gradually swelling and crowding us out of the house. I make wholly inadequate attempts to get rid of them. They seem placid and unmoveable. I grow irritable each morning on seeing them. They have grown in deeper by evening. Now Gibbs has taken on the job of fighting them, but is no more successful than I. The old stove probably owns the house. It may be hopeless as well as wicked and dangerous to try to get it out. Perhaps we should have it bricked in where it stands and maybe then we could deal with the little one.

To ALICE ACHESON

This time Alice Acheson made her summer escape to Duxbury, Massachusetts. In this letter DA gives her the news from Harewood Farm, the Acheson country retreat 18 miles north of Washington. "John" and "Gertrude" are Judge and Mrs. John Sternhagen, close friends of the Achesons, he a member of the U.S. Tax Court's predecessor body, the Board of Tax Appeals.

Saturday
August 27, 1928

Dearest Al:

. . .

Mr. Beale has been after me to be chief marshal at the Fireman's Carnival on Sept. 5. I told him that I would let him know the first of the week and I am rather inclined to do it. It won't interfere with any plans I may have and it may not be a bad thing to do in connection with the campaign.

After leaving you Jane and I went to the fair and rode unsuccessfully in our class. Then we watched some races and rode home. Got a bath and supper and went back in the Overland with Robert Hill as the return chauffeur. We rode on the Merry-Go-Round, threw rings over prizes, threw balls at milk bottles and saw the mermaid, the circus and the fireworks, returning home late and enthusiastic. Last night we slept ten hours.

I have put $450 in your checking account. Your Murphy check of $403 included your Am. Can dividend. So I was told. Your bonds are back in the box.

John is spending the night with me. Gertrude is entertaining some people he doesn't like. Jane wants to swim but I don't know whether your Manor Club card is still good or not. Perhaps I can take her to the river.

To-morrow Mme. is going in to the Russian church for some special party and Dorothy is going to stay on all day. They fixed it up and I acquiesced.

Tell us your adventures and think of us occasionally. We discuss your probable activities at great length. Also have a grand time so far as possible. I shall be definite about myself soon.

Love and lots of it.

To A. B. DICK, JR.

A. B. Dick, Jr. ("Jun") was head of the A. B. Dick Co., manufacturer of mimeograph machines and supplies. He was a Yale classmate and close friend of DA. The A. B. Dick Co. was DA's client, and here we have a passing glimpse of the grist of law practice. Joe Walker, President Coolidge's visitor, was also a classmate and close friend of DA.

March 16, 1929

Mr. A. B. Dick, Jr.
720 West Jackson Boulevard
Chicago, Illinois

My dear Jun:

We shall do nothing about the customs matter until we hear further from you. After you win the case in the Court of Appeals, as I am sure you will, we can, if necessary, invoke the powers of the Tariff Commission to prevent further imports of Arlac stencil paper.

We had Joe and Eleanor Walker here in Washington over Washington's birthday and enjoyed seeing them a great deal. They brought their 2 children down to show them the workings of the Federal Government and had several exhausting days watching the House and Senate operate and seeing the other things which are supposed to be educational. We arranged for them to meet Mr. Coolidge and this almost produced a crisis. At the last moment little Joe decided that he was not going to shake hands with Mr. Coolidge. After a great deal of argument in which Joe was assisted by the White House attendants, little Joe decided that he would shake hands with Mr. Coolidge but that he would not speak to him. This, of course, was perfectly all right with Mr. Coolidge who did not intend to speak to little Joe anyway. Pretty soon you will have to undertake the same job for Albert and Helen.

I am afraid that this winter is going to get by—it is already practically spring here—without our seeing you and Helen in Lake Forest. The tariff readjustment which is now before the Ways and Means Committee and the change of administration will probably keep me pretty busy for another couple of months.

Last night at Trubee Davison's we met Dave Ingalls, the new Assistant Secretary of the Navy for aviation. Perhaps you know him, he comes from Cleveland and looks most extraordinarily young for the job. He seems to be a nice person.

Have you made any plans for the summer as yet? Last year you had some thought of spending the summer in England. We are planning to spend the month of August in the Adirondacks and the rest of the summer at the farm.

Please give our love to Helen.

As ever,

To A. B. DICK, JR.

Here DA attempted to interpret the 1932 election of Franklin Roosevelt for A. B. Dick, Jr. As to cabinet appointments, DA's crystal ball was somewhat clouded. Of those mentioned by him, only Frances Perkins was a winner, and he was too uncertain to venture a flat prediction of her appointment.

November 14, 1932

Dear Jun:

When our people make up their mind they certainly make it up. There is very little doubt as to what the country, as a whole or in particular localities, thinks about the present situation. Or rather, I should say, there is very little doubt what they think about Mr. Hoover. There is tremendous doubt what they think about everything else. Down here there seem to be the following general conclusions emerging from the flood:

1. The Republican leaders in most of the states were thoroughly fed up with Mr. Hoover, were convinced that they were going to be beaten, and lay down with the idea that an overwhelming defeat would remove Mr. Hoover from Republican politics forever. The view is that this has happened and that he has ceased to be a factor of importance in the Republican party.

2. The sweeping defeat has been of great benefit to the Republican party in removing 5 or 6 gentlemen who had been completely covered with barnacles for the last decade and have hampered the intelligent development of the party. These are Smoot, Watson, Moses, Bingham, etc. It has also eliminated Bill Donovan. Some of the young men like Dave Ingalls and Trubee Davison have received black eyes but they will recover from these.

3. Probably the reorganization of the Republican party will center around a man like former Senator Wadsworth of New York, who has re-

turned to the House. This reorganization ought to take the form of a positive Tory liberalism. In other words, the party is now faced with the same problem with which Disraeli was faced in the middle of the last century. He had to adapt conservatism to the industrial revolution. The new leadership in this country has to adapt conservatism to the technological revolution in industry and to the altered position of the United States in the world. Policies which emerged from the Civil War have got to be thrown overboard.

So much for the Republicans.

4. The Democrats should found their policy upon a complete realization that the majority was not given for them but against Hoover. This, in one way, is an advantage to Mr. Roosevelt if he is capable of using it. The greater part of his majority in Congress comes from very doubtful districts. Almost 150 members are new members. They will tend to be timid. If Mr. Roosevelt will exercise a strong and ruthless leadership in Congress he can intimidate the newcomers and terrorize everyone who comes from the doubtful districts by threatening to go into their districts in 1934 and oppose them in the primaries. If he does not do this his majority in the House will run away with him.

5. *Cabinet.* The "consensus," as the race track tipsters have it, is as follows:

State will be offered to Newton Baker and then to Norman Davis. Treasury, probably first to Owen Young and second to Mr. Baruch. There is some question whether Mr. Traylor, who would have a good chance, has not been slightly damaged by the Insull publicity. For Attorney General the betting is on Governor Ritchie. Miss Frances Perkins is talked about for Secretary of Labor. There can not be any intelligent guess on the other positions.

6. *Policies.* The guess is that an attempt will be made to settle the beer question in the short session. Also to reach some solution, temporary or otherwise, of the foreign debt questions. If this can be done, it will be with the hope of avoiding an extra session until the fall of 1935. If an extra session has to be called, the hope is that it will only be after a definite program has been worked out and with the idea of jamming this through Congress while that body is amenable to discipline and before Mr. Roosevelt has exhausted its patronage.

This is enough for one dose. My best to you and Helen.

As ever,

To JAMES P. WARBURG

Warburg was a New York banker with an active interest in government monetary and fiscal policy, a writer in that field, and outspoken commen-

tator. His active mind and engaging personality were much appreciated by DA. The latter had just completed a brief tour of duty as Under Secretary of the Treasury. "Lew" was Lewis W. Douglas, a Congressman from Arizona who had just been made Director of the Budget.

January 7, 1934

Dear Jim:

It was nice of you to think of us at Christmas. We much appreciated your telegram. One of the few respects in which my present life is not as desirable as the one I had a few months ago is that I don't see you any more. This, I agree, will have to be repaired by my coming to New York rather than by your coming here—unless like a proper father you come to see April at the school. If you do come down remember that we shall want you here very much.

What do you think about the present trends in monetary policy. It seems to me that your activities contributed largely to slowing up the President. But I wonder now whether he isn't setting forces in operation by his expenditure program which will carry him along to paper inflation irrespective of argument. Once you start paying subsidies to great sections of the country I don't believe it is easy to stop and the President doesn't pick out the hardest thing to do. Lew seems to me to be in a bad spot if the alleged control over all these expenditures is put under him. In the first place I don't quite see what that means. The budget is made and if the appropriation follows just what function does Lew perform except possibly to fuss with details and certainly to be saddled with the responsibility for all the turmoil. I think they have put him in a most unenviable position by a rather adroit maneuver. He can't stop the spending and he can hardly criticize it.

Alice and I had a complete rest and most delightful time in Bermuda. I have hardly any desire for but am under the necessity to work, and am going to do this with my old firm here. Before long I hope to get to New York and see you.

With all best wishes.

As ever,

To ARCHIBALD MACLEISH

This letter appears to be directed to a criticism of Lewis W. Douglas that MacLeish either published in a Fortune *article or had drafted for publication. DA defends Douglas as the classic, conscientious conservative, an interesting foreshadowing of a role that DA himself sometimes played later in life.*

April 6, 1934

Mr. Archibald MacLeish
Fortune
135 East 42nd Street
New York, New York

Dear Archie:

. . .

As I recall it, you said that to many people it was curious that a person of Douglas' ability should be so insensitive to the intellectual currents of his generation. Now, in the first place, the word curious is something of a weasel word. Up on the Hill senators arise and say that it is curious that an official drawing a salary of $5,000.00 lives in a large house with fifteen servants and has four Rolls-Royces. What he means is that the official is undoubtedly and notoriously corrupt, but that for the moment the proof is lacking. Similarly, the word insensitive rather connotes a culpable hardness of the mind to meritorious ideas.

As I understand it, the facts on which you were commenting are that Lew is one of the only living conservatives of the time. When most of the young are willing to scrap the whole political, industrial and financial structure, because a combination of corruption, nationalistic madness and ineptitude have produced bad results, Lew believes that the foundations of capitalism, individualism and democracy can be preserved, and at the same time the evils which have produced the damage can be eliminated.

It is always unusual to find a man holding firmly to his convictions when an articulate minority are filling the public mind with different ideas, but I don't think that it is curious—certainly it would not be curious in England where such creatures are produced in each generation—and I do not think that it shows intellectual insensitiveness. Furthermore, I do not think that it indicates that Lew has become a dissenter, using that term as you seem to do as the opposite of a leader, or, as one might apply it, for instance, to Henry Adams.

. . .

I think that Lew is a leader. At the present time a combination of loyalty to the President, a desire to have his views heard in a place where for the immediate present they can be most effective, and the hope that the situation may swing around to his point of view, makes it impossible for him to lead in public debate in opposition to the whole program. I think that he understands perfectly what the advocates of a planned and regimented national life want to achieve. If the fundamental, intellectual and moral conceptions of this generation are the worth of the individual and the predominant right of society, I think he shares it. But he does not believe

C.1

that these values will be permanently furthered by the methods which the Marxians and Fascists want to employ. He doubts whether the administrative capacity, the intellectual stability and the moral character exist, which are essential if the entire life of a country as large as this is to be controlled in every detail by a centralized government. I don't think that it is true that he believes in laissez faire and the Manchester School of Economics without more. He would insist that the principles of neither had been in operation for half a century and that in the program which he would advocate they would not be put into effect without changes so far reaching as to alter the whole conception. He does believe in the necessity of international economic organization, and in the necessity of preserving the principle of competition in the industrial structure.

I am delighted to have *Fortune* and have reread your article on the Administration with pleasure. I think that the conception is good and that most of the detail is good. The part about Henry Morgenthau was much improved, although I was surprised to learn that he was tactful. That had not seemed to me to be one of his outstanding qualities. You were more than generous to me, which I appreciate.

. . .

My love to Ada. I am hoping to be in New York sometime toward the end of the month and will see you then.

As ever,

To WILLIAM H. WOODIN

Woodin had been Secretary of the Treasury, 1933–1934, and DA's chief. In his illness DA tried to cheer him up with some light gossip with historical overtones.

April 23, 1934

Mr. William H. Woodin
Two East 67th Street
New York, New York

Dear Mr. Woodin:

I saw Walter Cummings and Steve Gibbons last week and, as you may suppose, we talked of you. I was much distressed to hear from them that your winter in Arizona had not brought about the complete cure which we had all hoped would result from it. They tell me that you have been suffering again from your old throat trouble since you have returned to New York, but that the doctors now have a new treatment which they think will finally defeat it. I earnestly hope that it has already started its good work, and that this miserable consequence of your strenuous days of a year ago will soon be gone for ever.

The other day I saw in the paper that Henry Morgenthau had removed the portrait of your old friend "who could say no with a smile" as you used to say, and put in its place the portrait of Roger Taney. Your room would hardly seem the same without Mr. Gallatin to give a light touch to our more strenuous moments. That, however, would not be the most important change. I cannot think of that room without thinking of you sitting at the desk.

I wonder if Henry knows about the circumstances under which the gentleman whose portrait is now hanging there was appointed. I looked the matter up a day or so ago and found an element of humor in it. It appears that exactly one hundred years ago last fall Jackson decided to withdraw the deposits from the United States banks and put them in the state banks. Mr. Duane, the Secretary of the Treasury, thought this highly improper and said that he would not have a hand in it. The Cabinet was also opposed to the scheme, all except the Attorney General, Mr. Taney. As a result Mr. Duane's resignation was requested and given. Taney was appointed Secretary of the Treasury and removed the deposits.

I am trying a case for the DuPont Company, which may take me to New York within the next two or three weeks. If it does, I shall telephone your house in the hope that you will feel well enough to see me for a few moments. It would be a great joy to talk with you again.

With kindest regards,

Most sincerely,

To JAMES GRAFTON ROGERS

Jim Rogers had served the Hoover Administration in Washington. Here DA expresses skepticism about the celebrated Keynesian thesis of economic stimulation by deficit spending. Arthur Ballantine was DA's predecessor as Under Secretary of the Treasury.

July 5, 1934

Mr. James Grafton Rogers
Boulder, Colorado

Dear Jim:

. . .

I should be much interested to know what you think of the present situation from the cool and detached heights from which you observe it. Here, we are so hot and so confused by the legislation of the last ten days of Congress that we hardly know what to think. Mr. Keynes spent a few days in Washington about a month ago and, apparently, started the President off again on the theory that he can bring about recovery spending more money and spending it faster than we have done before. This has produced discouragement in circles with which you are familiar. The end of the fiscal year shows a deficit even greater than the one you used to talk to Arthur Ballantine about, and, what is worse, shows that there will probably be an even greater deficit for the fiscal year 1935. My own feeling is that none of these efforts are going to show sufficient results before the election and that when the President comes back we may expect some new effort to produce an artificial stimulus to business activity.

. . .

Our love to you both.

To **EMERSON TUTTLE**

Tuttle was Master of Davenport College at Yale, a member of the Yale class ahead of DA, and a close friend. Here DA's strong instinct for the analytical approach to problems emerges.

October 27, 1934

Mr. H. E. Tuttle
271 Park Street
New Haven, Connecticut

Dear Em:

I shall be glad to be with you in New Haven on the evening of November 27, and speak at the Davenport Dinner.

I have been turning over in my mind for some time the kind of thing which I could say. So far there seem to be two possibilities which may have some merit. One of them is the idea about which I talked to Archie sometime ago, that is, a discussion of the conflicting functions which are operating on the personnel in the executive departments of Government, on the one side the spoil system, on the other side the necessity for the development of a higher civil service to carry on the complicated programs in which all governments have to engage. I could talk a little about the experience with this in England and France, and the possibilities for developing it in the United States.

The other idea is wholly different. Its theme would be The True Function of a University in Connection With the Social and Economic Problems of Today. I might point out that the universities have largely shared the general attitude toward the New Deal, that is, an emotional attitude. One is apt to be either for everything, in which case he is a liberal, or against it, in which case he is regarded as a Tory. Passion and moral judgments seem to be the chief stock in trade, and everybody is talking about the various "isms," either with moral enthusiasm, or from the point of view that they are undermining the Constitution, and what is regarded as "Fundamental principles of Anglo-Saxon Government." The universities are, largely, not only sharing in this attitude, but also taking part in the actual day to day conflict, either by having their teachers work full or part time for various branches of the Government, or in writing books against it. This tends to remove the only agencies which can give calm and long range thought to the fundamental problems.

I should then like to point out that some of the basic questions of today are questions as to which one's attitude should be determined, not by whether one is liberal or conservative, but depending upon one's judgments as to the causes or results of acts in a field where knowledge is very limited. To my mind, the function of the university should be to devote itself to learning what has been and is happening, and to developing a body of knowledge as to what result one might expect from specific acts in specific situations. I should like to point out for instance that present trends in agriculture are merely the accentuation of trends which have been developing for more than fifty years. That one of the matters on which there is little or no learning, is the importance of the correlation of various time factors in connection with economic change. For instance, if a million people are displaced from agriculture at just about the time that the automobile is invented, you have one social situation. If, however, these two phenomena of this economic change are not correlated, you have a wholly different social problem.

I think you see the general idea. It tends to change the connotations which have accompanied the words academic and practical. The greatest thing that a university can do is to be academic and not be practical.

Do you think either of these will do. If not, since you know more about the occasion than I do, can you give me a lead?

Sincerely,

To JANE ACHESON

DA's older daughter, Jane, was away at Miss Hall's School in Pitts-field, Massachusetts. Duffy was Mary Acheson's pet Schnauzer, a bad actor destined for conflict with DA. Laura, Johnson, and Anne were the Acheson's cook, butler, and maid. Jeanette was Mrs. Raymond Lee, a close friend.

October 1, 1935

Dearest Jane:

Mary and I are all alone now, holding the fort with stout but lonely hearts and speculating about all of you who are out seeing the great

world—and having oodles of fun. A great word that! We trust you learn
some others equally eloquent of culture to overcome the somewhat re-
stricting effect of that one on your vocabulary. But to get back to our mut-
ton—I am very sad about Miss Hall's lack of desire to see me at
Thanksgiving. If Mr. Peabody [headmaster of Groton School] shows the
same enthusiasm I shall have to break down and make a speech at Yale
which I am now using you as an excuse to avoid. Mary and I are much interested in the Thanksgiving costume which you want completed. So far it
is a scarf and a hat. A very fine foundation for any costume, which alone
would get a girl a long way—but not in a New England school where everyone else wore black bloomers. You are clearly right in sensing that the costume is incomplete. The problem is what to add. At dinner to-night we
discussed fans and bubbles but felt that they lack coziness after the snow
flies. Whoever saw Priscilla Alden going to church in hat, scarf, fans and
bubbles on Thanksgiving. The Indians would clearly have shot the bubbles.
So that was ruled out. Then we thought of skinning Duffy and sending the
hide to you—particularly as he got me up this morning at five o'clock by
howling at the shambles which he had made of the sitting room, then, when
put out, bringing an old box under the sleeping porch and knocking it lust-
ily to pieces for an hour. On the whole, I think you get Duffy, pickled in his
own brine.

I have had two days in court trying a particularly dull case, and so, with
the fatigue of thinking about your costume, am all worn out. Write to us
some more. We have a great time hearing about your adventures. Laura,
Johnson and Anne send their love and are full of interest in your reports.
Jeanette has a 7 pound baby girl and is well. Write to her.

Devotedly,

To JANE ACHESON

DA had a low boredom threshold, as this letter shows.

*The reference to the Italians' "African show" is to the Italian invasion
of Ethiopia, which brought the Emperor Haile Selassie into the spotlight at
the League of Nations.*

[undated]

Dearest Jane:

We had one of our less good tea parties this afternoon which left me in
a poor state of mind. We then were misled into going to a movie called Java
Head. The book which you may by some strange chance know is, I think,
very fine, but this British effort was a flop. Anna May Wong who is very good
if given a chance seemed to have the idea that she was meant to be a

mummy after the first ten thousand years and had all the gaiety which that part would produce. The other characters had only been buried from one to five thousand years. So a good time was had by all and now we are home again.

We thought yesterday that Mary had broken her arm but the X-rays seem to show not. She has been doing some spirited head stands from her roller skates, two of which on two days on the same hand seem to have bent her arm in an odd way. If it isn't broken it must be a mild case of rickets.

There is no news—and very little gossip—here. The betting seems to be more and more that the Italians will get away with their African show; that sanctions will be too slow in effect to stop them; that England will not go in for military measures and that after Italy gets about what she wants the League will have to find a formula to sanctify it.—Unless Europe blows up first, which it well may.

Good night, my love.

Affectionately,

To **DAVID ACHESON**

Some of DA's reflections about Europe are here expressed. David Acheson, DA's second child, was a student at Groton School in Groton, Massachusetts. "Raymond" was Colonel (then) Raymond E. Lee, U.S. military attaché in London and a very close friend of DA.

May 4, 1936

Dear Dave:

. . .

I am sending you separately a pamphlet which Raymond sent to me containing some speeches which were made in London about the German crisis. I don't suggest that you read all of them but merely the first one by Harold Nicolson. He suggests what seems to me to be a very sound view of the present state of mind of Germany. Harold Nicolson is a very able man, the author of some of the best books on international affairs, and at present a member of Parliament. You may remember that he wrote the life of Dwight Morrow most recently. You will find that in what he says he is rather partial to the French point of view. Everything that he says is true. The difficulty is that he leaves out some things. He leaves out, for instance, all reference to the French Invasion of the Ruhr in 1923, which, I think, was the most disastrous single step taken in Europe during this century. That is possibly an extreme statement, because the declarations of war in 1914 were pretty calamitous. However, the invasion of the Ruhr, which brought on the German inflation, made the Nazi movement inevitable and revived in

Europe the conviction that the only basis of international politics was force, was almost as terrible a blunder as the War. And the French were responsible for it. However, the important thing in thinking about international affairs is not to make moral judgments or apportion blame but to understand the nature of the forces which are at work as the foundation for thinking about what, if anything, can be done. From this point of view I think you will find the first article most revealing and suggestive.

. . .

As ever,

To RANALD MACDONALD, JR.

This is a fair summary of DA's views on the court-packing controversy, expressed to his classmate and friend, MacDonald.

March 11, 1937

Mr. Ranald MacDonald, Jr.
115 Broadway
New York City

Dear Ranald:
Thank you for your note and for exempting me from those who incite to violence. I think all of us must agree with what Mr. de Madariaga says. I am no advocate of direct popular sovereignty. In fact, I can think of no more delightful period or place in which to have lived than middle 19th century England, when the country was run by a small group of highly intelligent and quite largely disinterested men. But I do not think that our present judgment can be based upon nostalgic yearnings. The fact seems to me to be that the Court has created a situation which is not acceptable to those who have power to change it. This presents the question whether the country should be split by a last ditch fight on questions of theory or whether some reasonable compromise can be reached which will deal with the present difficulty and leave the ultimate solution as it must be left to the degree of culture which we can achieve. I said the other night that I think the country must lose if either side of this controversy wins by a knockout. The only way the country can gain is by approaching the situation calmly seeing what the immediate difficulties are and going no further than is necessary to correct those. The present difficulty seems to me to require some present representation on the Court of the current overwhelmingly held point of view. I think that it would be most undesirable to have an immediate majority for this point of view, but I do not think that the Ark of the Covenant would be rent if two men were added to the Court who understood the pre-

sent temper of the country. After that we can approach soberly the question of basic changes.

Two mild changes seem to me acceptable to everyone. First, that by amendment, judges should retire at 70 in order to make possible a more even turnover in the membership of the Court. Second, that some orderly method be brought about for determining whether or not a Constitutional amendment is acceptable. The present method permits a proposal to drag on for years and come up at different times in different parts of the country in a highly haphazard way. I fail to see anything destructive in giving Congress the power to appoint a particular day reasonably close to the date of the proposal of the amendment on which its adoption or rejection shall be finally determined. And finally, I should like to see some change—and this I concede as highly controversial—in which questions of ultimate policy can be discussed in terms of ultimate policy and not in terms of lawyers' talk. This involves limiting the power of the Court to declare acts of Congress unconstitutional. I am not dogmatic about this because I find people whose judgment is better than mine on opposite sides of the question. I think, however, that it can and should be discussed not in terms of horror but in terms of practical operation.

. . .

My best to you both,

Sincerely yours,

To JAMES P. WARBURG

This letter contains further enlargement of DA's philosophy regarding the court-packing controversy and the limits upon judicial power.

March 12, 1937

Mr. James P. Warburg
40 Wall Street
New York City

Dear Jimmy:

I have read the pamphlet and Mr. Aldrich's speech with interest. I have no reason to doubt that the historical material stated by him is correct, but I think that it misses the point. The present difficulties have largely been created in the last forty years. They come from the perhaps inevitable narrowness which the sterility of the legal mind has brought into the interpretation of what is essentially a political document. Marshall understood and said that it was a *Constitution* which he was construing. Recently the Court seems to have forgotten that and cannot resist the temptation to declare unconstitutional measures of which a majority strongly disapproves.

Let me take a few illustrations. The Constitution gives to Congress the power to regulate commerce among the several States. The first Child Labor law provided that articles manufactured by child labor could not be transported from one State to another. Here was a clear regulation of commerce among the States. However, the Court invalidated the Act, because it said that the purpose of Congress was to deal with employment wholly within a State and that since it could not do this directly, it could not do it indirectly. This is pure policy making. The minority took what seems to me the unanswerable view that as long as Congress was regulating commerce among the States, it could do so for any purpose it thought desirable. Since that decision the Court has applied the same reasoning to invalidate half a dozen statutes.

Another clear field of policy making has been occupied by the Court in interpreting the Due Process of Law Clauses of the 5th and 14th Amendments. Neither Congress in the District of Columbia nor the States within their areas may regulate the hours of labor in a bakery nor minimum wages for women nor prevent the discharge of employees because they join a union nor refuse injunctions against peaceful picketing nor prevent speculation in theatre tickets nor impose sanitary conditions in the manufacture of bedding nor regulate employment agencies. All of this because the Court finds that such laws interfere with "liberty of contract." No such phrase is found in the Constitution. The Court has distilled it from writings of 18th Century Frenchmen who misunderstood the term "law of the land" or "due process of law" as those phrases have been used in Magna Carta and other English political documents to describe procedure in a criminal trial.

I could multiply illustrations, but instead of doing so, enclose a copy of a speech I made last summer in which some of them occur. I think it safe to say that if every case in which the Court has declared unconstitutional an Act of Congress, had been decided the other way—this is certainly true of every case which was decided by a divided Court—we would not, on looking back at them, see any violation of sound Constitutional practice and the Federal Government would today have ample power to deal with those questions which a great majority in the country believe make urgent demand for national treatment.

Now this being so, I believe that something has to be done to remedy the situation. This something I think requires having upon the Court men who will not be entangled in the Talmudic tradition of imposing gloss after gloss upon a simple document but will do what all judges say that they do, uphold any Act of Congress as long as there is any reasonable basis for doing so. It also requires, I think, some sort of an amendment which will give sanction to this return to basic principles and protect the men who do it from the charge that they are mere puppets. I believe as strongly as anyone that judges must decide impartially and independently, but under enacted law. For this reason I think it undesirable that the President should demand an immediate majority but he is entitled to representation. The precedent can, of course, be used to destroy the Court, but it need not be so used, and I see no reason for basing policy exclusively upon fears. This policy of fear now so prevalent existed also at the time of the Constitutional Convention. An interesting example of it appears in the quotation from Mr. Hamilton on page 10 of the pamphlet. In speaking of the necessity of judicial review of legislation he says: "It not only serves to moderate the immediate mischiefs of those which may have been passed, but it operates as a check upon the legislative body in passing them; who, perceiving that obstacles to the success of iniquitous intentions are to be expected from the scruples of the courts, are in a manner compelled, by the very motives of the injustice they meditate, to qualify their attempts." The conception of the Court as the angel with the flaming sword standing at the gate of the Garden of Eden protecting us from the iniquitous intentions of the legislature and the President was as overdrawn then as it is now.

As ever,

To **DAVID ACHESON**

A brief glimpse of how DA spent his spare time in the prewar period. References to the Douglases and "the park" are to Mr. and Mrs. Lewis W. Douglas and the Laurentide Park in Quebec, where many trout were called, but few were caught. References to Mr. Thacher and Mr. Taft are to Thomas Thacher, a distinguished New York lawyer, and to Senator Robert A. Taft, both members of the Yale Corporation as was DA.

April 12, 1937

Dear Dave:

Thank you very much indeed for your birthday telegram. I also got one from Jane and appreciate having both of you think of me.

Alice and I went up to New York on Thursday, where I went to a class dinner and she went to the theater. We stayed with the Douglases. We then went on to New Haven and had a very pleasant time there. I spoke to the law students on Friday evening, and later went back to another law student meeting, where Harold Laski was carrying on a competition in being bright with some of the more vocal young men. He patronized Mr. Thacher, Mr. Taft and me, which gave him a great deal of pleasure and did us no visible harm.

On Sunday morning we motored up to Middletown to spend the day with Mother. This was very pleasant, although quiet, and I think that it pleased her to have us come there.

This morning I got in the mail some folders on rods, reels, and trout flies which I thought might bring back memories of Quebec to you. If we do not get carried off to Europe in spite of our protests, you and I will have to try the other end of the park this summer.

With love from us all and many thanks for your telegram.

As ever,

To **LT. COL. R. E. LEE**

DA's hoped-for solution of the controversy over FDR's proposal to en-large the Supreme Court was to see some of the more dedicated opponents of New Deal legislation retire, and let their places be filled without altering the court structure. Events shortly moved along that course. "My old chief" refers to Justice Brandeis.

April 23, 1937

Lieutenant-Colonel R. E. Lee
38 Eaton Square
London, S.W. 1
England

Dear Raymond:

The pressure for the reformation of the personnel of the Supreme Court is still going forward here. Arthur Krock and Lowell Mellett tell me that recent conditions have not altered the situation and that the President will press forward with his plan. They also believe that he will achieve the substance of it, although concessions of form, they believe, may be made. A good deal of the hostility to the plan and the resentment which it has caused in some quarters would, I think, be mitigated if some of the old gentlemen would gracefully retire. My old chief, who is eighty, would, I think, be wise to do this. I do not think that further service will add to his already great reputation, and one does lose touch with affairs when one is eighty and has been on the Supreme Court for twenty years. There are three others who could well do the same. But I am afraid that they may get into a fighting frame of mind and produce a result which will not do them, the Court, or the Country any good.

As ever,

To **RANALD MACDONALD**

This letter is one of the most concise expressions of DA's distinctive pragmatism coupled with a strong sense of the standards to be pursued.

September 29, 1937

Dear Ranald:

Thank you for your note enclosing the editorial from the *New York Times*. I do not differ with it. I understand your difficulty in classifying me as either a pro- or anti-New Dealer. I couldn't classify myself. I know however that I am not a convert, recent or otherwise. It seems to me profitless to be for or against things in broad categories depending either on the persons who advocate them or upon general principles of a great and sweeping nature. It seems to me that Walter Lippmann tends to do this in his recent book, at least as far as I have gone. It is much more satisfying to me to consider specific proposals from the point of view of whether they are practicable methods of dealing with immediate problems. If the collateral damage is great, they ought to be rejected, but not because someone can tag them with a philosophical classification.

So far as Black is concerned, he is not the kind of man whom I would like to see on the Supreme Court, but neither are half of the judges there. I think that the considerations which lead to his selection are those of adroitness and smartness, which are always a mistake. The formal membership in the Klan does not seem to me to add much to what was known before, except that it is the kind of thing which would have defeated him if it had been known. My chief reason for not joining with those who condemn him in an unqualified way is that those who do it would approve an appointment just as bad provided the social and political background of an appointee were different.

We ought to have on the Supreme Court great judges of the stature of Holmes. That is almost impossible, but there are those who approach him such as Stone, Brandeis, Cardozo, Chief Justice Waite, and in some respects Taney. When we get away from this and get political appointees in the best sense, we have always had to put up with drawbacks which look serious at the outset but which turn out to be serious only insofar as they are indications of limitations which cannot be surmounted.

. . .

My love to Anne.

As ever,

To **DAVID ACHESON**

A colorful vignette of a regal affair put on by the President (Seymour) of Yale.

December 13, 1937

Dear Dave:

. . .

Alice and I have been in New Haven. I had to spend Wednesday and part of Thursday there working on a revision of the By-laws of the University. I then returned for Friday evening and all day Saturday for Corporation meetings. On Saturday evening Charlie Seymour had a dinner for the Corporation and reception at his new house. The house, which was left to the University, has been remodeled at tremendous expense to it and is much too grand. However, some people seem to believe that a college president should live like a Sultan of Bagdad. We certainly have provided such a background. The evening which started out as a great success ended in a minor disaster. The Seymours gave us a beautiful dinner, one item of which was the lobster. This destroyed the President, although the rest of us survived. In the midst of the reception at the School of Fine Arts, when he was shaking hands with several thousand people, he became the most beautiful green color and had to be taken home and put to bed.

My love, as ever,

To **COL. R. E. LEE**

Here is a taste of DA's work at the bar in private life. The revelation of Richard Whitney's peculation produced an investigation in which DA represented the New York Stock Exchange. The last paragraph of the excerpt would appear to describe a phenomenon not limited to the period of the letter.

July 12, 1938

Dear Raymond:

Your letter of last May was much enjoyed by the whole family. My reply to it has been delayed by compulsions of law practice and difficulties of getting five temperamental people—of whom Jane and I appear to have been the most temperamental—to agree on plans for the summer. We have come to a breathing space in both activities.

As to the first, I have finished one big job and am just about to go into the final sprint on another. The British American Tobacco Company brought suit against the Federal Reserve Bank to recover an amount, which would have seemed colossal in the old days, for gold which it turned in to the Bank in 1933. The Company wanted to be paid at the rate of $35.00 an ounce instead of at the pre-devaluation rate of $20.67. Since the gold had been delivered on account of orders which I issued when I was at the Treasury, the Bank retained me to defend it. We tried the case in the spring and recently the United States District Court decided the case for us on all points. It took a great deal of time and energy, and so you may be sure that the result is most pleasing.

The other matter is the one to which you referred in your letter, the unhappy affair arising out of Mr. Whitney's indiscretions. The Securities and Exchange Commission held protracted hearings to find out the facts about that affair. I was chosen to represent the Stock Exchange and developed into something in the nature of a friend of the Court, since I felt that the proceedings should not be of an adversary nature but that the Exchange should be as interested as the Government in clearing the matter up. We finished the hearings sometime ago, then wrote a report which we felt gave the facts impartially, and are supposed to receive tomorrow the draft of report prepared by officials of the Commission. When I have gone over that and said my say, I think I am through with this employment. Suggestions were made at one time that I should go to New York to represent the Exchange continuously. That, however, did not seem to me to be the kind of thing that I wanted to do so that if I represent them again it will be here in specific matters. My concern with the report is not to defend or protect anybody but to eliminate from it anything which is sensational, sarcastic, smart, or warped. The standard which I have been trying to get the Commission to adopt is two reports which you once sent me by British investigating bodies, one the episode of the budget leak when Mr. J.H. Thomas resigned, and the other the investigation into Sir Christopher Bullock's indiscretions.

In this country the bright young men have a leaning toward sarcasm and innuendo which tends to defeat the purpose of a report so far as any enlightenment is concerned and to divide readers into cheering camps, some for the Government and some agin it. This sort of thing seems to me to get nowhere very fast.

. . .

To JANE ACHESON

A lively glimpse, here, of vacation life. The reference to the chateau is to the site of a bizarre stay in France experienced by Mary and David Acheson and DA's sister's daughter, Nona. Dick Wilmer, a classmate of DA's, was a distinguished lawyer of eminently respectable tastes. His son, Grant, was David Acheson's lifelong friend.

August 11, 1938

Dearest Jane:

I hope that all goes well with you and the stock company. We are enjoying ourselves for a week in Paris before starting off with Margo and Gardiner to motor to Monte Carlo for several days of tennis and swimming. We have been bicycling for a day in the country, looking at modern painting of a particularly wild sort, seeing very few people, and having a good time. The children are, with Nona and a Russian boy named Maxy—John Emmett is also there—at a chateau on the Loire, which Mary describes as a bug house. She says that there is a crucifix there "with real human skin"! The lady seems to be slightly mad and the children don't get enough to eat—but they really are enjoying the oddity of it. They ride bicycles, play tennis and swim as well as work a little at French.

We go to England on the 20th where we hope to hear from you. Ranald and I were very gay on the boat—which was about ⅓rd full. We played tennis on a lovely full sized tennis court, danced, and picked up such girls as there were. The Wilmers were on board. Dick disapproved of us, but Grant thought we were the tops. We shall tell Raymond and Jeanette all about you and shall all miss you in doing so.

Good luck to you, my love, we shall look forward to seeing you in a month.

Much love, as ever,

To GEORGE RUBLEE

DA's senior partner, George Rublee, had accepted a mission to represent President Roosevelt in interceding with Hitler's government on behalf of the German Jews. DA's report gave Rublee some news of related and unrelated developments in Washington.

January 17, 1939

Mr. George Rublee
Intergovernmental Committee
No. 1, Central Buildings
Westminster, London, S.W. 1
England

Dear George:

I did not see Justice Brandeis a week ago Sunday, as I had expected to. He was taken ill on the preceding Friday and is only now able to get up a little while each day. The official bulletin says that is was influenza, but I gather that for several days they were quite nervous about him and are much relieved to have him well again.

He sent me a message through his secretary that he did not believe it wise to make any economic concessions to Germany. Yesterday I had a talk with Ben Cohen, and Ben, as he always does, took a calm and moderate view. He said that he fully understood the tremendous difficulty of your position and in what he was about to say was not attempting to suggest how the problem could be solved, if it could be solved at all, but only what he thought was wise from your point of view. His suggestion was that so far as possible you attempt not to identify yourself as an advocate for any suggestion which may come out of your Berlin visits. He said that he found among Jews with whom he had talked a strong feeling against concessions to Germany. He felt that the State Department might regard any such concessions as contrary to the spirit of Mr. Hull's trade treaties with their Most-Favored-Nation clauses and that you might find yourself battling alone to put through a program. I told him that you felt a tremendous responsibility for the people for whose benefit you were carrying on these negotiations and in fact you seemed to have a greater feeling of responsibility for them than anyone else, but that I would pass along his views to you.

I could not write you last week because, as you may have seen, Felix asked me to represent him here in the hearings before the Sub-Committee of the Judiciary Committee on his nomination to the Supreme Court. We had three days of hearings. Two were given over to the oddest collection of people I have ever seen. All were fanatical and some were very definitely mental cases. One poor old fellow informed the Committee that this country was founded on five principles Christianity, Masonry, checks and balances, the Trinity, and God. This is the kind of thing we listened to for two days, interspersed with vicious misrepresentation of Felix's views and undisguised anti-Semitism. The last day Felix appeared after I had carried out some negotiations with the Committee. He did a superb job; was vigorous, dignified, and did not try to be adroit, and made an excellent impression. Both the Sub-Committee and the full Committee have unanimously endorsed him, and I expect that he will be confirmed today or tomorrow.

Our love to you and Juliet.

As ever,

To SENATOR GEORGE L. RADCLIFFE OF MARYLAND

When DA went to bat, he went all the way, and here he was on one of his favorite subjects.

June 13, 1939

Honorable George L. Radcliffe
Senate Office Building
Washington, D.C.

Dear Senator Radcliffe:

I am writing to you as a member of the Senate Committee on the Library in wholehearted support of the President's nomination of Archibald MacLeish to be Librarian of Congress. What I say about Mr. MacLeish's qualities of mind, personality, and character is inevitably colored by one of the oldest friendships and deepest affections of my life. But it is also based upon intimate knowledge of him for almost thirty years. We came to Yale together in the fall of 1911, were classmates there and afterwards at the Harvard Law School. We have been constant companions, sharing together our experiences of life, both the good and the bad, during the twenty odd years since our graduation. I have known and been devoted to Mrs. MacLeish since she was a girl, and I have known his children and he mine since their births.

In our college and law school days there was no question that Archibald MacLeish was preeminent among us in the field of literature, scholastic work, and as a leader of courage and character. He was not only the outstanding poet of our particular time but ranks with the greatest which our generation has produced in this country and in England. It did not need the Pulitzer Prize for his poem "Conquistador" to establish this among those who knew his verse. At the Law School he was a leader both scholastically and in the intellectual life of the School. He had in those days, as he has now, the gift of friendship, and there are few who can spend a half hour with him without catching the fire of his enthusiasm and wanting to go with him on whatever task he has in hand. His courage has been shown on the football field, as an officer in the Field Artillery during the World War, and by his willingness to stand for the right as he has seen it against any opposition.

After leaving the Law School, he practiced law in Boston, where he soon attracted the attention of the leaders of the Bar and seemed destined for a brilliant and successful career as a lawyer. He determined, however, that this was not his chosen career and withdrew from practice to devote himself to literature and scholarship. He became, as you know, one of the Editors of *Fortune Magazine,* where he wrote penetrating articles on both business and government, and for the last year has been Curator of the Nieman Fellows at Harvard University. In this latter position he has the function of guiding a group of active newspaper men who have been given a year's leave of absence to make use of the intellectual resources of a great university.

In short, from the time that he was a young man, Mr. MacLeish has been outstanding among his contemporaries. He has rare gifts of mind and character and understands as few people do the function and methods of scholarship as applied to the problems of our age.

. . .

To **EDGAR S. FURNISS**

DA became a member of the Yale Corporation in 1936 and was a devoted and thorough student of Yale's affairs. This letter indicates the DA manner of coming to grips with Yale's educational problems. Furniss was Provost of Yale University.

October 25, 1939

Dean Edgar S. Furniss
Woodbridge Hall
Yale University
New Haven, Connecticut

Dear Ed:

I have been thinking over your letter of October 18 in which you ask what kind of information about the Graduate School would be helpful for members of the Educational Policy Committee. The following would be very helpful and interesting to me.

(1) A brief historical description of the origin and development of the Graduate School in American universities. I understand that it is a peculiarly American phenomenon. What caused it, and in general how do universities in other countries accomplish the same ends?

(2) An historical description of the Graduate School at Yale. When did it start? How has it grown? You might have some figures on the total enrollment over a reasonable period and over the last few years we might go into the numerical development of the various departments of study. This ought to give us some idea of the function of the Graduate School. Is it a professional school for teachers or is it part this and part something else?

(3) Financial data about the Graduate School. At present its finances are included in the faculty of Arts and Sciences. It would be interesting to have some idea of the receipts of the School from tuition, dormitories, rent, etc; the costs, so far as they can be separated out.

(4) A statistical appraisal of the length of time students stay in the School and the amount of this time which they spend on the work of the School and how much they have to spend on teaching or other form of self-support.

(5) We might then start with the most important (in point of numbers and expenditures) of the departments of study in the Graduate School and

have a pretty exact report of what the students and the members of the faculty do in that department. We might then attempt to appraise the result in terms of its effect on the faculty. Does the Graduate School serve as a place for important and scholarly research work by the faculty?

The last suggestion is along the lines we are following in our Committee here on Administrative Procedure. Our Committee sends a member of its professional staff into an agency and has him report exactly what the agency does in detail and quite objectively. We are not concerned with what it should do but with what it does in the first instance.

Take the English Department, if that is the largest one in the School, and tell us how many students and how many members of the faculty work in that Department. Who are the members of the faculty? Then tell us exactly what happens. I am, for instance, familiar with how undergraduate teaching is carried on and how Law School teaching is carried on. But I haven't the faintest idea of what happens on the first day that the Graduate School meets, how the work is organized, what the people read, why they read it, whom they talk with about it, and what they do. I should like to have this described as though you were telling a man from Mars about it.

This is a large order, but may be useful in giving you some idea of the depth of ignorance with which you have to deal.

As ever,

To PRESIDENT ROOSEVELT

The exchange set forth here marked a turning point in DA's life, and charts the reconciliation with FDR which brought DA back to government (DA broke with FDR in 1933 over monetary policy and left the Treasury in disfavor).

October 2, 1940

Honorable Dean Acheson
Union Trust Building
Washington, D.C.

Dear Dean:

I am perfectly delighted to read your letter in the paper this morning particularly since your support of me is based on consideration of world conditions and a recognition of their serious import to our American future. Quite aside from our own personal friendship, I am glad that you have publicly taken this much more important view.

My best wishes to you,

Always sincerely,
Franklin D. Roosevelt

October 4, 1940

The President
Washington, D.C.

My dear Mr. President:

I deeply appreciate the kind note from you which came to me this morning, particularly as we all know the great burdens which you carry. It was a joy and a duty—which Justice Holmes says are all one—to say publicly how essential for our country it is to have you at the helm. Beside my fullest support, may I add every wish that you may have the health and strength to meet the heavy strain of the days ahead.

Most respectfully,

To JEREMIAH M. EVARTS

DA explains his support of President Roosevelt to a friend who must have been of another persuasion.

October 8, 1940

Jeremiah M. Evarts, Esq.
50 Grove Street
New York City

Dear Jerry:

I am sorry to learn that my letter in support of the President shocked you and that you thought it at variance with the truth. It is quite plain that we can never agree on what you call facts, much less on conclusions.

You say that the President has done nothing for seven years to improve our defense. I say that the fact we have a first class navy rescued from the decay of disarmament policies of 1921 and 1930, greatly increased and in fighting trim, is due to him alone.

You say that although the President and the State Department had sources of information of the danger ahead before war came, he did not warn the country. I point out to you this is exactly what he did do in the summer of 1939 when he called the leaders of both parties to the White House. At that time it was a distinguished Republican who insisted that he had private sources of information superior and contrary to the Government's, defeated the repeal of the Neutrality Act at that time and greatly hampered its subsequent modification.

You say that the President has "screamed" at the Dictators and you refer to their opponents as "so-called democracies," and to our attitude as "partisan." Perhaps this suggests the greatest difference between us. You give me the impression that you see nothing in the war in Europe and Asia beyond a military conflict. If I do you an injustice, forgive me. As I tried to say in my letter, the inestimable value of the President's leadership, to my mind, is that he has aroused the country to the nature of the danger we face, to the grim fact that it cannot be avoided, and to the necessity of meeting it at the most advantageous point for us. If this is partisanship, then I am for it.

Most sincerely,

To DAVID ACHESON

DA's son David (then in the Navy) had come upon Don Marquis's Ar-chie and Mehitabel, and draws from DA an appreciation of that classic and a wry report of life in the Department of State (DA was an Assistant Secretary).

January 17, 1943

Dear Dave:

Your words about our vestigial youth are most heartening but they are undone by your telling us about Don Marquis's Archie. That character was a fragment of our youth and it was definitely in the past. Appreciation of Ar-chie was the mark of a true intellectual even before Krazy Kat broke us into the funnies on a high plane. It is good stuff and I am glad that you agree.

. . .

We are having revolutionary activities in the old Dept. of State. First of all, we now "speak." "The State Dept. Speaks" is a series of four radio pro-grams at 7 PM on Saturday nights. I go on next Sat. with my buddy Mr. Berle and two others. We tell all, to the wonderment of the populace, the despair of our own friends and the exasperation of the *Washington Post*. I am told that the public eats it up. If it does indigestion lies ahead. It is not as good as the Aldrich family and not as bad as Arthur Godfrey at 7:45 AM.

Aside from this we are also reorganized. It is quite a newspaper suc-cess. We have a chart with squares and lines and nearly everyone has a new title, but the same old faces peer over the ramparts and no one has yet had that salutary shot in the back, "pour encourager les autres." I am supposed to have more reponsibility and at the same time greater freedom from detail. Perhaps—but Monday was much like Saturday (which was supposed to be B.C.).

. . .

I have a letter from Ned Burling tonight in which he says that the talk is that I am to be transferred to Solicitor General. This is, I think, the old talk which Francis Biddle started. I have had nothing to do with it and shall not. They may do with me as they deem best—and it probably won't be. Somewhere today I saw Washington referred to as the "City of Magnificent Differences." Why that should come into my mind now I don't know, except that I can see why some people would be pleased to see me go to the scholarly seclusion of the Solicitor Generalship where I would argue every day before—but not with—Felix. We still walk down together every day. On Saturday he threw his back out leaning over to buy a *N.Y. Times* and I had to send him off to the doctor. It shows what Arthur Krock can do to a man, doesn't it.

Much love,

As ever,

To ELEANOR G. ACHESON

DA, writing to his mother, captured the environment of an international conference on postwar relief at Atlantic City, with the eye of a painter or caricaturist.

November 27, 1943

Dearest Mother:

Alice telephoned me that I had a letter from you and read it to me over the telephone. You were very sweet indeed to think of me and to do what you did. I am most grateful for the present and shall use it for something really special. I have found out over the years that it is useless to tell you that you should not do these things, especially when you have your own serious financial troubles, but you are incorrigible and I am continually grateful.

I have thought of you many times during these last weeks here in Atlantic City. On the rare occasions when I get out of the Hotel—and sometimes days have gone by when that was not possible—I have passed the shooting galleries or their successors which you and I used to frequent and where you used to so amaze the proprietors. The place has changed a great deal since those days. The Marlborough Blenheim is next door to where we are staying and is still as ugly as it used to be. Some of the old rambling, wooden hotels are still here, but for the most part everything is larger and more garish. As you know for a time the Army took over nearly all the hotels and still has some of them. As a result the old boardwalk demonstrators of potato peelers, etc., have disappeared, and I have not seen in operation any of the auction rooms, where people used to find themselves the possessors of objects for which they had no earthly use. But the wheel chairs are still here and people who carve in sand have not forgotten their art.

The Conference itself has certainly been strenuous, and I hope and think has been a success. The original plan was that I should open it and that a delegate from one of the smaller countries, possibly the Netherlands, would be elected the Permanent Chairman. However, trouble immediately started. The Russians took the view that, if I were not the Chairman, then one of the great powers (that meant themselves) should be Chairman. This was impossible because their delegation had not arrived, and it would have meant opposition from other countries. As soon as word got abroad that a small country might have the chairmanship, there were many candidates. It looked as though we might begin proceedings with a brawl. As a result, a meeting of the four great powers decided that I should be Chairman and I agreed. Fortunately we never know what we are in for when we make these decisions, or I think my courage would have failed. It has meant that, in addition to attempting to run a large and somewhat unwieldy American delegation, I have had to take on the responsibility for the Conference and the endless meetings and discussions in which we persuade and cajole people not to do foolish things. It looks as though this were having a successful result, although I shall have my fingers crossed until the last drop of the gavel. The unpredictable element is what our Russian friends may do and what they are thinking. They are extremely reticent, and several times have come out with decisions which have all the possibilities of trouble and which take many hours of midnight discussion to get into safe channels. This has resulted in my falling into a troubled sleep somewhere between two and three o'clock every night and the most colossal strain on my digestion. I have to go to or give a lunch nearly every day and recently a dinner almost every night. The delegates of the various countries have to be entertained at cocktails in parties small enough to make them feel that they are having personal attention, which means frequently enough to cover over one hundred or one hundred and fifty important delegates. This requires an iron constitution which, as you recall, I have not always had. But I seem to be bearing up fairly well and hope for the best.

Today we are finishing up the committee stage of our work. This is really the heart of the whole matter and, should we get through today without trouble, the rest ought to be formal; but, as I said, you never can tell. The whole Council is planning to meet in secret session on Monday to adopt the final recommendations and on Wednesday in open session to make the closing speeches and to adjourn.

One of the trials has been the press. On the whole it has behaved fairly well, with the exception of the *New York Times,* which has had an extremely troublesome fellow, who seems bent not on helping but on injuring the Conference. I have to have a so-called press conference every two or three days and see dozens of them in small groups in between. The press, of course, thrives on controversies. There is always a disgruntled delegate who likes to intimate that some row or other is brewing. This produces a great flurry and requires an hour or more to calm down. It also makes no difference at what hour of the day or night one of the reporters gets an idea. A few days ago my telephone went off at about 2:30 in the morning and I was cross examined in a somewhat dazed state by one of them who was trying to get a story in for the late editions of the next morning's paper. But this is all in the days' work.

We are hoping to be back in Washington on Wednesday, and I shall endeavor to catch up on a little sleep before going back to the Department. I had hoped that I could pay you a visit before going back, but so much has developed here and in Washington so much has accumulated that I must put in some time there before going away again.

You might be interested in knowing what one of the full sessions of the Council is like. The meetings are held in the large ballroom of the Hotel. The delegates sit at a large U-shaped table, with the Chairman in the middle of the closed end, flanked by the Secretary of the Council on the left and by the Director General on the right. The countries are arranged in alternate alphabetical order, beginning on either side of the Chairman and going down to the very end of the U, where Yugoslavia and Venezuela bring up the end. The microphone is in front of the Chairman, and emits groans or squeaks depending on its emotional level at the time. Each meeting has an agenda of the business to come up. The Chairman states the items, the Secretary reads the various documents, and discussion on each item then ensues. One of my greatest difficulties is in understanding what the delegates say. This is due partly to acoustics and partly to language difficulty. While all of the delegates, except one, speak English after a fashion, their command of that language tends to weaken under emotional stress. There is also a tendency to become involved in parliamentary tangles. Since I have never before presided at a large gathering and have never to my knowledge read anything on parliamentary law, I have to do a great deal of improvisation. Some of my rulings remind me of a remark made by a judge of our trial court in Washington, who said, "This Court is often in error, but never in doubt." So far everyone has accepted the presiding officer's efforts with good nature and, except for the Norwegians who have been consistently difficult and never wise, I think that there is general good will toward me.

I shall call you up when I get back and expect a full report on your health and activities. In the meantime if you could drop me a line on either or both it would be most welcome.

With much love, dearest Mother, as always—

Devotedly,

To **DAVID ACHESON**

DA's son was serving in the Pacific Theatre and DA sought to give him a sense of the war as seen from Washington. The reference to "another's stubbornness" was clearly to FDR. The "Monetary Conference" was Bretton Woods. "D" Day in Europe was a fortnight earlier.

June 20, 1944

Dear Dave:

I cannot tell you how much excitement and pleasure your letters produce. We all go over them singly and collectively and then read appropriate parts to enthusiastic addicts of yours like the little judge. Keep them up. I shall hope to do better myself. Exhaustion and spiritual degeneration are my present difficulties. My daily walk with Felix helps but does not repair the obsolescence. But to get down to business, let me list the news.

. . .

I have to go to the Monetary Conference on July 1 for 3 weeks as one of the U.S. delegates. Neither I nor the other delegates know what the hell we are doing and we can't get the Treasury to take time off to work it out with us. But somehow I think we can get along. Henry Morgenthau and his boys will do their best to frustrate themselves and all of us. Fundamentally they are stupid and rude—a bad combination—but have what Judge Covington used to call "low cunning." It doesn't get too far.

. . .

The invasion is going well and the radio tonight tells of a great impending naval battle in your region. The soldiers and sailors are doing a good job. The statesmen have a less clear record. In the immediate offing are two main challenges. The 1) French situation and the 2) organization to keep peace.

On the first we are in a mess. It comes, I think, from letting personalities obscure more fundamental factors. We are rightly antipathetic to De-Gaulle. He is a difficult, mystical, ambitious and narrow man. But he is only a man and not the French Comité or the determining factor unless we make him so, as we probably now have done. Furthermore we cannot govern France and if we try to do so we shall greatly prejudice the war. By strengthening the Comité we would play down DeGaulle and take the only available means of administering France until she can get her own government. This was the idea on France in the Secretary's speech of April 9.

But by Churchill's bad handling, by another's stubbornness, by De-Gaulle's unwillingness to seek a solution and by bad luck we are in an awful mess. I can only hope that men who are said to be great realists will prove to be so soon. If not, we shall have lost battles just as important as that of Normandy.

. . .

My own work is—so it seems to me—in mangy shape. Sometimes I'se up, sometimes I'se down, sometimes I'se almost to the ground. The problems are too big for me; the people are too small; I wrestled with both too long. If the voters return us all to private life I shall doubt whether they will do better, but be willing to say—Thy judgments are true and righteous altogether.

Much love to you from all of us jointly and severally.

As ever,

To DAVID ACHESON

DA reports here on the Bretton Woods conference which established the international financial institutions and arrangements which (with some significant changes) exist today. In the last paragraph, the reference to "this show" was clearly to the war. The "hell of a shove" was to come in October at Leyte Gulf and in Europe not long after.

August 1, 1944

Dear Dave:

. . .

Bretton Woods turned out to be even more strenuous than Atlantic City—and more confusing—the latter conference I ran, so that if there was confusion I knew why—this one ran itself with help here and there, and as merely one of the delegates I was perplexed a good part of the time—But the result was good and I hope important—if the country and Congress will support it—that will be affected by the election—

Our physical set up would have amused you. Instead of offices and suites, our immediate State Department group lived in a hotel, some four miles away. Transportation was always in default, so that when we got through work about two o'clock in the morning we couldn't get home and to bed. This led to excessive alcoholism. Our office was a badge of this. No room could be found for Miss Evans, Miss Ambrose, Pete Collado and myself. So a corner of the ball room of the hotel—used as the main meeting room—which had been fitted up as a bar, was partitioned off with canvas—and there we set up shop. Of course, we were right in the middle of every meeting, which was punctuated by our telephone and typewriters; our filing cases were the sinks and shelves of the bar, but our spirits were good and the product excellent.

Our delegation was large and, as the Baltimore Sun once said about me, uncontaminated by previous contact with the subject matter of its new duties. This led to the catch-as-catch-can method—mostly can—and a certain amount of free wheeling. But even this calls for effort and most of the boys and girl—one—couldn't stay the course. So, in the end, a little group in a smoke filled room wrote the ticket. Large sections of the ticket I couldn't understand—some of it will surely make *The New Yorker*—but we put it through by main stamina and violence in the end, and everyone seemed happy. I shall try to send you a copy of the final Act if the mail will carry so bulky a parcel.

I hope that we are getting to the end of this show and can all be together soon. Everyone is getting tired and out of sorts. My hope is that if we give it another hell of a shove something may break—Anyway that is my story and I am sticking to it.

Much love to you from every one of us.

As ever,

To DAVID ACHESON

DA reported here on the new line-up at the State Department under Secretary Stettinius. As this letter shows, DA's supply of enthusiasm was ebbing.

December 27, 1944

Dear Dave:

I am distressed that your radio bulletin has not given you the details on the six new assistants who have caused all the commotion in the Senate. We have had quite a lot of excitement. First of all, at Ed's request, Berle, Long, and Shaw resigned. The result of this was to leave me in solitary grandeur and with a considerable amount of paper work. It would not have been so bad if it had not cost me five dollars for a bond to assure the Government that I would be reasonably honest. I was a little hurt by the amount of the bond, since the Government did not believe that I would steal more than $5,000. The Secretary then got the Congress to authorize two additional assistant secretaries of State. The President nominated Joe Grew to be Under Secretary; Jimmy Dunn to be Assistant Secretary in charge of geographical areas other than the Western Hemisphere; Nelson Rockefeller to be in charge of Western Hemisphere relations; Will Clayton to take over economic affairs which I have been doing, plus aviation, shipping, and telecommunications; Archie MacLeish to have public and cultural relations; and Brig. Gen. Holmes (late Vice President of the World's Fair in New York and now Chief Civil Affairs Officer in France) to be in charge of the administrative services of the Department and visa, passport, and sleuthing work. I remain to be a sort of legislative counsel, dealing with our relations with Congress, the preparation of legislation, conduct of hearings, etc, and with a somewhat vague assignment to supervise and coordinate our participation in international conferences. This is the new set up. We can only end with the words of the well-known Christmas anthem "Fall on your knees!"

To DAVID ACHESON

In this letter appears an early sign of DA's misgivings about the proposed United Nations and about the postwar conduct of the Soviet Union.

April 2, 1945

Dear Dave:

It is far too long since I have sent a word to you, and in the meantime you have been very generous to us, and I have also shared some of your observations to Felix. But since I have written you, I have had to cover a good many thousands of miles and poured out almost an equal amount of words.

. . .

Since I last wrote you my own activities have been somewhat intense. There has been a good deal going on on Capitol Hill. We started off the session with hearings before the Senate Foreign Relations Committee on the Mexican Water Treaty, which developed into a fight between California and the rest of the country. California had appropriated $75,000 for the purpose of defeating the treaty, and they certainly have exercised a great deal of ingenuity and perseverance. It isn't at all clear that they won't yet be successful. The hearings went on for weeks, during which practically every red herring in the barrel was dragged several times across the trail and a considerable amount of misrepresentation of fact was indulged in. The California effort seems to me pretty thoroughly unscrupulous. The treaty is most advantageous to the Colorado River Basin states as a whole and is acceptable to Mexico. The interests of the country as a whole are all in favor of its prompt acceptance. Ultimately Mexican claims are bound to increase and the total American interest can only suffer. However, it appears to be the California view that, if they can defeat a settlement now, they may be able to improve their individual situation even though the total American position suffers. I think they are wrong in this analysis, but whether right or wrong it is not a very commendable position. The Treaty is now before the Senate and by the time this letter reaches you the vote will probably have been taken. We are engaged in trying to work on a few critical Senators. No one who has not worked for several years in the field of foreign affairs in this country can possibly understand the stultifying effect of the two-thirds rule for the ratification of treaties upon the whole conduct of our foreign relations.

After this we became involved in a brawl about the aviation agreements. The question was whether they all had to be ratified as treaties or whether only one out of the four had to go through the gauntlet. It was finally decided, we thought, with sufficient acquiescence on the Hill to submit only one and to accept the other three as executive agreements. Then there were charges of misunderstanding, etc., and it looked for a time as though we might have an ugly row with the Senate. This called for innumerable meetings; maneuverings, etc. I hope that we are now out of the woods, but you can never tell.

We submitted the Bretton Woods agreements to Congress, after having had a good deal of difficulty in working out a legislative vehicle for them. Various small, but powerful, groups of bankers have come out against them. Hearings have gone on for two weeks before the House Committee on Banking and Currency. I have made three appearances and am due for a fourth. The tide of battle ebbs and flows. In the meantime we are attempting to build up support in the country. It was for this general purpose that I went out to the Pacific Coast to make a series of speeches, and I have two more fairly large ones to do in the East—a speech before the Economic Club at the Hotel Astor in New York on April 16, and a speech in the Armory in Baltimore on April 12.

. . .

Some recent activities, as you may well guess, are causing us lots of trouble. The President's recent statement confirming the leaks about an agreement at Yalta by which the Ukrainian and White Russian Republics were to have votes on the Assembly, in return for which we might have British and Russian support to claim three votes, has been very serious indeed. The failure to disclose this at the time, the affront to the small nations, the cynicism which to many people it implies, have had a pretty generally shocking effect. When one adds to this the failure of the Russians to send Molotov and the present demand that the Lublin Committee without change be represented, it begins to look as though the whole program had received some pretty damaging body blows. The added trouble is that all of these things seem to be so inexplicable. They make so little sense from the point of view of any real interest of any participant and therefore become even more difficult to explain. However, I think that granted a reasonable amount of good luck the situation can be more or less straightened out.

Molotov, obviously, is not coming, and nothing can be done about that. It remains to be seen what it represents. If the Russians are merely playing a very cautious game, no great harm will be done. If they are preparing more surprises, then of course we can only hold our hats. . . .

. . .

Much love to you from all of us.

As ever,

To **DAVID ACHESON**

Here are DA's reflections on the death of President Roosevelt.

April 30, 1945
Dear Dave:

. . .

Much has happened outside the family circle since I wrote you. You spoke in your letter of the President's death. That was a major shock throughout the country. Some of us have known that the President's health was failing, but we had not known the extent. He had not been in Washington very much. Ed Stettinius, who saw him on his way through Washington to Warm Springs, was deeply shocked at his appearance. It was most impressive, as the news of his death went out, to see the effect on people everywhere. . . . As you listened to conversations on the street car and on the street, you began to realize what I had known intellectually but never appreciated; that is, the tremendous place which the Government and the Presidency, and particularly the late President, played in the lives of everybody. There was with millions of people practically a parent relationship in the psychological sense, and the sudden shock of his death leaves people completely at sea.

. . .

You will be interested to know that shortly before the President's death he decided to make me Solicitor General and so informed the Attorney General. This was all worked out between the Attorney General, the Secretary of State, and myself, and the President was to act upon it when he returned to Washington on the 19th of April. I assume that the matter is, of course, now completely past history. No one has spoken of it again, and I have not raised it and do not intend to. However, it is pleasant to have that last memory of the President.

I am sending you a collector's piece. The enclosed pamphlet, which may interest you on its merits, was sent by Professors Chafee and Maguire of the Law School to Felix. Felix sent it to Lefty Lewis, and you will see Lefty's comments throughout. The verse on the back is by Lefty himself. In case you can't read it, we enclose a translation.

By the way, you may be puzzled as to why I am writing you from Washington. It had been expected that I would go to the Conference at least for a while, although I really have no function to perform. However, Joe Grew has not been at all well and may have to go to the hospital at any time. So we talked it over and decided that I would stay here so as to be ready to become Acting Secretary if Joe should not be well and also to help him. Most of the other brethren are in San Francisco. Archie, who was there, came back for a day or two and tells me that it is considerable of a madhouse. I have no desire to be there and am very glad indeed, in view of the events of the last week, that I was in Washington.

. . .

Much love from all of us.

As ever,

These lines are the product of Wilmarth S. Lewis on reading the following sentence from a publication of the Harvard Law School, entitled "A List of Books Prepared by a Committee of the Faculty for Prospective Law Students Now in Service": "We hope that servicemen will learn elsewhere about books of poetry."

Song of Outside Reading for the Front

Before you land at Harvard Square
We hope you'll find the time
To think of us and read with care
A book or two in rhyme.

CHORUS (by Chafee and Maguire)

When you're lying on your belly
There's nothing quite like Shelley;
Better, far, than drowning
Is an evening with Browning;
The Tropics' torrid heats
Are cooled with lines by Keats;
And wherever you may go
Read Edgar Allen Poe.

To DAVID ACHESON

One of DA's major concerns at this time was the Reciprocal Trade Agreements bill. This letter reported an important milestone.

Department of State
Washington
May 31, 1945

Dear Dave:

Here is something to amuse you for a few minutes—a family "Information Please" prepared last Sunday at the farm.

You may have seen that last Saturday the House passed our Trade Agreements bill. I spent about eight hours at the Capitol sitting in the gallery during the final day, when all the amendments were voted on and the final passage also. The critical moment came when the House sitting as the Committee of the Whole had before it the Republican amendment to strike out Section 2 of the bill, which conferred additional authority to reduce tariffs upon the Secretary of State. We had known that this was going to be the real test, and on Friday afternoon, not only did the issue seem to be in doubt, but even those who were optimistic would not predict more than a margin of ten votes. The Speaker, Will Clayton, and I worked out a letter for the President to send to the Speaker. I got this prepared Friday night, saw the President Saturday morning, and went up to the Capitol with the letter in my pocket. It was kept a great secret. The Speaker did not tell anyone that he had it. He arranged to take himself the last five minutes of the debate on this amendment. During this time he made a most effective speech to a hushed House and then brought out the President's letter. It was one of the few things which I have seen on the Hill which actually changed votes. We came through that amendment with a majority of 23. Every other amendment offered was voted down. But while there were one or two close calls, we never went below 23. On the motion to recommit, on which the Republicans made a last desperate attempt, our majority went to 31 and on final passage it climbed to 86. We all went down after the House adjourned to have a drink with the Speaker and to telephone Mr. Hull. He had just heard the news and told us that he was drinking a highball to us.

The fight in the Senate is very difficult indeed. The Finance Committee is against us, and we have the very puzzling problem of finding the least damaging way of getting the bill to the floor.

I imagine that the House Committee on Banking and Currency will bring out its report on Bretton Woods today. They voted to report it by the excellent majority of 23 to 3. Bretton Woods will go through the House, I think, without trouble and with a large majority. I have similar hopes for it in the Senate.

We get good news from Mary, who writes gay letters and who is handling this whole trying situation beautifully.

We miss you deeply and continually persuade ourselves that some good fortune will bring you back here at least for a thirty days leave.

With much love from all of us.

As ever,

To **MARY A. BUNDY**

There follow a series of excerpts of letters written in 1945 to Mary Acheson (Mrs. William P.) Bundy, who had contracted tuberculosis and was recuperating in Saranac, New York. These comprise a good log of the daily life of a Congressional relations officer, and a variety of candid intelligence.

May 8

Jeanette [Mrs. Raymond E. Lee] had a thoroughly Lee story about her French governess the day the President died. She was overcome and went to stand in front of the White House in her new straw hat. It rained and ruined the hat which gave her great comfort. "This is a trifle to bear in the face of so great a loss." When she came home she found that Jeanette had bought a new puppy, which was crying. "I can find no tears," she said, "the puppy will weep for me." So she took it to bed with her and they have been inseparable.

May 17

Eddie Miller called from San Francisco to say that Stettinius, who was to speak on Monday night on the radio about the Conference and then give a big plug for Bretton Woods and the Trade Agreements was going to walk out on the latter because his Republican colleagues would be offended. I blew up and gave my opinion about the Secretary of State. I suppose this was all taken down, and the Gestapo will fire me. I hope so.

Friday, May 18

I heard a dreadful rumor today that the President thinks well of me and wants to appoint me to an awfully sour job. I shall run like a rabbit if it is true, but I hope not. My great hope now is to get through what I am working on now and get out! It seems like Paradise, though I shall probably hate it.

Saturday, May 19

I enclose the first draft of a speech I am working on for the President. Don't print it in the Saranac *News*. How do you like it. It has to be in the three-sentence-to-a-paragraph style. His Nibs has asked me to dinner on the 28th. I wonder what that is about.

Wednesday, May 23

We have had all kinds of going on today. An obscure assistant attorney general from Texas [Tom Clark] put in Francis Biddle's place. A nice congressman from New Mexico [Clinton Anderson] whom I know and like, put in Wickard's place—a clear gain. A former Senator and Judge [Lewis Schwellenbach] put in Miss Perkins's place—probably a gain again. Poor Francis Biddle has insult added to injury. It looks bad for justice in the abstract and for judgeships in particular. Probably Bob Hannegan will rule the roost.

I have again forgotten to bring home a copy of the revised draft of the President's speech. Tomorrow will do, since the Conference will not end until the first full week in June.

The enclosed column carries some of the venom which all the press feels. Archie gives me lyric accounts of Snow White's [Stettinius] performances, which are beyond belief. The department is beyond belief and God knows how long any sane man can or should stand it. The whole thing would have an intensely humorous side if it were not so terribly serious. We have had luck so far. I'm sure it will hold a little longer until, even in a world of soap operas, reality can catch up with fiction.

Monday, May 28

I have been having a great debate with Joe Grew, who seems to me the Prince of Appeasers. We had it out hot and heavy today, but so far all is well.

DA Note: This refers to a strong difference of opinion between Grew and me regarding the future of the Emperor of Japan. Grew argued for his retention as the main stabilizing factor in Japan; I argued for his removal as a weak character, who yielded to the military demand for war and who could not be relied upon. Grew's view fortunately prevailed. I very shortly came to see that I was quite wrong.

Wednesday, May 30

I am getting full of years and venom in the Department. Not giving a damn for my betters I shall probably get fired but enjoy a freedom of expression not given to more cautious officers. The Acting Secretary gives me the most acute pain.

Sunday, June 3

On Saturday—this is secret—Judge Vinson [Fred M. Vinson, Director of the Office of Economic Stabilization] asked me if I would be willing to take over Leo Crowley's job [Director, Foreign Economic Administration]. He did not offer it, since it isn't vacant. I said that I would think about the matter, but was inclined to say no. I thought that I was not really equipped to do that job, that the job shouldn't exist, and that I had to go back to practicing law anyway. But I shall give it real thought some time. I know not when.

Monday, June 4

John Dickey thinks that I should go out to San Francisco to try from there to prevent them from imposing the veto provision on the amendment clauses. He thinks, I guess rightly, that they are making the charter absolutely unchangeable and insuring that the organization can never take a position to unify the world in the face of a major threat of war. He thinks that it will not prevent wars as it is. Unless it can fight a Lincoln war "to preserve the union" it offers no hope of progress.

Tomorrow the House takes up Bretton Woods. I think that will go well. Thursday the Senate votes on Trade Agreements. That will catch hell.

Sunday evening, June 10

On Saturday I went to the White House to talk to Judge Vinson and try to escape with honor from the Foreign Economic Administration menace. I said that I was out as a possibility and suggested that he have Truman appoint Clayton as head of FEA, keeping him also as Assistant Secretary. Clayton could have Willard Thorp actually run the FEA. This arrangement would rule out conflicts between the State Department and FEA and would strengthen Clayton's position very much.

Vinson thought this was a smart idea but he asked what I would do if the President continued to insist that I take on this job. I said that I presumed that the President would say this to me, in which case I was sure that I could convince him of the wisdom of the Clayton appointment. If there were valid reasons why it could not be done, I would very reluctantly accede to the President's request. There is a strong possibility that nothing will be done until the budget is through on July 1.

Monday evening, June 11

Yesterday afternoon it appears that the White House was raising the roof trying to find me, telephoning B. Evans, the Department, everywhere except the farm and the house, where he was told I would be at definite periods. My curiosity is almost too much, but superstition prevents my calling to find out what it was all about. If I do, it will turn out to have been something which I don't want to have catch up with me.

One of the amusing and ironic episodes in this strange life of Washington is the hell which we are catching for arresting the man who was making off with our secret papers. Of course, those like Drew Pearson who are nervous at the possibilities are easy to understand. But the rest of the citizenry seem to be provoked that we didn't find some one else in the chickenhouse when the lights went on. The idea seems to have been that we should have apologized and turned the lads loose when they are not Drew Pearson or whomever the speaker dislikes most. Also some of our own boys who have shown papers to the press under instructions are beginning to get worried about their own position. Will their superiors stay hitched when the time comes?

It all shows that service of the Republic is no bed of roses. As one of our colored drivers said—I think I told you—"The army does the fightin' but we kinda does the brain work." Or do we?

Monday, June 18

This was Eisenhower day. . . . He rode to the Capitol and there delivered what I thought was a rather dreary speech which said everyone was wonderful. He didn't mention the State Department; but would have, I am sure, if some one had called it to his attention.

The crack of the day: that Churchill like Caesar, believes that de Gaulle should be divided into three parts.

. . .

Tuesday, June 19

. . .

My friend Archie [MacLeish] has telephoned to me again about going out to San Francisco; but I have fought him and an order from the Sec. of State also. I can go along in my own simple way. But Ed Stettinius is not going to tell me what to do or where to go as long as I can navigate for myself.

Friday, June 22

My life has become complicated by a press story that I am to succeed Mr. Crowley. The only happy feature is another story that Oscar Cox is going to do the same thing. This helps to confuse the issue. It all depends, as the New Yorker says, on what paper you read.

Senator Barkley is throwing a lunch at the Senate for Clayton, Charles Taft and me on Monday. In Senate circles this means that we have arrived and become one of the boys—or, perhaps, three of the boys.

We are off to an evening at the Fulbrights—and more Senators!

Monday, June 25

Just before I left the Department my nerve was almost shattered. Barbara [Miss Barbara Evans, DA's secretary] opened the door while I was signing papers and came in with all four propellers full steam ahead. For some reason the heel of her shoe came off and she came down like the Queen Mary running into the Statue of Liberty. I had to be fanned and given sedatives for some time. I asked her for God's sake to get up on the table and dive off where I could see her and not slide for third base behind me. I practically came right out of my shoes.

Sunday, July 1

We have been told officially that our new Secretary will be Mr. Byrnes of South Carolina. This does not move me to any enthusiasm. Felix [Frankfurter] thinks very well of him and, I am sure, rightly in the light of his experience on the Court. But in this field of foreign policy, I have seen several problems put up to Byrnes and he never seemed to understand the criteria for judgment. I think, however, he will do his wowing without me—which is probably in accord with his own wishes.

. . .

Thursday, July 5

This has been quite a day—politically and amusingly. Henry Morgenthau is out. Justice Roberts is out. As a piccolo solo Thurman Arnold is out. Ben Cohen is in—the State Department. Life is in a whirl!

Yesterday I told the new Secretary of State that I was leaving; and he said I wasn't; and we argued for a while, and he asked to postpone the decision until he came back from Europe. To which I agreed, without changing my view.

Saturday, July 7

We have a great plan for the Supreme Court vacancy. The President should appoint Bob Taft—thus removing him from the Senate. The Democratic Governor of Ohio appoints Charlie Taft to the Senate. Then Bob Taft, Bill Douglas, and Hugo Black destroy one another! Pretty neat!

Saturday, July 14

Yesterday the Senate Committee on Foreign Relations reported out the Charter 20 to 0. It will come up on the floor July 23rd. Bretton Woods comes up on Monday. The House yesterday passed our Export-Import Bank bill with only 6 dissenting votes. We hope to get that through the Senate before it adjourns. So far so good. A pretty fair record.

Thursday, July 19

Today another chapter closed. The Senate approved Bretton Woods 61 to 16. This only came after a last minute close squeak when Joe Ball [D., Minnesota] proposed a diabolical amendment which would have defeated the whole thing and which was defeated by a majority of only 17. My nerves are shattered but happily so.

We shall have a day or so of frantic effort to get the rest of our legislative program through. Tax treaties with the UK, the Food and Agriculture Organization, the Export-Import Bank. And then the Charter [U.N.] which I have always thought was the easiest of all.

When it is over, I shall be glad to take a bit of a rest. It has been a rather long grind and, I think, a rather successful one.

Friday, July 20

We have a law a day these days. Yesterday Bretton Woods (today the House agreed to the Senate amendments); today the Export-Import Bank Bill; tomorrow the the Food and Agriculture Organization Act and two tax treaties. This, with the Charter, winds up our program for the season. It has been a big job.

We are getting worried about Joe Grew. He is tired, worried, and very out-to-lunch. We are trying to devise a system to find out what he is doing so that he will not make some really bad gaff before Byrnes comes home. But it isn't easy, since he resists all attempts.

Sunday, July 22

The Food and Agriculture Bill was passed on Saturday. The Charter comes up Monday.

To **DAVID ACHESON**

DA was about to resign as Assistant Secretary; reported a close shave in Senate ratification of the U.N. Treaty. "Johnnie" was John W. Castles, father-in-law of David Acheson ("Dorothea" was Mrs. Castles, "Pat" Mrs. David Acheson).

July 28, 1945

Dear Dave:

. . .

As Alice has probably told you, Johnnie called us to invite us to go to their camp in Canada with Dorothea, Pat and himself. They are going off on the 5th of August to be there until the end of the first week in September. They want us to go as soon as we can and stay as long as we can. Johnnie is reserving air accommodation for us from New York to Ottawa on each Monday in August.

The matter is not as simple as that from our side. First of all, I am under some obligation to stay until Mr. Byrnes returns from Europe and we can reach some decision about my leaving. I have told him that I wished to do this. He has asked me to wait until I talk with him before reaching any decision. In the second place it would be a simple way of surmounting the travel difficulties to fly from New York to Ottawa. However, we had planned to spend such vacation as we got near Mary in Saranac and therefore it seems essential to us that we should go to Ottawa through Saranac in both directions so as to see Mary at least twice. This is a very difficult operation, and I don't know whether we can arrange it. So we are marking time until matters clear up a bit.

I have forgotten exactly where we were on our legislative program when I last wrote you. It now looks as though we were within a few hours of the end, and I hope that the end will be as successful as the rest of the program. Last week we ended by getting the Bretton Woods Bill passed and a few minor amendments concurred in by the House. We then got the Export-Import Bank carrying new lending power of $2,800,000,000 passed by both Houses, and finally on the same day the international organization setting up the Food and Agriculture Organization was gotten through. If, as now seems likely, the treaty will be ratified with practical unanimity today, that will bring us to the end of the first of our principal steps.

This week there has been only one operation requiring any degree of skill, which was to get us out of the unfortunate position into which Mr. John Foster Dulles placed us by stating that the subsidiary agreements under the Charter would be by more treaties requiring ratification by two-thirds of the Senate. This position was acquiesced in by Senator Connally and apparently by the rest of the Committee through silence. If everyone had continued silent through the debate, we would have been placed in the absurd position of making a treaty to make a later treaty, upon which all the opposition would center its fire at a time when public enthusiasm had quieted down and attention was directed to other subjects. This, I believe, was one of the principal reasons why the isolationists decided to go along with the ratification of the Charter. We went to work on this problem and by organizing a group of young Turks in the Senate who made strong and able attacks we have now gotten the matter to a point where the introduction of a letter from the President saying that the subsequent steps will be by statute seems to me to practically settle the matter in the way we want it settled. This has somewhat ruffled the great era of good feeling which was going on, but I think it has transformed the act of ratification into a meaningful one from a mere gesture.

. . .

With much love from all of us.

As ever,

To **MARY A. BUNDY**

DA commented on Churchill's removal from office by the British voters, and upon the pains of terminal tenure of office. The reference to Potsdam is to the "Big Three" conference there, where Truman, Churchill, and Stalin met. Secretary Byrnes was there also.

Monday, July 30, 1945

You ask about the British elections. I regret the result, not because I worry about the Honorable Winnie and his ultimate just reward. He has had much of that in the joy of command in war. I regret it because I think that it may make things harder all around. It will make our own problems with the British a little harder to solve because our rather conservative officials and politicians may be frightened of these more woolly lads. Then it will raise hopes all through the Mediterranean that new and leftist governments will come in. This is likely to cause disturbances on the lifeline to India and the British will react strongly, only to be denounced by Moscow. A leftist government in England will find it harder to work with Moscow than a rightist one. A paradox perhaps, but true.

Then in the abstract it seems to me that England will need some very sensible people at the helm in the next few years. Even the Conservatives would be socialists, but they have more experience.

Finally, any government in control now must make a failure because the problems are insoluble and the movement from failure will be to the left. I am in favor of giving more time to rightists to flub the ball. Perhaps we can stop them without two moves to the left.

These are my general thoughts—not too clear, somewhat colored by feeling tired, and a knowledge that these things are very tough and that a glib fellow like Harold Laski will not help us much.

I can hardly wait for Mr. Byrnes to come home and release me. I know that I shall probably die of boredom. But you know how you want an event to happen, even though you don't like it.

Thursday, August 2, 1945

Life has become very difficult for me. By Tuesday it was plain that with Congress gone, with gents in Potsdam telling us no word of what they are doing, and with the Department entirely without leadership, I had nothing to do. I do not want to start north until I can see Byrnes and get released from my job and we don't know when he is coming back—probably next week. So I just decided not to go to the office. So far the plan has been frustrated. Yesterday I found that a Congressman had come down from New York to lunch with me. So I went, though late. Today a dinner at the Meyers' [Eugene Meyer, Publisher of the Washington *Post*] for Fred Vinson takes me in—again late. Tomorrow is free. And Saturday—of all hours—7 to 7:30 Archie and I have to broadcast on the NBC University of the Air.

To PRESIDENT TRUMAN

DA's wartime service as Assistant Secretary of State ended with this letter.

August 8, 1945

The President
The White House

My dear Mr. President:
    I herewith submit my resignation as Assistant Secretary of State.
    The work for which I stayed on at the time of the reorganization of the Department has been finished, and, after four and one-half years of public service, some attention to my own affairs is long overdue.
    For the unfailing kindness and support which you have given me I am deeply grateful, as well as for the opportunity to have served the country in these eventful years.
    May I assure you of every wish for your continued success in the leadership which you are giving to us all.
                                                            Very respectfully,

To **FELIX FRANKFURTER**

DA's plans for resignation were on the eve of fulfillment, but an O. Henry ending was to follow.

> Assistant Secretary of State
> Washington
> August 9, 1945

Dear Felix:

Before the Secretary went away I had a talk with him about the necessity of my returning to practice on his return. He very kindly urged me to stay. Yesterday we talked further and he, after again urging me to stay, was most understanding of my problem, which is urgently financial, agreed to accept my resignation and transmit it to the President. This is being done to-day.

We are off tomorrow to Saranac Lake, N.Y. (Hotel Saranac) to be with Mary on her 21st birthday—Aug. 12th—also Alice's. We plan to go on to Ottawa on Wednesday and on Thursday to John Castles' fishing camp in Ontario—Camp Madawaska, Lake Victoria, Madawaska Station, Ontario, Canada—to be there until Sept. 7. Then back to Mary and on home again.

These last few days have been bewilderingly full—The Bomb, the Russian declaration, the fading power of Japan. I feel too weary to try to figure things out and hope that the Secretary has some good talent in mind.

Various people have talked to me about rumors of other public employment for me. But I am very clear that I do not want any for a while and cannot take any. So I should be happy to have a good rest in a remote spot and then observe and work at some simple matters.

Our love to you both.

> As ever,

To **FELIX FRANKFURTER**

DA succumbed to the blandishments of Secretary Byrnes and agreed to return to public service as Under Secretary of State.

> August 20, 1945

Dear Felix:

You were good to write us as you did. It has seemed almost impossible that the unacknowledged, never mentioned anxiety which came popping up every time the telephone rang at night is over. It is too good to be true. Dave will be back, we believe, in about a month.

Mary we found in wonderful form—more beautiful than ever, gay and happy, and almost best of all with a new X-ray which shows her cavity gone. Dr. Price is tremendously pleased with her.

My own affairs you must have thought were odd. The Hon. James brought me back to Washington by air and told me that I had caught him in a weak moment and he didn't mean any of it. I had not escaped, I was not to be allowed to and that the President would draft me by virtue of Title something section something if I resisted. I have no strength of character anyway, and certainly not when anyone is as charming to me as his honor was. He really seemed to want me and to understand that the past four and a half years had not been too agreeable. So on condition that I could have a week to relax, I surrendered. That it will turn out badly I have no doubt.

. . .

To **HENRY L. STIMSON**

The reference to "this baffling institution" is to the Department of State, of which General of the Army George C. Marshall had become Secretary, while DA was still Under Secretary.

January 25, 1947

The Honorable Henry L. Stimson
Highhold
Huntington, Long Island

Dear Colonel Stimson:

Thank you very much indeed for sending me a reprint of your Harper's article on the decision to use the atomic bomb. General Marshall had spoken to me with enthusiasm about the article and I was looking forward eagerly to reading it. I did so with mounting enthusiasm. The simplicity and power with which you presented the essential facts and considerations which led to the use of the bomb not only make this complicated matter wholly clear to the reader but leave no doubt as to the wisdom of the decision. This exposition was badly needed and it is superbly done.

There is one matter which I think will receive growing attention as the article sinks in. I had suspected it but not known it. That is that the two atomic bombs which we dropped were the only ones we had ready and that our rate of production at the time was very slow. It seems to me that this fact and the questions which it raises as to the present situation will become increasingly important both at home and abroad. It will be interesting to see whether this is true.

General Marshall has taken hold of this baffling institution with the calmness, orderliness and vigor with which you are familiar. We are all very happy and very lucky to have him here.

The latest news from Mary continues to be very good.

With warm regards to you and Mrs. Stimson, in which Alice joins me.

Most sincerely yours,

To **MR. AND MRS. EDWARD G. MILLER**

The arrival of a new daughter to Mr. and Mrs. Edward G. Miller (assistant to DA) was noted by Miss Evans to DA, who requested a telegram sent, of his own invention.

Department of State
The Undersecretary
February 15, 1947

The Eddie Millers have a new daughter, apparently some weeks early, but everything is quite all right.

Please send a telegram.

A world without a solid pillar
Is gladdened by another Miller.
Like Judge Picard we look with favor
Only on productive labor.

If you think we can get away with it.

To **JANE ACHESON BROWN**

DA often rose early at his farm. On this occasion, he took the opportunity to thank his daughter, Jane, for a birthday present and to transmit gossip. Once more, he was pointing toward resignation, to be succeeded by Robert A. Lovett. John, Kate, and Hattie were the Acheson servants, of whom the first two preferred city living.

Harewood Farm
Sandy Spring, Maryland
Saturday, May 3, 1947

Dearest Jane:

I am sitting here early in the morning—everyone else asleep—clad in your beautiful red plaid shirt, with no pen and a keen desire to write you. The family consists of Alice, with a very sore throat, Mary in health and spirits, Hattie and the old man. John and Kate insist that the farm is too cold for sleeping purposes, so they commute during these week-end visits.

The rest are I hope asleep. Mary has found the city rather a noisy place and was most excited about the peace and beauty of the farm when we got out here yesterday. This morning at seven a tractor started to plow directly behind the house in the big field and sounded like the fall of Berlin—So I padded out in my pajamas and hired the fellow to quit until 8:30.

Your shirt, my love, is most beautiful. I am deeply grateful to you for it and for your constant and, I may say unique, remembering of April 11th. You are very sweet to me. I have tried the shirt on before and paraded before mirrors. But today is its first appearance in the gardens and woods of Harewood farm. Mary has never seen it and should be impressed.

The present plan is to announce my resignation on May 15th to take effect June 30. Bob Lovett's nomination will be sent up the same day. When Bob has been confirmed he will come down here and work as an assistant to Marshall or me until he and Marshall are ready for him to take the oath as Under Sec—not later than June 30. I feel very sad and somewhat panic stricken to be going back to the Union Trust Bldg. I like what I am doing and have some sense now of sureness of touch and of a willingness on the part of others to let me drive—Then, of course, one grows into an unconscious acceptance of the side and nonsense of a cabinet position.

But that is the end of a chapter certainly and probably of a whole section. It has been hard and fascinating. I don't think that the republic has been the loser on the whole.

I have been having a lot of fun with the story of Joe Grew's speech to the Red Cross women working on the annual drive for funds. The theme—the Red Cross stands for duty, service. The symbol of these is George Marshall—Review of career—early life, adherence to army duty through long and obscure years—chief of staff stuck to that hard course denying himself soldier's dream of commanding allied army—Then China when duty called again. Peroration—"And this great man has only one ambition—to retire to Leesburg and spend the rest of his life with Mrs. Eisenhower."

Mrs. E. was on the platform and the next speaker. I have become the world's greatest teller of this story, but give all my rights to you. Mrs. Eisenhower, who is a great girl, says that in some respects I have improved on the original, although, she says, the first impact of breathless and then hysterical horror can never be equalled. I have also given Gen. Marshall a good rendition—But not Mrs. M.

Mary is in good spirits and looking well and beautiful. She is staying with us for two weeks.

Love to you and Dudley who was good to write us.

Devotedly
as ever,

To ARTHUR H. VANDENBERG

Senator Vandenberg was the Minority Leader of the Senate and a key figure in the effort to conduct a bipartisan foreign policy. DA's letter shows that flattery was not too poor an instrument to serve foreign policy.

March 3, 1948

The Honorable Arthur H. Vandenberg
United States Senate

Dear Arthur:

Thank you very much indeed for your note on Senator Wherry's comments about me in yesterday's debate and the *Record*'s misquotation of your reply. It is comforting to hear from you what I had already deduced from my knowledge of you—that the unhappy reporter had made a mistake. Your thoughtfulness in writing so promptly is another kindness to be added to an already long list.

Your leadership in the battle for the Recovery Program has been and is superb. Each move and each speech you make seems to me the perfect one. I marvel at how you maintain your good humor, your strength, and your zest for the fray.

With warmest regards and deep appreciation.

Cordially yours,

To ARCHIBALD AND ADA MACLEISH

As he often did, DA used this thank-you note as a vehicle for gossip and rumination. The reference to "Pauline" is to Mrs. Dwight W. Davis, the widow of a former Secretary of War and donor of the Davis Cup for tennis. Senator William Benton had recently joined the State Department. DA became Secretary of State a year previously.

The Secretary of State
Washington
January 3, 1950

Dear Ada and Archie:

Your telegram cheered us mightily. This Christmas, with Mary and Jane away, and the knowledge that Mary was having a very rough time, had a sadness about it which made your message very good to read. Your present to us, too, has solved a real problem—how to pass the variety of cocktail biscuits and still hold a drink in one hand. It is now all marked out so that the process of absorption need not stop. It is very charming and I join in the gratitude.

Pauline outdid herself again on New Year's Eve. This year with the women all in red or white—and the President as the guest of honor. The latter innovation held me down to a working role—even with which limitation, I still found plenty of good cold water acceptable on the following morning. So I took myself off to the farm all alone for contemplation, fasting and release from the impact of too many, too highly pitched voices.

Tell Archie that his friend and successor Bill Benton was sworn in today amid celebrations in which I joined. Senator Benton had lost some weight, and I hope had gained some wisdom in the years since we had met. We shall soon find out about the latter, and the former, I fear, will equally soon be undone. However, for the present he has lost that egg shape which so worried Archie.

My own troubles are off to a good start. China, Spain, the British dollar crisis, the American dollar gap, Germany—off they go again as people talk too soon and too much about what they know too little. Formosa is the subject which seems to draw out the boys like a red haired girl on the beach. It appears that what you want most is what you ain't got.

The motto for the day I read in a low, but amusing, book the other night. "Well," as the Madam said, "Let's get to work, girls, the piano isn't paid for."

You did us good. We miss you badly. Our hearts are with you.

Much love, as ever,

To **HENRY L. STIMSON**

Here DA acknowledged a helping hand.

The Secretary of State
Washington
March 27, 1950

The Honorable Henry L. Stimson
Highhold
Huntington
Long Island, New York

Dear Mr. Secretary:

I was deeply touched by your letter which appeared in today's *New York Times*. My gratitude on my own part is beyond expression.

I have tried not to let the present barrage of charges and innuendoes go below the surface or to deflect me from the main business at hand, but it is not possible to prevent altogether their having a depressing effect. Your letter has given me renewed courage.

Even beyond my personal gratitude is the gratitude I feel for the service your letter will render to the country. The strong voice of one of our wisest patriots will persuade many of our people of the urgent need for "basic steadiness and faith."

With my affectionate regards.

Sincerely yours,

To ALICE ACHESON AND MARY BUNDY

The reference to General MacArthur relates to MacArthur's message to the Veterans of Foreign Wars taking public issue with the Administration's policy, which sought to keep Chiang Kai-shek out of the Korean War.

The Secretary of State
Washington
August 29, 1950

Dearest Alice and Mary:

My correspondence has suffered latterly for reasons which must be clear to you in part from the press. What is not clear is a maze of decisions and discussion preparatory to the Ministers meeting, the NAT Council meeting, the General Assembly. The weekend which I had hoped would give me a moment or two to write you was made a nightmare by the Mac-Arthur matter, which I shall relate to you someday in detail.

In all that has been happening my admiration and affection for the President grows daily. He has courage and steadiness and loyalty, which are priceless assets. His judgment has been, in my opinion, just what it should be.

But these are tough days. I have still not had the hearing for which I returned ten days ago. They say tomorrow, as they have said for three weeks. It is likely to be a real rip snorter.

UNDATED SCRIBBLE

Apparently, this was the expression of a passing melancholy moment.

Department of State
The Secretary

Can't drive car:
Can't order lunch.
Got no program:
Don't have hunch.

Got no brains
Got no mem'ry
Call his friends
Tom, Dick or Henry.

Can't read cables
Can't write name
As to speeches
'Bout the same.

To A. WHITNEY GRISWOLD

Griswold became President of Yale in 1950. DA's letter was written during his service as Secretary of State, when he also continued to serve on the Yale Corporation. The reference to "Mary" is to Mrs. Griswold.

January 5, 1951

Dear Whit:
    Your Christmas letter brought me true "comfort and joy." . . .
    You, Archie and the other friends who have stood by me in these very troubled days have made the difficulties seem to have much to be said for them. One knows the value and meaning of friendship—and who the friends are. I shall think long of your sitting in deserted Woodbridge and sending me your words of cheer.
    Lefty who was here last week is lyrical about you and the new order at New Haven. I wish that I could be of more use to you and d.v. shall be. John Dickey who dined with me last night hears only good of you.
    Alice joins in warm and affectionate greetings to you and Mary.

As ever,

To A. WHITNEY GRISWOLD

This letter was another of thanks for moral support. DA was Secretary of State at the time.

June 27, 1951

Dear Whit:

I am doubly touched by your good note. By your words about my work here which lifted a spirit which sometimes flags; and by your saying that I have not been wholly useless to you in your work, as I have often feared.

The troubled scene in which I move has some brighter spots and some darker ones. On the domestic side I think things are looking better. The Malik development may be a useful one for Korea—though it is too early yet to say. Iran is very critical, and everything in Europe seems to move with maddening slowness.

But, as John O'Brian's old Vermont lady said, the best thing about the future is that it only comes one day at a time.

Alice joins me in warm greetings to you and Mary. Get a good rest.

As ever,

To FELIX FRANKFURTER

DA had taken up cabinet making and had acquired some timbers torn out of the White House during the renovation and had made a table from the wood.

August 21, 1951

Mr. Justice Frankfurter
Charlemont
Massachusetts

Dear Felix:

Many thanks to you for sending me Bob Menzies' letter. It was a wonderful tonic, coming during a weary week of hot weather and long hours and Congressional frustration.

Last week I took a few days to stay out at the farm. It was not too successful because of various harassments that brought me into town for a time every day. But it helped, and I got a table made out of the White House wood, of which I am, as usual, very proud.

. . .

With love to you both.

As ever,

To GEORGE C. MARSHALL

DA admired no one more than he did General Marshall and here tried to express his towering respect for that great man. Marshall had become Secretary of Defense in September 1950, succeeding Louis A. Johnson. At this writing he had just retired.

September 13, 1951

The Honorable George C. Marshall
Department of Defense

Dear General Marshall:

Yesterday was a day of sadness for all of us who have felt your presence close to us in the last year of grave peril to our country. It was so right for you to be there—giving all of us confidence that great wisdom and experience steadied all of our vital actions and decisions through the last twelve months.

There is no use pretending that there will not be a void. The fact that we can face this leave-taking with some joy in our hearts that you will have the leisure you so richly deserve, is due entirely to your great and lasting contribution to the building of our strength and security. If you had not been with us this last year to guide and chart the course, the tasks now confronting us would be far more difficult.

You have given me a great deal during the years I have worked in close association with you, and I shall not try to put into words how deeply your letter touched my heart, nor what courage and resolution it gives me to face the problems still ahead.

Alice joins me in heartfelt thanks and in every good wish to you and Mrs. Marshall.

Sincerely yours,

To ARCHIBALD MACLEISH

DA tried to comfort MacLeish over the latter's ulcer by undertaking to have one himself.

Harewood
Sandy Spring, Maryland
June 21, 1952

Dear Archie:

. . .

I can only explain our plans for the next two weeks as springing from a sympathetic determination to share an ulcer with you. Tomorrow we start off for London and another round with Schuman and Eden. Thrown in are an Oxford degree and honorary benchership in Lincoln's Inn. Then on to Berlin to lay the cornerstone of an American Memorial Library. Thence to Vienna to return Figl's visit—no business only speeches and such.

From Vienna by way of Dakar we fly to Recife to pick up Eddie Miller and the Brazilian Ambassador and then to Rio for a reception of three days which Neves de Fontoura says will be brilliant—whatever that is in Brazil. After Rio knocks itself and us out, we go on to Sao Paulo and do it all over again. The remains are then returned to Washington for interment in the State Department. Only a bright boy could think up a two weeks like that.

Our love to you and Ada—we long to see you.

As ever,

To FELIX FRANKFURTER

Fresh from his moving visit to Brazil, DA expressed his profound impression in this letter.

Harewood
Sandy Spring, Maryland
July 10, 1952

Dear Felix:

We are home again intact but exhausted. Alice in our last day in Brazil was hit by a cold and also amidships and is spending a day or so in bed. I am functioning but purely theoretically. The President has characteristically sent me home for the weekend to rest.

It has been a tremendous experience. As I come back to the radio from Chicago, it seems unbelievable that these supposed adults can be so blind to the majesty and magic of the position of the United States in the world and play with so great a thing in so small and reckless a way. Even our enemies do not do this.

England for all the beauty of Oxford and the careless dignity of Lincoln's Inn left me sad and depressed. There is much sorrow and anxiety in store for us there. But Berlin, Vienna,—even Dakar—and especially Brazil were emotional experiences of a progressively high order. I had no idea what a visit by a person holding my office meant to these very different people. And when the person and his wife involved, despite their forebodings derived from the American press, responded to friendliness in a human way, the whole business threatened to get out of hand in a big way. It came to a head in Rio when in the House of Representatives I put my prepared speech on the speakers desk "for the record" and spoke off the cuff. We had a near riot. And in Sao Paulo the Mayor made me a citizen of the city—without warning—I remembered St. Paul's statement that he was a Roman citizen and said that from now on I, too, was a Paulista. This simple business produced pandemonium. But beyond these things, the amazing greatness of Brazil one has to see to apprehend. It is altogether fantastic. Like the U.S. just before the Civil War and without that threat developing. Great, undisciplined, as full of energy as a colt, rich, vulgar, cultivated, poor, technically competent, naive, administratively hopeless—every contradiction, every possibility. I am in love with it. And it almost killed me with enthusiasm and kindness.

Science permits too much to be done to one too quickly—

Our love to Marion

As ever,

To LUCIUS D. BATTLE

After nearly four rewarding years with Luke Battle as his executive assistant, DA decided to assign Battle abroad so that he would be out of the line of fire when the administration turned over in six months' time. This was a "non-farewell note."

Harewood
Sandy Spring, Maryland
July 19, 1952

Dear Luke:

Thank you very deeply for your note. We shall not have a good-bye. It would punish us unnecessarily. We shall just pick up again in another phase, and go ahead.

We—Alice and I—are sending you a small object to fix something of these past three and a half years before time rushes on. There is one significant word engraved on it. It brings you and Betty our love. That is what these years have produced. You have been to us as close, as devoted, as loyal as our own son. We think of you as we think of David.

You must get happiness as you think back over these past years because you have done every part and facet of this task perfectly. It hasn't been easy. I am not easy. The whole setting has been somber. There have been major and minor prima donnas at every turn. You have had—after all—a life of your own to get on the road. But you have never in any minute way—so far as I know—wavered from your concern for me and my duties. I have always been sure that the Battle area was secure and sound. I have also known that, at any hour of the day or night, a knock on your door brought an understanding and gay friend to share whatever misery had to be digested.

Your devotion and the quality of your service to me has been, in the well known phrase of the medal of honor citation, above and beyond the call of duty. From us it has brought the same sort of response. And so we send you engraved upon this small gift

Our love.

As ever,

To ADMIRAL ARTHUR W. RADFORD, COMMANDER OF THE PACIFIC FLEET

DA believed Admiral Radford's services to have been crucial to the success of the ANZUS conference. In this thank-you note, DA expresses his deep conviction that alliances are kept healthy by a perceived regard of each ally for the concerns of the others.

The Secretary of State
Washington
August 15, 1952

My dear Admiral:

I shall send with this an official letter thanking you and your officers for all the help and kindness which you gave us so freely in our recent conference. But I want you to know from my own hand how deeply I value the part that you played in our meetings, how grateful I am to you and Mrs. Radford for your kindness to my wife and me, and how great a regard I formed for you.

. . .

The meeting, I think, succeeded because we were able to carry to our friends a sense of conviction that what we proposed was right for them. Their belief in you was a very great—I think the major part—in this. This is the greatest part of our role of leadership. We cannot do it through our power, or our capacity to deny them help, or by exhortation to our view of righteousness. We have to do it by carrying the conviction, which must lie in truth, that we do understand their problems and that the interests we serve are broad enough to include their interests too. Sometimes we have not understood this, and it always produces trouble.

I am deeply grateful to you and have told my feelings both to the President and Bob Lovett.

With warmest regards, in which my wife joins me, to Mrs. Radford and to you.

Most sincerely,

To **FELIX FRANKFURTER**

The "passport order" was an attempt to bring objective criteria to the granting or withholding of a passport.

The Secretary of State
Washington
September 9, 1952

Dear Felix:

. . .

I'm glad you liked the passport order. The great trouble will come, as always, in administration. We tried in the order to get into the administrators' heads that they should look at what people had done and were still doing rather than what they might be thinking. But it is a hard struggle. These cases and the visa ones are the most distasteful part of this job.

I am off on Thursday to Kansas City to talk to the machinists. I could wish that they were not striking a jet plant at the time. The speech will probably set the pack after me again but that is nothing new.

Another meeting in two minutes.

As ever,

PART

II

1953–1959

To **EDWARD B. BURLING**

DA wrote to his senior partner from Antigua, West Indies, where he had gone following the Eisenhower inauguration and the close of his service as Secretary of State.

Antigua B.W.I.
February 2, 1953

Dear Ned:

The Stanley Baldwin book is a fascinating one and has given me two very happy days. What a curious and absorbing person he was and how gently, wisely, and justly G.M. Young deals with him. That is the way to write biography. One of Young's sentences is unforgettable, "Statesmen," he says, "are not architects but gardeners dealing with such materials as only nature can provide." That says a lot—perhaps not all, but a lot.

We are resting deeply and happily. This is the ideal place to make you unable to remember what you came to forget.

I shall bring the book safely back to you. In the meantime my thanks and our love to you and Louise.

As ever,

To **HARRY S TRUMAN**

With this letter DA began a correspondence spanning almost two decades with the former President. This correspondence shows the deepening of their affinity and mutual respect as they both continued in active political roles after they left office.

Little Deep
Mill Reef Club
Antigua, B.W. I.
February 10, 1953

Dear Mr. President:

You and Mrs. Truman have been constantly in our thoughts these last three weeks. We see glimpses of you in papers weeks old and read fragmentary reports of you. But you are more vivid in our minds. We have spoken often of that last poignant day together and shall never forget the sight of you on the back platform as the train grew smaller and smaller down the track. We wish that you would both escape to the peace and privacy for a while of a place like this enchanted and blessed isle, where the sea and air and all around us combine to make rest and relaxation inevitable and delightful. We read and sleep and swim—Alice paints—we keep the world and its doings away from us. But we talk about the great epoch in which you permitted us to play a part—and which now seems ended in favor of God knows what.

One of the glorious things which I have read—and which you probably know—is Paul Wilstack's edition of the correspondence between John Adams and Jefferson. If you do not know it, by all means get it. There were two robust old codgers, I think one gets a wholly new affection for Adams.

We are here, I hope, until the end of March. This note brings to both you and Mrs. Truman our devotion and solicitude. I know that these are difficult weeks for you both.

Affectionately,

To **JEFFREY C. KITCHEN**

Jeff Kitchen had succeeded Luke Battle as DA's executive assistant at the State Department and had served in the last year of DA's tenure of office. Writing from Antigua, DA had an opportunity to tell Kitchen of his gratitude and to revel in his enjoyment of freedom from responsibility. "Barbara" refers to Barbara Evans, DA's trusted secretary and assistant.

February 13, 1953

Dear Jeff:

We could return you here to the natural state of man—much discussed in the Eighteenth Century—which, as the marriage service says, is
an honorable estate. It precedes the social compact, and, in my case, would
preclude one. I wouldn't agree with another damn soul on any proposition
which would take me out of the state of nature and into the mad house
known as man in the social state. I am brown, saturated with sun, salt water
and rum; possessed of only three articles of clothing—shoes, shorts and
shirt (I am about to discard shoes and shirt as I get used to sun and coral
sand); and full of reading such as I have not done for twenty years. Day follows day without any real working (since I sleep whenever I feel like it regardless of light or dark). If there ever was a lad relaxed or on his way to it,
and fast, it is yours truly. As I just read in Holmes to Laski—"At 90 it is time
to begin to learn golf and possibly to resume horseback riding—but the
world is all before you."

And what a world it is. The *N.Y. Times* a week or more late is thrust
upon me, by kind friends, against my will. It reads to me with all the current
urgency of the messages of General Gage or the Earl of Sandwich. The appointments intrigue me more than anything else. Do you know Browning's
Caliban on Seteros? Read it again and watch Caliban playing God on the
beach as the crabs march by—letting one pass, crushing another, tearing
the flipper off the next, etc., etc. I mourn for the victims (up or down) but
the very irrationality of it makes it seem remote and unreal.

My real life is in that hazy realm where the well being of the animal
merges into the life of the mind created by books so that one feels detached
from person, or time or place and lives several lives—quite inconsistent—all
at the same time. I have written Barbara of some of my enthusiasms—John
Adams—Jefferson—Thoreau—but you can tell her that I am on deeper and
more dangerous seas now, Edith Hamilton's book on the prophets of the old
testament (and great lads they were too, almost in the class of Marshall
Shulman).

A long round about way to send you and Helen our love, and to tell you
that I can never tell you of my gratitude—deep and understanding gratitude—of all that you did for me and meant to me in those trying months of a
dying administration when the full burden of the task remained and the
power to carry it was the greatest and rarest—the sense of honor. You are a
real partner for tiger shooting and God bless you.

As ever,

To **DAVID ACHESON**

DA was reading the Holmes-Laski correspondence and found mention of his own name in letters dated in the 1920s.

Antigua, B.W.I.
February 19, 1953

Dear Dave:

. . .

I continue chewing away at Laski and Holmes. To suddenly read about yourself—particularly when you have forgotten the episode entirely—gives the strangest sense that you are dead and the consciousness reading the book is another's. Laski is a gay rascal, probably often dealing in the realm of fiction, but erudite, facile and really fond of Holmes. He gives the old man a sense of living which in those last years he got nowhere else. With all the discounting Laski was a remarkable mind, but it always seemed to me that he produced very little, he rearranged, criticized, reemphasized. But his views, certainly about the U.S., seemed to me pedantic rather than perceptive.

. . .

To **PATRICIA (MRS. DAVID) ACHESON**

DA, still at Antigua, was well into a very eclectic pile of reading.

Antigua, B.W.I.
February 22, 1953

Dear Pat:

. . .

My reading has now carried me into Thomas's one volume life of Lincoln. I think it very good. It gets the irrelevant, and often analytical, detail out of the way so that the structure of the man's character and motivation begins to make some sense. I can recommend it. A book on Kate Chase (Salmon P.'s daughter), called "Proud Kate," I would skip. It is sloppy and, I am sure from a few glaring errors, inaccurate. The Laski-Holmes letters continue fascinating. Another Josephine Tey mystery—Brat Farrar—keeps me up late. And we go on getting sunburned. Kenny MacLeish and Caroline will be down next week so that he and Archie can go off with their goggles and spear fish hunting, around the reefs. This is not for me.

. . .

To **E. B. BURLING**

The reference to William English presumably is to the writer of a piece of DA's vacation reading supplied by E. B. Burling.

Antigua, B.W.I.
March 8, 1953

Dear Ned:

What a man you are to take off on such a motor trip in the great West. You have far more energy than I have. I hope you enjoy it thoroughly.

It is a great joy to be the forgotten man. I clasp Mr. William English to my bosom and refuse to be parted from him. Everything conspires to protect my anonymity including Stalin's taking off. I have had fun speculating on its consequences. One has to think about it in terms of an equation. On one side, the communist elements of the problem; and, on the other the Western elements. As to the first, I should guess at two effects; for some little time—though not beginning at once—a worsening of Soviet effectiveness abroad as the various individuals spar for position and possible purges take place. I doubt whether the announced succession will be permanent without trouble. This might, for a time, confuse Soviet direction in the satellite states and weaken the capacity for adventure, e.g. in East Germany and Indo-China. But after this is over I should expect the regime to be more intransigent as the more limited minded men who have grown up in the last thirty years take over.

If there is a period of decreased pressure it may have dangerous effects on the other side of the equation. If the Austro-Hungarian Empire was held together by external pressure, so has been the Grand Alliance. It will take skill to keep it united and maintain progress toward strength. Here adventures on our part will have a contra-productive effect—tending to unite the Russians and produce discord on our part. But a lull used wisely by us to change the relative power positions could be of vast use in moving us ahead on the road to more stable arrangements in Europe and Asia.

What are your thoughts?

I have also been amused over discussions between Holmes and Laski over one of your favorites, Santayana. Holmes has a sneaking liking for him. Laski is strongly hostile. Examples: Holmes on Feb. 17, 1924—"In a general way his thinking more than that of other philosophers coincides with mine. But he has a patronizing tone—as of one who saw through himself but didn't expect others to." Again on April 18—"I think our starting point put in plain words would be similar or the same, but there is such a mass of literary arabesques and variations that though the book may gain as literature, I think it is diminished in philosophical significance (the book is Scepticism and Animal Faith). I spoke of the tone of patronizing irony—and thought it an echo of Catholicism. Bertrand Russell said: more of the Latin—Santayana thought the English good for football, but thinks that speculation should be left to the latin races. Whereas we agreed that most of the improvements since Descartes had come from England." The quotation from Laski which I wanted I cannot find. Its general effect was that S was superficial and dominated by the R.C. Church.

These letters will give you much amusement.

Last week John Cowles flew us in his plane to Barbados. On the way we went low over several islands including Dominica. I thought of Andrew Green and, of course, of you. The island has great natural beauty but little signs of the work of man—Perhaps for the best.

Our love to you and Louise. We are all well but I am lethargic. We start for home on March 24th.

As ever,

To HARRY S TRUMAN

April 14, 1953

Dear Mr. President:

The message from you, Mrs. Truman, and Margaret, as I came around the bend into the seventh decade, touched me and delighted me more than I can ever tell you. It brought back all your kindness and thoughtfulness through so many years. Alice and I shall never forget how you and Mrs. Truman shared with us all our worries for Mary when she was so very ill in 1950.

Well, I am a spry and very lazy lad of sixty summers. After nearly three months off, the very thought of work is repulsive to me. That is, work in an office. Out here on the farm Alice has me painting the porch furniture, plowing the garden, wheelbarrowing manure for her roses, building a new wood fence and taking the grandchildren down to the next farm to see horses, cattle, pigs, and puppies. Aside from that I just lie around all day.

I am also getting pretty steamed up about the way the pupils whom you had us teach so carefully are really fouling things up. Two samples are enclosed of men, who used to spend their time making our lives hard, now having a field day with our successors.

So far it seems to me that the worst side of the whole thing has been the terrible retrogression which has taken place in the processes of government and in dealing with the personnel of government. Ike is presiding over something which is corruptive on a really great scale.

The folly of his supporting Senators and Congressmen who would cut his throat if elected one could put down to total lack of experience in politics and in government. But the studied appeasement of the Hill which is now going on at the expense of the best civil servants we have—certainly in State—is not only criminal but frightening in what it may mean regarding the quality of advice which the Secretary of State, and ultimately, the President will receive. Just last week Dulles has separated Paul Nitze, the head of the State Policy Planning Staff, who did, as you remember, such fine work on the NSC series under which the rearmament took place and under which Ike himself operated in Europe. I understand that he is being sacrificed to the Hill demand that all who worked with me be changed or fired, and that he may be picked up again by Wilson in Defense.

This seems to me plain cowardice and utter folly. Ike knows better than this. He would never tolerate it for the uniformed members of the armed services. But it is the established policy for all the civilian departments—the exact opposite of everything which you tried and did bring about.

This brings me back to your book, as I long to see it. A book to show how good government is carried on at all levels from the county to the White house. And it is not the way things are being done now.

But I should not disturb your vacation in the quarrelsome way. It is the first time I have blown up in months.

Alice joins me in most affectionate greetings to Mrs. Truman and Margaret and to yourself.

Most sincerely,

To **HARRY S TRUMAN**

The context here is the Eisenhower Administration's handling of foreign policy in the wake of Stalin's death. "The lady you refer to" was Evelyn Walsh McLean, premiere Washington hostess for many years and wife of the erstwhile publisher of the Washington Post.

May 28, 1953

Dear Mr. President:

The well known envelope with your name in the corner and your handwriting on it lying on our hall table always quickens my heart. Yesterday's letter was no exception. It was a delight in itself and because it brought the good news, which I shall treat as confidential until I see it released, that you will be here in the week of June 22 and that I shall see you. You must let me know when you will arrive so that I can have again the joy of meeting you as you step off the train. Will Mrs. Truman come with you?

Alice and I will be overjoyed to do anything which will make your visit more enjoyable. We should love to have you stay with us, being emboldened by the knowledge that you do not like air conditioning which we do not have. But we can also understand that you will wish to see many people and that the anonymity of a hotel might be more useful for you and your callers. If so, perhaps Mrs. Truman might wish to escape from your meetings to our house. We can arrange a dinner either at P Street or in the country. Let us know your convenience and we shall do the rest. Most of all we must have some talk.

What you say about the Great General is frighteningly true. I had a letter from a friend who writes: "I am anxious and worried increasingly from day to day as that fumbling silence in the White House seeps out over the country like a cold fog over a river bed where no stream runs." Ike's abdication has given us that Congressional government, directionless and feeble which de Tocqueville feared would result from the Constitution. And it comes at the very time when your policy of building strength and unity would have paid great dividends as the Russians ran into the period of weakness and division which the succession to Stalin inevitably created. You remember that we used to say that in a tight pinch we could generally rely on some fool play of the Russians to pull us through. Now that is being exactly reversed. They now have, as invaluable allies, division, weakness and folly. As an example of the latter Bob Taft's latest thinking aloud should get a special prize. It gives one doubt as to his state of mental responsibility.

And it is not only Congressional government, which must always fail because it cannot provide an executive, but Congressional government by the most ignorant, irresponsible, and anarchistic elements—anarchistic because their result, if not their aims, is to destroy government and popular confidence in it.

I think that you are quite right that you and I are very likely to be in for another period of attack and vilification. This is also Jim Webb's opinion based upon the belief that Taft will turn McCarthy loose on us sufficiently before the 1954 election to provide distraction, to revive suspicion of the democrats and to get sufficient right wing republicans to free the administration from the need for Democratic support and to give Taft the kind of a Republican majority which would insist on a policy which Taft would control, and which would make Ike the captive of the right wing. But as you say we have won many fights in the past and need not fear others in the future. It is, none the less, a distateful waste of time and effort.

As to the book, I shall, of course, be delighted to help in any way you think I can be useful. Call on me whenever you think best.

Lister Hill called me this morning to ask me to meet with a group of Democratic senators to talk about foreign policy on June 8. Unfortunately I have to be in New Haven on that day but said that I would be available at almost any other time. He will let me know. I think the time may be coming when they should keep the record clear that the Administration's words and its acts are not going along the same track, and that the conduct of foreign policy is not a mere matter of words.

I was amused this morning to read the man "who spells Lip with two ps" tell the world how successful were the policies of the past four years. He can't remember who the people were who did these things. The lady you refer to was a fabulous creature. It used to disgust me to see how people who should have known better used to fawn and prey upon her at the same time.

Alice sends her love to Mrs. Truman. We are looking forward to seeing, I hope, both of you very soon.

Most sincerely,

To **ARCHIBALD MACLEISH**

An amusing tidbit about the complications of getting through the day.

July 4, 1953

Dear Archie:

. . .

I returned yesterday to find a certain complexity to life. The Express Company was attempting to deliver at P Street a large, rapidly perspiring salmon; the cook had departed; Alice had run her foot into a pitchfork; and the water system at the farm had given up the ghost. Today's bulletin is better—the salmon is frozen, Alice is convalescent, the cook is still a.w.o.l. and we have a limping and sporadic infusion of water from the old barn well until independence is celebrated and Monday dawns. I shudder to think of what Princeton may have in store for me next week. Don't send me a Shetland pony about to foal.

. . .

My love to you both, and Alice's and Jane's.

As ever,

To **HARRY S TRUMAN**

DA commented on what could and could not be expected of the Kremlin in the wake of Stalin's death.

July 21, 1953

The Honorable Harry S Truman
Kansas City 6
Missouri

Dear Mr. President:

I am most grateful for the last Cabinet picture, which came to me from you. It brings back the most poignant memories.

All of us here are still talking of your visit. I see the boys from time to time when we meet to discuss Library affairs and last week I had a long and most pleasant luncheon and talk with Oscar Chapman. He is a sound man and most loyal one.

In case you have not seen it, I am enclosing a clipping from last Sunday's *Washington Post*. The story by Eddie Gilmore, who, as you know, has just come out of Moscow with his Russian wife, gives his reflections on the attitudes in Russia since the death of Stalin. I am doubly impressed with them because they accord with many of Chip Bohlen's thoughts.

It is important, I think, not to over-estimate nor under-estimate the change which Stalin's death has produced. It does not in any way mean, in my judgment, that the USSR will be any less of a totalitarian, Communist, police state. There will not be any lessening of the danger in the world if the West is foolish enough to weaken itself and make aggression seem the road to profit with little or no risk.

What Stalin did to the Russia of Lenin was to impose upon it a personal, oriental, despotism, in which the whims, fears, and ideas of one man and a small coterie greatly enlarged the field for intrigue and the uncertainty of life for everybody from the highest officials to the man in the street. As both Bohlen and Gilmore say, there was almost an audible sigh of relief when Uncle Joe died, and a great yearning for what was nostalgically thought of as "the good old days of Lenin" (which had become somewhat rosy-tinted in retrospect), in which there was plenty of dictatorship and ruthlessness, but in which the government was run by an oligarchy, the head of which had great power but was not deified. This tended toward committee government and greater scope for discussion and greater need for carrying some sort of acquiescence in what was done.

It is Chip's guess—and only a guess—that it was Beria's (the super cop's) passion for intrigue which made him unable to accept the new movement and got him into trouble. The fact that he could be dealt with as he was and that a man who had been in high position for twenty years could be denounced universally as a scoundrel from the start is both very Russian (see the book called *A Journey for Our Time*) and was evidence that authoritarianism has not appreciably declined.

It may be that the Russian leaders will have to make greater concessions to the Soviet and satellite people. If this is so, they will want a period of relaxation in foreign affairs. And if this in turn is so, we may be faced with proposals in regard to Germany and perhaps even Korea and Indochina which may alter some of the factors—i.e., the openness of Russian hostility and willingness to use force against weakness—which have strengthened the allied will to effort.

But it would be a great mistake, I believe, to think that the essence of the problem is changed. That essence, which influenced the thoughts which you and I have held for so long—that essence is that it isn't merely the imminent threat of aggression from the Soviet movement which causes instability and the danger of war, but the capacity for successful aggression whenever the mood or the desire to engage in it exists. Therefore, our policy was to create strength by binding ourselves and our allies both economically and militarily. It is essential to continue that policy.

I think now that the country is faced with a problem which you and I faced early in 1949, when the Russians raised the blockade in Berlin and asked for a meeting of Foreign Ministers. The first was a gesture toward relaxation, which you and I thought came from a desire on their part to extricate themselves from a failure and a weak position. The great question was how far the Russians were prepared to go. We, therefore, accepted the proposed conference promptly and with an agenda which gave the Russians a chance to show their hand one way or the other.

The first week of the conference was devoted to forcing them to expose their hand fully. It turned out that they were not ready to propose anything constructive and in the resulting propaganda battle they lost heavily. This, I think convinced our allies of the true situation more than any amount of speeches and enabled us to go forward together to meet the ensuing danger and hardships with a common appreciation of the facts.

1953 has much in common with 1949. Again it isn't a time for meetings by heads of states, a situation which puts more pressure upon the democracies to have what at least looks like a favorable result than upon the Soviets. But it is a time for a four-power meeting, at which the Russians must be thoroughly smoked out. Much preparatory work should be done with our allies. The White House must discredit the demagogic isolationist wing of the Republican Party which wishes to insult and separate us from our allies.

If the Russians propose nothing which makes a really free unification of Germany possible, I think that again, as in 1949, the Allies can be brought together on a program of building strength. If they are willing to make real concessions, then a most delicate and difficult period ensues. We cannot—and would not wish to insist—upon a continued division of Germany, but we must be very careful about what kind of a Germany we are unifying and what its place in the Western world is. I think this could be handled if there were understanding and wisdom in Washington and if I had any confidence that in the present constitutional and political situation in France that country was able to accept any solution, whatever it was. Since both of these matters are in doubt, I think the future gives rise to real anxiety.

All of this, I know, you have thought of yourself; but it gives me comfort to talk with you in this way.

I have been urging some of Stevenson's friends to get him back here in the near future. His voyaging seems to have been over-prolonged, and I hope that, if he is wise and tactful, he can help to bring Democrats of various shades closer together on some lines of policy which will be a little more positive than the Congressional minority has been able to achieve so far. I should hope that you and he would find yourselves pretty close together and that some of us who might be called in a World War I phrase "the old contemptibles" might be of some use.

Alice joins me in the warmest messages to you and Mrs. Truman. I hope that her hands are better and that I am not in her black books.

Most sincerely,

To **THE REVEREND NEWMAN FLANAGAN**

Father Flanagan was founder and long-time head of "Boys Town," a Catholic orphanage for boys.

July 27, 1953

The Reverend Newman Flanagan
3012 Jackson Street
Sioux City, Iowa

Dear Father Flanagan:

Your delightful note of June 10th came as close as any note could to bringing you into my room.

Your Gestapo, as is always the case with him, was entirely correct as of the date of the report. Since then I hope and believe that there has been improvement. It appears, or at least so the doctors say, that somewhere along the line of my extensive travels in 1952, an amoeba, with a fairly large family, came to live with me. He repaid my hospitality in a most unworthy manner. Hence the decline that Frank reported. It took some time for the medicos to identify the culprit and then to eliminate it. But this they have succeeded in doing. At any rate I feel much better.

There was one good outcome of this whole endeavor, which was that during the course of it I lost fifteen pounds which I badly needed to do. I do not recommend this method, however. It is too reminiscent of Charles Lamb and the roast pig. I am sure that your prayer came just at the moment when frustration was overcoming me and turned the tide of battle.

. . .

I hope that you have a thoroughly delightful journey. My father used to have the most wonderful time in Ireland. He delighted in travel and delighted in Ireland and went there many times. He loved particularly the small places because he said that the quality of the arguments was the best in the world. One did not have to search for them. They were everywhere. Furthermore, they had the easy flow which came from not being confined in any logical strait jacket and they were embroidered with the artistry of unequalled wit. I doubt whether times have changed and I am sure that you will enjoy every moment of the journey.

. . .

My warmest regards and best wishes.

Cordially yours,

To LUCIUS BATTLE

Writing to his former aide, DA commented on the poor morale in the State Department under the new Secretary, John Foster Dulles.

August 6, 1953

Dear Luke:

. . .

Our own life is a strange one. Like the man who was getting deaf and warned against alcohol, I find that I like what I drink better than what I hear. And I hear a lot. What is happening to our friends in the Department—and to the place itself—is very bad and gives one a contempt for the cowardly fools who are doing it. A great institution ought to command respect from anyone who is given the responsibility of command. Not awe, but respect and the desire to learn, inspire to better work and to leave the show better than one received it. It isn't a personal possession, or the mirror for one's ego. This hasn't been understood. Dulles's people seem to me like Cossacks quartered in a grand old city hall, burning the panelling to cook with.

On the broader front we seem to be in a state of flux and weakness on both sides in which any broken field runner might have a chance to score. It seems to me not unlike the CFM of May 1949 when we had to find out first what the Russians really had in mind—which then was nothing—and then move in on our allies and the Russians with real power. The show needs more daring than it now shows. Imitation is truly flattering, but they follow us too slavishly. Something new might be called for; and, if not a new departure, perhaps a deeper commitment in Europe to revive the momentum.

Since your letter I have seen President Truman and had long talks with him. He is in great health and spirits. I have been trying to get Stevenson back here and help to work out arrangements for the two men to get together in a really harmonious way with the Congressional leaders—so-called. There are too many who are sowing thistles in this garden for my comfort.

As ever,

To SIR OLIVER FRANKS

Sir Oliver Franks was the British Ambassador to the United States during DA's tenure as Secretary of State. The two men were friends and each held the other in highest esteem. Hume Wrong, formerly Canada's Ambassador in Washington, was also an old and close friend of DA.

December 28, 1953

Dear Oliver:

We are delighted beyond words to have your letter—just received and eagerly read. We have missed you both sadly and comfort ourselves by much talk of you between ourselves and with Felix. News of you is a good tonic. But it has its bad side too. Your energy with the removal of the herbaceous border renews Alice's charge that my complacency in the face of encroaching honeysuckle is a sure sign of onrushing senility. I insist feebly that one must choose one's enemies as carefully as one's friends.

It is good to know that you are settled happily—and that the girls are—in your new house and work. As you say, it is not an easy transition. We have had, on the whole, a good and restful year. My wretched body has had to go to the repair men of the medical profession for too much of the time. But it has been mostly a bore and now seems—good old tough chassis that it is—to be a pretty good used car job.

Only today I was writing about you. It was à propos of an honorary degree at Yale for Owen Dixon. I said that second only to you he had been pre-eminent in inspiring complete trust and confidence in us in his disinterestedness, wisdom and integrity. Those were good and curiously happy days of work and a sense of accomplishment.

The present takes time in developing reality. Princeton is interesting but retrospective. My professional life is stubbornly slow in developing. The environment of Washington is that of the tomb. Ideas do not live here any more. Mark Twain's advice has been forgotten—"Do right. You will surprise some and amaze the rest." The mediocre is king in the country of the third rate. It is the dullness of it which is so depressing.

But my father used to quote St. Paul—in which I believe to have been an apochryphal statement since I have never been able to find it—to the effect that one should not think on those things that are behind but those which lie before. This is not very encouraging either except for two things. One, your alluring suggestion that you and Barbara may be coming to inspect the heathen. You remember that there is an abode here whenever you want it. The other is that Alice, our daughter Jane and I leave on Saturday for three weeks in Antigua, B.W.I., for sun, sea and the MacLeishes. We are all excited beyond words at the prospect.

You may have heard that Hume Wrong has been very ill. I am glad to add quickly that he is well on the road to a recovery but, as yet, of uncertain extent. It has to do with high blood pressure and trouble in his good eye. He is out of the woods but may not be back on the job—in all probability never the job of deputy minister—He writes cheerfully and amazingly well without being permitted to look at the page.

I have one commission for you—to tell Professor G.M. Young what a great admirer he has in me. He knows, I think, that I admired his life of Baldwin—or him in it. I have just read his *Portrait of an Age* and have become little short of idolatrous. It is the overflow of a rich and understanding mind, when one has been used too often to the last drop squeezed from some pithy skull. Some day I shall come to Oxford to stay with you and lay a garland at his feet.

What I would give for what Holmes called a "jaw" with you. But I have had the next best thing and am content.

May all good things come to you, you and Barbara, and with them the deep affection of Alice and me.

Yours ever,

To HARRY S TRUMAN

The "group discussions at Princeton" refer to seminars that were held over entire weekends in the period of 1953–1954 at which DA and his former lieutenants attempted to reconstruct the circumstances and motives for decisions taken while DA was Secretary of State. A transcript of their discussions is available in the Truman Library.

February 5, 1954

Dear Mr. President:

What joy your letter brought to Alice and me! I took it home and read it to her. Right at the start we stopped at "Charlie's Aunt Margaret." I, in my ignorance, claimed that it was just a general expression for anyone not involved in your memoirs. Alice said, not at all—that you knew, and when you said his Aunt Margaret, you meant it.

So down came the Britannica and, sure enough, there she was—the daughter of the Emperor Maximilian and Charlie's aunt all right. I have been trying her out on some of my highbrow friends, and their degree of error is very comforting to me.

From the whole letter we could picture you full of energy and eager to get your hands on the work of building for the future with all your resources of knowledge of the past and understanding of the present. Whenever you want to blow off steam, we claim priority in being blowee, as the lawyers would say.

I know how bored you get in concentrating upon your own actions years ago. In a way I have been doing the same thing in these group discussions at Princeton and I do find that one can only do about so much a day. To do too much at a time gives me a strange dreamlike sensation of living in two periods almost at once.

As I look back over your administrations I do not see much to regret in any of the great decisions, but do see many, many times when I am amazed at the boldness, courage and insight of decisions. Comparing those years with the present, I am amazed, too, by the way in which we assumed that vigorous leadership was just normal, and how in the face of the most awful brawls with the hill you made the Congress do things which the present crowd would not dream of attempting.

The problems which tended to defy solution came, I think, from an erroneous decision which you inherited, and from another which you were swept—almost forced—into making or agreeing to in 1945.

The inherited error was the total destruction of Japanese and German military power and, in the case of Germany, of any German state at all. This completely withdrew all local containing power on both sides of Russia. Our own great power might have acted in large part as a substitute if we had not dispersed that in 1945–6.

Power is at the root of most relationships—by no means the only factor, but one of vast importance. A balance of power has proved the best international sheriff we have ever had. Many of our troubles—or perhaps better to say, many troubles, came from the dissolution of our power and the destruction of any balance capable of restraining the Russians from acts which weakened the West greatly, although we did deter them from direct attack on us or Europe. This is an interesting field to speculate about. For instance, how much did Stalin change his plans about China and Korea, when to what must have been his utter amazement, our army, navy and air force simply melted away. Cracked as he was, I think his talks with Wallace and Hurley must be read in the light of our power at the time he was talking— Not that he was sincerely adopting a line of action on which anyone could or should rely, but I doubt whether he believed that we would permit him to adopt any other course and *then* we had the power to make our will effective without the necessity of using the power.

These thoughts I write during a day spent without food or water having my insides X-rayed. This leads to contemplation but not to powerful flights of imagination—I hope this is to be the wind-up of almost a year of trying to get rid of some amoebae that I collected somewhere probably in Africa or South America.

When this Berlin fiasco is over—and it seems to be following the exact pattern of the Paris meeting of 1949—some attention ought to be given to the "new look," "that precious intangible—the initiative" which, believe it or not is exercised by "retaliation," etc, etc. This is in reality the policy we had to follow before you began the rearmament in 1950—and at a time when we had the monopoly of the atomic bomb.

I should think it unwise to raise the matter stongly while Berlin is still going. Partly not to attack a man who is representing us abroad, and partly because Dulles may well be crawling out of this speech now if he really hopes to get the French and Italians to ratify the E.D.C. Also I am not sure that peoples' minds generally would be as open to an analysis by you or me, as they would to someone who would not be charged with responding to de-fend their own work against direct action. If Stevenson would do it and stay on the line he would get a real audience and then Senators and Con-gressmen could pick it up. Sam Rayburn would be an ideal person to do it.

Our trip to Antigua this January, although shorter, was in some ways more fun than last year. We felt better and we had our daughter Jane Brown from Milwaukee with us, who is a pretty good vacation just in herself. We had a great time swimming, eating, laughing and drinking some good rum together. Everyone returned brown and happy.

Our deepest affection to you and Mrs. Truman. We hope her hand has recovered and that all is well. I wish I were seeing you in N.Y. tonight.

Most sincerely,

To THOMAS BERGIN

DA was in favor of a sojourn at Yale by former President Truman, as Chubb Fellow.

July 12, 1954

Mr. Thomas G. Bergin
Master, Timothy Dwight College
Yale University
New Haven, Connecticut

Dear Mr. Bergin:

Your letter of July 1st interests me very much. As you readily under-stand President Truman's illness relegates our discussion to what the cur-rent jargon calls the "planning stage." All that he has planned—centering around his book—will be delayed several months and he is in no state now even to consider engagements. But we can think about it and discuss it. I am eager to do so because I should like to have him come to Yale, and I think he would like to come under the right circumstances.

Mr. Truman is deeply interested in and very good with the young. His point of view is fresh, eager, confident. He has learned the hard way, but he has learned a lot. He believes in his fellow man and he believes that with will and courage (and some intelligence) the future is manageable.

This is good for undergraduates. He is easy, informal, pungent. He should not be asked to do lectures for publication. The pressures on him are too great, and it is not his field. It is not what he says but what he is which is important to young men and this gets communicated.

What you tell me is not enough to give me the feel of what you propose. I should like to talk with you, Professor Fesler, and Mr. Griswold about it. I should want Mr. Truman to be received at Yale with honor, with simplicity—not as a show, not with controversy, not as lecturer in a field which I do not believe is yet a discipline, "political theory or science"—but as one who could, if in some way we were wired for spirit, give our undergraduates more sense of what their lives were worth (how to spend them for value) than anyone I know.

I can understand that you may think this letter not responsive. It is not immediately so, and cannot be. The cast is a good one. Let us elaborate the fly.

With kindest regards.

Sincerely yours,

To **FELIX FRANKFURTER**

July 12, 1954

Dear Felix:

It was good to hear from you through your letters of June 23 and July 5. I am returning the clippings in the second letter.

. . .

Last week I went to the Library of Congress to lunch with the executive assistants of the Democratic Senators and Congressmen. They have a club known as the Burro Club. There I sat between the President of the Club, a Harvard Law School man from Florida, named Jack Bryan, and a wonderful person from Jersey City, John Murphy, the assistant to Al Sieminski. Murphy explained that the people in Jersey City took a very simple view of life, had firm principles, which amounted to three. As a result they were deeply attached to Mr. Truman and to me. I pursued this intriguing

idea and elicited the three governing principles of Jersey City as the following: One, never make a pass at another man's wife; two, never say anything
disrespectful to or about a priest, rabbi, or minister; three, no matter how
terrible your mother may be, always be nice to her. I said that I could see in
a broad general way how believers in these principles would think of Mr.
Truman, but the facts of my private life being somewhat obscure, how did I
rate Jersey City approval? "Well," he said, "there is a fourth corollary which
doesn't rise to the height of a principle, which is in Jersey City you are for
any poor S.O.B. who gets kicked around." This clearly let me in. . . .

I gave the Burro Club about half an hour along the general lines of the
Introduction enclosed herewith. They were very excited about it, including
some Congressmen who had been allowed by their assistants to attend.

. . .

As ever,

To **MRS. FRANKLIN D. ROOSEVELT**

*Eleanor Roosevelt served as a member of the United States delegation to
the United Nations when DA was Secretary of State.*

October 11, 1954

Mrs. Franklin D. Roosevelt
345 East 46th Street
New York, N.Y.

Dear Mrs. Roosevelt:

My wife and I send our warmest greetings to you on this important
birthday. May your vigor and inspiring spirit guide and encourage us for
many years to come. Never was it more needful and never did one fulfill
more completely than you the admonition of St. Paul—"whatsoever things
are true, whatsoever things are honest, whatsoever things are just, whatsoever things are of good report—think on these things."

With all good wishes.

Most sincerely,

To **CHARLES M. O'HEARN**

*Charles O'Hearn was Assistant to the President of Yale University.
Clem (Dr. Clement) Fry was the psychologist at the Yale University Health
Department. The roll of honor in Woolsey Hall refers to the list of Yale men
who died in World War I and subsequent wars.*

October 26, 1954

Mr. Charles M. O'Hearn
Assistant to the President
Woodbridge Hall
Yale University
New Haven, Conn.

Dear Charlie:

I am most interested in your letter of October 21st and its enclosures. It is indeed a good thing to have a Conservative Society in the Yale Law School or anywhere else. If this one is, as you say, "dedicated to inviting outstanding conservatives to address students," its start indicates a certain semantic problem. Are Clarence Manion and Felix Morley outstanding conservatives? I should have thought Lord Hugh Cecil, whose monograph on "Conservatism" is still a classic, would have required some persuasion of this. However, I am clearly disqualified to judge as an ex-New Dealer—"ex" because I was once expelled from the ranks as being too "conservative."

The directors of this effort are indeed rugged fellows. For them no glittering generalities to catch the masses. Generalities—yes; but glitter—no. "The conservative," said their first speaker, "believes that the world is not perfectible, and that we poor fallen human creatures, here below, are not made for happiness, and will not find happiness—at least, not if we deliberately pursue it. . . ." Calvin, himself, could not do better. This man wants no braying bands and torch light processions falling in behind him.

This pursuit of happiness business has always caused trouble. The Veep used to say that the pursuit was all right enough but that we ought to catch up with it once in a while. But I guess this is a liberal idea and probably corrupting. Come to think of it, it's probably a sound idea to tell people they're not made for happiness if they're not likely to get any. "Children, candy is bad for your teeth and besides there isn't any." Pretty good—if you can put it across.

Perhaps the best part of this sentence is the part which follows what I have quoted: "*therefore* (mark the 'therefore') he (the conservative) is not inclined to believe that any single fixed system of political concepts can bring justice and peace and liberty to all men everywhere." Now, curiously enough, I don't believe that either. I'm not even inclined to believe it. I strongly disbelieve it. And yet I don't get to this pretty sensible conclusion via the conviction that we poor fallen creatures couldn't do with just a little happiness and shouldn't take out after it if teacher isn't looking. Something seems to be wrong here. Perhaps I'm a conservative and don't know it—or an unorthodox conservative—or just have some common sense.

Do these conservatives of yours plan to have someone at the door on meeting nights to ask each entrant, "Do you believe in happiness? You do, hey? Well get the hell out of here." If they have a large meeting after this, you had better call in Clem Fry.

But this isn't the half of it. "Conservatism does not breed fanatics," he said, "If you want men who will sacrifice their past and present and future to a set of abstract notions, then you must go to Communism or Fascism." Careful, Brother, you are getting pretty close to that roll of honor in Woolsey Hall!

And in the last week before election, what do you think of this: "Kirk explained that conservatism is a word defining a state of mind, not a program. 'Conservatives always differ a good deal among themselves as to the better solution for any particular program,' he said." Dear, dear what a pretty kettle of fish. He sounds just like Mr. Harry S Truman himself.

I wonder whether these conservatives have looked into their security arrangements. It looks to me as though they had been penetrated.

Anyway, better luck next time.

Sincerely,

To **HARRY S TRUMAN**

DA had little patience for the columnist, Walter Lippmann.

January 20, 1955

Dear Mr. President:

Walter Lippmann has a new book out in which he makes the amazing discovery that the weakness of the democracies today comes from encroachments on the executive power by legislative bodies pandering to an ignorant and volatile public swayed by mass media of communication. If he had known this and used his power—which isn't much but something—to support the executive when we really had one instead of joining the chorus of misinformation, I could read him with more patience. One of the editors of a great weekly told me the other day that the feather bed which the whole press and radio, TV, etc. put under this administration was quite unbelievable. He said that if we had done one quarter of the fool and other things which this crowd has our great free press would have gone utterly crazy with denunciation. Perhaps some day the populace will see that the king has no clothes on—

Our most affectionate greetings to you both.

As ever,

To **DANIEL R. FITZPATRICK**

A ditty in response to a Fitzpatrick cartoon in the St. Louis Post-Dispatch *featuring the character "Sec."*

April 6, 1955

Mr. Daniel R. Fitzpatrick
St. Louis Post-Dispatch
1111 Olive Street
St. Louis 1, Missouri

Dear Mr. Fitzpatrick:

> Sec. is wonderful
> In a world so blunderful.
>
> And Fitzpatrick himself isn't bad,
> Even though a mere strip of a lad.
>
> But Knowland and Nixon, that's who
> I'd like to see on Quemoy or Matsu.

Yours,

To **THOMAS PIERRE HAZARD**

Hazard was a Yale classmate of DA's and the reference is to a class reunion.

June 28, 1955

Mr. Thomas Pierre Hazard
The Homestead
Peace Dale, Rhode Island

Dear Pierre:
    I am deeply touched by your letter. The days at Peace Dale were sheer joy. I quite agree that conscience made cowards of us all at New Haven and that we spent much more time doing what we thought we should do than what we wanted to do. However, it brought me one nice colloquy between Joe Walker, Bayne Denegre, and Bayne's brother, Dr. Bayne-Jones, on Saturday morning. It went something like this:

WALKER: Bayne, you were drunk last night.

BAYNE: I was not what I call drunk.

DR. BAYNE-JONES: There speaks a man with real standards.

. . .

With warmest regards.

As ever,

To **HARRY S TRUMAN**

The former President, writing his Memoirs, asked DA to comment on the manuscript. This long letter was DA's effort to clarify and strengthen Truman's analysis. It touched on many dramatic and controversial issues of the Truman Administration, particularly in the realm of foreign policy.

Covington & Burling
Union Trust Building
Washington 5, D.C.
July 25, 1955

The Honorable Harry S Truman
Federal Reserve Bank Building
Kansas City, Missouri

Dear Mr. President:

I have now finished reading your manuscript and return the last volume with my suggestions.

This manuscript volume flows along more smoothly than the last one and is most interesting. I congratulate you on it. For your generous references to me, I am profoundly grateful.

My comments are divided into two groups:—minor and stylistic suggestions; and, suggestions going to substance.

. . .

Pp. 554–557. Blair House meeting on Korea, June 25, 1950. The best account of "Why we Went to War in Korea," is in the *Saturday Evening Post* of November 10, 1951, by Beverly Smith. He wrote it after, by your orders, he had seen all our notes and papers. You should read it and then revise these pages which are skimpy on the greatest story of the 1949–1953 Administration and sometimes not altogether accurate.

To begin with, method—which was one of your strong points—is wholly left out of your story. It was this: Louis Johnson and Bradley were away, flying back from Tokyo on that Saturday night. Over the phone you told me to get together with the Service Secretaries and the Chiefs of Staff and get working parties started getting recommendations for you when you got back. These obviously could not be cleared with Louis and Brad and so the first order of business after I reported on the state of affairs was to lay out the recommendations for discussion. They formed the framework of the whole evening. It was not, as would seem on page 556, a series of off-the-cuff, disjointed observations.

One other preliminary observation. You did not permit any discussion until dinner was served and over and the Blair House staff had withdrawn. Then you asked me to report on the situation and recommendations. This I did first before anyone made any observations.

The situation report is what you have up to the top of 556. Then I reported the following recommendations for immediate action:

1) That MacArthur should evacuate the Americans from Korea—the dependents of the Military Mission,—and, in order to do so, should keep open the Kimpo and other airports, repelling all hostile attacks thereon. In doing this, his air forces should stay south of the 38th Parallel.

2) MacArthur should be instructed to get ammunition and supplies to the Korean army by airdrop and otherwise.

3) The Seventh Fleet should be ordered from Cavite north at once. We should make a statement that the Fleet would repel any attack on Formosa and that no attacks should be made from Formosa on the mainland. (At this point you interrupted to say that you agreed that the fleet should be ordered north at once, but that you would sleep on the statements until the fleet was in position. You expressed no opinion on them on the merits.)

4) The situation was not clear enough to make any further recommendations that night.

After this report you asked each person in turn to state his agreement or disagreement and any views he might have in addition. Two things stand out in this discussion. One was the complete, almost unspoken acceptance on the part of everyone that whatever had to be done to meet this aggression had to be done. There was no suggestion from anyone that either the United Nations or the United States could back away from it. This was the test of all the talk of the last five years of collective security. The other point which stands out in my mind from the discussion was the difference in view of what might be called for. Vandenberg and Sherman thought that air and naval aid might be enough. Collins said if the Korean army was really broken, ground forces would be necessary. But no one could tell what the state of the Korean army really was on that Sunday night. Whatever the service estimates might be everyone recognized the situation as serious in the extreme.

After listening to the discussion, you directed that orders be issued carrying out the recommendations as modified by you.

Louis Johnson has said that he and I had a debate on Formosa that night; he for protecting it, I against. That is completely untrue.

P. 559. Throughout Monday the situation in Korea deteriorated rapidly. You called another meeting at Blair House Monday night. The same persons were present, except that Assistant Secretary of State Matthews took Rusk's place and Secretary of Navy Matthews was not present.

The decisions taken that night were announced by you the next day, Tuesday, June 27th. The draft was prepared by me and adopted by you with minor changes. They were:

1) U.S. air and sea forces to give Korean forces cover and support.
2) Seventh Fleet would neutralize Formosa.
3) Our forces in the Philippines would be strengthened.
4) Aid would be accelerated to Indo-China.
5) Senator Austin was to report all this to the U.N.

Meanwhile the Security Council of the U.N. met again and adopted the Resolution (on June 27th) calling on all members of the U.N. to give assistance to South Korea. That morning you met with the Congressional group.

P. 564. On Thursday (our time) MacArthur made an air reconnaissance of Korea and during the night on the wire with Collins asked for permission to move in a regimental combat team as the beginning of a two division force since the Korean army had dissolved. Permission was given and later general agreement with your action was voiced by the NSC and a meeting of Congressional personnel.

The clear skeleton of this story of progressive decisions as events called for them does not come out clearly in these pages which are interspersed with too much conversation about who said what. The important thing is to get the bones in—because they are glorious bones—and let the conversational flesh come along afterward.

. . .

P. 590. Your description of the meeting is not as I recall it. My notes of it are: "When we came into his office the President had in his hands some yellow sheets of newsticker paper. He told us to sit down. He was obviously angry. He read aloud to us the whole MacArthur letter, his voice getting harsher as he read. He said that this letter had been sent by MacArthur to the Veterans of Foreign Wars over the open telegraph; it was now on the AP ticker. He didn't see how this could be done without somebody in the U.S. government knowing about it. He was going to ask each one of us in this room whether we had anything to do with it, whether they knew anything about it or were in any way whatever involved in it. He pointed at each person in turn around the room. Each answered, 'No, sir.'

"By the time the President got through it was a pretty thoroughly intimidated group. He turned to Louis Johnson and said, 'I want this letter withdrawn. I want you to send an order to MacArthur to withdraw this letter. That is an order from me. Do you understand that?'

"Louis said, 'Yes, sir, I do.' The President said 'Go and do it. That's all.' Everyone went out and disappeared very fast."

Pp. 599–600. This is a very important and critical point in your revelations with MacArthur. There is more to the matter of orders violated than you make—as I recall it. But my recollection and notes should be checked against the papers you have.

I was in New York on September 28, at the U.N. You sent for me to return to Washington. I got there that evening. The next day, Friday, September 29, after a cabinet meeting, General Marshall and I went to Blair House to lunch with you. When lunch was over and the luncheon things cleared away, an officer came in with a large map on which were the troop dispositions. General Marshall explained the military situation. He said the North Korean army was dissolving. The question was what orders should MacArthur be given. He told us of a tentative order sent by the Joint Chiefs to MacArthur for comment on, I think, the 27th. He now laid it before the President. The idea, as I recall it, was that MacArthur by amphibious and other operations would occupy, fortify, and hold the line Pyongyang-Wansan, running southwest to northeast across Korea. North of that line only Korean troops might operate.

This was discussed by the three of us. All the points which later became important were considered; i.e., as we might move north of this line, our supply line and air support would become longer and more difficult, the enemy's easier and shorter. The danger of Chinese intervention would increase. We came nearer to the Soviet border which would involve greater risks. The President concluded,—General Marshall and I were in complete agreement—that MacArthur should stand on the line mentioned and not go further north with UN troops—only Korean units might be used for policing and pacification if that proved possible.

I do not have and cannot find in the hearings before the Joint Congressional Committee the directives of September 27 and September 30, although they are discussed and certain portions of them are quoted in the Hearings before the committee by General Collins on pages 1216, 1230, and 1239. I believe that my recollection of what they contain is correct, but it would be most important to have this verified. They came up a month later, as I point out below, when on October 25 the Joint Chiefs protested against the general advance order which MacArthur had issued without consultation with them on October 24. This is a very important matter, because it was this advance, which, according to my recollection, was contrary to his directives, which brought about the disaster in North Korea. I think it now seems plain that, if MacArthur had kept his army where he was told to keep it, in a strongly fortified position, it would not have been disorganized and routed by the Chinese intervention.

Then followed the Wake Island meeting. On October 15th MacArthur told HST that 60,000 men could not possibly get across the Yalu.

On October 24, 1950, without consultation with Washington and contrary to the order of September 30, MacArthur ordered a general advance of all his armies to the north. His dispositions were amazing in view of the possibility of Chinese intervention. The 8th Army and the 10th Corps were separated. Then the 8th Army was divided into four or five separate columns out of touch with one another. The 10th Corps was divided into three widely separated forces.

On October 25th the Joint Chiefs protested against this departure from the September 30th order. MacArthur replied that "military necessity" required his actions; that he did not read the September 30 telegram as an order but as advice; and that the Wake Island conference had covered the situation.

The Joint Chiefs and Marshall fumed, saw the danger involved, but, in view of the tradition since Grant of the authority of a U.S. theater commander, were not willing to order MacArthur back to the September 30 line. They thought they were too far away. (There was also MacArthur's prestige.)

Now this was a critical point in history. The defeat of the U.S. forces in Korea in December was an incalculable defeat to U.S. foreign policy and destroyed the Truman Administration. If we had had Ridgway in command this would not have happened.

The extraordinary stupidity of MacArthur's action is shown by chronology. This divided, seven-pronged advance was ordered by MacArthur on October 24.

October 26, first Chinese prisoners taken.

November 4th, MacArthur reports Chinese intervention distinct possibility in an intelligence appreciation.

November 5th, in special communique to U.N. MacArthur says North Korean forces have collapsed and "the most offensive act of international lawlessness ever known in history" has occurred in Chinese intervention in power into Korea.

November 6th, MacArthur in special report to U.N. complains of Chinese intervention. This was debated in the U.N. on November 7th and 8th. (But the advance north continued.) We in State were almost wild by this time because in our meetings at the Pentagon no one could explain what MacArthur was thinking of.

By this time, unknown to him, MacArthur had over 100,000 Chinese in his rear. See S. L. A. Marshall, "The River and the Gauntlet."

November 8th. The vote to put Chinese intervention on the U.N. Security Council agenda was 10 to 1, Malik voting no. The Red Chinese were invited to appear and rejected invitation on November 11.

Meanwhile we met frantically at the Pentagon and with you—November 2, November 6, twice, November 13, November 14, November 17, November 29, December 1, December 2, December 3, December 4, etc.

November 21. 7th ROK division reached Yalu.

November 21. MacArthur flew to Korea and announced on November 24, general assault which would end the war.

By November 28–29–30, 8th Army and 10th Corps, were in headlong retreat. This was the worst defeat of U.S. forces since Bull Run. The generalship was even more stupid.

MacArthur's true nature was never plainer than in defeat. He first lost his head and said the game was up, and then started to blame his government for his own assininity.

December 1st, MacArthur replied to a telegram from *U.S. News and World Report* that the limitations imposed on him were an enormous handicap, unprecedented in military history. On same day he telegraphed Arthur Krock speaking of odds unprecedented in history.

December 6th, President sent his directive to submit statements.

December 11th, MacArthur made a statement that UN command was in fine shape having carried out "tactical withdrawals."

You have in the text his telegrams on (a) extending the war and (b) being unable to defend Korea and Japan.

Collins and Vandenberg went to Korea and Ridgway took over in place of Walker. By January 17 the situation had improved.

While we were approaching the 38th Parallel for the second time and discussing policy with our allies, MacArthur, I think in February, issued a statement that from a military standpoint we must materially reduce the existing superiority of our Chinese communist enemy engaging with impunity in undeclared war against us, with the unprecedented military advantage of sanctuary protection for his military potential against our counterattack upon Chinese soil, before we can seriously consider conducting major operations north of that geographic line. This was open defiance again of the Government's position.

On March 7th, he said, "Vital decision have yet to be made—decisions far beyond the scope of the authority vested in me as the military commander, decisions which are neither solely political nor solely military, but which must provide on the highest international levels an answer to the obscurities which so becloud the unsolved problems raised by Red China's undeclared war in Korea."

In other words: war against China.

Then came the episode of the President's proposed statement and MacArthur's interference. (Your text, page 722.)

Another order to MacArthur to make no statements.

He immediately made one to the effect that he had ordered the army to cross the parallel at will. This brought violent reaction from Nehru and others.

Then the letter to Martin, released April 5th. At the same time the *Daily Telegraph* published an interview with British General H.G. Martin, who quoted MacArthur to the same effect.

Senator Ferguson proposed that a congressional committee go to Tokyo to learn from MacArthur his views on how war should be conducted. Smith of New Jersey supported him.

P. 738, et seq. I have made some notes on the margin of your account of the meetings preceding General MacArthur's relief. The following is an account put together last year by Averell and me from our notes and recollections.

Pursuant to messages received from you on the afternoon of Thursday, April 5, there met with you in your study from 11:30 to 12:30 Friday morning, April 6, following the Cabinet meeting, General Marshall, General Bradley, Harriman, and myself. We discussed the question for an hour, and it was apparent that everyone took the most serious possible view of the situation. It was apparent that General Marshall had not come to a conclusion and wished to reflect further; also that General Bradley would have to confer with the Joint Chiefs of Staff. I believed that General MacArthur should be relieved, but thought that it was essential that you should act, if possible, with the unanimous advice of your military advisers—General Marshall, General Bradley, and the Joint Chiefs. Therefore, at this meeting, I analyzed the situation, without stating any other conclusion than that it should be thought over very carefully because it was a matter of the utmost seriousness. Harriman argued very strongly for the relief of MacArthur.

The next morning, Saturday, April 7, at 8:50 AM, the same group met for a short further meeting with you in your office. At that time you requested General Marshall and General Bradley to confer with the Joint Chiefs of Staff and be prepared on Monday to make a final recommendation to you. On Sunday, the 8th of April, you sent for me to come to Blair House, discussed the matter briefly with me, and told me that you had consulted

Snyder and, I think, Vinson. You said that you would be prepared to act on Monday when Marshall and Bradley made their report.

We met in your office at nine o'clock on Monday morning—Marshall, Bradley, Harriman, and I. Bradley reported that the Joint Chiefs had met with him on Sunday, and it was his and their unanimous judgment that MacArthur should be relieved. General Marshall said that he had come to this conclusion. I said that I agreed entirely, and Harriman re-affirmed his opinion of Friday, to the same effect. You said that your own conclusion was the same and you directed General Bradley to prepare the orders and confer with me, since the office of Supreme Commander, Allied Powers, was also involved. The same group returned to your office at 3:15 on Monday afternoon, April 10 with the drafted orders, which you signed. It was decided that the notification of these orders should be given to General MacArthur through Pace, who was then in Korea, we thought at 8th Army Headquarters. You directed me to send the orders with a message, also prepared, to Pace, through Muccio, directing him to go to Tokyo at once and convey the orders. Our message was delayed in reaching Pace, both through mechanical difficulties in transmission and because Pace was not at Headquarters but was at the front with Ridgway. About ten o'clock Monday night I was informed that, due to this delay and to the fact that Bradley had reported the rumor of a leak, you had thought it best to send the message also by direct Army wire to MacArthur. I was instructed to, and did, inform Congressional leaders and also got Dulles to come to my house, telling him of what had occurred and asking him to go to Japan to assure the Yoshida Government that the change in commander would not in any way affect our policy of pushing the Japanese Peace treaty to a speedy conclusion. This Dulles agreed to do.

This is the story according to the best recollection of Harriman and myself. I think it important that you should have it because it differs in some respects from the account which appears in your manuscript. Both Harriman and I were convinced then and now that your mind had already been made up, but it seemed to us then and now that you acted very wisely in not expressing your opinion to anyone until you had the views of all, which happily turned out to be unanimous. This proved to be a very strong point in the hearings which later occurred before the joint Congressional committee which investigated the MacArthur relief.

. . .

These suggestions were written under great pressure for time and are not very tactfully put. I hope that they won't offend you. The book is a fine job. It ought to be sound as a bell on every point, and is on most of them. My points are intended to raise a few points which I hope you can consider when you go over the galleys, though this may be difficult. I did not realize that you were so far along until your last letter, when my work was nearly done. So I send it along anyway.

Our most affectionate greetings,

Most sincerely,

To ANNIE BURR LEWIS

Annie Burr Lewis was the wife of DA's friend and fellow member of the Yale Corporation, Wilmarth S. Lewis.

Harewood
Sandy Spring, Maryland
November 1, 1955

Dear Annie Burr:

It was good to be one of the tugs which pushed and nudged the good ship "Lefty L" into the berth of a new decade. It seemed to buck the tide now and then at a critical moment, but in a few days you will have everything made fast and secure. How good of you to let him have all the fun of sending me the comb! These are the touches which make Indian summer the ideal time of life.

Yesterday I had Mr. A.E. Stevenson for lunch and the afternoon at P Street. My impression was that my line of thought seemed to him not what the customers are asking for now-a-days. And that may well be true. Now I am bracing myself for the flood of words which my own act will unloose on me this coming week. Well, the quiet life was good while it lasted.

Saturday and Sunday were good days, as are all spent in Farmington.

Our love,

As ever,

To HARRY S TRUMAN

This is one of a number of letters DA wrote to the former president discussing various Democratic candidates for the presidency. The first volume of Truman's Memoirs *had just appeared and Acheson's own book* A Democrat Looks at His Party *was being well reviewed. The Warren referred to is Earl Warren, then Chief Justice of the United States.*

November 23, 1955

The Honorable Harry S Truman
Federal Reserve Bank Building
Kansas City, Missouri

Dear Mr. President:

．．．

In connection with the publication of my book there was the inevitable barrage of requests for appearances on television and radio. I insisted that these be cut down to two—one on the Dave Garroway show on NBC; the other on the Bill Leonard show on CBS. I thought that I had an understanding with both men that I would not go into personalities and discuss candidates for the Democratic nomination in '56. However, Bill Leonard departed from this and asked me what I thought of Adlai's announcement of his candidacy. I thought of—who was it?—Mark Twain's? admonition that it was better to tell the truth because it was then easier to remember what you said. So I said that I had been for Adlai in '52, had reiterated the view that he was the best candidate when asked in '53, '54, and so far in '55, and I saw no reason for doubting that view now. I was sorry to be asked this, not because I have the slightest reluctance in saying what I think, but because, under the present circumstances, I thought it might unnecessarily wound Averell, to whom I am devoted. However, I am sure that he is broad enough and experienced enough to know that he cannot be involved in politics and harbor resentment for those who honestly believe that somebody else is a better candidate.

You know far more about these things than I do, but it would seem to me that Averell's greatest usefulness now lies, not in the possibility that he will be nominated and elected, but in the effect that he can have on Adlai, keeping him pointed up close to the wind and not letting him fall off with phrases like "the relentless pursuit of peace." With Eisenhower out of the picture, as I suppose he is, I should look with undisguised horror at any of the present Republican candidates being in the White House. (Warren, I exclude, because he is a man of honor and of his word, and I believe would not accept the nomination whether drafted or not.) In that case a Democratic victory seems to me of the greatest importance to the welfare of the country, and Adlai seems to me the best person to achieve it. How do you feel about all of this?

The visit which you and Mrs. Truman paid to New Orleans sounds delightful, and I know that your hearts were touched by the reception you describe. I think that every day and every year the affection of the American people for you rises. You typify for them—and rightly—the healthy-minded, direct, generous, courageous, friendly person, who is Mr. American for them.

Let me end up this rambling letter with an episode which illustrates my cold and frigid manner, which has been so often described in the press. Last Thursday morning I was walking east on 38th Street in New York from a friend's house to the air terminal and was not quite sure that the terminal was on 38th Street. On Third Avenue there were four or five men with picks and shovels digging up a broken place in the pavement, surrounded by the yellow barricades with "Men Working" which give them a little island of safety. I stopped there and asked one of them whether I was on the right street for the air terminal. One of them looked up from his work, beamed broadly, and said, "For the love of God, if it ain't Dean Acheson. I seen you on the Dave Garroway show on television yesterday morning." At that point they all threw down their tools, shook hands with me, and we discussed for five minutes the prospects of a Democratic victory in 1956. None of them seemed to be dismayed by the cold exterior.

Alice sends her most affectionate greetings to you and Mrs. Truman, as do I.

Sincerely,

To ARNOLD WHITRIDGE

Arnold Whitridge was a friend of DA, of many years and of many Yale associations, a distinguished educator, scholar and author, and a Republican.

December 27, 1955

Dear Arnold:

I am delighted that you liked my book [*A Democrat Looks at His Party*] and that your points of disagreement produced so thoughtful a letter to me. They relate entirely to chapters two and three and not to those on foreign affairs and the pressure to conform.

What I say in chapters two and three deserves criticism because it conveys the impression that I discern a difference between individual Democrats and Republicans—perhaps even between the "good" and "bad" sides of a mugwump's nature, good when he votes for FDR, bad when he votes for DDE—the Democrat rejoicing in the breadth and catholicity of his views; the Republican, a Scrooge before his reformation. And you rightly say, how explain the hold on the country of the Republican party if that is so. How can the party be made up solely of business men when, rain or shine, it polls within a few million votes of its rival?

So far as my conscious thought is concerned, I tried to repudiate the doctrine of innate characteristics—the liberal and conservative birthmark of Mr. W.S. Gilbert—on pp. 59, 60. But it has crept in to bother you and may even be deeper in my thought than I believe. The view I was seeking to expound was that the control, the center, the provider of funds, of personnel, the drawer of lines beyond which the politicians could not go was, for the Republican party, business. Now this is a very different thing from saying that every Republican holds the same views as Mr. George Humphrey. Next week we shall see a large Communist vote in France, of which only a minority will be Communists, and only a minority of them will direct the party. I do not wish to add insult to injury by comparing the Republicans to the Communist party—only to stress that the controlling interest upon which a party may be centered is often quite different from the views of those who vote the ticket.

In France the discontented by tradition vote the ticket farthest to the left. We have our traditions and historical causes, too, as you point out. For years Lincoln, Rum, Romanism and Rebellion, the protective tariff and the full dinner pail were effective Republican vote getters. But—so my thesis runs—the *dominant* interest, not the only interest, served by the party when in power is the business interest.

Now the Democratic party has its controlling machinery too. The big city bosses and the Southern politicians are a formidable lot, particularly when they are together. But what I was arguing is that no single interest dominates or controls this machinery. There are many interests and groups which have to be harmonized.

I have added no new persuasions but only attempted to make the skeleton of the argument stand out more starkly. As you say, I think I would insist that this domination of the business interest—which seems to me here in Washington to be more stark as General Eisenhower has become in these last months a dim, off-stage figure—does limit the scope for experimentation for the Republican politicians. As for imagination in foreign policy in the years before the wars, I don't think either party showed much of any. FDR's "Quarantine" speech in Chicago was a blossom quickly killed by the frost.

I do hope I provoke you to another letter for I greatly enjoyed your current one. Alice joins me in warmest greetings and good wishes to you and Janetta.

As ever,

To ROBERT A. LOVETT

Lovett was a partner in Brown Brothers, Harriman, a former Under Secretary of State, a former Secretary of Defense, and a close friend of the Achesons.

January 16, 1956

Dear Bob:

Your letter has been an escalator of the spirit unknown around these parts for years. I am almost ready to begin to believe that the damned book had some merit. What it really needs is a few sea shells, or, at least, some sea weed. Just drift wood won't do.

We had just heard about your return to the hospital when here you are out again. You are quite right about where the strength in the race is really to be found. This year Alice's Christmas performance exceeded anything know[n]. It began right after Labor Day and there is still a blush in the West. A sort of Voodoo dance with Santa Claus, the drums beating faster and louder until a frenzy of whirling, wrapping figures sucks all of us in, the way a whirlwind does leaves. It was something to see.

I hope we are seeing you and Adele at the Dickeys in two weeks. And, we have our reservations for Antigua for Feb. 25, down, and March 10, back.

Our love to you both—and stay away from Foster's verge.

As ever,

To ADA AND ARCHIBALD MACLEISH

This letter shows DA's effort to make a "come back" as a lawyer. "Banana twerps" was a MacLeish/Acheson term for banana quits, small yellow land birds of the Windward Islands.

February 9, 1956

Dear Ada and Archie:

That fragment of our hearts which is not utterly broken is filled with bitter disappointment. After months of sitting around and doing writing which can be done anywhere, today a client walked in (over the telephone) and hired me to do a job in the Supreme Court which must be finished by March 16—if the Court gives me that long. I should gladly have told him to jump in the lake if I were paying my way in this outfit. But since I am not and am trying to come back as a lawyer, I must take the job. And that means staying here. No Ada, no Archie, no banana twerps, no rum buds, no lovely ocean and glorious sun. It is maddening and frustrating. It is being tripped up just as we start down the aisle. It is hell on wheels. We shall miss you, my dears, most dreadfully, and all the fun we have just being together—which we haven't been for far too long a time.

Alice is out somewhere and hasn't heard the bad news yet. She has been working, as she can do, like a little beaver to get all her pictures finished, framed and in New York for her show in the middle of March. All the invitations addressed, etc., etc. She even has some snappy new bathing numbers to knock our eyes out. The worst of it is that she will be quite nice about this and not give me hell at all.

This damned case is an important one which the Court 5–4 decided quite wrongly (Felix fortunately being right) and it will have large financial repercussions in the utility industry. The job is to get a rehearing—a tough one—and the client wants me personally and not the firm. So I cannot take it and turn it over. What wretched luck! A little later and I would have gone. A little earlier and I could have done it and still have gone. As Adlai said on election night quoting Lincoln—I am too old to cry; and it hurts too much to laugh.

Think of us kindly, dear MacLeishes, and remember that you have our love, even without us. This summer we shall get together or bust. . . .

Poor Alice—She has just called and I have told her the bad news. She sends a Stoic's love and regret.

As ever,

To CHARLES E. WYZANSKI, JR.

Charles E. Wyzanski, Jr. was Judge of the United States District Court in Boston and a writer of occasional essays on jurisprudence.

February 27, 1956

The Honorable Charles E. Wyzanski, Jr.
United States District Court
Boston 9, Massachusetts

Dear Charlie:

You need never, as I am sure you know, feel any trepidation about writing to me about anything. But I for one would feel a good deal of trepidation about writing on LDB's inner nature. And for two reasons. In the first place, I would feel like saying, Brandeis is in his grave; after life's fitful fever he sleeps well. And I should have the greatest repugnance to intruding upon the citadel of that privacy he guarded so vigilantly. And to what end? Suppose he has been the subject of some undiscriminating praise. He is worthy of the urge which led to it. Suppose he had his vanities and was not proof against the constant drip of adulation. I have seen that iron man, General Marshall, be somewhat less than iron on occasion. All that is so minor and unimportant, so irrelevant to what he did, to what he stood for, to the effect which he had upon the times in which he lived. There is nothing here to expose. There is no sham, or pretense, or hypocrisy lurking in the background. There is no need for a Lytton Strachey to show that the picture of The Lady with the Lamp left a good deal of the real Florence Nightingale out—and to overdo it at that.

Which brings me to my second reason. A friend of mine used to have a file into which he put certain papers. It was labeled "Too Hard." I would put the project of depicting the "true" LDB into that file.

In your paper I do not see the man I knew—not so well as some others but still pretty well. And the informants you quote in the notes seem to me very wide of the mark and remote from the matters on which they testify. For instance, I am strongly persuaded that (1) Hughes's influence was a great element in keeping him on the Court, not the reverse; (2) that he withdrew from social life in Boston and Dedham because of Mrs. Brandeis's invalidism, not because he was dropped; (3) that he wrote thousands of letters, all longhand; (4) that he read a good deal of poetry; (5) that his surroundings were as they were because he wished to live a simple life as an example of revolt against excessive materialism and because the form of it was left to Mrs. Brandeis; (6) that his maturing views were his own and came from inside him and not from Mrs. Brandeis or her sisters. The opinions of Judge Hand and others are entitled to respect, but they are not mine. So often people treated LDB—particularly as he became "venerable"—as an oracle and were disappointed at many of the utterances. But he could be relaxed too, and could and would talk simply and even listen to gossip without pain. In short he was not an institution or an enigma, but a man, albeit a magnificently disciplined and able one. Humor could come through and fire could come through, and so could affection. But, when one finished with all analysis and description, the likeness is still not there; and I question, again, the utility of the effort. There is enough in the public and published material for hot arguments pro and con about what he said and did without chasing the will-o'-the-wisp of what went on inside and why.

This is negative help, but, I hope, not altogether useless. I just don't believe that this project has in it the possibility of success or of doing anyone any good.

I am sure you will want your papers returned and so enclose them.

Sincerely,

TO **HARRY S TRUMAN**

President Truman's daughter Margaret had become engaged; DA's letter touches on comparative experience.

March 27, 1956

Dear Mr. President:

Consolation is just what I can give. In the first place about Margaret's choice. She has always had good judgment and has shown it again here. Alice and I had dinner with them here on his birthday—just a year before we celebrated it in Independence with you—and were completely captivated by Clifton Daniel. He has charm and sense and lots of ability. On the way home I told Alice that there was romance in the wind and that I was all for it. She somewhat acidly remarked that I had so monopolized Mr. Daniel that she hadn't been able to get any idea of Margaret's view of him, and that I was getting to be an old matchmaker. This only made my triumph all the sweeter when the announcement came. I stick by my guns and am sure that the man Margaret has chosen is first class and just the one for her. Marriage is the greatest of all gambles. But character helps and my bets are all on the success of this venture.

Now as to the behavior of daughters and the position of the father of the bride. Daughters, I have found, take this business of marriage into their own hands and do as they please. So do sons—or perhaps some one else's daughter decides for them. I explained most lucidly to Mary and Dave that they should wait until the end of the war to get married. So they got married at once. All in all, the father of the bride is a pitiable creature. No one bothers with him at all. He is always in the way—a sort of backward child—humored but not participating in the big decisions. His only comforter is a bottle of good bourbon. Have you plenty on hand?

At any rate all this will take your mind off politics which seem to me royally mixed up—at least on our side. One thing I don't understand. Some of the wise men say—and I hear you quoted to this effect—that the desirable thing is to have an open convention where the nomination can be worked out. But why isn't this a pretty sure road to getting some one whom nobody wants? The only real possibilities—good possibilities—seem to be Adlai and Averell. Adlai, if nominated, would seem to have the better chance to win—though not a very good chance. Averell, if nominated and defeated, might, as the Governor of the most important Democratic state, [be] able to maintain a vigorous party committed to liberal principles through the difficult years until 1960. But by then he might be rather old for another try—and not realize it. At any rate, isn't that about the choice? And wouldn't it be good to have it made before rather than attempt it in the confusion of the convention. If you ask me, made by whom? I don't know. What I need from you is some political education. This is a fair exchange for consolation.

Alice sends her love to Mrs. Truman and to you. Her exhibition in New York has been—at the halfway mark—a great success. She has sold nine pictures. The latest purchaser Mrs. Herbert Lehman.

Affectionately and sincerely,

To MRS. JENNINGS WISE

Mrs. Wise's gift related to Acheson family roots in Edinburgh.

April 19, 1956

Dear Mrs. Wise:

How very kind of you to think of me and to give your thought such charming form. I am delighted to have the "Book," Old Houses in Edinburgh, and have, of course, already read all about my ancestor's house and admired the drawings of it and the other old houses. Books are not made like that today—such lovely paper and delightful and bold type. My father has spoken of the house many times and Sir Archibald's wife's name, Margaret, is my sister's also. Even after three centuries and over three thousand miles of water I still feel the strong attachment to that spot in Edinburgh.

I am most grateful. Please accept my thanks and my most earnest good wishes.

Very sincerely yours,

To ROBERT MENZIES

Robert Menzies was Prime Minister of Australia and leader of the Liberal Party.

April 20, 1956

Dear Bob:

I hear through our Australian underground, which is Owen Dixon to Felix to me, that you have had a mean fall in the most dangerous mantrap yet devised—the bath. The report goes on that you have had a lot of pain from it. For all of this I am most distressed and send you the most affectionate commiseration. I had a roommate in the law school who insisted that it was bathing that undermined the Roman Empire, but he got killed by an automobile. So I can't promise that giving up the practice will keep you out of trouble. But I can say, along the line of current political discussion by certain parties hereabouts, that even flat on your back you are head and shoulders above any of your upright competitors—even broadening the field by divorcing that word of any but physical connotation.

I have thought what I could do to speed your recovery and concluded that, if you had my book, confinement with it would soon force you into an ambulatory condition.

The British edition seems better for the purpose. The dust cover is particularly bilious and uninviting; and, then, it keeps you right in the Commonwealth. It goes to you separately.

Our own politics are running true to form under Republican Administration. The Democrats engaged in bitter internecine strife; the Republicans, wallowing in inane banality. Perhaps we shall make more sense than now seems possible.

My warmest and most solicitous greetings.

Sincerely,

To **FRANK ALTSCHUL**

Frank Altschul was a New York financier.

October 4, 1956

Mr. Frank Altschul
730 Fifth Avenue
New York 19, N.Y.

Dear Frank:
Thank you very much indeed for your two letters with your and Mrs. Goodhart's kind and generous words about my recent speech. I appreciate them very much indeed.

What you say about more—and better—being needed in the campaign on foreign affairs seems to me wholly right. I would think Adlai wise to maintain reticence on Suez while it is actively under discussion in the U.N. While we were always attacked in the course of an operation, it seemed to me at the time not only wrong but ineffective and unproductive from the attacker's point of view. By the middle of the month it ought to be clear whether anything will be done. My guess is that nothing will be done. Then Adlai is free to criticize. Some material is ready for that purpose if he wants it.

I have read your memorandum, which presents the situation well and powerfully. I am not critical; but I have some doubts, an opinion as Felix once wrote, "dubitante." You are quite right that this whole matter has been wrapped up in lawyers' talk, which obscures the issue, and that the equities have also been obscured and, perhaps, changed by Foster's very silly and clumsy attempt to wound Nasser by the withdrawal of the Aswan dam offers. But enough remains to stand on the position that Nasser has broken a pledge, renewed at the time of the base evacuation, to leave the canal alone until 1968. He did this by force and to strike (back, it is true) at the vital interests of the European powers. Force could quite justifiably have been used to prevent this and restore the status quo ante.

By "justifiably" I mean in accordance with good morals and also with a good prospect of success in accomplishing the purpose and without setting the Middle East afire. Firm, immediate, and overwhelming action—followed by very speedy evacuation—would have been a highly defensible, and perhaps the best, policy, calculated to produce little resistance and inspire respect for covenants freely made.

But the force to do this did not exist—so I am authoritatively told—the opportunity passed, and *that* opportunity will not recur. Now England is divided; France is motivated by collateral interest and not much judgment; the Arab states are aroused and united. Now force means something different from what it meant in July. Undoubtedly enough force could be got together to overpower Egypt, but I imagine a good many people would get killed and they might not all be Egyptians. Aramco has got six thousand people inland in Saudi Arabia.

So I have doubts whether force can at this stage accomplish the desired end. Then, too, there is some question as to the precise question which we will have to decide. Will it be whether or not to back our allies? May it not be whether or not to advocate force to allies—or an ally—who are undecided? This is a very different matter and a different measure of responsibility. The French may well be ready to precipitate a conflagration in which their own humiliations and frustrations will disappear. But what about the British? The *Economist* tells us that the Cabinet is divided. The Labour Party certainly is not (on this issue). New provocations might well pull the country together. But without them will it, in cold blood, after the first flush of indignation has passed, take all the risks which force involves? I very much doubt it.

The dog now has the bone firmly in his teeth, and I don't see anyone stepping up to take it from him. Meanwhile vast damage is being done to the Western alliance—which is probably more serious than any risks from Nasser in the canal. But because the ills are clear and great, it does not follow that the remedy is. There are some problems without a solution. At any rate I do not believe that I know enough about all the essential facts to resolve my doubts. And the duty and responsibility of resolving them is not upon me. So I observe, with deep apprehension, a series of steps which seem ineffectual and unguided by any purpose except to move from one untenable position to another.

These are my comments—and most unhelpful ones at that.

Most sincerely,

To **HANS J. MORGENTHAU**

Hans Morgenthau was professor of international politics at the University of Chicago. DA set out his views on the handicaps to lawyers in the administration of foreign policy.

January 3, 1957

Professor Hans J. Morgenthau
5542 South Dorchester Avenue
Chicago 37, Illinois

Dear Mr. Morgenthau:

Thank you very much for sending me your *New Republic* articles. They are very good; the analysis penetrating and the writing pungent.

You have, I gather from some of my young friends, set the cat among the pigeons by your remarks about lawyers as makers of foreign policy. But let not your heart be heavy for you have a good point. An outstanding example to support you is Sir John Simon, one of the greatest lawyers and most indifferent of Foreign Ministers. I have in the past put the point a little differently, and not as flatly as you do.

In considering foreign policy, a lawyer's training and experience brings him one advantage and several handicaps. The advantage comes from the mental discipline of logic, the training in relevance which comes from any schooling in the philosophical disciplines. Oliver Franks has it to a high degree.

The main disadvantages are three. Even in a large law office a lawyer works with very few assistants. The utilization of a large staff with many different points of view is confusing to him. Both Mr. Hull and Mr. Byrnes had this difficulty. But more important, I think, is that in a lawyer's experience his thinking starts from a point of view rather narrowly given him by his client's interest. I know, of course, about Brandeis being "counsel for the situation," etc. But there are not many Brandeises about; and he was not senior partner of Sullivan and Cromwell. It does not do to say that a Secretary of State has the whole country, or even the government, for his client and there is no real difference from the viewpoint of a practicing lawyer. There is a vast difference in the scope given for judgment. It is here rather than in the episodic nature of "cases" that the difference lies. Counsel for the New York Central Railroad System may not have "cases" and may enjoy the continuum of effort you mention. But his purpose and scope is delimited for him, even though he has scope within the limits.

But in formulating foreign policy one has a really great sector for thought and action. While the predilections of the client may limit execution, they have no part in determining what ought to be attempted. There is not in foreign policy the self-starting, energizing, and directing force of an all-embracing interest. Responsibility, will, and direction must come from the devisers of policy.

Then there is a final and less important handicap. High among the conditions of a lawyer's judgment is the possible approval or disapproval of some person or group—the client, a tribunal of some sort, a board of directors, stockholders, etc. The element of his proposed action's adaptability to advocacy—an important element in public life, too—rates very high. But in determining what is wise foreign policy, this consideration should rank very low. This perhaps puts all the greater demands on advocacy later on, in rendering the unpalatable acceptable. Many of us remember very well Mr. Hull's Sunday morning sessions in the Old State Department, which bewildered the newcomer. The old gentleman would move through three hundred and sixty degrees around a question, himself arguing every point of view, with the gallery chiming in freely, either in agreement or dissent. Gradually we could see him settle on a point of view in which he felt comfortable and secure. There are worse ways of deciding matters of policy; but there are better ways, too.

It would be a pose should I pretend that I did not notice the sentence about myself, did not appreciate your generous adjectives, and was not puzzled by its content, in two respects. You suggest that we failed in our task because we failed to marshal public opinion in support of sound policies. I was not conscious that any of the policies had failed for this reason. Recently in the *Yale Review* I said something which I thought was true:

> The Eightieth Congress, with which President Truman had his fiercest battles, worked admirably in foreign affairs; and many of those who demanded the dismissal of the Secretary of State in 1950–52 joined in passing all the major legislation he laid before the Congress, including the Japanese and German treaties on the very eve of the campaign of 1952. Mutual respect is more important than affability.

Do you disagree?

And then you add that we compounded our failure by, in the end, embracing unsound policies without gaining popular support. I confess that what you have in mind escapes me, unless you mean our handling of the loyalty-security matter, which I myself have publicly deplored. Perhaps there is something else which my subconscious had been suppressing—if that is the right lingo.

I congratulate you on the articles. You have given us much pleasure and light.

Sincerely yours,

To HARRY S TRUMAN

Covington & Burling
Union Trust Building
Washingon 5, D.C.
January 15, 1957

The Honorable Harry S Truman
Federal Reserve Bank Building
Kansas City, Missouri

Dear Mr. President:

I wish it were possible for us to coordinate our efforts a little better on foreign policy matters. Your article in last Sunday's *New York Times*, the first of your North American Newspaper Alliance articles, has, I am afraid, cut a good deal of the ground out from under an effort to put some sense into the Administration's foreign policy and to put some fighting spirit into the Democrats.

Your article says that "Congress has no alternative but to go along with the President in this program." If this is so, then I spent four useless hours before the Foreign Affairs Committee and a good many useless days of work in devising what I thought an excellent alternative, and one which was thoroughly in accord with steps which had been taken during your Administration.

The article says later on, "Now that the President proposes to adopt a clear-cut policy of action, we should do everything to back him up." I do not think that, upon reflection, you will really regard this as a clear-cut policy. In fact, there is no policy about it at all, as I tried to show in the statement before the Committee, which David Lloyd sent to you.

Again, the article says that "We must at this stage accept the President's assessment of what the situation is, for only the President is in possession of all the facts." This seems to me a wholly artificial view to take. I don't think we have to accept the President's assessment; and I doubt very much that he is in possession of more facts than the rest of us here. Certainly he is not in possession of any more than Dulles told him about, and I would hesitate to rely on that source of information.

Finally, the article says, "The proposals made by the President, when approved by the Congress, will strengthen the position of the free world." Again, I don't think they will strengthen it at all. There are alternative courses of action which would strengthen it far more.

However, the main purpose of this note is not to stick on what has been done, but to urge that in the future we try to get together and not be at cross purposes. I had thought that we were in agreement when you were in Washington. Of course, I did not know that you were about to publish an article saying that you would, if you were a Senator, vote for a proposal which I was about to urge Congress to supplant with a better one.

I hope that Mrs. Truman is completely over all the pain and discomfort of her accident. Alice and I send our love to her and to you.

As ever,

To HANS J. MORGENTHAU

January 16, 1957

Professor Hans J. Morgenthau
Department of International Relations
Yale University
New Haven, Connecticut

Dear Mr. Morgenthau:

I am replying to your kind and interesting letter of January 14, not to prolong a correspondence which I know makes inroads upon your busy hours, but to give two impressions of my own for whatever they may be worth in your appraisal of the two situations which you mention.

You suggest as an illustration of the last Administration's not doing something wise for fear of public opinion its failure to work out a negotiated settlement with the Soviet Union while we still had a monopoly of the atomic bomb. I was pretty close to the center of the Truman Administration's decisions on foreign policy throughout its tenure. We did not believe that there was an opportunity for a negotiated settlement. The experiences of both Secretary Byrnes and Secretary Marshall impressed this strongly upon them, and I believe that both Chip Bohlen and George Kennan would agree fully. My own first-hand attempt to work out something in regard to Germany in May of 1949 added me to the list of those whose experience convinced them that so long as it appeared in Russian eyes that there were soft spots, those soft spots would be probed. This was a matter which was discussed many times, and we always concluded that whatever might be agreed to would be of no value whatever, since the Russians would take whatever they got through the agreement and push on wherever the opportunity seemed open. Therefore, I am convinced, first, that the opportunity was not missed because it did not exist; and, second, that, if it did exist, it was missed, not because we were afraid to seize it, but because we did not believe that it was there.

Then you suggest the failure to recognize Communist China as being caused by our fear of adverse opinion. Toward the end of 1949, prior to the Colombo Conference, we had long talks with the British on this subject. It seemed to us at that time that it was premature to go to recognition in the absence of some assurance (and none was forthcoming) from the Chinese that they would honor their international engagements, including decent treatment for our nationals in their power. I don't think that the British really differed from this view, but Ernie Bevin, who was not well, was pushed by Nehru and did not wish to have it appear that British policy was being determined by India. Therefore, he parted company with us and recognized the Communist government either before or at Colombo. The Truman Administration was immediately, in January, faced with the seizure of our consulate property in Peiping by the Communists in direct violation of treaty rights. I do not suppose that anybody would have thought it wise to recognize the Government under these circumstances. While this matter was under discussion through the agency of the British, the attack on Korea started, with enthusiastic Chinese support through propaganda and later by military intervention. Although I may be wrong, I do not see any point at which it can be said that the Truman Administration was wrong in not recognizing the Chinese Communists; and certainly I do not see how it can be said that they failed to do so through fear of public opinion. I am, of course, open to the charge of special pleading; but, even so, it occurred to me you might like to have the impressions of one actually concerned in the matters about which you wrote.

With kindest regards.

Sincerely yours,

To JOSEPH N. WELCH, ESQ.

Mr. Welch had been counsel to the Department of the Army in the hearings held by Senator Joseph McCarthy. The latter was the subject of this letter; he had died not long before.

May 16, 1957

Joseph N. Welch, Esquire
Hale and Dorr
60 State Street
Boston 9, Mass.

Dear Joe:
Thank you very much for your generous words about me and my liter-ary offspring. I am proud to autograph your copy of the book which is on its way back to you.

The demise of one who has played a part in both your life and mine has brought me a curious bit of information new to me. When queried by the press, I said *De mortuis*, etc., which seemed to me colorless in the extreme. A flood of abuse has descended on me by mail and telegraph, the central point of which seems vaguely to be that the words were latin. Apparently my use of the ancient tongue of the Church of Rome implies to my critics the assumption of a superior attitude which infuriates them. One constantly learns and rarely profits by it.

Sincerely,

To **HARRY S TRUMAN**

The Michael referred to is Michael Bundy, one of DA's grandsons. The Foreign Affairs Committee of the Democratic Advisory Council was estab-lished to present alternatives to the Eisenhower Administration's foreign policies.

June 5, 1957

Dear Mr. President:
There is no better way for me to start the summer than for you to start it by writing me—and you pleased us both mightily by what you said about the children's party for us and about Michael. He is the only source of en-ergy I know of which equals the atom. After he had spent a month with us while his parents went around the world Alice reports saying to me "Don't you miss Michael?" and my exhausted reply "Not yet." I feel sure that if he ever landed in the White House no puzzled countryman would have to ask "I wonder who lives there now?"

The boys finally twisted my arm until I agreed to be Chairman of the Foreign Affairs Committee appointed by your Advisory Committee, about which you telegraphed me. Charlie Murphy was eager to have me do it be-cause, he said, the party was getting over the foolish attitude of backing away from the Truman administration and that I would help the reform by joining the Committee. What the Committee can do still puzzles me, but then if it doesn't do anything it won't do any harm, which for some Democrats these days is a big achievement. Paul Nitze has agreed to be Vice Chairman. . . .

This recent flap about the Khrushchev interview is a good example of what I talked about once as "total diplomacy"—that the diplomacy of a democracy was not at all restricted to what the government did, including the disorderly performances of the Congress, but included the press, radio and television, the movies, churches, labor unions, business, women's clubs, etc. Here comes CBS blundering into the picture with three interviewers who act as though they had never finished the sixth grade and give Khrushchev more free propaganda—which he used admirably—than he could have obtained in a year. As I see it, he had only one point to make—which happened to be untrue but which he put over to the Queen's taste—that the Russians were willing to "ban the bomb," move out of Europe, get on with mutual travel and cultural exchanges, trade, etc., etc., but that the Americans seemed to be afraid to do so. Communism was, he said, bound to win and we knew it. So we remained frozen like frightened rabbits. All the early part of the interview where he flubbed around with the agricultural situation, about which he clearly knew little, gave the impression—and was intended to—of a simple, honest fellow doing the best he could with great problems. He gets the prize for 1957 and CBS gets the dunce cap—and probably a big boost in income.

I shall, of course, be with you on the sixth of July. Alice says she has "every hope of being with me." I ask what that means to which she replies with exasperating calm that it is too early for her to say absolutely that she can come. So I shall make a plane reservation for her anyway and, if the temperature is under a hundred I think that she'll go.

I am doing a piece for a European magazine on NATO which I think you will like and will send along soon. Our most affectionate greetings to Mrs. Truman and to you.

As ever,

To **CHARLES B. GARY**

An early appraisal of Henry Kissinger by DA. Gary was a retired naval officer of flag rank who had served on the wartime staffs of the Chief of Naval Operations, the Joint Chiefs of Staff, and the Combined Chiefs of Staff, and a long-time student of and writer in politico-military affairs.

June 20, 1957

Mr. Charles B. Gary
37 Riverside Drive
New York 22, N.Y.

Dear Mr. Gary:

Thank you for your kind note about the advisory Committee on Foreign Policy. . . .

I shall be asking you for help. In fact I begin now. You and I talked a while ago about drawing a line between nuclear weapons and all other weapons as instruments for the last ditch all-out war and limited war respectively. I took this view at the Air War College. They argued but did not shake me. Now Mr. H. A. Kissinger in his new book *Nuclear Weapons and Foreign Policy* (Harper's) has shaken me. It is a hard book to read because of its repetitive Germanic style and the first section is infuriating because of its academic superiority. But the damned cuss has brains and has thought a lot. How well I want to know from you.

I have asked Harper's to send you a copy.

With warm regards.

Sincerely yours,

To **ALEXANDER BICKEL**

Bickel was professor of law at Yale University and had produced a book of the unpublished opinions of Justice Brandeis.

June 28, 1957

Dear Alex:

I am most grateful for the gift of your book and its very generous inscription to me. You have done a most impressive piece of work and the Belknap press has printed it very well indeed. At first I was worried about printing this material for fear of what it might do to the confidential relationship of the Court. But the Justices seem to have attended to that job themselves and what they have overlooked Mr. Mason has supplied. Perhaps Humphrey Wolfe's observations in another field are apposite:

> "You cannot hope to bribe or twist,
> Thank God, the British journalist.
> But seeing what the chap will do
> Unbribed, there's no occasion to."

Some of the things I seem to have written surprise me. I not only don't remember many of them, but, by and large, they are better than I could do now.

My very warm thanks and good wishes go to you.

Sincerely,

To CASS CANFIELD

Cass Canfield was Chairman of the Board of Harper & Brothers, publishers.

August 2, 1957

Mr. Cass Canfield, Chairman
Harper & Brothers
49 E. 33rd Street
New York 16, N.Y.

Dear Cass:

Apropos Mr. Martin's projected book, there is a terrific tale which Ambassador George Allen, now in Greece, told me a good many years ago which ought to be gotten direct from him. It is about our consul in Tabriz, Persia at the beginning of World War I. With the cables cut, no mail and no work, forgotten by the Department, he took to the bottle in a big way. Into his dilapidated office-living quarters one day came a bareback rider from a stranded French circus, since the U.S. had taken over French interests. No one seemed to be around until she discovered the consul dead to the world in a bottle-strewn bedroom. Having nothing else to do, she moved in, cleaned up the place and when he came to got him to eat something for a change. For a year or so they lived happily together, in the course of which she got him off the bottle and into pretty good shape. About then some missionaries got themselves captured by tribesmen and held for ransom. At her urging the consul rode out alone and effected a spectacular release.

As the missionaries were about to take the circus lady back to civilization, he asked her what he could do to show his deep gratitude to her. She, of course, said, "Marry me," which he did. In all these years, receiving no salary, he had drawn drafts on the United States which local merchants cashed at a proper discount. When these eventually got to Washington the war was over and he was summoned home to face charges of grave financial irregularity.

One of the missionaries turned out to be the sister of V.P. Charles Dawes, who moved to the rescue like the U.S. cavalry. The consul was offered the rewards of a hero, but he said that his wife had always wanted to live in Paris and could he be consul-general there. The end is a tear-jerker of his devotion to her through a long illness and of his desolation after her death.

My son reminds me of two other stories you might want to look into. One can be told by former Ambassador William Phillips, now living in Boston. As I recall it, it is mentioned in George Kennan's book. It has to do with the final abandonment of Petrograd. After the safe was emptied, code book and papers burned, they were about to leave the building with the safe open. Billy had an idea that commended itself to the others, which was to take his silk hat, put it in the safe, and lock the safe so as to give the Bolsheviks something to discover when it blew open.

The second story has to do with Ambassador Joseph Green, who lives here. He was captured by the Bolsheviks during the Archangel expedition. Dave says that as he recalls it, Green was condemned to death, and he and a colleague were finally brought before a firing squad, from which they were rescued after the command to aim had been given. Dave recalls that Joe's clearest recollection of the last few seconds was that all the guns were aimed at his stomach and he had a strong desire to put his hands over it, which was frustrated by the fact that they were tied.

Yours,

To SENATOR LYNDON B. JOHNSON

Here DA refuted criticisms of the compromises necessary to passage of the first major postwar civil rights legislation.

August 13, 1957

The Honorable Lyndon B. Johnson
United States Senate
Washington, D.C.

Dear Lyndon:
Thank you for your kind note of the 8th. I am very glad to have been of some help.

Now you can help me to understand something which has been baffling me. We Americans are most patient people. We accept a great deal of shoddy performance in many fields with good nature and even without much protest when we are told that it is what we are supposed to like. But when we do something outstanding, as usually happens in human affairs by a rare combination of good luck and good management, we can't believe it. We are filled with suspicion of our own action and immediately deprecate it. Why are we doing this about the civil rights bill which you have just passed in the Senate?

As I read the papers I get the impression that intelligent and liberal opinion regards the bill as probably the best compromise. Compromise with what? I don't think it an exaggeration to say that the bill is among the great achievements since the war and, in the field of civil rights, the greatest since the Thirteenth Amendment. The bill as passed by the Senate is in every way an improvement over the bill the Senate received—and I mean improvement from the point of view of the actual achievement of civil rights.

The elimination of Part III was undiluted gain. It made the bill a voting rights bill which everyone can understand and no one can or will oppose on its merits. It enlists on the side of the citizen seeking this elemental right the whole power of the United States, acting through the executive and judicial branches. He is no longer clothed with theoretical rights but with no practical way of turning them into reality. The elimination of Part III saved the government from the vain attempt to enforce two Reconstruction statutes which no majority of the Supreme Court has been able to interpret. Before anyone is permitted to bewail the demise of this Part he ought to be forced to read the innumerable opinions of the Court in *Screws* v. *The United States,* 322 U.S. 718 and *United States* v. *Williams* (3 cases), 341 U.S. 58, 70, 97, which, for my sins, I have done. If he can understand what the statutes mean he will be an unusual man. If he can persuade four others of his view he will be more successful than was any justice of the Court.

For Congress to have directed the Executive Branch to enforce these incomprehensible statutes would not have advanced civil rights. It would have produced endless litigation and given a perfect excuse to avoid any further legislation which experience may show to be necessary. Worse than this, it would have invited the Court to legislate, as all sloppy and vague acts of Congress require it to do, and then, when it does state the law—as it must—bring down upon it the condemnation of large sections of the community. This sort of Congressional irresponsibility can do vast harm to the judicial branch and to confidence in it. The Senate amendments avoid all this.

About the jury trial amendment I have already commented in my letter to the *Washington Star* which you had inserted in the Congressional Record. This, too, seems to me an improvement in the bill. The talk of horrendous and vague consequences in other fields of the law has no foundation. If some remote and yet unimagined consequence needs correction, the legislative process will still be operating.

The bill as passed seems to me the legislative process operating at its best. Legislation ought not to be an opportunity to record postures or attitudes. Its function is by agreement to get practical things done for the benefit of our society. To do this requires restraint and respect for views different from those of the majority. Respect means not only that they be heard, but that those who hold them and whose loyalty to the result must be won, shall believe that they have been heard with respect and have had an effect in the result.

In my judgment this was done in the Senate during the last few weeks. It was done in the best tradition of our republic. It resulted in a bill which, if made law, will, I believe, work effectively in those sections of the country where alone, as a civil rights measure, it has importance. Law does not lie, as a great judge has said, at the end of a policeman's stick. It is not merely a matter of the orders either of a dictator or of a majority of our people and the Congress. A wise and sympathetic observer of our history has warned that in our "vast country, of continental range and variety, with sectional interests, traditions, passions to be allowed for . . . the imposition by a numerical majority, of its views and interests and passions on such great minorities, spread over great territorial areas," might create "in those regions a sense of outrage dearly bought by a symmetrical party programme." This, too, the present bill avoids.

Why isn't all this more widely sensed? I understand, of course, that all these matters raise political questions of a party and personal nature in a most acute form, but these do not explain the attitude which most puzzles. Politics are of the essence. To regard the phrase "playing politics" as a dirty phrase is silly. Those whose attitude I am speaking of understand this. They understand, too, that politics have no honorable place in two areas, the security of the United States and in securing to our negro fellow citizens the basic right which we have promised them for nearly a century—the right to speak for themselves.

Can't we for once be proud of ourselves when we do the right thing?

Sincerely,

To **HARRY S TRUMAN**

The reference to "the bill" is to the civil rights legislation in the Congress that summer. (See letter to Lyndon Johnson, August 13, 1957.)

Covington & Burling
Union Trust Building
Washington 5, D.C.
August 14, 1957

The Honorable Harry S Truman
Federal Reserve Bank Building
Kansas City, Missouri

Dear Mr. President:

Thank you very much for having sent the letter to Congressman Carnahan, with copies to Sam, Lyndon, and John McCormack.

After I wrote you, as a result of Sam's canvassing the field it was decided to strike out the loan authority altogether, and merely authorize appropriations for two years. All those concerned, therefore, thought that as this rather disappointing compromise would go through Congress without much help, they would not use your support now but would save it for what may be the very tough period when it comes to the actual appropriation itself. When the time comes they are to let me know and I shall get you on the telephone. The same letter can be used with some very minor changes toward the end of making it appropriate to the new situation. Everybody is most grateful for your willingness to help.

I think you will be interested in a copy of a letter to Lyndon which I wrote him today at his request. He and Sam have been having real difficulty with some of the Northern liberals, although I think most of them are now beginning to see the light. He wanted a letter which would express what I had been saying to him the other day that the bill is not a mere compromise, not a second-rate article which has to be taken in lieu of something better, but is in reality a better bill than the one originally proposed. It will be a tragedy of the greatest order if well meaning but ignorant people are made the dupes of cynical politicians to destroy this really fine effort.

Alice is trying to get Clifton to come down this fall to speak to the Women's National Democratic Club. To this end she is hoping to induce Margaret and Clifton to stay with us. I pointed out that this is a delightful idea but leaves out one member of the family of the greatest possible importance.

With warmest greetings.

As ever,

To A. WHITNEY GRISWOLD

The opening of this letter refers to an article by DA which he had instructed Griswold to send on to Jane Acheson Brown, DA's daughter, but which Griswold wished to keep.

August 17, 1957

Dear Whit:

All right, all right. Keep your ill gotten gains and I shall send off another copy to Jane. I have modified some of the text to indirect discourse to mitigate the assurance which *Harpers* felt that they would be sued by ASCAP. They seemed so terrified that I am trying the milder version on the *Reporter*.

If you think you are working, boy, you should see me. Five hours even on Saturdays and Sundays on this damned new book in which I have the absolute by the tail and can't let go.

Have you read David Cecil's *The Fine Art of Reading*? The essay on Shakespeare's Comedies seems to me superlative. Is it all old stuff to you? For me it opened dusty windows on delightful landscape.

My love to Mary.

As ever,

To ANNIE BURR LEWIS

Burlingham was a prominent New York lawyer. "Marion" refers to Mrs. Frankfurter; Juliet Rublee to the wife of Acheson's former law partner, George Rublee.

Harewood
Sandy Spring, Maryland
September 17, 1957

Dear Annie Burr:

Mr. Burlingham was—in his hundredth year—full of beans. He disposed of Marion in one flash of his scimitar, and then turned to Juliet Rublee. "She had," he said, "the worst fault any wife can have—she answered questions addressed to her husband." Alice insists it works the other way, too. But I know of no authority for so extreme a feminist view.

. . .

As always,

To HARRY S TRUMAN

The "lesson of Little Rock" refers to Eisenhower's failure to back up a Court order desegregating the Little Rock schools until the very last moment, when the National Guard had to be brought in to restore order.

October 8, 1957

Dear Mr. President:

Your good letter tells me that you are off to Sam Rayburn's Library opening. . . .

I shall miss you at the [Democratic Advisory] Council meeting on the 19th but approve your choice of a wedding to a wake. For me it will be another lost week-end. At least, my role of presenting the Foreign Policy statement will have the merit which John G. Johnson found in staying at the bar instead of accepting Cleveland's offer of a place on the Supreme Court. "I would rather talk to the damned fools," he said, "than listen to them."

We have worked out a pretty good statement with some sense to it. But I suppose your brethren will want to clutter it up with a lot of words about peace, disarmament, Israel, Poland, etc. to produce the old futile attempt to appeal to nationality groups—like the 1956 platform.

We are, I think, getting in bad shape internationally. The combination of distrust of Dulles, our defense policy, which more and more rests on a relative nuclear position which we do not have and can never have, and no economic policy for the undeveloped countries is isolating us. It could easily pave the way for a quite unmanageable international situation.

This frightens me because of the lesson of Little Rock—a weak President who fiddles along ineffectually until a personal affront drives him to unexpectedly drastic action. A Little Rock with Moscow and the SAC [Strategic Air Command] in the place of the paratroopers could blow us all apart.

My lectures try to get at the inwardness of our predicament and suggest lines of policy. Sometimes I am frankly over my head. But as I study I become increasingly depressed. The escape from Götterdämmerung will take a vigor of mind and leadership which I do not see in either party, even on the distant horizon. And for three years it seems impossible to do anything at all—God rest ye merry gentlemen!

This is hardly a gay letter. But you are proof against depression.

Our warmest greetings to you and Mrs. Truman.

As ever,

To PHILIP H. WATTS

The paper referred to is "A Proposal for St. Paul's School." Watts was a friend and neighbor of DA and, as a member of the St. Paul's School Alumni Standing Committee, prepared the "Proposal" as a paper for that committee. The Vice President was Richard M. Nixon.

December 9, 1957

Mr. Philip H. Watts
1513 28th St., N.W.
Washington 7, D.C.

Dear Phil:

This is a good paper. From my point of view it can be made better. My comments have to do with the method and angle of approach. I am allergic to evangelicism; also, to the Vice President, particularly as prophet and spiritual leader.

I am all for young (and also old) men of quality going into public life and government service. But why do they have to be "dedicated men"? To dedicate means to set aside for the service of a divine being or for a sacred use. Secondarily, it means to set aside for any definite use. In this sense men who go into public service are, of course, dedicated to it by going into it. The word is redundant. Used as a color or image word to suggest Sir Galahad, it is worse than confusing. There is nothing divine or sacred about public service, any more than about dentistry.

Both are important. There have been times in my life when a dentist seemed to me more important than the President or the Pope. But because we *need* dentists or doctors, or scientists or bomber pilots is not a compelling reason why any of my grandsons should become one, or why their schoolmasters should try to steer them toward one of these careers. And yet I would be eager to see them steered toward a career, perhaps a life, of public service, as some of their ancestors were. Why? Not because I see the gleam of a halo forming about their heads, or because I am persuaded that they are under any duty to sacrifice their lives for Jimmie Hoffa's children, but because there is no better or fuller life for a man of spirit. The old Greek conception of happiness is relevant here: "The exercise of vital powers along lines of excellence, in a life affording them scope."

This is the geiger-counter which tells us where to dig. It explains also why to everyone who has ever experienced it the return from public life to private life leaves one feeling flat and empty. Contented, interested, busy— yes. But exhilarated—no. For one has left a life affording scope for the exercise of vital powers along lines of excellence. Not the only one, I am sure. Undoubtedly Einstein, Michelangelo, Savonarola, Shakespeare, and a good many others could give interesting testimony on other lives. But outside of aesthetics and teaching religion belongs to both—the requirement of "scope" is hard to come by in this age, outside of public life. Surely vital powers are exercised in the whole vast task of feeding, clothing, housing us, as I am sure Mr. McElroy was aware in making soap and being handsomely paid for it. But I am equally sure that he now feels a zest, a sense that the only limitation upon the exercise of all his vital powers is his own capacity, that he never felt before.

I am in danger, perhaps, of overstating my point. So I do not want to draw a picture of public life as a perpetual marijuana jag, or to leave out its colossal obstacles, some of them killers, as not a few of our close friends have found out. But, painted with all the warts, it is a life of scope for the exercise of all one's vital powers, even though one may become a casualty in exercising them.

This has not always been true. For instance, in Athens of the fifth century (B.C.) public life offered the greatest scope for men of talent in all Greek history; in the fourth century, after the defeat and humiliation of Athens, it presented none. In the last half of the nineteenth century, public life in England reached its most luxuriant and brilliant flowering, while in America it sank to depths not plumbed before or since. It did so because in this country the real scope for the exercise of vital powers (perhaps not altogether in the direction of excellence) lay in exploiting a continent and building industrial and financial empires as glittering as dreams of Cathay. Today much of the glitter and the semblance of the rewards (the reality is hidden in expense accounts and management participation plans) still exists, but the power, and with it the scope for action, of business and finance have faded with the rise of the dangers and the demands of a two-camp world. Today, more than ever before, the prize of the general is not a bigger tent, but command. The managers of industry and finance have the bigger tents; but command rests with government. Command, or, if one prefers, supreme leadership, demands and gives scope for the exercise of every vital power a man has in the direction of excellence.

How, then, does one present to the boys at St. Paul's a life of public service? Not, I am sure, as an evangelist appealing to the young squires to turn their backs on the world and dedicate themselves to a sort of secular order for ministering to the peasants, nor as crusaders led by Mr. Nixon to bring communist infidels to capitalism or the sword. Rather, I think, one educates them to know the world in which they live, to understand that government will go on whether they take part in it or not, that command is too important to be entrusted to the ignorant, even though they may be well-meaning and dedicated, and to an understanding of the good life, of happiness as the Greeks saw it, of the joy of exercising vital powers in a life affording them scope, of the limitless scope of governmental responsibilities. In addition, they might learn, as an authority on the process of revolution has pointed out, that "Brave men are not uncommon in any system, but there is a tendency in most systems to make courage and a disciplined openness of mind to the significant facts mutually exclusive. This is the immediate cause of the downfall of every ruling class that ever falls."

Against a background of this sort I wholly agree that visits of public men can do much to sharpen and focus images of a world not yet experienced, and possibly—though not probably—give an occasional boy the sort of hero that T.R. was to me.

With warm regards.

Sincerely yours,

To **HARRY S TRUMAN**

DA and the former President found amusement with the middle initial in Truman's name.

December 20, 1957

The Honorable Harry S Truman
Independence, Missouri

Dear Mr. President:

In your letter to me of December 5, 1957, spurred by your incurable (thank God) curiosity, you asked me this question:

"Do you know the word meaning an initial
   standing in a name but signifying
   no name itself, as the 'S' in
                       Harry S Truman?"

You know, and so do I, how to get at a question of this sort. In my youth an advertisement used to say, "Ask the man who owns one." So I asked the two people who might know—and, of course, they were women—Elizabeth Finley, the librarian of Covington & Burling, past-president of the law librarians of the country, and Helen Lally of the Supreme Court library. Their reports are enclosed.

The essence of the matter is that we are blind men, searching in a dark room for a black hat which isn't there. The "S" in Harry S Truman (no period after "S") does not "stand for anything." Therefore, it cannot have a descriptive noun— "vacuum," "nothing," etc., are already pre-empted. But, more positively, it *is* something—not representatively, but absolutely. You are "S" (without a period) because it is your name. For instance, you appointed an Associate Justice of the Supreme Court (may God forgive you) whose name is "Tom." Now "Tom" usually stands for "Thomas." But not in this case. There it stands for nothing—absolutely nothing—except, of course, Tom himself, which may—who knows?—be the same thing.

So, you see, "S" is your middle name, not a symbol, not a letter standing for nothing, but an inseparable part of the moniker of one of the best men I have known in a largely misspent life. The same, for that matter, could be said of "Harry."

"Harry" stirs all my deepest loyalties. The senior partner, who brought me up, was christened "J. Harry Covington"; and what a man he was! After years in Congress (he was one of the men who, in 1912 in Baltimore, brought about the nomination of Woodrow Wilson), he had a phrase which to me epitomizes the political obligation, perhaps among the most honorable obligations because resting on honor alone. He never said of an obligation—"I have to do it." He always said, "I have it to do." What a vast difference! In the first, one is coerced into action; in the other, a free man assumes an obligation, freely contracted.

This has a good deal to do with politics—about which you have always thought I knew nothing—in those reaches of it which fit men for government. There are some reaches which unfit them. Honor is a delicate and tricky concept. It does not mean standing by the unfit because of friendship. But it does mean standing by in time of trouble to see a fair deal, when the smart money is taking to the bushes. All of this I learned from the old judge, and relearned again from you in unforgettable days.

So I say that "S" is a good name as it stands, and I am for it. Should either of us have the good fortune to have another grandson, let's agree to persuade his parents to a middle name of just plain "S" with no period, and no explanation.

Indeed, no explanation is possible, because it is the most truly international name. In 1200 B.C. it appeared in the Phoenician as a sort of wobbly "W," but was, unhappily, pronounced *sin.* By 900, in the Cretan, it looked like a 3 and had become *san,* a great improvement. For the next 500 years the 3 was turned around. Then the Latins, Irish, and Saxons, for some odd reason, turned it into a "V." Finally, the British, as they have so often done, got the thing straight in a wiggle, from right to left to right, but not until our colonial ancestors, Ben Franklin included, printed it half the time as an "f" to you and me.

That again is why I like "S" for you. It has had one hell of a tempestuous life.

As ever,

To **WILLIAM TYLER**

William Tyler was a senior Foreign Service Officer serving with the American Embassy in Bonn. DA often corresponded with him about the German situation, especially after Khrushchev's ultimatum of October 1958 initiating the sequence of events culminating in the Berlin crisis of 1961. The "Summit" refers to speculation about a meeting of Khrushchev with the three Western heads of state. "George" is George Kennan, a close and valued associate of DA in the State Department days, whose written advocacy of a disengagement of the U.S. from its military commitment of Western Europe brought about more than one sharp response from DA.

Covington & Burling
Union Trust Building
Washington 5, D.C.
February 25, 1958

Mr. William Tyler
American Embassy
APO 80, c/o P.M., N.Y.
Bonn, Germany

Dear Bill:

Thank you very much for your note of January 26 and its enclosures. I have been after poor George again in an article in *Foreign Affairs*, in its next issue. It does a more detailed, more restrained, but perhaps even more cruel dissection. I am told that he has been ill, which makes the whole operation seem more regrettable, but one can hardly do as much damage as George has done and then rush off to immunity in the hospital.

As one looks around these days, there is very little on which to build much hope. The poor French seem to be making a worse mess of things every day. England seems to me to be weakening visibly, and now I read that the Chancellor's cancellation of his South American trips means that the Summit is right around the next peak. Even Mr. Eisenhower's growing difficulties and the almost certainty of a much larger democratic majority in the House and Senate next fall do not promise much but continued paralysis in the government.

We have had a weekend of democratic jubilation and today have to face the sobering reality, in a meeting that Mr. Truman and I will address, that our own democratic policies of foreign economic aid and liberal trade are in the gravest trouble in Congress.

In this dark hour I have moved to the higher fields of morality and enclose my latest effort. I hope it may give you some amusement.

Please give warm greetings to the Bruces, the Allens, and the Tylers from both of us.

Sincerely yours,

To JACQUELINE KENNEDY

In a speech at the University of Florida, DA criticized the then Senator John Kennedy for his position on the Algerian revolt against the French. This is DA's reply to Mrs. Kennedy's remonstrance.

March 8, 1958

Dear Jacquie:

Thank you very much for your note about my speech. That you like the style of it pleases me very much.

Your last point has been buzzing around in my mind and raising questions which I put up to you. Is there, as you suggest, a dichotomy between being Olympian and being personal? The Olympians seem to me to have been a pretty personal lot. Think of all the trouble which came to the unhappy Trojans because Athene got her feelings hurt about that golden apple. And Zeus himself was a good deal more personal than would be wise for an FCC Commissioner to be.

But passing that, what is being personal in argument? Surely the argument ad hominem is. But is vigor personal? Is the denigration of the opposing position, which one believes wrong, personal? Perhaps lawyers, who are always contentious fellows, are too hardened to be sensitive to these things. But I had always thought that the practitioner of politics was no less tough than the practitioner of law.

And then you suggest that differences of policy are, of all differences, the least proper ones for insensitive words. But, surely you can't mean that. Our late differences with the Germans and Japanese, and our present ones with the Russians, are differences of policy. So are the differences between the Kohler Company and the U.A.W. My difference with the man who would take my wallet is over a sound policy toward private property.

So, you see, you have me very much mixed up. Shall I have to wait for the next snow storm to be set straight?

With kindest greetings.

Most sincerely,

To MRS. JANE A. BROWN

DA had broken his arm that winter.

April 16, 1958

Dearest Jane:

Home is the hunter, home from one hell of a week—to find your sweet thought of me on that solemn day which due to my absence only you and two others remembered, You are a dear to do it. In order to carry out your every instruction I write you fresh off the plane, and having had no opportunity to play the record. But I shall like it greatly.

Three days of Mr. Truman at Yale and two in Kansas City, and two more at Yale and a talk to the girls at Miss Porters, have really got me feeling all of sixty-five. After all, that's pretty darned old, when you think that it's about three times as old as Alexander the Great lived to be—or am I thinking of Chatterton? At any rate, I shall need some sleep before going into that any further.

Come down to cheer us and see my new 50% mobile arm. I can't raise it very high, but I can pinch!

My gratitude and love to you and Dudley.

As ever,

To FORBES B. HENDERSON

Mr. Henderson, not previously known to DA, had written to protest DA's published views that the President of the United States must inevitably act as party leader and political leader rather than be above the battle.

May 14, 1958

Forbes B. Henderson, Esquire
58 Meadow Lane
Grosse Pointe 6
Michigan

Dear Mr. Henderson:

I have your letter of May 7. It seems to me that your Boy Scouts are a little too easily shocked. Perhaps they ought to begin their education in American government by reading American history, and perhaps begin that by reading from the Founding Fathers, high among whom I would recommend Jefferson and Madison.

The office of President of the United States is, of course, the highest in the land. In this office are combined two which are usually separate in constitutional governments. The first of these offices is that of Chief of State, which in England is filled by the monarch; in France, Italy, and Germany, by the President. The second is the Head of Government. This is usually called Prime Minister or Chancellor. In all democratic, representative governments the Head of Government is a political figure, subject always to the most vigorous political criticism. The Chief of State is usually a symbolic and ceremonial figure.

The office of President should . . . be regarded with deference, and the President, when he appears as Chief of State, should be, and is, regarded with all courtesy. But it is equally true that the President, from the very beginning of American history has been, when he acts as Head of Government, criticized with the utmost freedom. This has been true of all the greatest figures in our history, beginning with President Washington, and no sensible person ever has found or ever should find fault with it. There have not been in the United States—and I hope never will be—generalissimos or fuehrers, to criticize whom is to court prosecution for lèse majesté.

I think it is also plain that throughout American history there have been a few great Presidents, a few more able ones, and a considerable number of poor ones. Mr. Eisenhower was, in my judgment, when elected, a lamentable choice, and has in the five years of his office demonstrated his complete incapacity to understand the role of leadership in a democratic society and to act vigorously upon that conception. I quite understand that, although a great number agree with me, a great number will disagree with me. This is the substance of politics. For the Boy Scouts to be shocked to hear such language as this indicates that their education has prepared them for life in some other world than this one, and it is high time that it should be rectified.

I take it that your letter does not call upon me to explain in detail why I think General Eisenhower is and always has been a poor President. I am sure that, if you wish to go into this with the Scouts, Mr. Neil Staebler [Governor of Michigan] will find a qualified exponent of my point of view to go into it thoroughly and at length.

Sincerely yours,

To **SENATOR JOSEPH S. CLARK**

July 17, 1958

The Honorable Joseph S. Clark
United States Senate
Washington, D.C.

Dear Senator:
    That article of yours in the June *Harper's* is a mighty good one. In my pedestrian way I have just gotten to it. I particularly like your deflation of the "art of the possible" cliché and insistence that what is possible is what leadership makes possible; also, your warning against those "who react to new challenges in obsolete ways." Along this line let me give you two quotations to have in mind when you must listen to that admirable man and hopeless leader, Bill Knowland.

> "Brave men are not uncommon in any system, but there is a tendency in most systems to make courage and a disciplined openness of mind to the significant facts mutually exclusive. This is the immediate cause of the downfall of every ruling class that ever falls."

"The attitudes influential in international relations are likely to be remote from any scientific analysis of *reality*. International relations is, therefore, in large measure relations between fantastic beliefs about nations not between actual nations, and is regulated by fantastic beliefs about the effect of acts and procedures not by the real effects."

We are hoping to get you both out to our retreat in Maryland before you adjourn. My wife will pursue this through channels.

Sincerely yours,

To ARCHIBALD MACLEISH

DA was planning a trip abroad in the autumn to give a series of lectures at Cambridge University. "Matilda" referred to in the letter was the Frankfurters' cook.

[undated]

Dear Archie:

You and Ada are good to think of us—and to tell us so. The week before last was a bad one. For Mother most of all. Death was not compromising or gentle at all. But that is the way things are.

Labor Day depresses us, too. I have all my take-off cold feet about the whole expedition—the stage of apprehension when all I think of is arriving in a strange place with the reservations fouled up and the bags lost. Anyone who has traveled at the taxpayers' expense and escorted by the taxpayers' minions ought to stay home thereafter and think about it.

But Alice, of course, has been reading Mahon and L'Estrange family history and now tells me that in her lineage are three generations of Catholic bishops—grandfather to grandson. Well, some people just have no pride—or no shame.

Just to cause trouble, why don't you and Ada spend Labor Day here. I know the answer—Felix comes to lunch tomorrow. When I upbraided Matilda for an extravagant lunch last week she said—"There's no use saving for a rainy day, when we got the rainiest days yet."

Love,

To **ANNIE BURR AND WILMARTH S. LEWIS**

In response to a letter of condolence on the death of DA's mother.

> Union Trust Building
> Washington 5, D.C.
> 31 July 1958

Dear Annie Burr and Lefty:

How good of you both to write me. These last weeks have been hard ones for Mother, poor dear, when everything—mind and body—just seemed to run down and stop. Every day she lived was a burden to her, but one which she would not or could not put down. As Annie Burr says, it is very hard to realize the fact of her death. She had so much quality and force, and it was obviously the longest influence in my life, that I constantly find myself wondering how she will like, or take, this or that. Even when she was very ill she would undo things which I had done almost as fast as I could do them. And then be both penitent and unyielding. She leaves a void.

I wish we were going to see you, but I fear there is too much to keep us here before we fly on Sept. 10th.

Our love to you both

> As ever,

To **A. WHITNEY GRISWOLD**

Griswold had written to DA following the death of DA's mother in July.

> August 6, 1958

Dear Whit:

How good of you and Mary to have such warm thoughts of me and to tell me so. As you say, there has been long warning that Mother was failing; and in the last two months the inevitable end was clearly imminent. But it has been a hard time. Hardest of all for her, poor dear.

I understand less than ever why the Prayer Book asks that we be spared from sudden death.

Alice and I are off on our travels on Sept. 10th. After various adventures in England and the Continent, including my four lectures in Cambridge we hope to be back on October 28th. So I shall miss the October meeting.

In the meantime my most affectionate greetings to you and Mary.

> As ever,

To **EUGENE V. ROSTOW**

Rostow was Dean of Yale Law School at this time. References to Bowles and Benton are to former advertising partners (Benton & Bowles) who had been rivals for Democratic nomination for a U.S. Senate seat (Connecticut).

August 14, 1958

Dean Eugene V. Rostow
Peru, Vermont

Dear Gene:
Thank you very much for the most unedifying correspondence of those late rivals for the U.S. Senate, Chester Bowles and Bill Benton. Brandeis used to quote in German a line, which I believe comes from Goethe, and was to the general effect, "One does not *say* such things." Time spent in the advertising business seems to create a permanent deformity like the Chinese habit of footbinding.

I wish that we were coming north again this summer and could accept, as we have so happily done in the past, the hospitality of Chez Rostow. But this year we have a different operation in view. We are going off to England on the 10th of September and are not coming back until the end of October. I begin with a meeting of the Bilderberg group at Buxton and end up with two weeks at Cambridge. In between, visits to Belgium, Luxembourg, and a little quiet time in the Italian lake country. When I go to Cambridge, Alice and Jane will meet and explore Alice's ancestral bogs in Ireland.

My love to Edna and the children and to the Dean himself.

As ever,

To **WILMARTH S. LEWIS**

DA wrote from King's College, Cambridge, where he had been invited to give a series of lectures.

King's College
Cambridge
[undated]

Dear Lefty:
My days at Cambridge are already half gone. They have been a delight. Until yesterday your warnings about the coming of the ice age seemed denied by some lovely Indian summer (St. Martin's summer here, I believe)

weather. But yesterday was your justification. I motored over to lunch with
David and Rachel Bowes-Lyon. The car was heated; but if General Electric
could get the secret of their house, the deep freeze would enter a new
phase. I shook so that I had to hold my cocktail with both hands. But today is
better again.

Cambridge has been wonderfully warm and hospitable to me. And how
right you were to urge me to come along. A big weekend is being put on for
Alice. But the eating in hall, the sherry parties (nauseous stuff for which in
my case they substitute scotch) the shy young men who come to my rooms
(I sleep in the Lodge) to talk about the world and themselves—much of this
I should have missed. And, then, I am flattered into euphoria—my lectures
are packed, with people on the floor, and in the aisles, and another lecture
room with a loudspeaker for the overflow. I am a curiosity—and when Mr.
Nixon attacks me he advertises me. One of the sterner dons told me that I
was lucky to be lecturing at the beginning of the year. "The new men," he
said, "haven't caught on yet, and go to lectures."

Love to Annie Burr.

As ever,

To **FELIX FRANKFURTER**

King's College
Cambridge
October 15, 1958

Mr. Justice Felix Frankfurter
3018 Dumbarton Avenue, N.W.
Washington 7, D.C.
U.S.A.

Dear Felix:

Last evening your descriptions of conversation at the High Table at
Balliol came vividly to my mind. I was seated between the Provost and a
young mathematician. Across the table was an older colleague, a classicist.
The young mathematician was describing to me the low opinion of science
which was held at Eton, the encouragment which was given to this view by
Oxford and, in his opinion, the unhappy consequences which ensued thereafter due to Etonians' capacity to get themselves important ministerial positions. Towards the end of this exegesis the older colleague leaned across the
table and, with the greatest courtesy said "My dear Fritz, I know how unpleasant it is to have facts brought to one's attention about a matter upon
which he has already made up his mind. . . ." He, of course, then went on to

take the opposite side. How delightfully civilized this was!

Yesterday afternoon the Provost took me to the ceremony of admitting the new Scholars. This, too, impressed me deeply, and for two reasons. One was the individuality of the ceremony and composition of the group. These Scholars had been chosen entirely for intellectual qualifications and without regard to a means test of any sort whatever. I am enclosing a copy of the list which I think you will find most interesting. One of the outstanding factors of it to me was the great predominance of the sons of schoolteachers and Civil Servants. When I mentioned this to the Provost he remarked that in the present state of society one must not be surprised that the children of intellectuals had intellectual training. Each boy was admitted separately. Each separately read the declaration to which I will refer in a moment. Each separately re-enacted the old medieval ceremony of kneeling before the Provost and putting his hands between the Provost's when he was admitted.

Perhaps, however, the most typically, to me, British part of this ceremony was a phrase in the declaration which each made to the effect that he would obey the statutes of the University and apply himself diligently to his studies. The engaging phrase was "as in me lies." I thought of the harshness of our Oath of Office in which we require to swear that we will do our duty "without mental reservation or purpose of evasion."

This experience at Cambridge is an enchanting one. I would not have missed it for anything. Even my first lecture, after the first nervous moments, was great fun. Some of the scholars raised their eyebrows over the insouciance of my history, but the audience was with me and we all had a good time.

My love to you and Marion.

As ever,

I go off to my first sherry party with undergraduates in a few minutes.

To A. WHITNEY GRISWOLD

DA was in Cambridge, England, as a visiting lecturer. In mentioning the Scotch at the sherry party, DA was alluding to a long standing, friendly difference with Mrs. Griswold about the appropriate refreshment for members of the Yale Corporation when they enjoyed Mrs. Griswold's hospitality.

October 19, 1958

Dear Whit:

To say that I am having the time of my life would be a vast understatement. This, and by this I mean all of Cambridge, is an enchanting spot and when the British start in earnest to be pleasant and use their gift for flattery, they are hard to equal. I sleep and have breakfast in the Provost's lodge where I am far more comfortable than I would be in the guest suite which has been given me in the College—There I read, work on my lectures and receive the undergraduates that want to talk. Four very nice Yale boys came in for a cocktail and a nostalgic gossip before lunch a few days ago. Walt and Elspeth Rostow are here, Denis Brogan and a number of old friends who could not be more hospitable.

The lectures are great fun. They have caught on, and are crowded. They also tend to become hilarious on occasion and since loudspeakers have been put up in other rooms, this requires magnanimity from other lecturers who are attempting to be heard at the same time. Dr. Kitson Clark has raised his eyebrows at some of my history, but the undergraduates love it, right or wrong.

Tell Mary that at the second sherry party given for me by a group of undergraduates, I was handed a scotch and told by my host that the remark was attributed to me that a man could not drink sherry and retain his self respect. Of course, it was a slander.

Here the great current issue is the admissions system. I wish we could send Art Howe over to talk with [people here]. Why not?

I start home in a week.

Yours,

To DAVID BRUCE

David Bruce and his wife were close friends of the Achesons. Bruce was the U.S. Ambassador to Bonn at the time.

November 12, 1958

Dear David:

Alice and I got home about ten days ago in time to warm up for the ballot casting match of last Tuesday. This turned out, as you have seen, to be quite an affair. There were some curious, and in a way curiously just, oddities. Averell's defeat in New York was brought on, as was Governor Leader's in Pennsylvania, by an attempt on the part of both men to be what they were not. They attempted to be smart political operators, which they were not, instead of being men of integrity and character, which they were. The people in the two states caught on at once and came to oddly different conclusions. In Averell's case they chose a man who seemed to them to be young Lochinvar, a man who presented himself as an honest liberal and high minded as well as energetic. In Pennsylvania they chose a man who presented himself as what he was, a machine politician. In Maryland we swept in all the Democratic ticket except Jim's opponent in the primary, D'Alesandro. Probably D'Alesandro is a better man than Beall, but there was certainly nothing in the public presentation to make one suspect it. And, indeed, the efforts seemed to be the other way. The press is now boring us to death with talk about 1960, like a child who has gotten through with Hallowe'en will now scream for Christmas.

Last weekend I spent in New Haven at a meeting of the Corporation. There we did something which may be of interest to you. We ordered President Whitney Griswold to take the month of April and the first part of May off and go to Europe for the purpose of intellectual refreshment, some time talking with his colleagues in European universities and getting a little rest in the Italian sun. In an afternoon's talk with Whit I got the impression that he would like to spend two weeks or so in England at Oxford and Cambridge, a few days in London. Then, if you think it would be advisable, he would be willing to go to the Free University in Berlin, make a speech, give a lecture or seminar, or whatever they might desire. Whit speaks German, is very much interested in the Free University, would very much enjoy doing this, and would then go on down to Lake Como or further south and just spend another couple of weeks loafing. He would be going with his wife Mary. They are delightful people in the first year or so of their 50's, very gay, amusing, interested in everything. I know that you and Vangie would enjoy them, and he might do something at the University of Bonn if you wished that done.

The real point is that he is high strung and has a puritanical conscience. In order to get him a real change and rest, we have invented a few things to give this enough aura of utility to satisfy his conscience. If you could work this out without inconveniencing yourself or causing trouble to anybody, it would be in a good cause, and you would meet two delightful people, although you probably meet too many of them anyway.

The town is getting in a dither about Archie MacLeish's play "JB" which opens here a week from Saturday night. He and Ada were planning to stay with us, but Ada thinks that he is going to be too keyed up to stay with anybody, so they will cool off by staying in a hotel with the producer and all the cast. That does not seem to me too bright.

Our love to Vangie.

As ever,

To **NOEL G. ANNAN**

Noel Annan was Provost of King's College, Cambridge, and author of a biography of Leslie Stephen.

November 13, 1958

N. G. Annan, Esquire, MA., O.B.E.
Provost, King's College
Cambridge, England

Dear Noel:

I spent the weekend at a Corporation meeting at Yale and out of it came some matters which give me an excuse, and, indeed, a little more, to write to you. I stayed at the Griswolds' with Lefty Lewis, and, of course, we talked much and long about Cambridge and King's. We also discovered that Whit Griswold needs very much to get a break in the course of this academic year and to find some intellectual refreshment out of the American environment and rest. Lefty and I devised and put through the Corporation a resolution requiring the President to take six weeks off beginning with the second week in April, 1959, and go to Europe.

In order to appease Whit's Puritan conscience, and also make my brethren on the Corporation feel that they were not misappropriating trust funds in the course of a worthy endeavor, I suggested that it would be highly desirable to have the President spend some days at Oxford and some days at Cambridge, comparing his problems with theirs and both learning and, if possible, giving wisdom in exchange. Whit has a good many friends at Oxford and can work this out for himself there.

I am appointing myself chief conspirator with you to determine whom he or I should approach for the purpose of providing the simplest and least troublesome way for his spending, say, four or five days in Cambridge, meeting the delightful people who inhabit that charmed spot, and talking about whatever matters you might think he could be useful about. He does not want to give lectures or anything of that sort. He would, of course, love to meet with Lord Adrian, yourself, Dr. D. Thompson, and such other people as the authorities might think he should. It occurred to me that you could usefully examine him at some length about some of the increasing problems which we are finding with regard to admissions and how we are attempting to handle them. It also occurred to me that Dr. Thompson, the Master of Sidney Sussex, as head of the History Department, might like to talk with Whit, an historian in the field of American history, about the organization at Yale of American history studies, and to hear some rather sensible and practical ideas which he has of how some American history might be introduced into Oxford and Cambridge, not by having American bigwig historians, usually specialists, come as visiting lecturers, but by having some of your younger historians work with us for a few years, by means of funds which it should not be too difficult to provide.

However, these are merely illustrative suggestions. What I really want to know is whether you will conspire with me, what your advice to me is, and who should do what next.

Whit Griswold and his wife are both charmers. Whit is 52; Mary, I should think, about 50. Discounting prejudice so far as I can, I think Whit is the best University president in the United States. He is also the most amusing companion, a great producer of Gilbertian verse, and a rather mediocre flute player. Mary and I retain deep mutual affection even after eight years of unending battle, in which she has tried to introduce sherry into University functions, and I have bitterly opposed it in favor of the coarser but quicker cocktail. Cambridge, I know, would give them great joy, and I think would get from them some in return.

. . .

Affectionately yours,

To **ROBERT MENZIES**

The Evatt referred to in this letter was Herbert V. Evatt, Leader of the Australian Labour Party.

November 13, 1958

Dear Bob:

Two sound reasons prompt this letter. First, I have never seen any reason for being neutral in Australian politics—at least, as long as you and Evatt are involved. So my warmest wishes that you give him hell go to you. The omens are good for sensible people. We have just given those who richly deserved it a royal trouncing and it looks as though Harold Macmillan would [win] next year. The Canadians, as usual, were wrong. But you will be right. Good luck.

The second is to recommend to you Charlie Dickey and his wife Catherine whom you are to see, so I am told, after the election. They are great friends of ours. Charlie is a partner in J.P. Morgan & Co., and a colleague of mine on the Yale Corporation. He has been doing some business in Australia, perhaps for your government. I forget. At any rate he is a delightful man and, although a Republican, is not too conservative to be without intelligence. Catherine and Alice are fond of one another which is a good recommendation both ways.

We are back just two weeks ago from a long European visit where we saw all sorts of people, talked a great deal—including my giving four lectures at Cambridge—and had a thoroughly good time. Europe seemed to me almost as flat as this country. No one seemed to care much about anything or to be going anywhere—no one, that is, except those in the three communities, Coal & Steel, EURATOM, and the common market. Here was the only sign of life and vitality. The British seemed to be scared to death of the common market and to be sabotaging it. My guess was that this would not succeed and that British fears were exaggerated.

Our warmest greetings to your lady and to you.

Affectionately,

To **ROBERT BROWN**

DA dealt here with a well known thesis.

November 19, 1958

Mr. Robert Brown
40 West 77th Street
New York 24, N.Y.

Dear Mr. Brown:

In reply to your letter of November 11th, President Roosevelt provoked the Japanese to attack Pearl Harbor in just about the same way that President Lincoln provoked Booth to assassinate him. This whole canard is the product of the ingenuity of the late Charles Beard's tortured and bitter thesis. It seems to me regrettable that the school authorities by assigning such a topic for a term paper suggest that this is a subject for proper discussion.

Yours sincerely,

To **ROBERT MENZIES**

December 9, 1958

The Right Honorable Robert Menzies
Prime Minister of Australia
Canberra, Australia

Dear Bob:

My warmest congratulations on the Australian elections. Your people are not only level headed but wise. Thank you for seeing Charlie Dickey. I should not bother you with another letter were it not to relieve some anxiety which you and Owen Dixon may be feeling about Felix.

As the press has announced, Felix has had what is called a "heart disturbance" and is in the hospital. His trouble began early in November with what the doctors thought was an impairment caused by a specific overexertion. They reduced his activities considerably, and he seemed to be showing improvement. He assured me that there was nothing to be alarmed about and that we would soon be resuming our morning walks. However, a little over two weeks ago, he had another disturbance or attack which was much more serious. This led to his complete isolation in the hospital, where for two weeks he saw nobody, read nothing and—severest of deprivations—was not even permitted to use the telephone. I think that he was quite sick. From the sick room there now emerge unquestionable sounds of recovery. He is permitted to read the dullest newspapers but may receive nothing from the Supreme Court on the sound ground that this may prove emotionally disturbing. In the past few days he has been permitted to receive notes from me on the ground that they could not possibly disturb anybody, and I am sure that you and Owen would be admitted to this innocuous company.

He will be out of circulation for some time. There is no use in speculating or prophesying about the future, because not even the doctors can tell how long his recovery may take or how complete it will be. But, as you can imagine, he is gay and confident.

And finally, dear Bob, you are quite right in viewing the American political position with a good deal of uneasiness, but your reason for doing so is quite wrong. You say, "How an administration can conduct any firm line of policy if it has a hostile Congress is beyond me." But the Administration hasn't a hostile Congress. My criticism of the Democrats is that they have gone all out in supporting the Administration. There hasn't been any opposition at all in Congress. In fact, it gave Ike last year an extra billion dollars for defense which he refused to use.

No, the situation is worrisome but not because of Congress. Ike and Foster could truthfully say, "The fault is not in Congress but in ourselves that we are underlings."

I want all of my friends to worry; but for the right reason.

Sincerely yours,

To FELIX FRANKFURTER

Frankfurter was convalescing from a heart attack. DA's letter appraised the alternatives facing the U.S. in the wake of Khrushchev's ultimatum giving the West six months to agree to a new regime for West Berlin.

2805 P Street
December 12, 1958

Dear Felix:

Barbara's capacity for worry and her propensity to peer into the future have put me on the R.R. to New Haven instead of a plane. She was sure it was going to snow, whereas it is a perfect day.

This has some bearing on my talk to Paul's school yesterday. There I pointed out that the cleverest part of the Russian note on Berlin was the six months given to think about it. Six days or six weeks would unify the West. But six months, leading up to the British election gives too much time for thought and talk—and worry.

I reviewed for them the background facts—historical, military and political—then the specific proposals and threats of the USSR, as distinct from the comments by East Germans and columnists.

Why was the note sent? It was, I thought, to peel the layers of the onion of resolution to demonstrate, if possible, that Western resolution would not be found at the core. If it were found to be there or pretty far in, the process could be stopped without much damage to the USSR. If we fail we are out of Europe—disengaged with a vengeance.

The Russians, I pointed out, are in the quandary in which we found ourselves in 1953–4. We had the hydrogen bomb before they had it. What should we do with it in the political field. Foster tried massive retaliation which fizzled. The USSR now has the ICBM before we do. They also see the US, UK, France and Italy pretty divided or distracted, or both. So they try Berlin.

The test they propose cannot be evaded by treating East Germans as Russian "agents," or by jumping over them with an air lift. 1958 is not 1948. The West Berlin economy is vastly more extensive and the impediments to air navigation can be greatly multiplied.

The test is put there so that it must be met. That is the whole purpose of the exercise.

Ask ourselves some questions. Should we start nuclear war rather than leave Berlin?

Answer. No.

Should we use force rather than deal in any way with East Germans? Answer. No.

Should we insist that present communications to West Berlin must be maintained and use force to remove obstacles?

Answer. Yes. This is dangerous. But there is some elasticity here. We shall be dealing, in first instance, with East Germans. The Russians may either then intervene diplomatically—in which case, their resolution has failed first—or militarily—in which case they can force the evacuation of Berlin if they want to. But a forced evacuation, bringing refugees with us, will do us far less harm than a surrender without a struggle. It will also tend to solidify NATO and worry the neutrals about Russian intentions.

In the question period I said that what I wanted from them was criticism of the analysis or better suggestions. There was not much of either. One had asked what I thought of Nixon's visit to London, to which I interposed the rule of relevance.

. . .

Affectionately,

To **LYNDON B. JOHNSON**

Johnson was Majority Leader of the U.S. Senate at this time.

Union Trust Building
Washington 5, D.C.
December 16, 1958

Dear Lyndon:

Felix let me see your moving letter to him. I simply want to say how much I admire the man who could have written it. One rarely sees depth of understanding and generosity combined with lightness of touch and the use of that other ingredient of the etcher's art, a little acid.

F.F. asks me in a note "am I wrong in thinking that I know of no other active political leader possessed of the qualities that lie behind this letter."

He is quite right in thinking so, as I am telling him.

You have done him a lot of good.

Yours,

To **FELIX FRANKFURTER**

Acheson here recounted a Hubert Humphrey story related to him by "Scotty" Reston and Stewart Alsop.

December 22, 1958

Dear Felix:

Scotty and Stew Alsop picked me up for lunch today (I asked whether this was a peace conference after Wally Carroll's border raid). Out of it came a story of Hubert Humphrey's about his eight hour conference in Moscow. When it happened, I had said to Scotty that, my mind being an earthy one, I wondered whether in the course of eight hours Hubert had had to take a leak, and, if so, what were the current conveniences in the Kremlin. This stuck in his mind. So he asked Hubert. It appears that the necessity did arise and H proposed to K that they take time out for the purpose. K had had the same thought. So all 3—including the interpreter repaired to the gents' room, which was disappointingly modern. H took the nearest stall to the door; K, the furthest from it. The interpreter occupied neutral ground between.

As they were buttoning up, H said to K that the situation reminded him of a story of Attlee's that in the War Cabinet days he and Winston had had to be excused, and found themselves at opposite ends of the stalls. "Isn't this unusual modesty for you, Winston,'" said Clem. "Not at all," said Winston, "I'm just suspicious of you Socialists."

Clem asked why. "Because," said Winston, "whenever you see a means of production in good working order you want to nationalize it."

This brought a great laugh from Mr. K. "I must tell that to our Armenian," said he, "Mikoyan, he's that kind of a chap, too."

. . .

Affectionately,

To **ROBERTO DE OLIVEIRA CAMPOS**

Campos, an economist, at this time was President of the Brazilian National Bank for Economic Development and was later (1961–1964) Ambassador to the United States. DA was interested in his views on Latin American development, especially with regard to the needs of public infrastructure.

December 29, 1958

The Honorable Roberto de Oliveira Campos
Apartment 402
Avenida Atlantica 778
Copa Cabana
Rio de Janeiros, Brazil

Dear Dr. Campos:

Through Eddie Miller's thoughtfulness I have read your excellent speech at the inauguration of the Brazilian Institute of New York University. It is refreshing beyond words to read a speech which says so much and says it so well, though not surprising when you are the speaker. There is a great deal to think about and to act upon in what you have written.

It is plainly ungrateful for me to ask more when you have given so much. But I am going to put myself in this position, and am doing so because I am trying to get a Democratic Party pamphlet written on inter-American relations. You have given me a lot of guidance. On one point, relating to the "Controversy On Investment"—pp. 9, 10, 11 of your speech—I need some more.

My need has to do with the use of investment funds. I have the impression that in Latin America governments are directing investment rather heavily to what we might call the private sphere—hotels, industrial plants, extractive industries, etc.—and neglecting the public sphere—schools, health and hospitals, low cost housing, roads, water, sewerage, ports, agricultural credits and research, etc., all of which are essential to supporting an industrial society with rising standards. Governmental credit and managerial capacity does not seem great enough to do both. The Venezuelan Government, for instance, is conducting over fifty enterprises in which billions of bolivars have been invested and billions more are committed for their completion and expansion. Many of them are and will remain losing ventures. At the same time, there are said to be half a million children in the country for whom no schools exist, and another forty or fifty thousand being added each year. There is a shortage of three-quarters of a million houses.

Without laboring the point, there is an obvious question of priorities involved. As you rightly say, much of the "social capital" funds needed must be furnished from public sources. If this is so, has the public lender some duty to perform, not only to lend for the higher priority items, but to induce the borrower to use its credit and governmental personnel for these purposes? Surely, there will be some national predilections which cannot yield to argument, as Brazil's for a government-operated oil industry. But, by and large, does wise economic policy in the hemisphere contemplate some restraining and guiding function in the creditor, and how can this be exercised without its being the cause of ill will as economic imperialism? No one likes to be restrained from his favorite follies. Similarly a bank understandably does not like to lend to one who insists that his right to plunge on the ponies is an inalienable one.

What wisdom have you for me on this matter? I shall greatly appreciate it.

With all good wishes for the New Year.

Most sincerely yours,

To **CATHERINE MEYER**

Miss Meyer was on the editorial staff of Harper's Magazine.

January 7, 1959

Miss Catherine Meyer
Office of the Editor
Harper's Magazine
49 East 33d Street
New York 16, N.Y.

Dear Miss Meyer:

I am enclosing the proofs of "The Great Fish of Como" with a few changes.

You ask about my "literary background, tastes and activities." This is a tough order because, having passed the mystic age of sixty, when Duff Cooper says old age begins, I have shed conscience about reading. For years I was constrained by the fetish that reading should "improve" my mind, and by the even more puritan idea that having begun a book I must finish it. All that nonsense fell from me like sea water from our distant ancestor emerging from it, when in a frenzy of boredom I hurled an offending book out of the bedroom window into a dripping garden. . . .

So I read what I like, stop when I like, eschew self-improvement, and, as far as what I "ought" to like or dislike, "the public be damned." There is no order or system or plan about what I read. There is only that fundamental aim of man which the Declaration of Independence rates so highly, "the pursuit of happiness"—all too rarely caught.

Sincerely yours,

To ROSWELL B. PERKINS, JR.

Unable to attend a meeting on the reform of laws on conflict of interest to which he had been invited, DA set forth his ideas on the subject. The problems touched on here are very much alive twenty years later.

February 10, 1959

Roswell B. Perkins, Esq.
20 Exchange Place
New York 5, New York

Dear Mr. Perkins:

Your meetings on February 27th and 28th sound as though they would be most interesting. I wish that I could be with you and appreciate very much your kind invitation. However, in the last half of February I shall be in the West Indies, which has an even greater attraction for me.

Your committee is doing a most important work and on a subject with which I have had frequent and often costly experience. May I make a few observations which may be of some use and which I would make if I had been able to be with you.

Point 1. The laws on conflict of interest and on profiting from governmental experience and connection should first of all be clear, which they are not, and secondly, in one place, which they are not, and thirdly, existing laws should be repealed. The present laws are almost impossible to understand and apply to any concrete situation.

Point 2. It is quite possible in the zealous pursuit of virtue to make it quite foolhardy for a professional man to serve the United States government for a temporary period. Among the problems which exist is that of a lawyer who finds himself faced with withdrawing wholly from his firm, being paid his interest, whatever it may be, and being taxed upon it as income. The result can easily be that the government takes almost all of what is really his capital and what little remains to him usually goes in trying to live on an inadequate salary. Or an official of a corporation may find serious inroads made on arrangements upon which he had counted for retirement, insurance, and things of this sort. It is not necessary to ruin a man in order to make him an honest official.

Point 3. No law can be drafted which takes the place of good judgment and common sense. It was, for instance, utterly foolish to appoint Charles Wilson of General Motors as Secretary of Defense. Therefore, the law should not be drafted on the basis that this kind of thing will be the normal appointment and thus require that an appointee must sell the bulk of his securities, with the taxation or loss which that may bring about. This is not required of judges, where the requirement of probity is equally great. In the ordinary case a sound rule of self-disqualification to act on a question where there can be a conflict of interest, with a notation in the record, ought to be sufficient.

Point 4. It is often essential to have for short periods experts from one or another industry. The State Department, for instance, has had frequent need to have the services of oil experts. Where laws are written on the basis that everyone employed in such a capacity will profit improperly, it is almost impossible to get men whose advice is worth anything. Latitude is required for people of this sort.

Point 5. Laws which operate on an official after he has left the employ- ment of the government fall within this category also. Here I think they should be clear and firm against the use of knowledge or connections ac- quired in Government service after that service has ended. In regard to knowledge I see no reason for not making the prohibition a permanent one and making it apply to any firm or association of any kind which the former employee may have entered into. An illustration of this sort of thing is the use by officers of the Department of Justice of information obtained in the Department in order to bring treble damage suits under the antitrust laws. Prohibition against appearing before one's former department or agency should be clear, specific and limited. Beyond that they should be left to good taste. There seems to me little sense in provisions of law which prevent a former officer from sharing in the income of a firm some of which may have been acquired through cases against the government which he himself could not have prosecuted. This sort of thing accomplishes little and merely makes complicated bookkeeping.

These are a few hasty thoughts which I hope may be of some use to you.

Sincerely yours,

To JOHN DICKEY

John Dickey was President of Dartmouth College.

March 18, 1959

President John Dickey
Dartmouth College
Hanover, New Hampshire

Dear John:

. . .

You may be right that the United Nations can be a more adequate political structure than it is. Frankly I do not see how it can be; and, as I get it from various writings of Dag Hammarskjold, as well as the talks I have had with him, he thinks of it more as an aid to diplomacy than as a political structure.

They tell me in the press that I am getting rigid. Perhaps they are right. At any rate I still believe that we are not going to get far in our dealings with the Russians unless they realize that the Free World has a basis of power to which they have got to adjust themselves.

With affectionate greetings to you and Chris.

As ever,

To MAX ASCOLI

Max Ascoli was editor of The Reporter *magazine.*

March 25, 1959

Mr. Max Ascoli
The Reporter
136 East 57th Street
New York 22, New York

Dear Mr. Ascoli:

Over the years one learns to be wary of questions from friends about themselves which begin, "Now tell me frankly. . . ." To be elegaic in response, rather than frank, is much safer. So in replying to your letter I shall be a little of both.

I am an admirer and constant reader of *The Reporter*. Its articles are about subjects which interest me and the viewpoints of its writers impress me as sensible. Could its articles, I sometimes wonder, be shorter and more interestingly presented? Virtue should not be incompatible with sparkle, irony, and humor. Mr. Miller, who wrote a memorable article about Eisenhower's philosophy as reconstructed from his speeches, has what I am suggesting. The (London) *Observer* and Sunday *Times* have it. To some extent the (New York) *New Leader* and *New Republic* have it also. I have complained to friends on the *New Yorker* that they must pay for their articles by the mile, and suggested that they dock their writers for every word over 1500.

In short, by all means lead us toward the intellectual kingdom of heaven; but let there be sound of pipes on the way.

Sincerely yours,

To WILLIAM TYLER

Exasperated by the Eisenhower Administration's handling of the Soviet threat to turn control of access to West Berlin over to the East Germans unless the West capitulated to Khrushchev's ultimatum, DA wrote a critical article which appeared in the Saturday Evening Post. *DA feared that Eisenhower was derelict in not strengthening the U.S. ground position and in relying upon Soviet fear of nuclear war to deter them from a showdown.*

Covington & Burling
Union Trust Building
Washington 5, D.C.
April 16, 1959

William Tyler, Esquire
American Embassy
Box 700, APO 80
New York, N.Y.

Dear Bill:

In my desire not to appear in any way an advocate of massive retaliation or of use of nuclear war as the solution for all problems, I apparently misled not only you but also David Bruce, whom I saw when he was here, in my article in the *Saturday Evening Post*. I did not intend to suggest that there was any realism in a battle for Berlin won by the Communists without global nuclear war. In fact, I tried to suggest as strongly as I could the line of policy which you state in your letter; that is, that we should immediately strengthen our ground forces, both American and allied components, insist that any interference by East Germans would be overcome by force, and be in a position to do this with such considerable power that the Russians must see that to oppose us with superior power would require bringing additional troops from the Soviet Union, which inevitably by the rise in tensions would lead to one or the other of the powers cutting loose with nuclear weapons. This, it seemed to me, was the best deterrent. In making my case, I was trying to show that its strength depended not upon our use of nuclear weapons but upon the uncertainty of the situation which would be created by substantial ground forces in actual conflict.

It seems to me that Eisenhower's position carries no conviction to Moscow at all. He says he will not contemplate a ground war, but obviously he would contemplate a nuclear strike. I cannot believe that anybody would believe this, least of all SAC which is not even able to maintain an air alert. I have had a new crack at the general situation in the *New York Times* magazine section of Sunday last, a copy of which I enclose.

Sometime when you get a chance, please tell me the inwardness of the Chancellor's decision to run for the Presidency. I have more than a suspicion that his performances with Von Brentano during the NATO meeting more than suggested whimsical senility and led to pretty strong pressure upon him to step down.

With warm regards to you both.

As ever,

To A. WHITNEY GRISWOLD

This letter affords a glimpse of the delicacy of some of Yale's affairs in which DA sought to help, while not always taking them altogether seriously.

Covington & Burling
Union Trust Building
Washington 5, D.C.
May 19, 1959

President A. Whitney Griswold
Yale University
New Haven, Connecticut

Dear Whit:

Yesterday I talked with one of the officials of the Visa Division about the problem of getting Iris Murdock (Mrs. John Oliver Bailey) a visa to come to lecture at Yale. I said that she quite frankly described herself as an "ex-communist" and that I presumed that, if they were satisfied about the "ex" now that Senator McCarthy had passed to whatever reward was awaiting him, she would be allowed in this country. He said that this was the case, and that there was a section of the statute, the number of which I cannot remember, which refers to people called, I believe, "defectors from communism." Upon filing adequate affidavits that such persons had as publicly denounced communism as they had previously embraced it, they would be given a clean bill of health and from then on would have no trouble about getting visas.

There is another section, so he said, which provides that, even though not satisfied as to the present views of the applicant, the consul could recommend that it is in the interest of the United States for an alleged ex-communist to come to the United States; and, if the recommendation is approved by the Departments of State and Justice, a visa will be granted.

I said that at Yale there was no desire to put a distinguished lady through a series of humiliating and tiresome exercises and that it would be better to leave the students at Yale and the citizens of New Haven in their gross and crass ignorance rather than to do so. He said that this was to take too dim a view of it, and he suggested that, armed with an invitation from you to lecture at Yale, she get the necessary papers from the nearest American consul, who I suppose is at London, and fill them out. He also suggested that, if she is to come for a short period only, it would be well to have this appear in the letter; since, if people are coming for a year, they have to have chest X-rays and, perhaps, even more intimate examinations.

It has occurred to me that, if, when you invite her, you also write to Jock Whitney, asking him which consul in the Embassy she should go to and have Jock flag the matter, the whole operation should not be too difficult.

I hope your voice has risen at least an octave and your cough entirely disappeared.

As ever,

To **HARRY S TRUMAN**

May 20, 1959

Dear Mr. President:

This morning's papers bring us two bits of very good news—one, that our hopes about the boss have been confirmed; the other that Margaret has another boy. I know how happy both of these have made you; what a weight of worry has been lifted from you.

We rejoice with you. Please give Bess our deepest affection and Margaret our warm congratulations.

For your amusement I am sending on to you my latest venture in the field of literature, a short story in the June Harpers. This ends me as a serious character and puts me down, to the surprise of a good many people, as the frivolous fellow I really am.

The day seems bright for the good news of both your girls.

Affectionately,

To **HARRY S TRUMAN**

May 27, 1959

Dear Mr. President:

I have a letter from Kay Halle from London who hears much of Sir Winston's disappointment that he did not see you on his farewell visit. When we lunched with him at the Embassy on May 7th he spoke of it. I told him of your being swamped by the jubilee festivities and held out hope that you might see him or talk with him in New York. Apparently this was not possible. Now the old man seems to brood about it as he is very fond of you.

Would it be a good idea to drop him an affectionate line? I think he would treasure it. It would be too bad for him to get the wholly wrong idea that you didn't care about seeing him.

Probably you have written him already and I should have minded my own business. But you have had enough on your mind to have driven out such ideas altogether.

We hope the boss continues to make great progress. When does she come home? Our most affectionate greetings to you both.

As ever,

To **KONRAD ADENAUER**

Konrad Adenauer was Chancellor of the Federal Republic of Germany.

May 28, 1959

His Excellency, Dr. Konrad Adenauer
Chancellor of the Federal Republic of Germany
German Embassy
1900 Foxhall Road
Washington, D.C.

Dear Mr. Chancellor:

I have been troubled all day trying to recall the aphorism attributed to you by Sir Ivone Kirkpatrick, which I mentioned to you during our conversation and which seemed to me to be very apropos of it. My secretary happily has found it, and I discover that it was even better than I thought.

Toward the end of a lecture given at Trinity College, Dublin, by Sir Ivone in February, 1957, he said: "My old friend Dr. Adenauer often said to me that God made a great mistake to limit the intelligence of man but not his stupidity."

This is too good to forget and neither of us must do it again.

It was a great joy for me to see you this morning and to have so unhurried a talk.

Most sincerely yours,

To **ROBERTO DE OLIVEIRA CAMPOS**

DA was never averse to employing flattery in a good cause—in this case how to make more development funds available to the countries of Latin America.

June 5, 1959

The Honorable Roberto de Oliveira Campos
Avenida Atlantica, 3778
Copa Cabana
Rio de Janeiros, Brazil

Dear Dr. Campos:

My delay in answering your vastly interesting and instructive letter from Geneva has been largely due, as you will see from the enclosure, to the time which I have spent searching for an opportunity to appropriate your ideas and use them, without even the shadow of an honest acknowledgment. This came this morning, when fulfilling an engagement made some time ago, I appeared before the House of Representatives Committee on Banking and Currency to support the Inter-American Development Bank bill. I hope you will find that in the shameless stealing of even your phrases and best mots there has been a rough honesty; that is, I have taken them as you wrote them, and have not injured them by any attempt to dilute them by my own words.

Your observations seemed to me so wise and right that I thought they deserved a wider audience than only myself. What could be better than the Congress of the United States, with the hope that they might ricochet around the Latin American Embassies and perhaps find their way south of the Equator. At any rate, I now express to you my great appreciation and gratitude for your letter and for the help which it gave me. I hope that what I have done with the letter will to some degree amuse you and that perhaps in some degree also you will approve.

Whenever you feel the spirit move you, please write me another such delightful letter. I assure you in advance that I shall confiscate your thought without just compensation but with immense gratitude.

My warmest regards.

Sincerely yours,

To **ERIC LARRABEE**

Eric Larrabee, editor of American Heritage, *appears to have solicited an article from DA.*

July 14, 1959

Mr. Eric. Larrabee
Executive Editor
American Heritage
551 Fifth Avenue
New York 17, N.Y.

Dear Mr. Larrabee:

I will have a go at it. As one of my friends heard the proprietor of a pet shop say to a lady who asked whether he could guarantee a particular monkey as a suitable pet, "Lady, a monkey is a monkey; and no one can't guarantee nothin'."

Just as I thought I was beginning a quiet summer, I have been made to work unconscionably. But even this will pass.

Yours sincerely,

To **GEORGE DIXON**

George Dixon was humor columnist for the Washington Star. *He and DA often amused themselves at the expense of the more solemn public figures.*

July 30, 1959

Mr. George Dixon
2523 P Street, N.W.
Washington, D.C.

Dear George:

I am worried about you. When I am just up the block from you, which fortunately is half the year, I try to help you with your writing, keep you from getting nervous, elevate your thoughts and generally see that you stay on the rails. Then I go away for the summer, all the twenty miles out to Sandy Spring, and we seem to lose touch. Not only that, but as I said, I get worried about what happens to you. I get worried because I don't quite know what you are up to except that you seem to be getting into hot water.

The trouble starts with the newspaper. In town I get it first, read you, and know the worst at once. But out here I fool around at one thing and another in the morning until you know who has the paper, is reading you, and what do I get? A torn sheet with a little egg and more Walter Lippmann on it. So all I know is that whatever Dixon is up to he shouldn't be, except it's doing him a lot of good. Then I read a lot of letters to the editor complaining about you.

As I get it you have been saying things about Wayne Morse and Paul Butler and quite a lot of writers think you have been mean to them. I have tried to find out what you wrote but the past copies have been laid out in the chicken house and this makes them hard to read, even though that improves them in some respects. Some people would think that not knowing what you said was sort of a handicap, but you and I have been friends for a long time and know that that doesn't matter at all.

The point, as I see it, is that the whole thing is a great big misunderstanding. You wouldn't, indeed you couldn't, say anything mean about Wayne or Paul, because you know how sensitive they both are, and how neither of them could possibly say anything mean about anyone else. And you wouldn't hurt their feelings for the world. The whole thing is absurd.

And then what they say you said! They just don't know you, so they misunderstand everything. Take what I hear you said about Wayne—that he wasn't a true liberal and that no true liberal would be seen dead with him. Anyone who knew what you think of liberals would know you were praising Wayne as your sort of a guy. Would you be seen dead (except professionally) with a true liberal? Would I be seen dead with you if I thought you were even a fellow traveler with true liberals? Well, you see how absurd the whole thing is when you just stop to think about it. But, then, I suppose Wayne hasn't time to stop and think. It's all too bad. As the man said, haste makes waste.

· · ·

To WILMARTH S. LEWIS

DA here discussed strategy with his fellow Yale Corporation member "Lefty" Lewis for raising new funds and for allocating them among the different academic disciplines. DA shared his perplexity with Lewis about important questions of educational policy. The references to "the E.P.C." and to "the Council" appear to be to the Educational Policy Committee of the Yale Corporation and possibly the Alumni Council.

July 31, 1959

Mr. W. S. Lewis
Farmington, Connecticut

Dear Lefty:

To our sorrow it is fated that we shall go through London, on our way home, after you have left it. This pains me doubly; to miss you and to be the occasion—not of my seeking—of trying the brethren by postponing the October meeting. I was hoping that you could have a preliminary canter as senior fellow to let the E.P.C. [Yale Educational Policy Committee] know what was to be what. I have to be in German-American meetings in Bonn and Berlin, which do not seem trivial, and then in London to learn whether the British have wholly taken leave of their senses, as they seem to do when the pressure is off. I had hoped that you—but not I—would breast the Niagara of words which would greet the fund raising plan.

This plan can be made as complicated or as simple as you like. Here is the prescription: Decide what we want to do in the next ten years beyond what we are doing now. Cut out nonsense; keep the goal to brass tacks and under $50 million—which is all we can get in a year anyway. Then rationalize it. If you have read, as I know you have, C. P. Snow's Rede Lecture at Cambridge, 1959, the objective is clear, and all we need is will and brutality to coerce the drily logical members of the Council, and the fund raisers. I had hoped that the first sip of this cup might pass from me to you. But that hope is gone.

The real problem, I think, comes during and after the period of money raising. Suppose we get the money, or some of it. What do we do with it? Here, again, read and think about Snow. You sent me the catalogue of the Divinity School to read and shudder at. But I need guidance in shuddering. I presume that the intellectual and cultural bases of the place, or lack of them, are what bother you. But how to train these people? Do you want them to read more in the humanities or in science? I should be in favor of the latter; but I don't think you would be. Would it shock you greatly to have me say that, whereas the congeries of Philosophy-Religion-Law and Medicine were once the basis of a university as against a collegiate school, I wonder whether today it is not more nearly true to say that the former should be centered around medicine and science. I don't say it. I only ask how shocked you would be should I say it, which is another way of asking how sure you are that it is untrue. And what you would mean, if you did think so, by *untrue*?

Will you think about, and write me, what you would like to see the E.P.C. tackle next winter. We shall have, and should have, our quota of *ad hoc* crises. It is good for both Whit and the officers that there be this catharsis. But, as a purposeful pressure, what do you say? Not subjects which are worthy of interest, but things that need to be done. Everyone from Whit through all the officers to Ed Roberts, who knows more than anyone what Yale really *does*—by what it spends its money on—are eager, as never before, for help. The question is, have we as a body the capacity to surmount our individual hobbies—the fear of bankruptcy, athletics, more and greater scholarships, the social system, radicalism in economics, the Church in Yale, and so on—to look at the whole, understand it, and give wise guidance to men genuinely desirous of it.

I do not take myself very seriously, but I should like to help, if I could, because, among many reasons, I am devoted to Whit and, knowing the good and the not so good, think he is the best we have had in my lifetime and may have in another. This is the best chance we shall ever see. So give me your steer.

As ever,

To PRESIDENT A. WHITNEY GRISWOLD

DA endeavored to elicit from President Griswold agreement on how the additional funds to be raised from the Yale alumni were to be spent as part of the justification for raising them in the first place.

August 27, 1959

President A. Whitney Griswold
R.F.D. 28
Vineyard Haven, Massachusetts

Dear Whit:

That letter of yours (August 18th) is a mighty fine one. I showed it to Felix at lunch last week. He not only agreed, but added that he knew of no other university head who could have written it. As we tried to make his remark specific, we concluded that we had given you too easy a field in which to excel. But even enlarging it did not furnish much competition.

But you cannot get off with mere adulation. To each of your reservations, I have a reservation. This reminds me a little of General Marshall's attempt in 1945–6 to get some progress into the negotiations of the two Chinese factions. Each proposal by either side would have three conditions attached to its acceptance by the other. The first side would then attach three conditions to each of the other's three. The other would impose three to each of the first's nine. And so on. The resulting confusion was so magnificent as to enhance my respect for Bret Harte's observation that, "For ways that are dark, and for tricks that are vain the heathen Chinee is peculiar."

So, to your objection to my simile of ten extra strokes a decade, as against "devising a continuous policy," I say use any words you will, but don't rationalize yourself into doing nothing different from the past. Looking at acts, not words, we are—at least, I thought we were—going to try to raise for the Independent Educational Resources Fund (by the way, "independent" of whom or what?) $50 million, over and beyond our usual annual intake of gifts and savings, in a period of one or two years.

It may be that this is a "continuous policy." I won't quarrel. But that phrase does not mean, I take it, that we are going to try to add to University invested capital each year our average for the past five years *plus* $50 million dollars. We may go out for special gifts for Art and Architecture, etc., etc., from time to time, or all the time, in the future. But we are, as I understand it, intending to make a special effort *now* for $50 million dollars for the I.E.R.F. Are we agreed on this?

If so, on to my reservation to your No. (2). You are wholly right about the aim being to make each culture, the traditional and the scientific, intelligible and useful to the other. You are right, also, about the impossibility of wholly closing the gaps between them and within them. The fund will, of course, support both, and, since we have a long start on the traditional culture and rather short roots in the scientific, we must push harder in the latter field for a while, anyway. Are we agreed so far?

My reservation has to do with misconceptions from language. The I.E.R.F. will be, of course, a part of the University endowment, all of which is used to strengthen, perpetuate and make the two cultures intelligible to one another. But how does it do this any differently from the rest of the endowment, some of which is earmarked for one or another educational purpose, and some not earmarked at all? Of course, the text of your proposal tells us some things you want to do with it. They are—asking your worship's pardon—a fairly heterogeneous lot of unfinanced desirables. The problem is how to give your request for them form. I made a suggestion. You objected for the reasons given above. And sound they are, if this fund is to endure forever. You counter with a phrase, the I.E.R.F., which has the advantage of meaning nothing, the disadvantage, that it will never launch a thousand ships—or one ship. If you had to express meaningfully in a phrase or be shot what you want this fund for, what would you say? Certainly not I.E.R.F. The Fund for Educational Advance? The Fund For the Next Decade? The Fund For Yale's Future? Something which *helps* explain your purpose and its importance.

This, I suggest as I duck, is not a pure matter of semantics. Could it be that the whole idea is not yet thought through to a conclusion?

Well, if it isn't, it will be by the time I next hear from you. It is my function—and I can't think of a better one in our circumstances—to say,

"Yes—but?" The "yes man" has had an unfavorable press, largely because attention has been centered on *legitimate* yes men. But there is a more useful, if rarer, type—the yes men who are stinkers. In this sense I subscribe myself.

> Your humble and obedient stinker.

P.S. As for Snow having an odor of Marx about him, I didn't get it. My partner, Hugh Cox, whose knowledge and judgment I respect, didn't get it either. I shall read Snow again with this point in mind. But I had best make a confession first. I have never smelled the true Marxian odor because I have never been able to read him long enough. My boring point is too low for Marx. I know him, of course, by hearsay and via some of his alleged disciples. But, if you say you smelt him and I don't, I will concede to you since my smeller is far inferior to yours.

P.P.S. I have from you Dean Simpson's report and will read it sympathetically.

P.P.P.S. I have just learned that Keynes, also, could never get through Marx.

To A. WHITNEY GRISWOLD

This letter affords an example of the amenability of DA's opinions to contrary evidence—as opposed to contrary opinion. The name "Carry" referred to Carrie Nation, the temperance activist of another day, as a humorous analogue for Mrs. Griswold, who served sherry rather than hard liquor as refreshment for the Yale Corporation, despite long agitation by DA to introduce the martini.

> Sandy Spring
> August 29, 1959

Dear Whit:

I have read [......   ....] report and think much better of him. It has humor, sense, and a good deal of iron.

Well, darn it, if I have to I shall part with a cherished prejudice. But it ought not to bother me with the fear of running out of them.

In an hour or so Alice for reasons which 42½ years still make unfathomable is having the whole damned county to a reception. I shall have to be polite, clean and dressed, triple outrages which I may mitigate by getting tight.

Don't tell Carry.

> Yours,

To **HARRY S TRUMAN**

One of a number of exchanges with the former President appraising the merits of and handicapping the various contenders for the 1960 Democratic nomination. References in the seventh paragraph are to the projected exchange of visits by President Eisenhower and "Mr. K," Secretary Nikita Khrushchev of the U.S.S.R.

August 31, 1959

Dear Mr. President:

I find it hard to believe that Winston would be so silly and so rude as intentionally to ignore your letter. He was certainly far from mentally acute when I lunched with him at the Embassy and it seems far more likely that he has forgotten it or that some secretarial failure is responsible. My suggestion is to get Rose to remind you well in advance that Sir Winston's birthday is Nov. 30 and write him a note in the course of which you can say again how sorry you were to miss him and hope that he got your letter explaining why. Then, at least, you can rest in the belief that you have done all you could to put things right.

I spoke to Sam Rayburn today about your concern over Paul Butler. Sam said he knows now that Adlai was right when he wanted to fire Butler and thinks less than nothing of him and his friend Ziffren of California. But the gossip Sam hears is that neither of them are for Stevenson. One of his authorities for this, so he said, was Pat Brown. Pat told me that the only Democrats who could carry California—aside, I imagine, from himself— were Kennedy and Stevenson.

My mind goes back to our talk the Sunday we lunched together with Florence Mahoney that the fruit of drift would be Stevenson. He still seems to me to be the most likely outcome, and I agree with you that it seems more likely than not that he would be defeated by either Nixon or Rockefeller. My analysis of the convention is that John Kennedy must win, if he wins at all, on a very early ballot. If he does not, there seems to me to be only two realistic next choices, Adlai and Lyndon. Humphrey is only an heir to Stevenson; and Symington, to Johnson. Stevenson would certainly get it if Kennedy would agree (having lost on his bid for the first place) to run with him. Tom Corcoran tells me that the only person with whom, according to Joe Kennedy, John would run under the circumstances mentioned is Lyndon. If, therefore, Kennedy threw his strength to Johnson, Adlai might be stopped and the Johnson-Kennedy ticket might be nominated. Lesser combinations seem to me of only theoretical interest, because they cannot win.

To me a Johnson-Kennedy ticket would have much more appeal than a Stevenson-Kennedy ticket, though the polls would give the latter a better chance. But the polls gave you no chance in 1948. I say, to hell with the polls, if we have real stuff against them.

Lyndon is the ablest man in national public life today. He has thousands of faults. But when we really take our hair down, he is a giant among pygmies. So I feel confident that if, with strong support and a united party, he took on the campaign, especially with Kennedy, we would have a chance for a fight in which I could join wholeheartedly, because there would not only be a real chance to win, but to win under circumstances where victory might really turn the tide for the great struggle of our time. My constant worry about Adlai is that all we accomplish by electing him is to accept the formal responsibility for ultimate defeat. . . .

As you know I agree with you about the dangers of the forthcoming visits, though I advised against either of us opposing them now. Because of Ike's neglect of the basic realities of power he has been forced to substitute improvisation for planning. He feels, as a beautiful woman might, that his charm must carry all. But as Norman Hapgood said of Maud Adams in *Chanticleer,* "charm never made a rooster." Averell thinks your recent article a mistake and that, of all the trips, Ike's to Russia may be the most important in undermining the picture of the U.S. which Mr. K has been selling to his people and limiting his capacity to build up war scares. But I have told him that he takes too serious a view of the effect of your piece and not to worry himself or you about it. This article has about it some of the mystery of the Virgin birth. I wonder what inspired it.

My own writing is taking varied forms. I have done an article for *American Heritage* about Arthur Vandenberg. Another for the *N.Y. Times* Magazine, called Time to Think, stimulated by Ike's speech on thinking in "the highest echelons" to the Foreign Service Institute. Both of these you will get in due course. Then I have written another story for *Harper's* about Italy like the one I had in last June's issue. It has all kept me busy and my mind from rusting. I hear that you are to write two books. That is real ambition and energy.

I am enclosing a triptych which came to me in the mail showing you in the company of your successors. How about a good law suit out of this?

We are off on Sept. 13th for Italy, Germany and England, part vacation, part meetings. We look forward to it eagerly.

Alice sends her love, and much of it, to Mrs. Truman (I always stumble over calling that dear lady Bess, as she has bid me) and to you, Excellency and Friend, as do I.

As ever,

To **A. WHITNEY GRISWOLD**

Here an experienced advocate counseled the President of Yale in the advocacy of presenting the case for a capital fund drive to the Yale Corporation. Tom Sappington was DA's trusted physician.

Covington & Burling
Union Trust Building
Washington 5, D.C.
October 20, 1959

President A. Whitney Griswold
Yale University
New Haven, Connecticut

Dear Whit:

This memorandum is for you only. It is my attempt to distill from the papers you gave the Corporation: First, what you want Yale to do that it is not doing, or to have it acquire that it does not have, and how much that will cost in capital and alumni fund increase. Surely this is where a logical mind ought to start. Second, to bring out that in some cases you will ask for funds for the new purposes directly, but in others you will try a carom shot. You will ask for endowment for existing activities in order to release presently committed general income to new purposes. Clearly one must understand this to understand the play. Otherwise we shall be tackling the player who appears to be carrying the ball, but really isn't.

Thirdly, I try to show to whom you expect the University to go to get what.

In some way you have got to make these facts clear to us in a simple memorandum and with understandable figures. As you will see from my figures, I cannot determine (except for new professorships and immediate new construction) how much ends up in exactly what new activity. Until this is clear, we are in trouble.

This is intended to help, but it may do the reverse. If so, forget it.

I am improving, my dear Doctor, but tomorrow Tom Sappington has a field day at my expense.

Yours,

To MANLIO BROSIO

Manlio Brosio was Italian Ambassador to Washington and later Secretary General of NATO.

October 28, 1959

His Excellency Manlio Brosio
Italian Ambassador
2700 16th Street, N.W.
Washington, D.C.

Dear Mr. Ambassador:

Returning from a European journey, the most pleasant part of which was spent in your beautiful country, I found your thoughtful letter about my Williamsburg lecture. You have caught my meaning exactly. Liberty is something very different from what the orators of today or the libertarians of the eighteenth century thought it was. The strain of conservatism which you so rightly find in liberalism is the element of restraint. I do not know the Memoirs of Cardinal de Retz. Is there an English translation? If so, I should like to get it out of the Library of Congress and make his acquaintance.

I have just read a most fascinating book published by Hamish Hamilton in England, made up of selections from Saint-Simon, translated by Miss Lucy Norton with a foreword by Miss Nancy Mitford. The title is *Saint-Simon at Versailles*. Here one sees the end of the process by which feudalism was destroyed in France by Richelieu, Mazarin, and finally by Louis XIV and the foundations laid for the Revolution. I could hardly put it down.

My week in Germany was an interesting one. There I met with a good many Germans in Bonn and Berlin from business and all shades of political opinion from the Chancellor to Carlo Schmidt. They had been shaken and bewildered by the Khrushchev visit here and by the somewhat unguarded remarks of President Eisenhower and Secretary Herter. I found far more attention paid to my remarks than they deserved, I suppose because they were more what the Germans were hoping to hear from Washington. But what I said seems to have upset Walter Lippmann, Jimmie Warburg, and others, who believe that if we call a retreat a negotiation, the element of consent prevents it from being a defeat and a loss. I am most unsympathetic to this sort of self-deception.

Most sincerely yours,

To **LYNDON JOHNSON**

DA here urged the Senate Majority Leader to eliminate a remnant of McCarthyism in the form of a loyalty oath that had been incorporated into the National Defense Education Act of 1958.

December 2, 1959

The Honorable Lyndon Johnson
297 U.S. Court House
Austin, Texas

Dear Lyndon:

While you are relaxing on your porch and watching the river flow by your door, or roaming your acres, or contemplatively absorbing a drop or two of Bourbon in the cool of the evening, will you think over the request of this letter? It has to do with striking out a portion of section 1001 (f) of the National Defense Education Act of 1958.

This Act, as you know, makes available to young men and women scholarships with the aid of which they can further their higher education. It is a good act and Congress deserves praise for enacting it. There is one feature of it which is causing a great deal of dissatisfaction. This dissatisfaction is not a matter of any great political importance. But it is a matter of intellectual and moral importance, and it deserves your sympathetic attention.

Section 1001 (f) requires a recipient of a government scholarship to do two things. The first is to take the Oath of Allegiance to the Constitution of the United States. This is quite proper, and no one with any sense objects to it. The other required act is an affidavit that the applicant does not believe in, and is not a member of and does not support any organization that believes in or teaches, the overthrow of the United States Government by force or violence or by any illegal or unconstitutional methods. This is the requirement which is causing more and more dissatisfaction and is leading more and more colleges to withdraw from participation in the administration of the Act, including the University of which I am now senior Trustee; that is, Yale University of Connecticut.

This is a silly, futile, and insulting affidavit to require of young people engaged in preparing for their future life's work. It is quite obvious that anyone who means what he says when he swears to bear true faith and allegiance to the United States of America and to support and defend the Constitution and laws of the United States against all its enemies, foreign and domestic does not believe in overthrowing the government by force and violence or by unconstitutional means.

I cannot believe that the Federal government is truly, or should be truly, concerned about the past life and beliefs of children of eighteen. It is concerned with their future, and, as to that future, they are required to swear, as is every officer and soldier of the United States, to bear true faith and allegiance.

As I have said, the faculty of more and more universities, including my own, are refusing to administer the Act for the reasons that I have given, and also because who knows what ephemeral organizations to which some youth may have belonged later on may be determined by someone else to be of proscribed character; again because this is to insinuate that the boy or girl holds beliefs which he or she cannot hold consistent with the Oath of Allegiance; and because it raises the whole shadow of McCarthyism again.

At the last session Kennedy and Javits attempted to rectify the situation, but did so in a clumsy sort of way, which ended in the proposal being recommitted. They started out with an amendment which would have repealed the whole section. This raised a furor about the Oath of Allegiance. They then decided to concentrate their attack on the affidavit, but in the meantime had confused everybody so much that they lost the battle.

I am sure that, if you would give your attention to this, the same group and others with your advice could do this without a commotion and to the great advantage of American education. Therefore, my dear friend, please give this more than passing thought. It is of more importance in academic halls than in Washington.

I saw that you were in town briefly to hear about the President's travel plans and that you said he would be accompanied by our prayers. This is a much wiser observation than the one which I made and will cause you less trouble than mine has caused me. However, I am willing to join in your statement on the ground that I feel about the future of the United States whenever the President starts out on his travels the way the Marshal of the Supreme Court feels about the law when he opens a session of that Court. You will recall that he ends up his liturgy by saying "God save the United States for the Court is now sitting."

With warm regards.

Most sincerely,

To **NOEL ANNAN**

Saarinen was the architect of Morse and Ezra Stiles colleges which introduced a radical new style of dormitory into the Yale scene.

December 21, 1959

Noel G. Annan, Esquire
Provost
King's College
Cambridge, England

Dear Noel:
The accompanying letter gives you all I know on the questions involved in it.
Now for the more congenial realm of gossip.

. . .

Whit has told me about your crises, both on Saarinen's plans and on the Latin requirement. I have not been able to thrill to the call to battle on either. I helped Whit get the Saarinen plans approved by the Corporation and pushed along the road to execution, but, while I do not admit it in Corporation meetings, I retain doubts. A good deal of improvement has been made in the plans in regard to such elemental requirements as getting the light from windows in places where it is needed rather than in some angle in the corner of a room, but the buildings do give me somewhat the impression of the Castle of Chillon, which we saw last year.
As for Latin and Greek, I remind myself a little of one of Alben Barkley's mythical Kentuckians, who was asked which side he was taking in a forthcoming election and replied, "I haven't made up my mind yet, but, when I do, I will be bitter as Hell." My bewilderment comes in part from the fact that, when I left Groton School, I could read Greek easily at sight and write it far more easily than French and only a little less easily than English. Today, not only have I forgotten it completely, but am not even sure about some Greek letters. I suppose this and Latin were good intellectual discipline. I suppose that what I read in Greek entered in some way into the formation of an attitude of mind, but I wonder a little bit whether it was all worthwhile, particularly as it was all done at the expense of never having any scientific instruction beyond trigonometry, so that I belong to that group of ignoramuses whom C.P. Snow confounds by asking them to explain the simplest proposition in physics.
Whit approaches all of this from the qualifications which he thinks the recipient of a Ph.D. ought to have. From that point of view he may be quite right, just as it may be highly desirable to have all Cardinals talk Latin. But I think for myself that I should be happier if my education had left me with a speaking as well as reading familiarity with one modern language, other than English, and its literature. The efforts which I have made in the last year with Italian show me how much I have really missed.

Most sincerely yours,

To MADELEINE AND PATRICK DEVLIN

Sir Patrick Devlin was Justice of the High Court, Queen's Bench Division, and at this time Chairman of the Nyasaland Inquiry Commission.

DA's criticism of the Eisenhower Administration was directed that fall against the inadequacy of its response to the Soviet threat to Berlin.

December 24, 1959

The Honorable Sir Patrick and Mrs. Devlin
West Wick House
Pewsey, Wilts.
England

Dear Madeleine and Patrick:

This autumn has been a confused, a full and unproductive one—slipping away without my having told you how warmed I was by the letters which we had from each of you. You touched me very much by what you said.

It seems to me that this has been an autumn of controversy for me. I have been critical of what President Eisenhower has said and has not done, and in this have been almost unique. This has given the eighty per cent of the press which supports him fanatically a single target at which to fire, and, while their shots have been far from lethal, they have not been painless.

Then there has been the even more thankless task of pointing out to my own party comrades that they have not been facing up to the decisions which should be made. They have been understandably resentful of this. I suppose—at least all the strategists say so—that a soldier of any sense does not fight on two fronts at the same time. I can testify to the discomfort of that position.

Then, too, I have fallen into a bear trap, dug for me by the Chief Justice. Felix also prepared the way by unctuous statements about the desirability of a lawyer's taking interest and pride in the technical side of his profession. No good, I was sure, could come of this. Then the Chief Justice informed me that the time had come for the review of the Rules of Civil Procedure in the Federal Courts and that in his infinite wisdom he was requesting me to be the Chairman of the committee to undertake this labor.

This situation has about it an undoubted humor. Perhaps the only person who knows less about the Rules of Civil Procedure than I do is the Chief Justice. At the last term of Court I argued the only case which I have ever had on the interpretation of one of the rules. It was never decided because we were so uncertain of our ground—as, indeed were our opponents of theirs—that we settled the matter out of court while it was *sub judice*. Apparently the residue left by this unfortunate incident in the Chief's mind was that I was an authority on the subject. Undoubtedly I shall be if I am able to survive the experience. During the course of what is now becoming a long, and what has undoubtedly been an ill-spent life, I have associated with many classes of people, but I doubt whether I have ever been with any who have impressed me as having less spontaneous charm than those teachers and writers of law who specialize on procedure. The juice seems to have gone out of them, and they are concerned with matters which doubtless have their importance, but seem also to have a distinct medieval aura. However, I am in for it and have got to put the best face on this matter.

· · ·

As ever,

PART

III

1960–1964

To **A. WHITNEY GRISWOLD**

A lecture visit to Knox College prompted DA to reflect on some matters pertinent to Yale. DA must have found his room equipped with stationery of a sister hotel.

Hotel Custer
Galesburg, Ill.
March 23, 1960

Dear Whit.

Why this hotel—where I enjoy the Sandburg suite (he was born here)—puts me in Nebraska, I know not. I am here for a week—two lectures in the Congr. church and tri-daily performances at Knox College. Several bits of intelligence seem worth transmitting.

This is a small place, 900 students, coeducational, mostly Anglo-Saxon and German stock, a pretty good faculty, a poor plant. The overall tuition, room and board charge is $2100. The endowment at market is $8 million. Income from it pays about half the instructional costs. The President [illegible], formerly dean of W&M, says the policy has been to pay high salaries and practice austerity on living and plant. They do. They are now having to replace some obsolete structures and build new and modern eating facilities.

Here they are strong on "social sciences" and political science especially. The psychologists are behaviorists and make no sense to me, but the political scientists resist this. One of them, a most attractive and intelligent chap, Herring, whose father is or was at Harvard, would warm your heart in his historical and literary approach to political theory from Plato on.

As I see how other people "make do" with far simpler construction than we think necessary, I wonder whether for classroom, laboratory and working library space we don't try to build too massively and for too long and for too fancy an effect. The Prospect street buildings are not a hundred years old; they will last a millenium and what a joy if some one would blow them up. Why not tuck some cheap and useful horrors of brick, plastic sheets and glass out of sight behind a lovely screen and scrap them after 50 years. Let tradition gather around the colleges and the old campus—

Well, you see what dangerous thoughts Satan can find for an idle mind.

My love to you and Mary.

Yours,

To HARRY S TRUMAN

April 14, 1960

Dear Mr. President:

I shall look forward to April 27th. Would you have dinner with me on that night or the next one? Alice is away on a trip with Adele Lovett to Greece. But we still manage to eat pretty well. If you are free, shall we have a stag party or give the ladies a break?

Your schedule sounds as though you were headed for trouble with the Boss. I have been running a pretty hard one myself and got pretty tired. While Alice is away I am going to ease up a bit and play a bit of hookey out at the farm to which spring has eventually come. One most interesting experience I had in March was a week of lecturing, seminars and student consultations at Knox College in Galesburg, Illinois, where—as you know—the fifth Lincoln-Douglas debate took place and where Carl Sandburg was born. It is a fine and gallant little place, though the town is pretty bad. They were all Republicans when I got there. But we certainly changed all that. What is all this anti-sit-down attitude of yours. Felix was asking me the other day, saying that his brother Whittaker takes the same view. I told him that Missourians are confederates at heart, and that while they—or some of them— accept the Constitution, and even defend it vigorously, they won't go a step further. There's nothing in the Constitution about how to run a drug store's lunch counter. Only we New England abolitionists find that reasoning irrelevant. Am I right in my diagnosis.

Now for a prophecy. If Jack Kennedy stubs his toe in West Virginia or elsewhere, the candidate will be Stevenson. I hate to say this but I think the only possible alternative is Stu and I doubt very much, though I am for him, that he can make it. He just doesn't seem to catch hold. Maybe we should all give Jack a run for his money—or rather for Joe's.

My warmest greetings to the Boss and to you

As ever,

To **HARRY S TRUMAN**

May 23, 1960

The Honorable Harry S Truman
Independence, Missouri

Dear Mr. President:

The first sentence of your letter to me of May 9 is a real puzzler. "I have been reading," you say, "the results of our situation in Asia east of the Caribbean Sea and I am very much worried." I have been worrying for some time that the Asia problem was creeping up on us, but I had not realized how close it had approached, and here it is now just a bit south of Bermuda. So I am worried too.

However puzzling your geography may have become, your meaning is perfectly clear, and I agree entirely that the President of the United States ought not to admit that he doesn't know what is going on. And, even more important than admitting this fact, it ought not to be a fact.

The day that our admission about the U-2 flight came out I was lecturing at the National War College, and a madder and more disgusted group of officers I never saw. There used to be a saying around in my youth that the Lord took care of children, drunks, and the United States of America. But it seems that now we are over taxing the omnipotence

Shortly before the Summit meeting the official attitude around the State Department was that the Summit would be a pushover. Khrushchev, they said, was under such pressures at home that in order to have a political success he must get an agreement and have Eisenhower in Moscow. So he would agree to a nuclear test ban and then adjourn the festivities to Moscow. I produced a great deal of merriment around town by predicting that the Summit would not last two days. I seem to have overstated it by one.

The official version has now changed. It is still said that Khrushchev was under great pressure, but this time it was pressure in the opposite direction. The State Department tells us that the pressure was not for a success but for a failure and came from the Army and the Chinese allies. Having learned of the firmness of Mr. Eisenhower and the unbreakable unity of the Allies, he had to end the Summit without a test of strength, and, in seizing upon the U-2 incident, he has overplayed his hand.

I think this is as erroneous as the first view. Mr. Khrushchev knew exactly what he was doing, and he was playing the game of the protracted conflict, as the Russians have always played it, alternating tension with detente. Peaceful coexistence is now abandoned for a renewal of the cold war, but the purpose is the same. It is to get us out of Berlin, get Germany out of the Western Alliance, and to get the United States out of Europe.

My guess is that, under the cover of the commotion which will be going on in the U.N., the East Germans will begin to tighten up on civilian traffic with Berlin, and sometime, when we are sufficiently distracted by attempts to prevent majorities or two-thirds majorities in the Security Council or the General Assembly, the treaty with the East Germans will be made.

Mr. Eisenhower, like a weary fighter, is maneuvering for the bell; and, whatever happens, he will do nothing about it, leaving these problems for his successor. The enclosed article from the *Yale Review* seems to me a pretty sound statement of the situation as it stands at present.

Most sincerely,

To MICHAEL JANEWAY

Mike Janeway was a student at Harvard.

May 24, 1960

Mr. Michael Janeway
Eliot H-33
Harvard College
Cambridge 38, Mass.

Dear Mike:

. . .

. . . Now for you and Holmes. You make me realize how little there is in that small Ark of the Covenant in which one keeps the most sacred vessels. There may be nothing in them after all these years. But the vessels are there, preserved through the eternity of one's life, like the vessels in an Egyptian tomb. Holmes was and is my chalice. Perhaps, when I come to Eliot House I should try to tell you of the fragrance and richness of the wine it held over forty years ago.

One of the slipperiest words I know is "great." But I think the "greatest" man I have ever known, that is, the essence of man living, man thinking, man baring himself to the lonely emptiness—or the reverse—of the universe, was Holmes. Brandeis was eminent, but not his equal. George Marshall was a peer and in some ways—in transfiguration through duty, for instance—their superior. But there the class closes. Even the most intense devotion cannot open it further.

Norman Hapgood always denigrated Holmes, said that we were all deluded by the beauty of his English prose style—an early manifestation of

George Kennan. Holmes, himself, would have understood this, and would not have been displeased. He used to say to pretty girls who came to flatter him and tell him how much they got from Euripides, "My dear, what you really like is Swinburne via Gilbert Murray."

But he was the master not the creature of his command of style. Read his dissent in the Abrams case (250 U.S. 616, 624) and try to write your own reply to Senator McCarthy. This opinion was written after three of his close friends on the Court called on Mrs. Holmes to persuade her to persuade him not to give the comfort of his vast prestige to subversives.

. . .

Don't patronize Holmes. Don't worry about his Lochner dissent. It means just what you think it ought to mean. Don't be disturbed by all the Jesuits have said about this most articulate and critical of agnostics. And, perhaps—only perhaps, throw your paper away and start over again.

I know that I sound like God saying, "Put off thy shoes from thy feet, for the place whereon thou standest is holy ground."

No one would have thought this sillier than Holmes. He used to tell us of Emerson telling him to hold Plato at arm's length and to say to him, "Plato, you have impressed millions. Let's see whether you can impress me."

This is right. And my guess is that, if you will stop being shocked, and identifying remarks of his with reading period notes and trying to classify him as this or that kind of a liberal, you might experience some of the richness which was showered so lavishly on me of knowing something of one of the immortals.

. . .

Yours,

To **WILLIAM TYLER**

DA's reflections here dealt with the collapse of the U.S.-Soviet detente of that time, a collapse preceded by a Russian discovery of an American U-2 reconnaissance aircraft and capture of the pilot.

Washington, D.C.
May 31, 1960

Dear Bill:
How fully I agree. Enclosed is a statement of the situation which for the first time publicly expresses my thoughts.

All the way through this affair two of our friends . . . have played a strange and harmful role. They led what Dick Hottelet called the euphoria of the State Department on the Paris meeting before the U2. It had to be a success because Mr. K needed Ike in Moscow to deal with the great pressure he was under from domestic critics of his policy of detente. So there would be no crisis over Berlin and probably an agreement on nuclear testing. After the collapse the explanation was that he blew up the conference under the pressure of these same critics. In other words, the U2 blew up an otherwise successfully planned meeting.

There is something about Soviet experts which makes them—in the Department, at least—dangerous reporters and advisers. Their hunches are uncommunicable and must be accepted by those who have not the same occult power of divination. Chip as much as said this to me. "Dean, you came to this field too late to be able to get the feel for it." How can a government get away from this? In part, I think by getting the judgment of more varied and less committed experts who can bring together more than *personal* impressions. This, I think, an organization such as the Rand Corporation can do.

What do you think about this? Our warmest greetings to you and Betsy.

As ever,

To **HARRY S TRUMAN**

Perhaps DA asking Harry Truman to observe verbal restraint in the 1960 campaign recalls a reformed alcoholic strengthening his own resolve by asking another to take the pledge.

June 27, 1960

Dear Boss:

As the Convention approaches we partisans are likely to become, shall we say, emphatic in our statements to the press. Could we make a treaty on what we shall *not* say?

On the positive side we can, and doubtless will, say that our candidate—yours and mine—has all the virtues of the Greats from Pericles through Churchill. St. Peter and the Pee-pul forgive this innocent though improbable hyperbole. But there are some things that no one should, and few will, forgive.

These fall into several groups, but the common denominator is the harm that comes from allowing the intensity of the personal view to dim a proper concern for the common cause. The list of the "It's not dones," as I see it, goes like this:—

    I. About other Democratic Candidates:
        (a) Never say that any of them is not qualified to be President.
        (b) Never say that any of them can't win.

(c) Never suggest that any of them is the tool of any group or interest, or is not a true blue liberal, or has (or has used) more money than another.

The reason: At this point public argument is too late—Deals may still be possible. I just don't know. But sounding off is sure to be wrong. If our candidate is going anywhere—which I doubt—it will not be because of public attacks on other candidates. And such attacks can do a lot of harm when they are quoted in the election campaign.

II. About the Negro sit-in Strikes:

(a) Do not say that they are communist inspired. The evidence is all the other way, despite alleged views of J. Edgar Hoover, whom you should trust as much as you would a rattlesnake with a silencer on its rattle.

(b) Do not say that you disapprove of them. Whatever you think you are under no compulsion to broadcast it. Free speech is a restraint on government; not an incitement to the citizen.

The reason: Your views, as reported, are wholly out of keeping with your public record. The discussion does not convince anyone of anything. If you want to discuss the sociological, moral and legal interests involved, you should give much more time and thought to them.

III. About Foreign Policy:

(a) For the next four months do not say that in foreign policy we must support the President.

The reason: This cliché has become a menace. It misrepresents by creating the false belief that in the recent disasters the President has had a policy or position to support.

This just isn't true. One might as well say "Support the President," if he falls off the end of a dock. That isn't a policy. But to urge support for him makes his predicament appear to be a policy to people who don't know what a dock is.

So, please, for just four months let his apologists come to his aid.

We have got to beat Nixon. We shall probably have to do it with Kennedy. Why make it any harder than it has to be. Now, if ever, our vocal cords ought to be played on the keyboard of our minds. This is so hard for me that I have stopped using my cords at all. By August they will be ready to play "My Rosary."

So I offer you a treaty on "don'ts." Will you agree?

Alice joins me in most affectionate greetings to you both.

Most sincerely,

To **HARRY S TRUMAN**

Arthur Summerfield was the Postmaster General in the Eisenhower Administration. The reference to Chicago is to the Republican nominating convention still to be held.

Harewood
Sandy Spring, Maryland
July 17, 1960

Dear Boss:

We are here for the summer, and I, a commuter. So your letter of July 9th, by virtue of your extravagance in putting a special delivery stamp on it, lay on the floor at P Street for about a week. Mr. Summerfield forwards ordinary mail but special delivery has him baffled, and it goes into oblivion through the mail drop until Alice or Johnson happens to go in to P Street.

But in this case it was just as well. Your letter told me of your penultimate decision to go to Los Angeles, which was happily reversed by the ultimate one, not to go. Had I gotten your letter I should have wasted the family substance on the telephone urging you not to do what fate was to prevent you from doing. I am sorry that your sister-in-law had to be sacrificed to keep you from so unwise a step. But it was in a good cause and I hope that she is now much improved.

I listened to your press conference and regretted that you felt impelled to say anything. Though what you said was better than what you first told me that you intended to say. It seemed quite inevitable that Jack's nomination would occur and that all that you and Lyndon said you would both have to eat—as you indeed have.

Poor Lyndon came off much worse, since he is now in the crate on the way to the county fair and destined to be a younger and more garrulous—if that is possible—Alben Barkley. It is possible that being a smart operator in the Senate is a special brand of smartness which doesn't carry over into the larger political field. Lyndon certainly behaved like a high school lad running for class president in 1956, and seemed to have retrograded by 1960. Jack and his team were the only "pros" in Los Angeles, so far as I could see.

The ticket seems to me about the best which under the circumstances—by which I mean Jack's determination to go all out for it and the absence of any opposition of comparable capacity and determination—the Party could put up. It will not raise great enthusiasm, but neither could any other ticket, and neither will Nixon on the other side. So far as a Kennedy administration is concerned, it would, I think, be better than what we have, than what Nixon would give; and I see no solid evidence on which to found a belief that Stu or Lyndon would do any better.

One current belief seems to me quite unfounded, that Lyndon as V.P. will continue to run the Senate and have great influence with Sam. I remember on the Hoover Commission urging on President Hoover that the V.P. should be selected and set up to be the Administration's agent on the Hill. The old man said, "It won't work. That is what I thought when I selected Charles Curtis to be my V.P. But I found the day after inauguration that no one, including his Senate colleagues, wanted to talk to No. 2."

Well, we're off to the races, after a little breather and a little more vulgarity and foolishness at Chicago. I hope that it is still true that the Lord looks benignly after children, drunks and the U.S.A. But he may think it about time that the last of the trio grew out of irresponsibility.

Our warmest greetings to Bess and you.

As ever,

To A. MAURICE LOVEMAN

William De Vane, whom DA defended, was Dean of Yale College.

July 19, 1960

Mr. A. Maurice Loveman
A. M. Loveman Lumber & Box Co.
1200 49th Avenue, North
Nashville 9, Tennessee

Dear Maurice:

Thank you for your note. I agree that the reunion was very good fun and share the hope that we all have the good luck essential to being on hand again for the 50th.

Mr. Sensing has taken Bill De Vane's remarks in quite the wrong way. Bill did not, as Mr. Sensing thought, attack free enterprise. He was attacking the complacency which led some people for over a century in England and this country to use the catchword as the excuse and justification for "voracious aggressiveness and ruthless competition" and for the defeat of child labor and hour and wage laws even for women. It is just this same blind indignation at any criticism of the *status quo* which has forced legal supervision of business practices from the Interstate Commerce Act of 1889 through the New Deal.

It is simply not true, as Mr. Sensing apparently believes, that the public interest is merely the sum of all the individual self-interests as seen from the point of view of the individuals, and particularly from the point of view of the most articulate and potent individuals in a society. There is a requirement, not always met, for persons who can and do take a larger view of the needs of the society as a whole than can be had by adding together the individual self-interests even when they are not mutually cancelling. If we do not all get a glimpse of this truth, the future will belong to Mr. Khrushchev's grandchildren, as he has prophesied.

I know Bill De Vane well, and do not know Mr. Sensing at all. Nevertheless, I will bet that in any meaningful sense of the word Bill is more deeply conservative than Mr. Sensing; that is, desirous of conserving those values essential to the freedom of the individual human being and to what we call Western civilization. As a sample of his mind and spirit, I enclose a speech of his, called "Yale Then and Now," which I feel sure you will find deeply moving.

Finally, as to your worry that Dean De Vane's speech will not help Yale in its campaign for capital funds, I would offer two consolations. First, it can only upset people when it is misunderstood, and this will not happen widely. Second, if it were necessary for Yale to believe and teach the view that our economic system has been as faultless as Mr. Sensing's political and spiritual attitude towards it implies, I should wonder seriously whether additional capital funds could accomplish any useful result.

With kindest regards.

Sincerely,

To **PHILIP HARING**

In this letter DA capsulized his view that foreign policy must be powered by high purpose and wise objectives, but not by what laymen call "a moral order."

August 9, 1960

Mr. Philip Haring
1145 North Cherry Street
Galesburg, Illinois

Dear Mr. Haring:

I'm glad that you "got started (in your letter of last May) and couldn't stop." My trouble is in getting started. In thinking about the world I feel the exasperated bafflement of trying to remember a dream. One almost has it only to find that it dissolves like mist.

You are right, of course, that military and economic power are capabilities which make action possible and qualify it. But you ask action for what? And answer "a new and moral world order to remedy unsatisfactory relationships of status, prestige, etc." But does this really clarify much? It seems to lead into Harry Luce's discussion of the need of national purpose, which pretty well demonstrated its own futility. In trying to find ideological tests for conduct, I wonder whether we don't take seriously as ends, what the communists regard and use as means to the end of power, the capability to impose one's will, to command, to dominate, which you regard as only a means to some more metaphysical end. So we whirl, our tail firmly grasped in our teeth.

The communists—the Sino-Soviet axis—want to dominate. We don't want to dominate; but we don't want them to either. We want a live-and-let-live situation in a world where order, progress, and quiet predominate. We are willing to put forth a good deal of effort and money, some of it downright altruistic, to get it. I could refer to our purpose more acceptably as the preservation of an environment of freedom and aid to other people to improve their lives materially and spiritually within that environment. But I suspect that your conception of a "moral order" is not met by this.

You want something more. But what? Have people in the mass anywhere at any time had as their aim the establishment of "a moral order"? I don't accept as an answer the eloquent and moving words of leaders urging their fellows on to action. My question goes to the motivation of the masses. I would think it more true that when "national purposes" or mass purposes have existed they have been hysterical manifestations of some fanatical, or other illusory or worse, human weakness. Islam as a political or military force, the revolutionary nationalism of France, Hitler, militant communism in Russia or China (or perhaps Cuba). Even the moral order of Christianity soon turned into the power structures of Western and Eastern orthodoxies.

Has this country ever had a national purpose, as such, much less a purpose to construct a moral order? There have been times when the rhythm of individual purposes led to the conquering of the continent and of those who stood in the way. Mr. Lincoln's purpose in 1861, as he expressed it, and half his fellow citizens accepted it, was to preserve the union and the future of a nation. This was politically desirable and wise, but not necessarily moral.

Individual purposes are a congeries, some moral, some instinctive and essential for preservation and reproduction, some esthetic, some intellectual, and some sordid and unqualifiedly bad. So are the purposes of 182 million individuals grouped in a society. In our common domestic life they all play a part; so do traditions like the impartiality and equal protection of law—not a controlling part, but, we hope, a growing part.

So when you tell me that to survive we must defend—and necessarily, therefore, create—a moral order, you seem to lay down an almost impossible requirement for survival.

Holmes used to say that the essence of the polywog was the wiggle. He could put it more elegantly: "Man is born to act. To act is to affirm the worth of an end; and to affirm the worth of an end is to create an ideal." This, of course, is pragmatism. But isn't there a good deal of sense in it? After man, through the discovery of fire, shelter, and clothing, began to create his own environment, he began to push it beyond his individual necessity.

What we want of the world, and try to make of a sizeable part of it, is an environment in which what we call western civilization can exist and prosper. Do we really care whether this is moral? It is, to us, pretty essential. To do it we need enough force to protect our environment and coerce those who try to subvert it. We also have to make that environment attractive to others within it, so that they would rather go along than buck it. It is important to "present" this so as to get as emotional an affirmation as possible. But this is the heart of the matter as I see it.

Your moral order bewilders me.

Yours,

To HARRY S TRUMAN

August 12, 1960

Dear Boss:

Your delightfully contrite letter has disarmed me wholly. To add to this, Alice and I read your letter just after looking at the *N.Y. Times* picture of you and Governor Abe [Ribicoff] under the caption "Truman Will Stump Coast to Coast for Kennedy." So I offered the thought that if the Lord is accurately quoted as having remarked "Vengeance is mine," He probably has a copyright on "I told you so," also. So I say no more. You have said it all, and said it with all your very good humor.

Now you are in for it. Just don't exhaust yourself through sheer remorse. Here is a thought which you might work in to get you into the merits of the Party as such. In the U.S. the registration is something like 60–40 in favor of the Democrats. When it comes to enlisting Americans of brains and character for all the multifarious tasks of democratic government, the Republicans proscribe all Democrats. This brings them down to 40% of available material—a minority to start with. Then they proscribed all Republicans who had worked for the Government under Democratic administrators [sic]. This brought them down to about 20% (the inexperienced fifth). You were old fashioned enough to believe that all Americans were needed and eligible for the great task which faces our country and you used them all. The Party will do this again. We don't have a means test in reverse, nor are we limited in our choices to big business executives who can only "afford" a year or two for public service—though that may be all that the public can afford of them.

Well, you see. This is known as the "high road." But it really is, you know. (You have to be ready to explain that Ike and Foster got by, even though they had worked for you, by getting out in time to denounce you.) All of this may make no sense but it could upset the calculations of the "truth squads" which the newspaper tells me will follow you around and read your preconvention statements about Kennedy. As for those they must have been made by another fellow of the same name.

I have a very depressed letter from Dirk Stikker. You remember him. He was the Dutch Foreign Minister from 1949–53, was their ambassador to London and is now the Dutchman on NATO. He says that the alliance—the only hope against Mr. K—is foundering for lack of U.S. leadership. Spaak tells him the next ten months will decide NATO's fate. In the absence of U.S. leadership de Gaulle, Macmillan and Adenauer each take their crack at some new idea which weakens the basic conception that it is Europe and North America which is needed to deal with the U.S.S.R. He urges that both candidates make strong statements that no plans for NATO can or should be made now but that immediately after Jan. 1961 the new president will confer with the NATO powers on an urgent and far reaching strengthening of the alliance.

I have some ideas as to what this should consist of, but now is no time for this sort of thought and, perhaps, ideas from me will not get very far at any time.

So far in 1960 Jack Kennedy seems to have handled himself very well. In his match with you, in his handling of Lyndon (who made quite a goat of himself), Adlai and the whole convention I find it hard to fault him. This is by no means the same thing as saying that he arouses enthusiasm. Neither candidate does that. If their joint appearances don't stir some interest, the campaign may turn out to be one of these pitchers' duels, where neither side gets a hit and the paying customers go to sleep. If enough of us stay awake we can still win—

Alice is 18 today.

Affectionately,

To A. WHITNEY GRISWOLD

DA was concerned about Griswold's delicate health and offered advice from the standpoint of one whose own health was none too good. DA's career as a writer was in full flower.

August 16, 1960

Dear Whit:

Many thanks for your note. I have had you much in my thoughts this summer hoping so much that you were getting some real rest this year at the Vineyard and not letting those fund raising blatherskites harass you with their interminal trivia. One of their documents is not trivia—your report on and explanation of the request for capital funds. This is very fine and greatly burnished since you showed me the early drafts. The illustrations, too, which we talked about, have come out just right.

Now for my mid-August advice—your last three or four weeks of the summer rest. In Brazil they say that "Brazil grows at night when the politicians sleep." In another sense Yale will grow if, and only if, you get a really recreative sleep in these months when you don't have to be turned up to the point of incandescence. So get a sense of duty about being lazy and unproductive.

We are staying here all summer and I find it very restful not to be going somewhere. My damned intestines, however, haven't gotten the word. They think that I am at Como eating Italian bread and drinking Suave, or at Torcello or Burano, poisoning them with octopus. Even that doesn't really bother me when I wake up and know that there isn't a damned thing to do.

Yet I am frightfully busy writing every morning and afternoon on a series of sketches from life, a short story, and revising a long and gloomy speech called "The nature of our times." Alice has her new studio and is no trouble—a picture frame once or twice a week keeps her as happy as can be—And my small granddaughter, Mary's Carol, is an exact reproduction of her mother, and lives only ten minutes away. We call on one another with mutual pleasure.

. . .

The world depresses me, but I pretend to believe that this is the era of the young men and that they are up to it. But I don't believe it, and chafe at being, as I definitely am, put out to pasture. One amusing interlude was my attempt to pursuade the honorable Harry Truman not to make a total fool of himself. I failed, but have had such delightfully abashed and contrite letters from him that it seems worthwhile. He ends "Don't give me up. I love your letters—and I love you, too." What can you do with a man like that.

Again, take it easy a while longer. We shall meet in about seven weeks and start in on an interesting year. In the meantime my love to Mary and to you.

Yours,

To THE WALLACE CARROLL FAMILY

Wallace Carroll, then Washington News Editor of The New York Times, *frequently sent DA amusing bits of doggerel. This response in kind by DA expressed his thanks for a visit and hope for another get together the following August.*

August 21, 1960

To Peggy and Wally, and Poesy and Pat
Go my love and my thanks. But what of the cat?
Pas de chat, pour moi. I am,
You've heard the phrase, a simple man.
All I ask are Carrolls, young
And younger still to sit among,
While talk slides in between martinis.
Potato, eggplant and zucchinis.
But not a vegetarian diet—
By no means that—for though a quiet
Man, I love to sink a tooth
As once in alien corn did Ruth—
But surely I have got this wrong
No gossip Ruth, like Susie Wong.
Better go back and straighten out
What this letter's all about.
It carries gratitude, affection,
And, by the way, in that connection,
A lively sense of favors yet
To come, when once again we set
Our course down wind Rehoboth-wards for fun
With Carrolls in August, sixty-one.

To **HARRY S TRUMAN**

DA complains here of the boring, war-of-maneuver character of the 1960 election campaign up to that point.

August 23, 1960

Dear Boss:
    Many thanks for your letters about the Bar dinner on Nov. 30. I accepted their invitation to get a chance to see you and Bess in Independence without the whole gang around which make Washington visits so hurried and hectic—except at P Street. So I shall get there perhaps the day before, or anyway early enough for a good visit with you.
    Do you get a funny sort of sense that, so far at least, there are no human candidates in this campaign? They seem improbable, like very life-like puppets, who, or which, are operated by most skillful technicians. Both are surrounded by clever people who dash off smart memoranda, but it is not all pulled together, on either side, by and into a man. The ideas are too contrived. No one believes a congeries so suited to his apparent "voter

need," as Madison Ave would put it. Even Bob Taft was heretical enough to be for government housing. These two are so perfectly suited to someone's idea of what they ought to be suited to that they bore the hell out of me.

This session of Congress seems to be bearing out a long held view of Alice's that Lyndon is not nearly as smart as he and a lot of his other admirers think.

Whew! What a lot of subversive stuff!

Affectionately,

To **WILMARTH S. LEWIS**

Mrs. Lewis was Jacqueline Kennedy's aunt by marriage; i.e., Mrs. Lewis' brother, Hugh Auchincloss, was Jacqueline Kennedy's stepfather. "Nin" was Mrs. John Ryan, a friend of Lewis and of the DAs at Newport, R.I., where Lewis was at this date.

Harewood
Sandy Spring, Maryland
August 28, 1960

Dear Lefty:

Hemmed in by lawyers, British, American, tall, short, bright and stupid—but all boring—I return to a hope which you and I temporarily abandoned a few years ago. To have Yale give Felix a degree. We decided not to push it because if some of our colleagues opposed it, we could never bear to see them ago [sic, again]. Now that consideration no longer has terrors for me. Most of them I shall not see anyway.

I should like to walk at my last commencement with Felix and am prepared to manhandle and mayhem (used as a verb, like implement) any slob who asks for it. I do not think that you need to join the fray except to maneuver one bit of skulduggery. I shall write you a letter making the proposal. If the Committee adopts the recommendation, fine. If trouble develops could you say that out of deference to me you suggest that the Committee express no view since I wish to make the proposal directly to the corporation. Or just withdraw the name and say nothing.

I should feel like a heel not to do this which is becoming more and more outrageously apparent. To hell with Fred Rodell and all his kind.

How is the step uncle-by-marriage of my candidate? One thing we can say for this campaign so far—only the fact that the year is divisible by four suggests that there is a campaign, or an issue of any sort or even a municipal election. It is quite possible that the whole country might just drift off into a sound sleep about November first—and wake up to find Coolidge

President. I know that it is all very critical and important, but somehow it just doesn't seem so.

Has the summer been better than your apprehensive forecast? I hope so. When you see Nin or the John Mason Browns, give them all severally our love.

I have another story in the *Reporter* about mid September and have started on a book of portrait sketches of people. Bevin is done. I am working on Schuman. There will be, perhaps, ten, with possibly a group one of "the old Court." It keeps me busy and is a sort of discipline.

Alice sends her love, as do I. A cheerful note from Whit suggests that he is profiting by a good rest. We hope that you are.

As ever,

To REUBEN HOLDEN

Ben Holden was Secretary of Yale University.

September 6, 1960

Mr. Reuben A. Holden
Secretary
Yale University
New Haven, Connecticut

Dear Ben:
Would you please do me the service of laying this letter before the Honorary Degrees Committee, temporarily without a chairman.

Gentlemen:
I present for your consideration for the honorary degree of Doctor of Laws, Mr. Justice Felix Frankfurter, Associate Justice of the Supreme Court of the United States.

I need not belabor Justice Frankfurter's eminence as that nearly unique figure in American life, "Scholar on the Bench," as his latest judicial biographer describes him (*Felix Frankfurter, Scholar on the Bench*, by Helen Shirley Thomas, Johns Hopkins Press, 1960). He is starting on his third decade on the Supreme Court. I doubt whether the influence that he has exerted as teacher and jurist on American public law over the past half century has been equalled by anyone, even the great Master himself, Mr. Justice Holmes.

This has, in part, been due to the fact that Justice Frankfurter has reveled in the give and take of oral and written battle. He believes with passion, not perhaps as much passion as he sometimes displays, but enough to be sure that vigor will attend the search for truth. So, quite naturally, Justice Frankfurter is what is called "a controversial figure." It happens that the same characteristic has been applied to me, perhaps for the same reason. At any rate, I have never seen reason to take offense at the term, particularly when one takes a look at the nature of the controversy and the controversialists.

In the present case, Professor Rodell of our Law School refers to Justice Frankfurter as "its (the Supreme Court's) most tragically wasted brilliant mind," while Judge Learned Hand regards him "as the most important single figure in our whole judicial system." You will note that both views employ superlatives. If anyone believes it useful to resolve the conflict, I, who think I know the most, or, perhaps, the more, important figures in our judicial system, will vote with Judge Hand.

Eminence, and scholarly eminence, on the highest bench, might be thought enough to warrant, at the age of seventy-eight, when character is well formed, that distinguished accolade, an honorary doctorate of laws from Yale. But I confess that to me it constitutes rather the lesser reason. The greater one is that Justice Frankfurter embodies to me all that I hope this University does, and forever will, stand for—the unquenchable energy and curiosity of the human mind, its restless searching, its stern and disciplined critical judgment, and finally its attachment to those principles of conduct and thought, those restraints founded in doubts of one's and others' infallibility upon which rests the freedom of the human mind and spirit.

In these qualities, I think, lie the answer to the puzzle which he has posed to the pundits. How is it that those "judgments and intuitions more subtle than any articulate major premise" which lie at the roots of the Anglo-Saxon law and institutions form the fabric of the mind of this Jewish immigrant boy from Vienna, who could not speak English until he was twelve.

These are the qualities and achievements which I ask Yale to honor in honoring Mr. Justice Frankfurter, for they epitomize the qualities and achievements of mind and spirit which it is, I hope, the purpose of Yale to instill and inspire in her sons.

Sincerely yours,

To ARCHIBALD MACLEISH

The references to "Mary" and to "Bill" are to Mary Acheson Bundy, DA's third child, and her husband, William P. Bundy. "Arthur S. Jr." is probably Arthur Schlesinger, Jr.

September 14, 1960

Dear Archie:

What a delightful letter to have from you. Alice and I are entranced with it and it has produced a vast amount of talk in this old house as the hurricane has been followed by wood fire weather. I agree that Durrell's novels are pretentious, though I had not thought of it until you said so. My analysis had been more blunt. I think they are a bore endless words which say nothing. . . .

I suppose blokes like us turn to the artist in letters to give us experiences which we have never had, but can dimly imagine, or to interpret for us experiences which we have had on the inevitably moving belt of life but have not apprehended. To me Durrell does neither. He opens nothing to me. And as for Justine, I was so damned bored with her I didn't care who slept with her, so long as it wasn't I. So much, perhaps too much, for him.

We are all, including Mary, still waiting for Mary's baby. Some one must have fouled up the abacus when no one was looking, for now all expectable dates have passed, and even Alice's witchcraft—picking Bill's birthday, for instance, has proved ineffective. I point out that any child as bright as one of Mary's and Bill's, being urged to enter this world at this time, would be pretty hard to coax down out of the high branches. All you would have to say to me would be "Lumumba" and I would take the freshman year over again. At any rate he, or she, won't show up—perhaps sitting out the election.

As for that, I don't think you really understand what is going on. Plainly the candidates are trying to bore the country into a coma by election day. What they are going to do then, I confess I do not understand. But that must be what the vast staffs of super-intellects are working out. For obviously they are not working out anything else.

This is one theory. The other is that both candidates are doing the best they can. I am told that Arthur S. Jr. feels that "he has been used" and left, that he would like to flounce back to Harvard, but that he has been given a half year's leave and hasn't a flounce left.

As you say, the Republic is in a hell of a fix. But it has been, as Mr. Lincoln would say, for just under half a score of years and has no place to go but up. The best campaign cheer I know is in the current gag, "Anyway, they can't elect *both* of them."

I am going to be in New Haven on October 7th and Alice and I are to be with Lefty on October 8th and 9th. Is Lefty going to be in Farmington on the 7th? Why don't you and Ada stay over?

Felix is well, delighted with the success of his book, and happy to have Oliver and now Venetia in this country.

Love to Ada.

To **JAMES BONBRIGHT**

Bonbright was the American Ambassador to Sweden at the time. The Swede referred to is Dag Hammarskjold, Secretary General of the United Nations.

October 5, 1960

The Honorable James Bonbright
American Ambassador
Stockholm, Sweden

Dear Jamie:

Thank you very much for reminding me of the paper that I was going to send you. I am ashamed to say that it slipped my mind—in fact to the extent that I am not sure which of two papers I was working on at the time was the one I mentioned. I hope to make amends by mailing both to you today.

The performance in New York is incredible. Nothing could more perfectly vindicate the judgment of those of us who strongly objected to the United Nations being in New York. It was the three master minds of Ed Stettinius, Nelson Rockefeller, and Warren Austin that put it there. Can you imagine how much more amusing history would be if Attila had been able to appear with immunity in Rome and tell off the ruling Caesar, or if Napoleon could have taken a packet across the channel and told the younger Pitt and the Prince Regent and perhaps the Iron Duke himself how he was going to bury them?

I saw Harold Macmillan last Saturday afternoon, who told me that even his experience in Moscow had not prepared him for the violent effrontery of K's performances at the United Nations. I did not say it to him, but I believe that Mr. K could not have picked a more useful man to insult than the Honorable Harold himself. It really shook him out of the pipe dream, which he has found so useful for political purposes in England. I did observe to him that when the United States, the British Commonwealth, and NATO found themselves fortunate to be saved by a Swede, the world had come to a pretty pass.

To **A. WHITNEY GRISWOLD**

DA had the capacity to regard his bouts with internal medicine with humor, if not detachment. He found ready sympathy from Griswold.

October 17, 1960

Dear Whit:

The prospecting team working from north to south finished today. The exploration from the south will be done next Friday. No report has been made by the grim-faced foreman as yet, but the terrain gives some evidence of having been thoroughly worked over.

Thank you for your solicitude which I know comes from the soundest foundation—how shall I put it? from the same emotion remembered in tranquility.

I speak to the Episcopal Theological Seminary on politics tomorrow—which is I suppose between heaven and hell.

Affectionately,

To **HARRY S TRUMAN**

November 22, 1960

Dear Boss:

Many thanks for your post election letter which came this morning. First a word or two about plans for our meeting in Kansas City. I am planning, if you approve, to stay over on Thursday, December 1st until the 4 o'clock through flight to Washington, to have some quiet time with you. The plane from here on Nov. 30th will not get in until after lunch—1:54 PM—and WDAF wants me to record a television interview in the afternoon. So there won't be much peace on Wednesday.

If you are free on Thursday we might meet at your convenience, say at the Library, and from there on do what you wish. If I could see the top Boss it would be a joy for me.

Alice is not coming as she did something to a muscle or nerve in her right leg which has been painful and incapacitating, though now yielding to heat and rest. She will send her messages and get her report through me.

This election is so unbelievably close that I wonder whether we really know the result yet. If the southern conspiracy should flower, and enough delegates—I mean electors—withhold their votes to prevent a majority of the total number, what then? Some electors are pledged by state law and some are not. Can they be ordered by mandamus to vote? To vote for the one to whom they are pledged? Suppose they violate the order and either refuse to vote, or vote for Lyndon. What then? I suppose that the court could put them in jail for contempt, but it can't vote for them. If it invalidates the votes for Lyndon the election goes to the House and Nixon has a majority of states with one vote each. Or perhaps if Lyndon were on the slate which went to the House he might get a majority should the Kennedy states switch to him.

It is all very speculative, but most interesting.

Do you really care about Jack's being a Catholic? I never have. It hasn't bothered me about de Gaulle or Adenauer or Schuman or DeGasperi, so why Kennedy? Furthermore I don't think he's a very good Catholic. But a Jehovah's Witness would bother me badly. The whole public health service would go to hell over night.

Another question. You are quoted as saying that you won't worry about the farmers anymore because they voted for Nixon. But did they. A lot of people in the farm states voted Democratic. What about them? Guilt by association?

That ought to stir up the animal.

Affectionately,

To DIRK U. STIKKER

Dirk Stikker was former Dutch Foreign Minister and representative of the Netherlands to NATO.

December 27, 1960

The Honorable Dirk U. Stikker
Palais de l'O.T.A.N.
Paris, France

Dear Dirk:

Your most interesting letter of December 19 and its enclosure have left me with gloomy thoughts. Almost everywhere the prospect is displeasing. In this hemisphere our relations with Canada are deteriorating seriously. And to the south of us from Mexico to Argentina there is a restlessness which has our best friends in Latin America gravely worried. From Japan and Laos, through India and Africa, to General de Gaulle and the British Labor Party, both in crisis, there is trouble everywhere. What you tell me about NATO and Spaak does not surprise me, but it does depress me.

. . .

Kennedy I have never known well, though I have known him over quite a long time. We had talked over the telephone during and after the campaign, but had not met in person for about a year. I was impressed by his air of calmness, of authority, of seriousness, and of modesty. He came to call on me at home to get my views and listened as though he were considering carefully what I said. We talked together for an hour and a half. He was quite willing to concede his lack of knowledge and experience in fields where this existed. He was eager to learn. I had a feeling he would be decisive.

He had made up his mind, so I was told by Bob Lovett, that in his judgment the opposition to appointing me Secretary of State would be considerable and he had quite early determined not to consider it further, if he had ever considered it at all. At the end of our talk he asked whether there was any position which I should like to have. I said that there was not. He then mentioned the NATO post. I said that I thought policies were more important than posts and that I could be of more help to him as an adviser and consultant than I could 3000 miles away talking about ideas which might or might not be the policies of the United States government. Dean Rusk raised the same question with me, and I gave him the same answer.

I quite agree that it is of the greatest importance that the United States should send a man of reputation and authority within the administration to NATO, and I think that this will be done, but I think that it is even more important that this administration should with the utmost speed possible develop a military strategy for the defense of the center of the free world and a political policy toward Europe and the Soviet Union which will complement it to fill the complete void which now exists.

. . .

But is it your view that to devise "a multi-lateral European nuclear weapons system" goes beyond the political purpose for which it has been proposed and provides an adequate military strategy for the defense and strengthening of NATO? I should think not. We seem to have gotten to the point where the best efforts of all the NATO partners in the nuclear field are unlikely to produce a counter weapon nuclear capability. Hence the reluctance on both sides to use strategic nuclear weapons will grow, and, without some other capability, the appeal of NATO will continue to decline. Here, so it seems to me, lies the problem for military and political inventiveness in the new administration.

I should like to see it solved along two lines: (1) within NATO to devise military strategy and capability with concurrent NATO political institutions to make these effective; (2) outside of NATO, and far broader, another *political* development involving Western Europe and North America in the interest of greatly increased production for three purposes—(a) the increasing needs of our increasing populations, (b) the needs of adequate defense, conventional as well as nuclear, and (c) the provision of export capital where it can be wisely used in undeveloped countries. This cannot, in my opinion, be done on a purely economic basis. Certainly, it cannot be done on that basis in the U.S.A. Here the Hull approach is dead. This country will move in a protectionist and economic isolation direction unless it gets some new conception of a national destiny which links us with the Atlantic community.

A purely economic approach to the problem of the six and the seven requires a low external tariff of the six in order not to penalize the seven. This, in turn, requires a lowering of U.S. tariffs. Every day opposition to such a policy is mounting, because the invasion of the South by industry, particularly the textile industry, has subverted the last stronghold of liberal trade policy. Also Labor, which twenty years ago was on net balance for liberal policies, is now turning against them as American capital goes to Europe to build plants which Labor believes (a) will supply markets once supplied by American exports, and (b) will undersell U.S. goods in this country. Hence the need for policies which will increase production for purposes which are in the common interest of the alliance and will not raise political opposition.

So we need new conceptions, military, political, and economic to meet the new developments of the sixties. The American people will respond to vigorous and sensible leadership. But it must be based on a broad grasp of new realities, realities based on Russian possession of nuclear weapons and a growing economic potential. Am I wrong in thinking that the Norstad proposal stems more from the effort—a necessary one, I agree—to prevent de Gaulle from doing something very foolish, rather than from a more long range military or political strategic plan?

Keep me on the right path.

With warmest greetings to Pauline and to you. We must see you both in 1961.

Sincerely,

To **WILMARTH S. LEWIS**

Harewood
Sandy Spring, Maryland
[undated]

Dear Lefty:

You have now infected me with your veneration for collections and libraries, with what may be substantial results. I may have told you of having been shown last October by Count Gustiniani his family library of the manuscripts and accounts of this Venetian family's trading and seafaring business covering almost a thousand years.

It has hardly been looked at. He cannot afford to have the documents preserved, catalogued and microfilmed. I asked him whether he would permit this to be done under his control by accredited American scholars financed by one of our foundations. He said he would if I would vouch for the people.

After many months Dean Rusk of the Rockefeller says he believes the funds can be provided. But what is the next step? I can handle the Count but who can do the job?

The technicians are not difficult. But the job needs scholars in Italian history and in economic history who understand the importance of what you have written about as the things so taken for granted in any age that no one mentions them.

Think of having the history of a business since not long after the rise of Islam! (If I am correctly informed.) Who can be trusted to find out?

Yours,

To LADY PAMELA BERRY

Daughter of F. E. Smith, 1st Earl of Birkenhead, and wife of the Honorable W. Michael Berry, editor-in-chief of The Daily Telegraph, *Lady Pamela was a keen observer and commentator on matters of politics.*

February 7, 1961

Dear Pamela:

Your gay letter and Christmas card of Mr. Franklin's works have cheered me in a period of most depressing winter. The ice age is returning, and I am in favor of giving this country back to the Indians and moving in with the Brazilians. They have lots of room and any climate you like. Have you ever seen Mr. Franklin's bread and butter letter to the English hostess who had had him in the country over Christmas and whose young daughter he has escorted back to school in London in the post chaise? He reports their conversation which centered on selecting husbands for her six sisters. I shall get the Yale Press to send you the volume of the cream of his correspondence which they brought out in celebration of his 200th birthday.

I have sent over to Hamish Hamilton two revised copies of the book, one for Michael, in which all of the thousands of errors are corrected and possible libel suits eliminated. It has a new last chapter on Vienna in 1952 and State visits in general, which seems to me one of the best. In the course of it Alice loses her petticoat at a state dinner in the Ballhausplatz with the utmost sang froid (She doesn't yet know that this is in the book. I may soon be a fugitive from justice—hers). If the *Sunday Telegraph* wants a third instalment this might be the one.

. . .

Please come over and seek serials. How would you like one by Jacqueline on "Life Among the Kennedys," or one by Ike called "Fore!" Your question about our top hats must have some good answer but I would doubt that it has a basis in foxhunting. We shoot one another while in search of deer and call that hunting. So far we have never shot the right people.

Here is a suggestion for a serial. The magazine called "Living History" is reprinting from the original documents *Harper's Weekly* for 1861. The type is dreadful and it should be reset but the drawings are good. A series chosen say from Lincoln's inaugural, the attack on Fort Sumter and perhaps the first battle of Manassas might be pretty good for 1961. Next year you could have a series on the Peninsular campaign before Richmond. 1963 would give you Gettysburg and Grant's battles on the Mississippi. 1964 "From Atlanta to the Sea." 1965 Appomattox and the assassination of Lincoln. Do you want to see a sample copy? I get a copy each week for the week just one hundred years ago.

Alice has been in the hospital having a bone removed from a foot—incapacitating but not serious. She comes home on Thursday, I hope, after two weeks.

Probably Hamilton will need prodding to give up your copy of the revised manuscript. When he does so you are clearly entitled to the older one.

We shall try to be in Europe this year. I have an argument at the Hague in April. But we should come again later. Felix is bouncing and adds his warmest greetings to ours.

Yours,

To **WILLIAM TYLER**

This letter marks the beginning of DA's renewed involvement in shaping U.S. policy toward NATO. Both Presidents Kennedy and Johnson called upon him for extended periods of work in the State Department in an effort to deal with problems in the European alliance created by passage of time and the policy of de Gaulle to withdraw from multilateral participation.

February 16, 1961

The Honorable William Tyler
American Embassy
Box 700, APO 80
c/o P.M. New York

Dear Bill:

Thank you for your February 10 letter. I am answering it not because I think that politeness requires it, but because I have something to say.

Your criticism of my rationalization of not going to NATO is probably correct. But there is still one flaw in your brief, contained in the sentence, "but I feel you underestimate the extent to which your going to Paris would have convinced our Allies that the U.S. meant business (otherwise you would not have accepted the job)." This indeed was one of the troubles. I did not underestimate the effect of my going to NATO. What I doubted was the honesty of the impression given. We will not know until I have completed my present exercise and the government as a whole has or has not accepted it whether the United States does mean business. I was asked to accept when the evidence on this point seemed to indicate that it did not.

The main purpose of my writing, however, was to say that I have talked with Foy Kohler about the importance of getting word to the Chancellor about a visit and find that he quite agrees and is at work on the matter. I also spoke to Dean Rusk about it.

Secondly, I have spoken to Foy about you and the importance of a good post for you. Here again he purports to agree and here again I shall speak to the Secretary. I think that Dave Bruce has already done so.

I find once again that, in being back in this building, dealing with intractable problems, the intractability appears to increase and that the more sweeping approaches of private life, so gratifying to Walter Lippmann, are really not very impressive.

Alice is rapidly getting about again after having had a bone removed from a foot. We are having our first dinner out together at the Averell Harrimans the end of this week.

Our most affectionate greetings to Betsy and you.

As ever,

To PRESIDENT JOHN F. KENNEDY

DA believed that the transition from colonial rule to independence in Africa was difficult enough without the United States harassing the colonial powers and whipping up resentment. President Kennedy, as Senator, had taken a public position in favor of Algerian independence and critical of the resistance of the French government. F.L.N. is the abbreviation for the French name of the Algerian National Liberation Front.

March 19, 1961

Dear Mr. President:

The enclosed *N.Y. Times* report of a statement by the U.S. mission to the U.N. may be an accurate description of the brief conversation before our meeting on Wednesday last between you and Dean Rusk regarding the telegram which he had previously shown to me. I do not know because I was not a participant in it; but I doubt it. I also hope that it is inaccurate, and since the statement has already produced mischief may I add a further word to what I said on Wednesday.

The point of impact of the vote last week—and more importantly of the statement, with its ominous note of warning for the future—was not primarily upon the Portuguese or the Angola crisis. The last paragraph of the enclosed dispatch, recent editorials in the *N.Y. Times* and the *Washington Post,* as well as the African reaction, give the vote and statement a far wider significance. Perhaps its most important impact is on a negotiation which everyone has hailed as very probably "the last best hope" for sanity in Africa, and certainly as one of utmost delicacy.

Even if General de Gaulle and the F.L.N. Algerian leaders did not each have explosive elements with which to deal, their difficulties would be enormous—the Sahara, the colons, bases, property interests, the civil service, etc. The General knows that the hour of independence has struck. He must be permitted to accept the inevitable without a humiliation which might well be impossible for him or which might destroy the regime and throw France into chaos. The stakes are enormous. What is needed now is that the F.L.N. shall be responsible and, if possible, even generous in victory. It does not need inciting. It needs sobering.

Indeed, throughout Africa the great necessity is not to push more peoples faster toward an independence which they are no more able to handle than are the Congolese. Independence for all these people is no longer an issue of any reality. The great and crucial problem is to prepare them with far more than deliberate speed to deal with their inevitable future.

Every statesman, soldier, and lawyer knows that the road to disaster lies in fighting on ground of some one else's choosing. One of the greatest traps in the U.N. is to allow small countries to maneuver responsible powers into voting on every conceivable issue. We are great enough not to do this. We can refuse to vote on alleged issues which do not advance solutions and our very greatness and responsibility requires us to look at every situation in the light of the whole. This is the "principle" involved in determining how we should vote or whether we should vote, and what we should say at the U.N. It is not some formulation on human liberty, about which we can nonetheless continue to take a favorable view.

Most respectfully yours,

To **HARRY S TRUMAN**

The "Cuban adventure" refers to the Bay of Pigs.

May 3, 1961

Dear Boss:

I am home just in time to thank you for your birthday note and to write you one wishing you all good things for this coming year and many to follow. I have seen some recent photographs of you looking sassy and full of fight.

Our trip to Europe was interesting, hard work and fun, all mixed together. The end of it, in which first our government and then de Gaulle's fell apart had its grim aspect. Why we ever engaged in this asinine Cuban adventure, I cannot imagine. Before I left it was mentioned to me and I told my informants how you and I had turned down similar suggestions for Iran and Guatemala and why. I thought that this Cuban idea had been put aside, as it should have been. It gave Europe as bad a turn as the U2. The direction of this government seems surprisingly weak. So far as I can make out the mere inertia of the Eisenhower plan carried it to execution. All that the present administration did was to take out of it those elements of strength essential to its success.

Brains are no substitute for judgment. Kennedy has, abroad at least, lost a very large part of the almost fanatical admiration which his youth and good looks had inspired.

Washington is a depressed town. The morale in the State Department has about struck bottom.

Nevertheless, I say again, "Many, many happy returns of your birthday."

As ever,

P.S. An inscribed copy of my book goes to you to-day.

To **WILMARTH S. LEWIS**

DA had recently retired from the Yale Corporation after twenty-five years of service.

Covington & Burling
Union Trust Building
Washington 5, D.C.
June 6, 1961

Dear Lefty:

. . .

Jackie outshines the Empress Theodosia, which proves that some good girls finish first.

Yours,

To **WILMARTH S. LEWIS**

June 30, 1961

Dear Lefty:

Thank you for missing us. We missed being there very much where so many of our favorite people were gathered. Some day I must tell you, "with expression," Jean Monnet's description of the slow dawning upon him that far from being a charming dilettante you were a "pro" of formidable proportions, running a scholarly operation which challenged even his lively imagination. "It is very impressive," he kept insisting. "That Lewis is a remarkable man. He is a great scholar. And he is an organizer, too. That evening was the high point of my trip to America." So you eclipsed even Yale herself. It was very good for [him]. He still harbors notions of Gallic superiority.

Thank you, too, for saying that you will miss me on the second Saturdays of most months. Of course, I shall miss you and Whit more than I can say. For a while the counterbalancing value will be release from the attempt to travel between two points which God intended to keep forever separate. But memories of weariness will pass, and homesickness will remain.

We should love to see you this summer at Newport, but when—and even whether—can not be clear just now. I completed yesterday the first phase of a task for JFK. The second now begins and my part in it is not determined. If it is light you and I will plan at once. If not, and if it should take me abroad, we shall have to wait a while.

Alice sends her love.

As ever,

To **HARRY S TRUMAN**

July 14, 1961

Dear Boss:

This, as you say, is a worrying situation. I find to my surprise a weakness in decision at the top—all but Bob McNamara who impresses me as first class. The decisions are incredibly hard, but they don't, like Bourbon, improve with aging.

There is also a preoccupation here with our "image." This is a terrible weakness. It makes one look at oneself instead of at the problem. How will I look fielding this hot line drive to shortstop? This is a good way to miss the ball altogether. I am amazed looking back on how free you were from this. I don't remember a case when you stopped to think of the effect on your fortunes—or the party's, for that matter—of a decision in foreign policy. Perhaps you went too far that way, but I don't think so. Our government is so incredibly difficult to operate that to survive in the modern world it needs the most vigorous leadership.

I will say for Kennedy that getting any good, clear work out of the present Joint Chiefs is next to impossible. But McNamara and General Taylor can help him mightily; and, as Holmes said, every day we must make decisions on imperfect knowledge.

The great point is that we ought to be acting now to bring home to Khrushchev that we are in deadly earnest about Berlin, which is only a symbol for our world position. This is what Khrushchev has under attack.

Affectionately,

To **LADY PAMELA BERRY**

*The Khrushchev reference is to Kennedy's June meeting with Khrushchev in Vienna. The ultrasecret proposal to Tom Dewey was the offer of
appointment as Ambassador to the United Kingdom. Truman had defeated
Dewey in the 1948 election and he did not want to embarrass him if he preferred not to be considered for the post. "Harold" is Harold Macmillan,
Prime Minister of Great Britain.*

[undated]

Dear Pamela:

The epidemic of security consciousness—e.g., Harold's threat to put
the press on a war footing—has carried across the Atlantic. Our top man
has been having a seizure, too. A paper of mine which put up to him for decision some very mean choices was deemed so secret that for a time not
even those charged with carrying out the decisions were given a copy, and,
then, only expurgated ones. Of course, this town is the worst place in the
world for leaks, and it is a curious fact that many of them come right out of
the White House. In fact, while JFK was giving us his lecture on security he
told us that newspaper men had even seen copies of his report of his talks
with Mr. K. This did not come as a surprise to me since one of them, a
neighbor of mine, told me that, over the weekend, JFK had read the best
parts to him and a colleague.

Mr. Truman once wanted to make an ultra secret proposal to
Tom Dewey. I offered to do it (being then Secretary). Mr. T said that it
couldn't be kept secret. I bet him that it could, provided he told no one in
the White House. He promised and to engage his sense of honor we bet
$20 that no report would come out. I won. Someday I must write the story
—but after a few more years have rolled by. Tom and I had code names. I
flew to N.Y. in an old bomber. Borrowed a friend's car, with an old-fashioned
leather top with no side windows, and a most discreet chauffeur, not telling
him the purpose. Tom and I met in the house of a friend of his which was
closed for the summer, guarded by state troopers, had our talk, and I was
in the office the next morning with no absence from Washington ever
suspected.

So it can be done. Again, when I became Secretary, Mr. Truman and I
made the arrangement on Nov. 22, 1948. It was announced on Jan. 7, 1949
(Gen. Marshall was ill and Mr. T did not want him disturbed about it). In
the meantime not a whisper was made and I wasn't even mentioned in the
speculative columns. When I went to Blair House (the White House was
being rebuilt) it was to consult the President as Vice Chairman of the
Hoover Commission.

As a result of these operations the President and I got an opinion of our capacity to keep secrets which was not always justified.

What a long digression that was!

Having been pretty much entangled with the new frontier and having presented more plans and proposals than they (or it or he) have been able to, or cared to, act on, we have decided to leave Washington in its Potomac miasma for a time and go off to Martha's Vineyard. Our girls will be there together for the latter part of August and some close friends including the President of Yale, Whit Griswold. We shall put the length of the island between the girls and ourselves—to give them a chance for liberty—and give ourselves up to swimming, gossip and moderate drinking. But no effort and no Berlin. Perhaps in the autumn we shall go to Europe again. I take it that once again since Caesar's time, England may—but very cautiously—be considered as included within the generic word, Europe. The Chancellor wants me to play bocca with, and after talking with Pereira here, I may have a look in on Lisbon.

. . .

Yours,

To FELIX FRANKFURTER

August 16, 1961

Dear Felix:

Many thanks for your note. I am sending this reply to Washington because my recollection is that you were to be gone a month, now about over. So you must be back in the heat from which we have just escaped to this pleasant island endowed with Jane, Mary, Bill and the children, as well as the Griswolds. I hope you have come home freshened in body and spirit, both of you.

Your question of who is at the wheel of the ship of state is a complicated one—or rather the answer is a complicated one. It often looks as though the answer should be, No one. But that would be misleading because the old ship has the very latest devices aboard her. She can be, and often is, steered by remote control, and, not infrequently, from several control spots at the same time. Adlai, of course, has a control wheel in New York which apparently he can detach and plug in from Paris, or some other spot. There are several around the White House which are not locked up at night, so that Caroline or some of the other children around there often play with them. Then, of course, Dean Rusk has one in the State Dept. But he hasn't learned to work it very well and when he asks his quartermasters for help, one will be porting the helm while another is trying to put it to starboard.

They often compromise by giving it a good spin one way, followed by another one the other way. This dodges torpedoes if there are any, but when there aren't it confuses the hell out of the crew and the rest of the shipping.

This, as you see, is the sort of talk which the Administration does not think at all funny.

. . .

Yours,

To **EELCO VAN KLEFFENS**

Eelco van Kleffens was the Netherlands' Ambassador to the United States from 1947–1950 and Chief Representative in the United Kingdom of the European Coal and Steel Community at the time of this letter.

September 6, 1961

The Honorable Eelco Van Kleffens
20b, Kensington Palace Gardens
London W.8, England

Dear Eelco:

Your compatriot's letter is most interesting and wise. I too have been an advocate of a policy designed to let us all live through the next twenty years, without prejudice even though without solutions. In order to keep ourselves from being hopelessly prejudiced in the process of gaining time (we could gain it, for instance, by giving in to the Russians at every turn) we have to act in a vigorous, as well as intelligent, way. Here is where the rub comes.

My hero, Mr. Justice Holmes, said "General principles do not decide concrete cases." Granting, as I do, the truth of all that your correspondent says, it gives us an attitude towards our problems—albeit a good one—and not much of an aid to, say, the problems Mr. K poses about Berlin. We can, of course, let him have his way. I take it that Lippmann, Stevenson, et al., who say that "there is no alternative to negotiation" on Berlin mean to let him have it. The negotiation would provide some decent covering for the nakedness of the submission.

In fact, there is an alternative to negotiation. That alternative is to use force to maintain our position. Its use might lead to a change in Mr. K's position. It might not. If not, it would create a risk of nuclear war.

Does your correspondent's principle help us to decide whether or not to accept the risk, and how to act toward Mr. K?

Mr. K is apparently ready to accept some risk of nuclear war, although, generally speaking he, too, wants to gain time which he thinks is on his side. Perhaps, if he found that we were ready to accept more risk than he was, he might adjust his position. Then we could go on gaining time without prejudice to the vital interests of free societies.

If Mr. K would only accept your correspondent's principle of gaining time by running no risks at all in the effort to speed things up, we should all be able to relax more and see whether Marxism is as dynamic as Mr. K says it is. The trouble is that he doesn't believe all that he says. Time is against him in East Germany if he lets things go on as they were going. So he doesn't want time; he wants decisive and definitive action.

It is true that Rome was not built in a day; but it is also true that it was burned in a night. I am all for looking at the long run, even though in the long run we shall all be dead. I am also all for giving the next century a chance. But these yearnings are of mighty little help in deciding today's problems in a bitterly divided and dangerous world.

Finally, I don't think it fair to say that "*most of the time*" American policy is the pursuit of the impossible. We often do things from rather mushy and romantic (I hate the word idealistic) reasons; but, if we have been pursuing the impossible, we have accomplished a lot of it since, say, 1941. If you add that our problems seem to have been increased thereby, I should only question the "thereby."

Send me some more thoughts. I am grateful for distraction from the immediate.

Warmest greetings.

As ever,

To EDWARD B. BURLING

September 20, 1961

Edward B. Burling, Esq.
Windsor, Vermont

Dear Ned:

When you spoke to me about Learned Hand, I knew that he had a grave turn for the worse but did not realize that the end was so near. I have written Mrs. Hand, but as no one knows better than you, it was not easy. The Judge was too complicated and special a person for the usual panegyric of the obituary.

Paul Nitze has, as you say, come to the fore and rightly so. He is a very able person and one with whom I find myself in agreement about 99 per cent of the time. The speech of his, excerpts of which appeared in the *Post* not long ago, was a good one. I wish I felt that his advice and mine was making a little more impression than I think it is.

I have just come back from a few days in San Francisco where I carried on fund-raising activities on behalf of Yale. Have you been there lately? It seems to me one of the most delightful cities in the United States. It is unusual too. A combination of its wealth and a more cosmopolitan and sophisticated atmosphere than exists in most American communities has made it quite unique. Did I ever tell you that when you offered me a job forty years ago, Alice and I had about decided to go to San Francisco to practice law? Here is something for you to speculate about. What would have happened if we had not known Norman Hapgood, who told you about a young lawyer whom you might hire for the Norwegian case?

Alice sends her love.

Sincerely yours,

To JANE (ACHESON) BROWN

A thank-you note for a Christmas present, as DA was about to commence a trip to Cambodia and the Browns about to cruise the Bahamas by sailboat.

2805 P Street
December 25, 1961

Dearest Jane:

The inside of your package entirely lived up to the anticipation which, as I wrote you, its outside evoked. What an engaging and delightful weather vane it is, cock and all! Did you invent it, or did some one unknown to me have the intriguing idea of our rooster always facing the breeze to catch that ill wind that blows no good. And I don't mean Adlai, either.

To put it up will, I see, require some skill. The north end of the studio where the ground rises suggests itself as avoiding perilous heights, but the nearby chimney may give the wind a deceptive twist if it comes from the north east. On the south end is a wasp's nest, a real hazard.

Then there is 1961's real gift to the farm—a brand new bath room on the guest house, taller, grander by far, than the old chicken house which preceded it. But your lovely weather vane should not surmount a bathroom; and who would look there for any but an ill wind.

No, I think the studio is clearly the right choice, and the north end at that, so that it is the first sight on coming through the gate. But, perhaps, before a final decision we shall ask Prince Sihanouk's advice for he is an artist—so our briefing paper says—or that of the Princess Monique, a charming lady (says the same source) even though only a commoner and wife of the second rank; or Princess Soraya his favorite daughter, oddly enough by his aunt, recently engaged to a young brother of his mother, who (i.e., the brother) was trained as a jet pilot in the U.S. All should be able to contribute to the solution of a problem simple beside the complexity of their relationships.

At this point your telephone call came through and we decided the question.

Be careful this winter in your explorations and don't take unnecessary risks.

My love to you and to Dudley as we go off to the other side of this uneasy globe.

Devotedly,

To JOHN B. DENAULT

Mr. DeNault had somehow formed the belief that DA was connected with the U.S. government's policy in the Congo.

December 29, 1961

Mr. John B. DeNault
10319 Lorenzo Drive
Los Angeles 64, California

Dear Mr. DeNault:

Whoever told you that your letter of December 14th addressed to the President "should more rightfully have been addressed" to me had a unique capacity for error. I had no more to do with the United Nations or United States policy in Katanga than you did. I have no position in the State Department. And, when you say that "not a solitary soul understands . . . you (i.e., myself) in the Katanga incident," I cannot see how you or any of the other souls *could* "understand" my views, about which you and they are uninformed.

Very truly yours,

To BARBARA EVANS

Barbara Evans was DA's long-time secretary. DA had been asked to serve as legal counsel to the government of Cambodia in its dispute with Thailand over possession of a temple near the frontier. This letter and several that follow were written during a stay in Cambodia in connection with that case.

Hotel Miramar
Hong Kong
January 14, 1962

Dear Barbara:

. . .

How right you were to give us two days in Japan—no more, no less. Any more would have killed us; any less would have deeply offended the Japanese. Just how I became a Japanese national hero I do not know, but there is no doubt about the fact. Our reception included the Embassy and the Foreign Office and went on from there. My old friend Takeuchi with whom I signed agreements and reestablished a Japanese diplomatic agency after the war (he is now Vice Minister of F.A.) became our constant companion and guide. The Foreign Minister had a Japanese style luncheon for us in a famous restaurant, after which I began nursing on my bottle of paregoric. Yoshida, with his charming daughter, Mrs. Aso, and Ikeda and wife as co hosts had a dinner (half western half Japanese to Yoshida's disgust). The Emperor and Empress gave us an audience at the Palace. The Empress is a cosy, chatty, smiley lady who kept up such a chatter with Alice, or vice versa, that the men's talk proceeded as in a boiler factory, to which was added the difficulty that the Emperor was inaudible and his interpreter only barely audible under the best of circumstances. He talked chiefly about his gratitude to me and about our trip to Cambodia and Prince Sihanouk's unpredictability.

After some time at this, we switched conversational partners and I got the Empress quite giggling on some foolishness or other. Just as I was wondering how we were going to break up (the Grand Chamberlain had suggested that it would be all very informal) and after the Emperor had made several ending up type of remarks ("Good luck on your journey," etc.) Alice took over management of the situation, got up, and said goodbye. All the rest of us were a bit dazed by this development; and I had to get an FF grip on her arm to prevent a break for freedom before their majesties and their entourage withdrew while we bowed in true western style, not with hands on knees, Japanese style. Whether this was a faux pas or not, Takeuchi said the chances were that everyone was relieved by direct and vigorous action.

On our first day Takeuchi in a cloud of secretaries and security officers took us up to Nikko in a snow storm. A special car was allocated to the party, as well as the President of the railroad, a Mr. Nezu, a collector of ancient scrolls and bronze and porcelain as we later discovered. After a drive in snow and icy air to the famous waterfall, it all began to come back to me. Particularly the Kanaya Hotel where we went to lunch. I told Mr. Kanaya, who is the eleventh generation of his family to run a hotel on that spot, that I was sure that I had stayed with his father in July 1915. He got out the old register and there we were all six of us signed in in Turnie Morse's unmistakable hand.

The next day Mr. Nezu took us through his private museum which would make the Freer green with envy, and then put on a performance of the Japanese tea ceremony, all very slow and solemn with a chief vestal and ministering acolytes. I was threatened with hysterics when it occurred to me that my father would have been outraged at it as a most blasphemous Japanese parody of the communion service.

We are leaving Hong Kong in a few hours for Phnom Penh. It is as fantastically beautiful as Mary said it was and as teeming with life. The view from the Consul General's terrace on top of the mountain across the water to the communist islands is quite breath taking. I shall write about it later.

Perhaps you would run off a few copies of this for MAB, JAB, & DCA. EBB & FF might like to keep up with us too. Your arrangements have been fine.

Yours,

To BARBARA EVANS

Cambodia
January 17, 1962

Dear Barbara:

We are on the plane to Angkor and before my memory fades I want to jot down some notes of a memorable morning. Last night the Prince invited us to attend his "audience populaire" to-day in the Pagoda de Danse where we had seen the Royal Ballet after his dinner party. The Pagoda is in the Palace grounds, an open-sided building with columns supporting an ornate roof, the floor raised a dozen or so steps above the ground. To-day the rugs and party chairs were gone, the tiled floor bare except for a small rug in front of the stage on which was a plain wooden table and an office chair. On the table was only a bowl of roses. In the back of the Pagoda were rows of wooden benches and a hundred or more people, many barefooted, [and] a small child who kept talking to its mother. On the sides were a row of chairs on which Alice and I, with our interpreter, were placed; across from us, about four rows of chairs to which petitioners were summoned as their cases were called from a docket. To the right of the table, facing it, were tables and chairs for the ministers and other officials who would be involved in the petitions.

The Prince bounded up the steps and into the Pagoda, energy incarnate, dressed in a western blue suit. He greeted us warmly, and then walked along the benches greeting the people. Everyone stood as he entered, many knelt as he approached them. He talked a blue streak, urging everyone to sit down, putting his hands over the hands held out to him with palms pressed together—a true feudal gesture last seen by me when Noel Annan received the scholars into Kings College. They, too, knelt before him.

After a brisk greeting, he went to his seat at the table. Officials in white trousers and long white Nehru coats approached, knelt and put folders on the table. An official took his place before a floor microphone and called the first case, a petition of workers in a state-owned plywood shop asking for paid holidays, better medical service at the plant, shorter hours and a pay raise. A dozen young men left the benches, knelt before the Prince and took the seats facing us. One of their number then stood before the microphone and compared their situation unfavorably with that of workers in a textile plant. They were, he said, only getting about $20.00 (U.S.) a month.

The manager of the State Industries made these points: (1) These people are apprentices, not regular workers. (2) Their hours are the same, so are their paid holidays as all other factory and office workers. (3) This plant cannot afford to pay anyone any more. (4) It is turning away applicants better qualified than this group.

The plant manager added that this was a trouble-making group. No one else joined their complaints or criticized the medical care. Plywood was in over supply.

At this point the Prince took over and made a long, loud, dramatic speech with gestures. It was a stem-winder. The point was not the status of the workers. He was against all status contracts binding the apprentice or state-educated technicians to a term of work. They were to be cancelled forthwith and no more made. "You men are free to leave your employment to-day. In a communist country this would not be possible (some of the group, it was whispered, were communists). This plant in which you work cannot sell enough plywood to pay you more; not that you cannot make more, but the supply is already too large and your product is far from the best. The State is not going to pay a deficit on the plant." Then followed a lecture on supply and demand, the evil of looking to the State for everything—à bas the welfare state—and the curse of factions and quarrels when the trouble lay in themselves and their product. If they wanted a different doctor they could have one. Finally a burst of oratory to the effect that the country was theirs as much as his. If they got out and worked for it as he was doing, instead of complaining all the time, they would all get somewhere. When the youths started to argue back the marshal pushed them out, some looking sullen.

Next case, a wife saying that her husband had served half his sentence and was entitled to parole. The Prince interrupted to grant the parole on a favorable report from the Ministry of Justice.

The case of the Monk's land. Petitioner claimed as lessee of a Cambodian monk, resident in Thailand. Respondent, magistrate of a lower court before whom litigation was pending, answered that the issue was whether the monk's uncle, through whom he claimed by inheritance, had sold the property and the purchaser had neglected to register his title. Petitioner claimed the alleged sale a forgery. Magistrate claimed he had already decided to the contrary in criminal suit instigated by petitioner. The Prince cried out, "You will kill me with these details. Let the case continue in the usual channels." Cert. denied.

The next case produced a ragged barefooted man who claimed to be broke and unable to get back to his village. The Prince gave him in charge of an official telling him to give the man money, to put him on a bus and see that he stayed on it.

An old woman, barefooted, claimed to have lent money to someone who refused to pay. "Now, now" said the Prince, "don't cry. We'll never get anywhere that way." Then he called for a lawyer from the Ministry of Justice and told him to take the woman to court, summon the defendant and see that Justice was done.

Last case, traffic court plus. Up came a one-legged man on crutches and two women, one his wife; the other, the wife of his opponent, who was absent working. The cripple claimed to have lost his leg while driving as a paying passenger with the car owner—i.e., in an accident caused by his negligence. Judgment had been recovered for riels 150,000 reduced to 70,-000 by the judge; but def. had paid nothing. Def. said a lot of people had been hurt and she was trying to pay them all off on the instalment plan but plaintiff wouldn't cooperate. Anyway, he would not have been hurt if he hadn't jumped out of the car window. Plaintiff jumped to his one foot with the aid of a handy chair and shouted that the defendant had not only bribed the judge but had given him his daughter in marriage. This brought down the house, including the Prince, who had to put his head on the table behind the bowl of roses to recover. The parties continued to shout at one another. The Prince outshouted them both and told a palace attendant to put the whole lot of them in a palace car, take them before a judge, who wasn't married to either family, and get the injured man paid off. He had waited a long time. The Prince wanted the matter ended, and ended pronto. The parties, who had cooled off a good deal, said that if it was all right with the Prince they would rather go to-morrow morning. There was a distinct whiff of settlement in the air. "Please yourselves," said the Prince.

I have overlooked one matter. A very ancient old chap, looking like a Chinese scroll painting, was led up by his son, who said that another son had been sentenced to two years for negligently setting fire to a building. Now that his sentence was about up he was sentenced to another two years.

This was not fair. The Minister of Justice replied that his sentence had also included a fine to be paid as damages to the owner of the house. The second sentence was only in the event of non-payment of the fine and was in accord with customary practice. It could only be waived if the prisoner's health would suffer. The Prince inquired about his health, was told that it was excellent, and informed the old man that he regretted that he could not help him.

We had been there an hour and a half and were due to fly to Angkor in an RKG airplane used by the Prince, a rather ancient DC-3. As we rose to leave, the Prince came over to say good-bye. I made flattering comments and wished that we could stay longer, asking how long these audiences usually lasted. He said about six hours—a fair day's work for any court, and here decision was instantaneous, without written opinion or dissent. I thought of St. Louis, Henry II under his oak, and Harun al-Rashid. It was the same process with considerably more restraint where courts were involved.

This has been finished at Angkor, where we have already been over part of the first tier or gallery of the Wat and seen a two-hour series of dances—a real dose—at night before the entrance of the temple. Some were gay and amusing, but one long one was without much of any movement except by arms and hands. One of the characters pretended to go to sleep on a couch. My performance in my chair was no pretense. We have to go again on Friday. Three evenings of classical dancing in a week is above and beyond the call of duty. The local populace were having a high old time about a hundred yards from the temple dancing in a modern Buddhist pagoda.

January 18th. Item: East and west meeting. At the beginning of the bridge to the entrance gate to Angkor-Thom, the Restoration was doing some filling in. This involved moving earth up a 15-foot bank and tamping it down. A mechanical conveyor belt moved the earth from the lower level to the higher. A man with a pneumatic tamper packed it in. At the bottom a man with a pick dug up the earth, another with a shovel put one shovelful in baskets carried on the hip by three women who sauntered about 25 feet to dump them on the belt. The delivery at the top was minimal. One hard piece of earth was emulating Sisyphus's rock on the belt, getting almost to the top and rolling back. The whole crew stopped work to cheer the climber on with gales of laughter, until it rolled off the belt altogether and was forgotten. In the language of official Washington, the Cambodians haven't found out about bottlenecks yet; or, if they have, they just don't care a damn!

My love to all. If we could mix your weather and ours we would all be happy.

Yours,

To **BARBARA EVANS**

Cambodia
January 18, 1962

Dear Barbara:

Since we have been seeing temples all day descriptions of which would be boring, I shall pick up an item or two from Phnom Penh.

I was too harsh in describing the place in an earlier letter. It is better than I suggested but no great shakes. On the other hand, they are trying pathetically hard to do a good job with the city and have intense local pride. The Governor of the City (who is also head of the department of Planning) took us on a motor tour just before we came up here to Angkor. This had been announced, with the result that people turned out along the route and clapped us genially as we passed with our escort. This tour showed a rather good city plan of broad dual-street avenues, with delightful gardens between them, going in the main directions—to the Palace, the R.R. station, the airport, the central market, and through the main areas set aside for business and those reserved for residences. The avenues are away ahead of the city, as I can imagine they could be in Brasilia and Canberra, and were in Washington.

Then, too, to get anything done, so the Governor said, is very difficult. Any plan gets fouled up, changed without notice, abandoned for something more interesting—even the plan of our travels. So I apologize to Phnom Penh, but have no desire to return to it as a town. As a country Cambodia is just too damned hot.

Le Diner du Prince: Informality was the keynote. As we came into the Palace, not his own residence, but the Queen's, he rushed up to meet us, talking volubly and propelling us into the room where the Queen had received us. All the guests, about 25 (that is, the male half) wore white dinner coats. He wore black. He and Alice sat on the Queen's golden sofa with the Trimbles and me around them. The other guests were a little way off. We presented our gifts—Alice's picture, my book, the gifts for Princesses Monique, his wife No. 2, and his daughter Soraya, neither of whom was present. He gave Alice a stole of green silk with gold thread and a silver piece. Alice's picture knocked the ball out of the park, and caused all kinds of sensation—and when Sihanouk makes a show it is a good noisy one. Everyone had to see and admire. We were too, too kind, etc. Meanwhile an orchestra played American popular music a little too loud for ease in conversation.

Speaking of conversation, the Prince's tone level in English, French or Cambodian is adapted to a public meeting. I sat across the table, a long fairly narrow one, and had to give up talking to my neighbors—one, a Cambodian lady with the traditional soft and gentle voice—while he was in full cry. But this was quite all right as it increased his immediate audience. The Prince has great charm. He is a gifted actor, moves quickly from mood to mood and understands the art of flattery by being one of its principal victims. He shouted his way through dinner, explaining to Alice that he ate too much, which explained why he was so fat and had to go to France every year to take the cure.

At the end of a long and rich dinner he rose and read a toast to me as the greatest international lawyer since Grotius, etc. To this I replied with what in Brazil Eddie Miller would have called a three Martini speech (though in this hot climate liquor is neither very attractive or effective). I forget what it was all about, but it nearly reduced the Prince to tears, and the company generally "could scarce forebear to cheer." After dinner the Prince and I talked for a while and I got over some ideas which for some reason Bill Trimble thought he should not state himself, that the U.S. would arm some more battalions if, as he said, he wished to strengthen his forces along the Vietnam and Laotian border, etc.

It was then time to go to the ballet. The Prince proposed walking; then found that it had started to sprinkle. Alice and the Ambassador had started off regardless, so led by the Prince with a good deal of noise the company followed along in an increasing shower, with ladies complaining and trying to protect hair-dos with scarves or their husbands' handkerchiefs.

A description of Cambodian classical ballet is beyond me. It has a sort of primitive charm but I cannot believe that it is an advanced art form. The dancers shuffle about to a sort of syncopated rhythm to which our young could do the "twist," furnished by xylophones and hollow-sounding drums, accompanied by the damnedest nasal caterwauling by old (so I am told) women off-stage that you ever heard. Every few seconds the dancers stop, stand on one leg and lift up the other one behind them, bent at the knee, with the grace of a cart-horse cooperating in being shod. The costumes are elaborate, the gilt headdresses rising in a long spike.

Movements of the hands and arms play a large part in the dance, the fingers being back almost at right angles and performing the most extraordinary rippling movements. A little of it goes a long way; and two hours of it, too long a way. In our case it called for a stiff nightcap at the Embassy before going home.

Unstatistical observations.

1. The Cambodians are great travelers. The autobus is ubiquitous, pack-jammed, the roof covered with baskets full of everything—half the population is on wheels.

2. The Cambodians are addicted to soda-pop even more than betel nut. Little stands are everywhere, even the poorest villages. On wheels, too. 7-Up is the big seller; has a bottling works here. Jim Farley Coke is a non-starter.

3. Bicycles everywhere and bicycle rickshaws. Pushers in the city; pullers in the country, where they are also used for cargo. You can pull more than you can push; but the passenger can't see.

4. While standards are low, there are more signs of consumer goods around than I would have thought—wrist watches, good clothes, gold teeth, cameras, etc. There are no banks in the country areas. People keep their money in the sock or in goods. The Governor of Siem Reap province, the largest in Cambodia, has no bank account and never has had.

5. Alice blocks traffic when she sketches, but particularly when out of her car. But the gazers are careful not to block her view.

Angkor-Wat
April 19

Cambodian Episode: We were urged to get an early start this morning since the helicopter would meet us at Siem Reap to take us to Bauteay Screi, a famous temple, twenty miles away. We were off at 8:30 with great effort. But there was no 'copter. Alice sketched. I was taken about town by the Governor. At ten-thirty the 'copter is reported at the airfield fifteen minutes away. We rush to the airfield and find that the 'copter has gone to the football field at Siem Reap. We return to Siem Reap. It is now after eleven o'clock. The French pilots cannot go to Bauteay Screi because they have too much gasoline. (This seems to be a non-sequitur. But that's what they said.) Therefore, we have to fly about for awhile to reduce the gasoline. We can see some temples from the air and see a bit of the countryside.

We are strapped in and told to stay that way as it is too hot to shut the door. A canvas strap is put across it and off we go. The pilot circles Angkor-Wat and Angkor-Thom, but so fast and so close that photographing is hard. He then mounts to a thousand feet or more, so that one gets only a sense of unbroken forest as far as the horizon—which is probably right—and then goes roaring around for an hour.

We have been down now for two hours and are just beginning to be able to hear again. In another hour we shall go up once more and deafen ourselves. One thing, however, is certain. While we were up there we were cool, even chilly, for the first time since coming to Cambodia. It was quite a treat.

Later.

The afternoon flight took us about twenty minutes to a clearing in the thick forest where there was a small patch of harvested rice paddies into which we descended vertically, stirring up a tornado of rice straw. The motor had hardly stopped before naked boys began emerging from the forest, followed by their fully clad elders, until quite a crowd gathered. No one had much interest, though some, in us but the Whirly Bird was something else again. We saw no village either coming in or going out, but another sizeable group of women and children were sitting and playing in the temple (to Siva) courtyard which we reached by a dusty track through great trees. The village must have been hidden in the dense forest.

The temple, a tenth century one, two centuries earlier than Angkor was small, delicate and beautifully carved, in some places into mere tracery and design, but elsewhere with scenes from Siva's (the Destroyer's) history. It is supposed to be peculiarly the women's temple; why, I dare not think. We sketched, photographed and had explanations from a mush-mouthed man from the Ministry of Antiquities and Reconstruction, most of which wholly eluded me. Tonight we are dining with the famous French archeologist, Bernard Groslier, whose father preceded him at Angkor, and may learn more.

Phnom Penh

January 21

Again I have slandered Cambodia. Yesterday and today have been lovely days. Hot in the sun to be sure, but Antigua weather in the steady breeze when in the shade.

Our last morning at Angkor was clearly our best. M. Groslier went around with us, taking us to several places in course of reconstruction. This was fascinating and left us amazed at the breadth of knowledge of this remarkable man. He is in his early forties. First the site has to be cleared of the jungle. The great banyan and silk-cotton trees have to be poisoned since their roots go all through the crevices in the stone sucking the minerals from the stone. To tear them out would be to destroy the soft sandstone of which the temples were built. The poisoning is done with arsenic. We saw a great tree in course of dissolution, which is just what happens. Then the stone is treated with antibiotics to destroy bacteria which have gotten into it and are destroying it. Usually the tree roots have toppled the walls and towers and weakened the foundations. The jumbled piles of stone have to be sorted out, placed in order—a jigsaw puzzle—and marked. Those still standing are marked as they are taken down.

Then new foundations of concrete are poured with elaborate engineering ties so that the downward thrust of the temples' weight is made to counteract the outward thrust against the retaining walls of the embankment. When the stones are put back, missing ones are replaced with concrete made of powdered sandstone and cement colored to match the wall. But no attempt is made to reproduce moulding or carving. This Mr. Groslier regards as faking. All he permits is to maintain the same volume and color as in the original.

One monastery has been made into what he calls a fake for romantic tourists. It is supposed to be the structure still in the grip of the jungle. But he said six feet of earth have been taken out of it and all the smaller vegetation. Otherwise, one could not see the structure at all. It is certainly romantic enough with great trees growing out of towers and their roots covering the structures like giant octopi. Camus's brother was shooting a movie there yesterday with "the most beautiful girl in Cambodia" in the leading role. She was glamorous all right. The whole movie paraphernalia, kleig lights, director with megaphone, was odd in this ghostly place.

Yours,

To FELIX FRANKFURTER

DA was writing from the Hague, the Netherlands, where the case of the Cambodian temple was argued before the International Court of Justice. Sir Frank Soskice represented Thailand, DA Cambodia.

Hotel Wittebrug
'S-Gravenhage
March 15, 1962

Dear Felix:

Many thanks for your note.

We limp along and may have another ten days of talk in us. We are now examining witnesses. Sir Frank continues to be, as my French colleague puts it, "very nice but not very clever."

But the Court does not help either. Last Tuesday at 12:30 Sir F finished the opening argument—of six days for his side. We were then to examine witnesses. At the end of the opening one is supposed to announce (why God knows) his "submissions"—these are more or less like the prayers at the end of a bill for an injunction, purely formal. Sir F who had run out of steam, mercifully, earlier than he had expected to, asked the Court to let him put these in after the testimony was finished. When asked by the President we said that we had no objection. Whereupon the Court adjourned until Thursday morning to consider the unopposed motion.

It granted it to-day; and we got started again. Sir F was crushed at the havoc he had wrought and could not have been more apologetic. I told him that growing boys never know their own strength.

Well, the young still believe, God forgive them, that international law has glamour and amounts to something.

Our love to you and Marion.

Yours,

MEMORANDUM OF CONVERSATION WITH THE PRESIDENT

The memorandum is indicative of DA's conviction that the American interest in the issue of the independence of the African colonies did not lie in a simplistic one-sided support for the African nationalists, but in moderating nationalist impatience while encouraging the European allies to speed up self-determination but avoiding U.S.-Europe confrontations.

April 2, 1962

Pursuant to the President's invitation, I was received by him at five o'clock today, upstairs in the oval sitting room at the White House. He sent for Mac Bundy and, before Bundy arrived, began his conversation.

First the President asked me what I thought of the Supreme Court's decision in the Tennessee districting case. I said that I thought the Court had taken on in the desegregation decisions about all the legislative and executive governmental work that it could handle for the time being, and it seemed to me unwise to pick out another task, the end of which no one could see. The President remarked that the legislatures would never reform themselves and that he did not see how we were going to make any progress unless the Court intervened. I said, suppose it didn't? It did not seem to me that the injustice resulting from the over-representation of rural areas was one of the tyrannical impositions which drove a people to rebellion. It was a long way from fascism. I did not believe that every injustice had to be corrected at once. As for the legislatures reforming themselves, a good deal had already been done in the state from which I originally came, that is, Connecticut; and more could be done if people really cared deeply. I had a strong feeling that they did not; certainly in Maryland at the present time the talk was more in the newspapers than in private conversations. The President remarked that mine was one point of view and dropped the subject.

He then turned to the negotiations with Portugal over the Azores base. He said that not much seemed to be happening and that he would be grateful to have me take the matter over and see if something could be done. I asked him for permission to talk about the situation for a few minutes and said about the following:

The Portuguese were deeply offended at what they believed was the desertion of them by the United States, if not the actual alignment of the United States with their enemies. The problem, it seemed to me, lay not so much in negotiations with the Portuguese as in the determination of United States policy. The battle would be in Washington, rather than in Lisbon. At this point the President intervened to ask whether the battle might not also be in New York. I agreed. It was largely, I said, a battle of personalities. Stevenson, Harlan Cleveland, and Soapy Williams believed that our relations with Portugal should be sacrificed to maintain the favor of the new African states. The problem was not so simple as this. I did not believe that a policy should be evolved either to retain the Azores as a military base or to gain the approval, if that could be done, of the African states. I thought the purpose of the policy should be to serve the best interests of the United States in its position of leadership both in Europe and in the world. I did not think our present policy was doing that.

If new policy was to be devised, I went on, there was going to be bloodshed in our government's ranks and there would be a good many casualties. I did not mind being one of them if it was to be in attempting a policy approved by the President and carried through. But I knew that if he made a decision against the African group, they would not accept it, but would leak to the press, stir up trouble on the Hill, and go out to eliminate me. The real question, therefore, was how much of a row was the President prepared to support.

The President then asked me why I was so sure that there was no room for negotiations under the present conditions. I said that, as he perhaps knew, we had in fact been subsidizing Portugal's enemies; and that they strongly suspected this, although they could not prove it. He said that the purpose of this was to try to keep the Angolan nationalist movement out of the hands of the communist Ghanians, etc., and keep it in the most moderate hands possible. I said that I quite understood this, but that it did not make what the Portuguese suspected any more palatable to them. We were also engaged in smuggling Angolese out of Angola and educating them in Lincoln College outside of Philadelphia in the most extreme nationalist views. Furthermore the head of this college had secretly and illegally entered Angola and on his return had engaged in violent anti-Portuguese propaganda. We voted in the United Nations for resolutions "condemning" Portugal for maintaining order in territory unquestionably under Portuguese sovereignty. I pointed out that the Portuguese were a proud people, especially sensitive because they had declined to such an impotent position after such a glorious history. They would rather proceed to the ruin of their empire in a dignified way, as they had in Goa, than be bought or wheedled into cooperating in their own destruction.

By this time Mac Bundy had joined us and asked me what I thought might happen in 1963 if no agreement were had. I said that I thought, if real efforts were made to improve the situation, we might be able to live under a tacit *modus vivendi* while trying to work out a more permanent solution. On the other hand, if the situation did not improve, and especially if it deteriorated, I thought that the Portuguese might request our forces to leave (without denouncing the permanent treaty which existed for the duration of NATO), and, if we did not leave, take the position that we were in occupation by force, like the Indians in Goa.

The President asked what I would propose. I said on our side, first, that we should completely refrain during the coming session of the General Assembly from joining in any debates and votes critical of Portugal; that we should take the position that we thought these were futile and that the interests of all concerned were better served by quiet and friendly discussions. Second, I thought that a plan for economic development, both in Portugal and Angola, under Portuguese direction could be worked out with Brazilian and German participation. I thought that Roberto Campos, the Brazilian Ambassador here could be of immense help, and I knew Franz Josef Strauss was deeply interested. On the Portuguese side, I said that the last two speeches of Ambassador Pereira, one at the Overseas Press Club here, the other at the Commonwealth Club in San Francisco, went almost far enough in the direction of not excluding self-determination to permit us to take the attitude suggested above. I thought that one of the great problems here was who should make the first overture and it seemed to me that the United States, being great and powerful, was called upon to do so.

The President said that it was all very well for me to take the attitude I did, but that I was asking him to make a very considerable change in policy and that he would be accused of doing so solely to get the Azores base.

I said that I saw the embarrassment in his position and could only make two observations: One was that I had made a suggestion for easing this embarrassment as much as it could be eased; and, secondly, that, if he became convinced that the policy he was following was not the right one, the best thing was to change it as soon as possible and accept the embarrassment of doing so.

He then said that the Portuguese had to do something to make the United States Government's position more tolerable. I said that I thought this expression, which I had seen in paper produced by Harlan Cleveland's division (there it said that the Portuguese *must* declare that they would permit self-government in from five to ten years), was a complete misunderstanding of the Portuguese character. They did not believe that there was anything that they "must" do.

The President said that it was plain that the present relation between Portugal and the provinces could not continue indefinitely and must inevitably develop into independence for the provinces. I asked him to listen patiently while I talked a little more about both Africa and Portugal, which he said he would do.

Surely, I said, the relation between Portugal and the provinces would change. One of the highest objects of policy was to have it change with the greatest advantage to all concerned and the least possible disruption—a change such as occurred between France and French Africa (aside from Algeria) would be what we would hope for; a change such as had occurred in the Congo would be bad, but in the case of Portugal it would be worse. Not only would disaster, bloodshed, and destruction be brought to Angola and Mozambique, which were today relatively quiet and prosperous, but people in Washington, and there are such people, talked about the overthrow of the Salazar regime in Portugal, having no recollection or knowledge of what Portugal was like from 1910 to 1928. With a revolution every six months during that period, it had been reduced to abject poverty, anarchy, and despair; and it was Salazar, whom everybody criticized now, who had produced almost a miraculous change in the country. He might have outstayed his time, but I urged the President to pause before he encouraged action which might throw the whole Iberian Peninsula into a violent revolution.

The upshot of the matter was that I told the President that, before I ever heard from him, I had made a date to lunch with Pereira the following day. He asked me to explore the possibilities of some more cooperative attitude on the Portuguese part, which I said I would do, and he told me that I would probably be hearing later either from him or from Dean Rusk. We parted amicably and Mac Bundy walked with me to Pennsylvania Avenue.

To JANE A. BROWN

Reference to Kennedy and the U.S. Steel Corporation is the latter's announcement that it was raising prices in the face of Kennedy's appeal to hold the price line against inflation. The company backed down.

April 13, 1962

Dearest Jane:

You were a sweet daughter to enliven the birthday which launches me into my seventieth year with the story of Louise de La Fayette, the mistress of a king who became a nun. It is high time that I knew about these things; and I have already started, with pleasure, on my education. Thank you very much, my dear.

Alice is off in two days, as she says she is writing you. I shall follow in three weeks, for an absence of three weeks, partly in London, partly in Sweden at Prince Bernhard's conference and then a visit with the Bohemans. I think it will be fun, although the month at the Hague was pleasant, too, despite some hard work and poor weather. We shall be gone I fear when you motor through here. If you want to stop off just commandeer the house. Johnson would love it. He gets bored just fighting with Anna. . . .

The President is trying to get me to take over dealings with the Portuguese. I am refusing to do so unless he will turn from the Africa firsters and agree to use some sense. He refuses to promise anything. So we are dead-locked; and I hope remain so. But I fear that Mac Bundy will think of some trick which I shall see through but will find it hard to denounce without calling JFK a double-dealer.

What a rooking he took from U.S. Steel. I have now known two Chairmen of the Board of that company, members of our Corporation. Both were bright but damned fools when a question of public responsibility was involved. Businessmen are more apt than politicians to be unfit for their jobs.

April 14

This morning comes the news of the Steel Companies volte face. What a victory for JFK! And what added proof of the fumbling incompetence of the giants of industry. If Khrushchev has any sense he will get a tape of JFK's press conference denunciation of the steel executives and play it daily to the uncommitted countries.

Alice has written you about FF [Felix Frankfurter]. Every day which goes by without added improvement adds to our deep worry. He must not be left as he is, poor little cuss.

Much love to you both.

Devotedly,

To ALICE ACHESON

Alice Acheson was traveling in Europe with the Jessups, leaving DA to the challenge of housekeeping. He had not yet commenced his autobiographical books, Morning and Noon *and* Present at the Creation, *and was rather at loose ends.*

April 28, 1962

Dearest Alice:

To-day has been the year's best day. And I almost used it to fire the cook.

But first the day. Warm, after ten days of warm (80°s) dry days, so that we have had to water the garden, it was cloudless with a strong south breeze. All the fruit trees were in a riot of blossom, even the apples a week early, and all sort of tulips, hyacinths, jonquils and lilacs. A dream day to plant, weed and paint screens. These are the days to be here! You can have Vence.

Then the cook. After giving us raw lamb chops and a raw roast beef last week, she gave us a steak to-night which she must have started on right after lunch—and indeed, after my speaking to her specially about it. So I gave her a good piece of my mind, after telling her to give the steak to any thin dog.

This summer I must figure out something to do. The speech, the only one I ever make, is beginning to pall. Another book has not yet begun to gestate. I have no cases and no job. And I really enjoy doing nothing rather more than your Presbyterian views are likely to approve. So I must think of something, but not until we get back from Europe.

. . .

Lots of love

Devotedly,

To HARRY S TRUMAN

May 3, 1962

Dear Boss:

Alice and I will be in London with the Bruces on your birthday. We shall drink your health and raise a loud cheer for you in the company of good men and true everywhere. All good wishes and many more years to spread the word and hearten the brave. We need it more than ever these days.

I have a curious and apprehensive feeling as I watch JFK that he is a sort of Indian snake charmer. He toots away on his pipe and our problems sway back and forth around him in a trance-like manner, never approaching, but never withdrawing; all are in a state of suspended life, including the pipe player, who lives only in his dream.

Some day one of these snakes will wake up; and no one will be able even to run.

So we are going away again. Alice has been in Cyprus doing some painting and being received by his Grace of the whiskers, Archbishop-President Makarios. (What a President you would have made if you had been an Archbishop into the bargain and had had whiskers down to your waist! The idea is a novel one but quite intriguing.) I am to meet her in London after she has a week or ten days in Southern France, in the small town of Vence near Grasse, a place for painters. After ten days we go on to Sweden where I attend a conference presided over by Prince Bernhard of the Netherlands. Then we shall both visit the Bohemans for a few days. You will remember him as the Swedish ambassador, a tall able fellow who always believed that agriculture would prove the Achilles heel of the Soviet system—that is, the limiting factor.

Again our most affectionate remembrances and greetings go to you and Bess.

Most warmly,

To FELIX FRANKFURTER

DA wrote from Europe where he was attending the Bilderberg Confer-ence. References are to Sir Frank Soskice (DA's recent opponent in the Cambodia-Thailand litigation), Hugh Gaitskell (prominent British Labor Party figure), and Princess Beatrix of the Netherlands.

May 19, 1962

Dear Felix:

I am taking advantage of a dull speech by an Italian in French to give you another bulletin.

You will be glad to know that we had a nice luncheon with the Sos-kice's at the Garrick with the Gaitskells as the other guests, and that, after proper preparation by Alice, I behaved very well indeed. No quarrel, no sharp words, nothing untoward at all. Sir Frank, also, could not have been more cordial. So that is all for the best.

The conference here has not been very exciting. As before, its best mo-ments are out of the meetings. Last night I had a good talk with Dennis Healey, who let me in on his views of his colleague Harold Wilson, also in attendance here. When I shivered at the latter being shadow Foreign Min-ister, he said that this was to separate him from the Exchequer which frightened everybody (i.e., HW's connection with it did). When I still shiv-ered he reminded me of an alleged remark of Winston's after the election of 1951 at the last meeting of the Shadow Cabinct.

"Well, gentlemen," he said, "this is the last time we shall meet—some of us."

The talk today is all about Britain and the Common Market. But under it all one can sense that negotiations are going on and each side—the U.K. and the Six—are painting their picture as a depressing one to encourage the making of concessions by the other side. So I find it only mildly interesting.

Perhaps, the most interesting episode to me occurred yesterday, lun-cheon with the Princess Beatrix, and a long talk with her about her educa-tion. Her father told me that she had asked to be allowed to attend as an observer, and the Steering Committee had approved. This delightful young lady—about 23, I would suppose—is bright, quick, amusing and intelligent. Like many of the young, she thinks that her education was thoroughly botched, and thanks (unlike most) her father for discovering the trouble and correcting it in time.

The original error was her mother's. She likes dreamy ideas, one of which was "modern education" on the Montessori model. It was a real mess. No one worked. Sometimes, they simply left school. They lied to the school and to their parents. She was unhappy and going to pieces. Finally her father found out about her problems and got a new school started on more old fashioned lines. This pulled her into shape and got her into the university with flying colors.

All this she said with the conviction of a reformed drunk telling you about A.A. But she had humor, too, and gave all of us at her table a very good time.

After this she gave me—à propos of the recent Greek royal wedding—a sketch of young European royalty. You will be interested to know that she regards them as living too sheltered a life which prolongs adolescence unduly. She finds the Greeks surprisingly cut off from their own people, unable to share their experiences both ways, and hence not really performing their royal function! (Quite an idea.) Of course, she said, the King's brother had been "kicked out" (her phrase), which doubtless made him cautious (again hers), but the new generation ought to have more confidence. This is quite a girl, as the Dutch will find out, if she has a chance to show them.

Barbara gives me good news of you.

Yours,

To WILLIAM LOEB

William Loeb was president and editor of the Manchester (*New Hampshire*) Union Leader.

June 14, 1962

Mr. William Loeb, President
Manchester Union Leader
Manchester, New Hampshire

Dear Mr. Loeb:

Thank you for your kind letter about and generous attitude toward our friend Felix Frankfurter in his present affliction. He was much touched by your message and good wishes and asked me to thank you for your kind thought of him. He is not writing himself.

It is sad to see beloved friends grow old and pay the tolls which each of the years exacts—and they are merciless tax collectors. Felix has been improving, slowly but steadily, since shortly after his second stroke. His will to recover is great. His wife, as you know, is now an invalid unable to get about, and he is deeply distressed at being separated from her. As you and I know, when he gets dead-set on doing something, he usually does it. The doctors are pleased with his progress but, wisely, won't set a date when he can go home.

I am surprised that Felix should have criticized any of his friends for "wandering from the 'liberal' fold," as you put it, and doubt whether he would do so now. He is impatient of labels—perhaps, for the quite human reason that they have been applied to him. He, too, has been charged with "wandering from the 'liberal' fold." So I think that today you could expect absolution and remission of this sin.

As I look back to my youth, it seems to me that the test of liberalism, then, was quite simple and rather innocent. One was a liberal if one was sympathetic to labor unions, employers' liability, direct election of United States Senators, the federal graduated income tax, maximum hour and minimum wage legislation for women, and if one read the *New Republic*.

It is a good deal more complicated now. Perhaps the words "liberal" and "conservative" should, by an article in a semantic disarmament treaty be towed out beyond the three-mile limit and sunk. Certainly a good many proposals, put forward under both descriptions, seem to me to fall more properly under the heading, "Damned Fool Ideas."

I have just received your note of June 11 with the editorial enclosed. Many thanks for sending it along.

With kind regards.

Sincerely,

To **ROBERT G. MENZIES**

DA wrote to give Menzies, a friend of Felix Frankfurter, a bulletin on the Justice's convalescence from a stroke.

August 14, 1962

The Right Honorable Robert G. Menzies
Prime Minister of Australia
Canberra, Australia

Dear Bob:

It is some time since I have written you about Felix, and I find it hard to know just what to tell you. There has been progress, quite a lot. Felix's speech improved quite rapidly and then seemed to get stuck. His voice is low, the speech somewhat slurred, some sounds quite elude him, and sometimes his mind just gets ahead of the articulation with a resulting pile-up and fresh start. His left arm has been the slowest affected spot to respond, but it is now doing so with little or no pain. The leg has done best. He cannot yet get himself up; but once put on his feet, he has been able for some weeks to walk ten or fifteen feet holding on to a rail. He is now learning to navigate with a cane, but is very unsure of himself and needs help at his elbow.

All this is pretty good. Until he came home, I had hoped (and I mean just hoped) that he might be well enough by October for perhaps a token appearance on the bench. But (for your information) this seems highly un-likely now. His will to recover was strong and his effort gallant. But lately he has seemed discouraged, as though he realized that it could not be done. I think that soon he will have to face the decision, which will be a bitter one.

Two weeks ago the President, at his own request, paid Felix a visit. The latter was in a rare flutter about it, and I was summoned to an almost daily meeting to decide some vital matter. Where should the President be received? In the living room. Should Felix stand when the President came in? Yes, he could and should with help. What refreshment should be offered? Tea. I must be there as Chief of Protocol. Agreed. It went off very well. The President behaved beautifully. He was warm and deferential, letting Felix have the floor and showing great interest in all he said. At the end he asked to be allowed to come again.

I thought that this visit would give him a great boost; and for a few days it did. But then, as I have said, the spirit just seemed to ooze out of him. It is heart-breaking to see that invincible vitality tamed at last.

My hope now is that, once the decision to retire is over, he will rally. Perhaps we can get him out of that depressing house and revive his desire to see people, which he has now quite lost. But it could go the other way. I think we are approaching a crisis.

This is not a happy report, but I thought you would like to know how things are.

We have followed the Common Market talks with absorbed interest. What impossible characters these French are! With warmest greetings to Dame Pattie and to you.

As ever,

To **SYDNEY WARREN**

Sydney Warren was professor of government at California Western University, San Diego.

August·14, 1962

Mr. Sidney Warren
California Western University
3902 Lomaland Drive
San Diego 6, California

Dear Mr. Warren:

Many thanks for your article in the *Saturday Review*. You ask for my thoughts about the piece.

Some time it would be interesting to do a piece on changing fashions in appraisal of the presidency. Going back only as far as Woodrow Wilson's

Congressional Government, one can trace three or four switches—one in Wilson himself—between the view that the role is only one for a chief civil servant to the opposite, that it is too strong for the survival of democracy in the Republic. It all depends on what the President is doing and the mood of the country (somewhat but not wholly interrelated factors) at the time of writing. My own view is that in the hands of a strong man who has the flair for the sort of leadership which combines the ability to educate and to inspire, the office is strong enough to deal with the problems of our day.

Underlying the question of the presidency, is the deeper one of the constancy of a democracy, its capability for continued self-discipline, the problems which de Tocqueville posed. Clarence Day has pointed out that ours is a simian world, and we might paraphrase Shakespeare's Caesar, the fault is in our tails, not in our institutions, that we are scatterbrains.

Sincerely yours,

To ELIZABETH FINLEY

Elizabeth Finley was the librarian at Covington & Burling, DA's law firm.

October 15, 1962

Dear Elizabeth:

Fancy you having a hole in your head! Almost anyone but you. Whenever some one says "I need a Democratic Congress like (people do say "like") I need a hole in the head," I shall remark that I once knew a girl who had a hole in her head, and she not only did not need it, but went to some trouble to have it filled up. It just goes to show that these old sayings come out of the wisdom of the race.

We have missed you on the sixth floor. That is, the elite have; the rest don't even notice that they are not there themselves. In the few days that you have been away I have learned something most revealing. This is that your great admirer and friend, Mr. H. Westwood is not, as I have often suspected, a real person, but a character out of a book. And I have found the book. He is out of J. D. Salinger's *Franny and Zooey.* Read the first part, called "Franny," and there you have, as Lane would put it, "the whole goddam thing as clear as for Chrissake." Well, that is a load off my goddam mind, so-called.

Stick to your determination to make your doctors come up with a diagnosis, even if it is the wrong one. No psychosomatic dodges allowed. If they waver put a few holes in their heads and see how they like it.

Our affectionate thoughts are with you.

Sincerely,

To **PRESIDENT JOHN F. KENNEDY**

This letter deals with the President's leadership during the Cuban missile crisis.

October 28, 1962

Dear Mr. President:

With proper precautions for warding off the ill-luck which is said to attend upon and punish premature statement, may I congratulate you on your leadership, firmness and judgment over the past touchy week. We have not had these qualities at the helm in this country at all times. It is good to have them again.

Only a few people know better than I how hard these decisions are to make, and how broad the gap is between the advisors and the decider. It may be that we are not out of the woods yet. I remember the fate of our high hopes as the Korean armistice was agreed to. But though the dangers of the fly paper of talk are clear, what has already happened amply shows the wisdom of the course you chose—and stuck to.

I am happy that you enabled me to participate in the events of last week.

Most respectfully,

To **JOHN COWLES**

John Cowles was owner and editor of the Minneapolis Star *and* Tribune. *The Achesons became close friends of the Cowleses in Antigua where they all went for a few weeks each winter.*

DA wrote following his return from Europe where President Kennedy had asked him to go to brief President de Gaulle and Chancellor Adenauer about the decision to impose a blockade in the Cuban missile crisis.

2805 P Street
Washington 7, D.C.
November 2, 1962

Dear John:

This is an interim report to let you and Betty know that we remain in a state of anticipatory excitement over your delightful December invitation, and are already prepared, in spirit at least, to take off at a moments notice. There were, to be sure, moments in the past two weeks when it seemed improbable that any of us might go. But that phase of this crisis seems over. I think the chances are good that we may get started before the next one is fully flowered. But flower it will.

My adventures in Washington and Europe have been lurid and can best wait until we can garnish them with rum under a tropic sun. Enough to say that I gained respect for the President, though I did not always agree with him, that de Gaulle, as on a previous occasion, was quite superb, and that the Chancellor, while not that, was very stout hearted and gave me a terrific workout. For 87 he is a thorough going menace. We ended in a hot argument whether a cardinal beat him at bocce because—as I insisted—the cardinal's prayers got to God faster, or because—as Der Alte insisted—he (the Cardinal) took off more clothes and thus became more supple. The Chancellor claimed that his prayers went as fast any anyone's and got as prompt attention. I enlisted him forthwith as our secret weapon.

The Supreme Court is setting a case of mine for argument in the session beginning Jan 7. I wrote today pleading to have it put in the week of Jan. 14th. We shall know before we leave. But, at worst, I may have to come home and go to work a few days before the Cowleses—and Alice, if she is wise.

Our love to Betty and to you.

As ever,

To A. WHITNEY GRISWOLD

Griswold, for whom DA had the greatest affection, had been stricken with cancer.

November 20, 1962

Dear Whit:

What foul luck you have! I know that happily the reports are as good as they can be under the basic circumstances, but I refuse to be gay about that. When I broke my arm I determined after a few calls from kind friends to murder the next one who said "Aren't you lucky that it wasn't your right arm." My view was that I was unlucky, period.

I see no reason why you and Mary don't repeat the 1960 program. Finish up the hospital a little earlier than before. Stay in Florida until late March or April. Go to Sicily to see the Greek temples. Follow the sun north to Rome. Home for commencement and a lazy summer at the Vineyard. Then go back for the next academic year—Lefty's last—just oozing fight. There's a program for you!

But, for the present, just lie there, sip a little Bourbon, and follow the example of Holmes. "When my brethren begin to talk about freedom of contract," he said, "I compose my spirit by thinking of all the beautiful women I have known." The hospital walls will just fade away.

I shall keep in touch with Mary and your progress. She has promised to call on me for any chore I can perform.

Good luck from now on.

Affectionately,

To **PRESIDENT JOHN F. KENNEDY**

*The memento described here was a calendar device memorializing the
dates spanning the crisis of the Soviet missiles in Cuba the previous month.*

November 30, 1962

Dear Mr. President:

How kind and imaginative of you to have designed and to have made
me a recipient of such a delightful memento of those stirring and critical
days in October. I am deeply grateful for it, and grateful, too—as I wrote to
you earlier—for the opportunity you opened to me to take part in the campaign so wisely conceived and vigorously executed. In its execution you
confounded de Tocqueville's opinion that a democracy "cannot combine its
measures with secrecy or await their consequences with patience."

Most respectfully yours,

To **LADY PAMELA BERRY**

*DA could distinguish between his admiration for de Gaulle as a person
and his opposition to de Gaulle's policies.*

*Franz Josef Strauss was leader of the Christian Social Party, the Ba-
varian affiliate of the Christian Democratic Union, the governing party of
the Federal Republic.*

George Brown was "shadow" Defence Minister in the Labour Party.

*Vassal was a British citizen reported to have been involved in Soviet
espionage.*

December 3, 1962

Dear Pam:

I look forward to Oliver Lyttleton and Deakin—the latter I do not know
about. Three things of my own are about to burst on the world—a leader in
the December issue of *Foreign Affairs* (Dec. 18, I think), a speech at West
Point (going to you by ocean mail) and a piece about my childhood in the
Connecticut valley in the 1890s, which the *Sat. Evening Post* will publish in
its issue of Dec. 15th. In due course I will send you reprints.

We are apprehensive that your brother will come and go while we are
away. I have written him that Alice and I have succumbed to La dolce vita
and are off in ten days time to spend three weeks in the West Indies with
the MacLeishes and the John Cowles. Part of the time we shall be cruising
on a schooner from St. Lucia to Grenada and will then have a look at Trini-
dad. We shall be back here by January 13th. So don't you come, too, during

our escape from Christmas. Come later when we are here, and be sure that we should love to have you at 2805 P St. if you would care to stay there.

My flight bearing the news of Cuba had a good many amusing as well as exciting moments. Some day I shall put them all down, but it would destroy my usefulness to do it now. As David walked with me from the command post of our SAC base to the car which was to run me back to our aircraft, he said, "Put your hand in my coat pocket." I did so, and felt a revolver. "Against whom?" I asked, "do you carry this artillery? Am I to be liquidated?" He did not know the potential enemy. "I was instructed to carry it" was all he would tell me. I am delighted that amidst all his duties he remembered my message to you.

De Gaulle could not have been better. He has a magnificent inner calm and serenity which makes all the nervous affectations of social talk unnecessary as well as any urge to make an impression or to charm. His dignity is real, like General Marshall's. We could not have had a more satisfactory talk. And as for der Alte, I always enjoy him and get on with him very well. He was here shortly afterward for an official visit which gave me another chance to see him.

While in Bonn I went to see Strauss of whom I am very fond. Strauss is a good man who unhappily lacks judgment. He is impulsive and could be more selective in choosing his friends. Two years ago I thought that he had a chance of succeeding the Chancellor. But, I fear that he has slipped to the bottom of the ladder and will have to begin all over again. Some years ago, in accordance with a Bavarian custom, we exchanged first names. He calls me Franz Josef and I call him Dean which confuses a company no end. I fear that our friendship may now languish for lack of nourishment.

You ask about George Brown. We dined with him and the McNamaras at my daughter Mary's when he was here, and no one could have been better behaved or talked better. We all found ourselves in harmonious agreement and having a good time. He seemed to be impressed by McNamara and very fond of Mary—both of which are sentiments I share.

Please do not have Mike Janeway on your mind. He thought you were very kind to him and was captivated by all your family. He wrote me a rather sweet observation about your boys. Judging from his own experience in his own family, he said, he was sure that your sons must believe that they should be in revolt against so dynamic a mother. But it was clear that they were so fond of you, that it was just not worth while.

The Vassal business puzzles me. Was it more than the usual spy story—a weak character caught by the Russians in their net and blackmail? . . . Our papers were pretty sketchy. They are now up in arms—with Joe Alsop in the lead—because McNamara has come down hard on leaks from the Pentagon. More power to him, I say.

Affectionately,

To **EUGENE V. ROSTOW**

DA was not underscheduled at this period. Cowles was publisher of the Minneapolis Star *and* Tribune *and a close friend. The West Point speech kicked up considerable dust because of its mention that Britain had lost an empire and not yet found a new role.*

December 13, 1962

Dean Eugene V. Rostow
208 St. Ronan Street
New Haven, Connecticut

Dear Gene:
     Belatedly the word comes to me that you have been ill, suffering from a painful and debilitating malady, to which I was subjected in a slightly different form thirty years ago. It is hell on wheels, and my deepest sympathy goes with you. I know how frustrating and infuriating it must be to be laid up when there are so many things that you want to be doing. But I am sure that the medicine men are right that the quickest way to be about again is to curb your impatience and cultivate serenity.
     Alice and I are off for three weeks or so in the West Indies with Archie. Then the four of us, with John and Betty Cowles of Minneapolis are going to cruise among the southern Windward Islands in a comfortable old schooner. I have to come back a little ahead of Alice for argument in the Supreme Court and then to prepare two more speeches, which I hope some guardian angel will prevent me from making controversial, to be delivered in California in place of the two which I was supposed to deliver when the President sent me to Europe. One of these was the controversial West Point one (a copy of which I thought you would like to see and had sent off to you the other day); the other is the leader in this month's *Foreign Affairs*.
     I am sorry that I have not been able to take on the assignments which you proposed to me. I do want to help, and, when I get this load off me, which I find more worrying than I used to, I shall be glad to go over with you various proposals.
     Felix does not, I am sorry to report, seem to be improving. It is hard to say whether he is holding his own or slipping a little. I think I find his speech a little harder to understand than I did a month ago, although this could easily come from his being tired at the end of the day when I usually see him. He has been very much exercised at the British press attacks on me and worries a great deal about how to ensnare the Establishment so that we may subtly arrange for my reinstatement as a friend and not Public

Enemy No. 1. This, I may say, is not one of my major concerns. But we have considerable discussion about it, because it appears to give him so much pleasure.

Alice joins me in love to you and Edna and in every wish that you may soon see the end of your present trouble. I have been sending the same messages to Whit.

Affectionately,

To HENRY A. KISSINGER

In a speech at West Point DA had referred to Britain's loss of a world role, and was loudly criticized by political figures and the press in Britain. "The General" is de Gaulle.

January 7, 1963

Mr. Henry A. Kissinger
Center for International Affairs
Harvard University
6 Divinity Avenue
Cambridge 38, Mass.

Dear Henry:

May I add my thanks to those Miss Evans sent for me. Your words of praise for the unfortunate West Point speech lost in the hurricane of British flap touch me and reassure me that, after all, it had a kernel of thought.

What you tell me of the General's remark also goes straight home. I came from my second mission to him saying the same of him, "Voila un homme!" He has true inner serenity from which all else follows.

Many thanks and warm regards.

Yours,

To KURT BIRRENBACH

This letter expressed DA's exasperation with the German government's lending itself to the Gaullist line that Western Europe could pursue security and its regional interests free of concern for its relationship with the United States. Dr. Birrenbach was a distinguished industrialist, member of the Bundestag and the Foreign Affairs Committee of the Christian Democrats, and member of the Bilderberg Conference Group convened by Prince Bernhard of the Netherlands.

February 19, 1963

Dr. Kurt Birrenbach
Düsseldorf
Königsalle 74
Germany

Dear Dr. Birrenbach:

I have delayed answering your letters of January 31st and February 6th for a variety of reasons, not the least to let some of the emotional elements of the situation subside. Let me try to give you my response to some of the observations in your letters.

Chancellor Adenauer made a mistake—and I think a serious one—in signing the French treaty when he did. You suggest two reasons for this: That he has not understood the implications of General de Gaulle's grand design for Germany, particularly so far as relations with the United States are concerned, and that he does not understand what you call the "idiosyncrasy of the two great Anglo-Saxon nations." Let us skip the latter, since the former is quite enough.

The Chancellor has never understood General de Gaulle's design nor the undignified and demeaning role designed for him and for Germany. He has believed that his place in history would be that of the reconciler of France and Germany—a place long since occupied by Messieurs Schuman and Monnet. Neither nation has today the power, interest, or inclination to return to the futile hostilities of the past. His real role, if he but knew it, was to cement together Western Europe and North America.

To sign the treaty with France after General de Gaulle's political manifesto and just before he vetoed (in defiance of the Chancellor and the other four parties) Britain's application to the Common Market was an act of singular imperception. The rejection of Britain was rested by the General on the ground of her alliance with the United States, a defect which one would have hoped would have been shared by the Six, including France whom we have for nearly two centuries proudly called our "oldest ally."

"In short," said General de Gaulle, "they (the Six) are united because not one of them (as contrasted with Britain) is tied to an outside power by any special political or military pact." We had supposed that all six were tied to us or—at least equally important—that we were tied to them by the most special political and military pact in our history, one which reversed the whole course of our foreign relations since President Washington's Farewell Address—the North Atlantic Treaty. Today that treaty, our obligations and all that we have done under it are the principal protection of Europe from subjection to Soviet will. Can the Chancellor seriously believe that rapprochement with France is the major purpose of German policy?

Twice again in the pronunciamento General de Gaulle returned to his obsession with the American impediment to European unity. Turning to economic matters, he pointed out that the entry of Britain into the Common Market would dilute its Continental purity.

"Moreover," he said, "this Community, growing in this way would find itself confronted with all the problems of its economic relations with a host of countries and primarily with the United States." The economic relations of the six nations, and especially France, with the United States since the end of the war have not been unduly difficult. They have been on the whole the relations of anemia patients with a blood bank. We are happy that our friends are feeling so invigorated and confident that they class the United States with a "host of other countries" with which they do not wish to be involved. But we wonder whether General de Gaulle really expresses a view which Germans want the Chancellor to accept?

Again, turning to military matters, General de Gaulle developed the same theme. Speaking of nuclear forces, he reiterated what he has often said of all French forces that, while he "by no means excludes the possibility" of French forces' being combined with those of allies, "integration is something that cannot be imagined." And why not? Because this "multinational force would be used to defend Europe and would be under the American command of NATO."

Unless the General objects root and branch to the combined command, organized through NATO, his dislike of it appears to center in the fact that the commanding officer is and has been an American. What other officer would he prefer? A German or Italian officer, lately in arms against him? Or perhaps a French officer, if he has one whose loyalty can be regarded as unimpeachable? One would sympathize with General de Gaulle if he felt about the present French army as the Duke of Wellington felt about some of his in the Peninsular War. "I don't know," he said, "what effect these men will have on the enemy, but, by God, they terrify me!"

In short, the General made it as clear as his considerable powers of exposition could that the United States' presence in Europe is unwelcome to him and that any close association with Great Britain raises a host of problems for him "primarily with the United States." Apparently a conception of "Europe from the Atlantic to the Urals" avoids these and raises no others for him.

After this disclosure of policy and on the eve of its dramatic inauguration, the Chancellor journeyed to Paris and there—doubtless after having been informed in the spirit of the new treaty of the General's plans—signed a treaty of close consultation and collaboration, a "special" Franco-German relation within the Six. This dismays you, but you can do nothing about it. You "cannot afford to choose between the United States and France" (which nobody in the United States wants you to do), but you find French policy "completely unrealistic."

Your solution of this, in large part, self-generated German problem is, to say the least, interesting. "All the parties in the Bundestag will urge the Federal Government to do the utmost to bring France to reason. It is, however, sure that the principal task to accomplish this objective will be yours." And what is our principal contribution to be? "To offer a limited and symbolic quantity of atomic warheads to the French Government."

I assure you that both your suggestions are quite futile. The first you dispose of in your second letter when you say, "the Federal Republic and particularly the Federal Chancellor are unable to exercise a decisive influence on the French President." The second would never be accepted by the United States Government, nor have, if it were carried out, the slightest effect in deflecting General de Gaulle from his purpose. He cannot be bribed, persuaded, or bullied. He can only in time, often too long a time, recognize the inevitable, as he did in Algeria.

But there is one thing that all three parties in the Bundestag could do to carry a clearer message to the French President—and incidentally but importantly to Khrushchev—than any that the Chancellor will send. This is to attach a reservation, if not an amendment, to the Treaty stating German determination to maintain the defense of Europe through NATO and the North American connection, to bring Britain into the Common Market, and to maintain the closest political and economic collaboration with the United States. This would remove Germany from the equivocal position into which the Chancellor permitted his government to be maneuvered. If, as all my German friends insist, these policies are as firmly rooted in German opinion as rapprochement with France, it can do no harm to assert them at the same time, and it could be a helpful reminder of them to both the Chancellor and the General. If either of them takes umbrage, that in itself would be interesting.

Sincerely yours,

To **PATRICK DEVLIN**

Although DA admired Kennedy for his performance in the Cuban missile crisis, he adhered to his own view that the risks of delay involved in the quarantine approach outweighed the risks of immediate air strikes against the missile sites.

[undated]

Dear Patrick:

Thank you so very much for your and Madeleine's kindness to our young friend, Mike Janeway. You gave him a very good time and furthered his enlightenment no end. We have become very fond of him. For the last three summers he and his friends have given us what you do not lack, the companionship of the articulate and irreverent young. Mike also shares with me what must be an illusion—that our daughter Mary is without peer. He is my reassurance against senility.

My senior partner—93 in Feb. 1963—says that I have the ideal life, participation without responsibility. But he has never had responsibility—or he would not have thought it an advantage to avoid it. It goes with the power of decision. This I have always found exhilarating. Do you remember Henry Nevinson's reference to a Greek definition of happiness, which I have never been able to run down, as the exercise of all one's powers in the direction of excellence in an environment giving them scope. I think it is in the preface to his *Changes and Chances*, a delightful volume beginning his autobiography. He was a real charmer.

At any rate, my involvement in the Cuban crisis led to my partner's comment. I was brought in at the start; participated in the councils of government, and was sent off as an Ambassador Plenipotentiary, returning to advise again until the Soviet decision to withdraw—what? Something anyway. My own desire was for more vigorous action than was taken. I never quite believed that my younger colleagues really understood the nature of the decision. They thought that the choice was between beginning tough, with some physical action, and risking its consequences, or beginning soft with the "quarantine" and, if necessary, working up to tougher measures. They did not realize—though they were warned—that it is almost impossible today to work up.

Every factor of domestic pressure, international pressure, general panic over nuclear war, ideological confusion (a Pearl Harbor in reverse), the hopeless fly-paper of negotiation which only a Korean veteran can appreciate—all this paralyzes effort. One never exceeds the altitude first gained. So I was in favor of destroying the missiles and the IL 28 bombers by low level conventional bombing and then dealing with the consequences. These might have been severe since a good many Russians would have been killed. We should have expected them to be severe. But if they were, then I thought that the Russians were ready for drastic action, anyway, and we would be better off to take the initiative than to await theirs later on. I thought that they might act in Berlin or Turkey, and that we must be prepared for war. My judgment, on which we could not bank, was that they would not react with spasmodic violence. Some disagreed; and I was prepared to accept their judgment and go ahead.

Both de Gaulle and Adenauer expressed the same view—that is, as their own. I expressed the U.S. Gov't view. However, I was only asked to express an opinion—which I did—and was quite prepared to accept the President's decision and go on from there. The trouble is that, as I had feared, we have not gone on. We are hamstrung by the U.N. and ~~anestest~~ (what a word) anaesthetized by Adlai's verbosity. However, my own talks were very dramatic and revealing of two great Europeans. Der Alte has just been here with equally interesting results. We swapped after dinner speeches at the German embassy to, at least, our own mutual delight.

. . .

Yours,

To MADELEINE AND PATRICK DEVLIN

The Devlins had sent a cable commemorating DA's seventieth birthday (April 11).

April 29, 1963

Dear Madeleine and Patrick:

Your cable brought me cheer on a significant birthday. I marvelled at your knowledge and deeply appreciated your thought. Our young put on a gay party for us and convinced me that I was not beginning a decade but only finishing one.

We also have hope of seeing you this year when we come to England in September for a meeting of the Institute of Strategic Studies in Cambridge during the third week in September. We do so hope that you will be staying soberly at home, and not be in India or Australia on a civilizing mission to the emerging peoples. Are you likely to be sitting or vacationing in the latter half of September?

I am being urged to go to the Continent in October to make some more speeches, but do not know whether I can bear it. The point has now been reached when I bore myself desperately. My respect for mankind declines as the species still tolerates the stuff.

We have been through a sad time. My great friend, Griswold, President of Yale, died ten days ago of cancer which has been stalking him for the past three years. He was only 56 and about halfway through a brilliant career, in which he was ushering our university into the modern world and at the same time leading our educational field in and towards the highest, and often sternest standards.

I spent the last afternoon of his life with him in an unforgettable talk.

My successor, as senior fellow, a great Anglophile, . . . has an idea that the job of President of a great University is a hopeless job, a combination of money raiser, alumni stimulator, compromiser of faculty controversy, general administrator, etc. . . . So he wants to do us over on the British model and have a Chancellor—of sorts—and then draft some member of the faculty to be a Vice Chancellor (Administrator) for four years, after which he would slip back into deserved oblivion.

Whatever can be said for the British system—and on the results, not much can be—it is that the universities, each a congeries of colleges, are Britain's experience of federalism. We have been strong for centralism, which is not the same thing as dictatorship. The Departments of Study have kept a strong *university* hold on all teaching and research; and the great university presidents of our history—in the last century, Gilman of Johns Hopkins, Harper of Chicago, and, in this century, Angell and Griswold of Yale and Conant of Harvard—have moved education into a new era preserving the traditions and standards of learning. To graft the product of British educational history onto a very different experience here will do only harm.

But I shall restrain myself, remember how we resented the interference of our retired brethren and let those who have the responsibility exercise it according to their own lights.

I am sending you the outcome of a recent return by me to the law courts. The Southern Railway retained me to argue this case in the Supreme Court. It seems simple enough, but the difficulty was that Black and Clark, JJ, believe that the barge lines are constantly menaced by the powers of hell in the form of railroads. The Chief, as an old populist, believes any evil charged against the railroads, and Brennan and Douglas usually go along to be "liberal." The task of advocacy was to picture the railroads as the true "liberals," friends of people, the consumer, the new South to split off the latter two, and to make a good legal argument for the four to whom that is a relevant consideration. It seems to have worked.

Felix produced quite a commotion in my absence last week by appearing at the induction of a young friend onto the Court of Appeals here and launching into a speech from his wheel chair. After twenty minutes of unhappy wandering and no signs of termination, someone wisely turned off the microphone. Someone else, believing the speech over began to clap, and FF's messenger wheeled him out amid satisfactory acclaim. It was his first really public appearance and caused dismay among the admirers who had not seen him since his illness.

Alice joins in affectionate greetings from our cold but beautiful spring.

Yours,

To **FELIX FRANKFURTER**

April 29, 1963

Dear Felix:

Thank you so much for your note to me about Whit. What you say of the effect of his death with me is quite right. Tennyson has Ulysses say, "I am a part of all that I have met." And so it was in our case, mutually.

. . .

Yours,

To **MRS. HOWARD F. ROSS**

Mrs. Ross was Chairman of the Giles-Johnson Defense Committee. The two Gileses and Johnson were young blacks under death sentence for rape.

May 21, 1963

Mrs. Howard F. Ross
Chairman
Giles-Johnson Defense Committee
319 Quaint Acres Dr.
Silver Spring, Md.

Dear Mrs. Ross:

In reply to your letter of May 2nd, I have given the matter very careful consideration, and have today written to Governor Tawes, urging that he commute the death sentences imposed upon the two Gileses and Johnson.

Sincerely yours,

To **J. MILLARD TAWES**

Here DA framed an unusual piece of written advocacy which was far removed from his usual concerns. Tawes was Governor of Maryland, the state of DA's residence.

May 21, 1963

His Excellency
J. Millard Tawes
Governor of Maryland
Annapolis, Maryland

My dear Governor:

Having been the recipient of a good deal of unsought advice when I was in office, I have been chary about offering it myself. I depart from this excellent practice now only because of deep concern in a matter which has been much on my mind and, I am sure, on yours—the execution of the death sentence for rape upon three negro youths, the two Gileses and Johnson. I shall try to make my points as brief and specific as possible.

They do not lie in any merits of these youths. Their conduct was thoroughly reprehensible and deserves severe punishment. But, although I have not had the benefit of reading the record, I have doubt whether their crime was that of rape, whether the punishment of death is warranted, and whether executing these men will enhance confidence, more than ever needed now, that Maryland administers equal justice under law.

It appears that the complaining witness did not resist, struggle, or raise a hue and cry. Yet, if she did not, the crime was not rape, unless her will to resist was overcome by having been put in fear of her life. She did not testify that she was so put in fear; only that it was no use crying out since there was no house near. In fact, there was one. Cross-examination of the witness on her habits and juvenile record was not permitted. This information, however, is available to you.

The significance of resistance and the excuse for non-resistance or no outcry was not explained by the Judge to the jury, which was left practically unguided in reaching its verdict. If this was not, as the Court of Appeals has found, ground for reversal, it surely bears upon the nature of the punishment. Death is very final. It leaves no place for second thoughts in the light of new evidence.

Finally, there remains the real doubt of the *equality* of the justice administered here. In cases in Montgomery County and the adjacent District of Columbia, not dissimilar to this one, where the convicted defendants have been white men, death sentences have not been imposed. At a time, like the present, when our negro citizens are acutely conscious and resentful of every appearance of discriminatory treatment, it is preeminently important not only that justice shall be equally administered under law, but that it shall carry every appearance and hallmark of equality. These sentences do not. They have about them the stigma of the reverse.

These crimes took place and the participants live in our general neighborhood. It is all a matter of intense but almost furtive interest there. I believe that the commutation of these sentences would be in the interest of our neighborhood and the relations of those who live there and are, in the main successfully, working out the problems of our common life. A sense of unequal treatment will inject new poison into that life and make heroes out of criminal offenders.

With appreciation of the opportunity of submitting these views, I am,

Respectfully yours,

To JANE A. BROWN

Walton Butterworth had been Assistant Secretary for the Far East in the State Department under DA and later Ambassador to Sweden. At this writing Butterworth was Ambassador to Canada.

Lester Pearson was Prime Minister of Canada and leader of the Liberal Party.

Harewood Farm
Sandy Spring, Maryland
July 15, 1963

Dearest Jane:

You are off chasing about on the sea, poor proletarians—the salt grapes of wrath type—migrants, with only one yacht to call your own. It saddens me—yet gladdens me—to think of you. You will rise to it and have a high old time; and I am damned thankful that the bouncing waves are not for me.

We have been bouncing around the heavens, at least we did so on our way back from Ottawa. Walt and Virginia asked us to come up for a dinner party they were giving for Mike and Marion Pearson. So up we went and stayed for three days of very good fun. One day of a swimming picnic for us four up the river at a friend's camp. Another day flying to Quebec to sight-see, lunch and home for dinner. It was quite enough and all very relaxed as Canada usually is.

Mike was recovering from losing a gland in his neck and from a Finance Minister's boner on the Budget, which nearly upset his government—about as stupid a performance as the Bay of Pigs. But he was laughing it off; and Marion was disliking power and position as much as she disliked its opposite. As for the rest, they were, as Walt said, a tribal society, naive, terribly serious about the wrong things and not at all aware of their real problems, which were worth being very serious about. Their best move would be to ask us to take them over; and our best move would be to say, no.

. . .

Yours,

To **JOHN COWLES**

August 5, 1963

Mr. John Cowles
The Star and Tribune
Minneapolis, Minnesota

Dear John:

You don't need to be straightened out on your views on foreign policy. They are all right; and your speech at Meadville is a good speech. You and I tend to concentrate on different aspects of the contemporary scene. They are all important aspects and it would be quite futile to try to estimate their various degrees of importance. I agree, of course, that the great undercurrents of population pressure, and the revolution of rising expectations, both of economic and racial advancement, will have—and should have—profound effects. They also call for urgent attention. I agree that the dispute between Russia and China is deep and important, but I do not foresee the developing consequences with the optimism that you seem to feel. In fact, I can't foresee them at all, nor have I found anyone in the State Department or in academic circles professionally qualified who does. So I don't know what you mean about "playing our cards right" and following "intelligent policies." No one, I suppose, would be in favor of playing our cards wrong or of following unintelligent policies. But what are the cards to play, and what is good or bad play, what are wise and what unwise policies are different and much more difficult questions.

From your statement about a connection between Khrushchev's retention of power and the lessened danger of nuclear war, I suspect (and it is slim evidence) that you may share the belief of some high placed persons here that "intelligent" policies would have one purpose "strengthening" Khrushchev against his domestic and Chinese critics, and as another through making agreements to "relax tensions" and "take steps" toward "better understanding" between Russia and the United States.

I confess that this line of thought scares me to death. The way to win the cold war may be difficult and unclear—though I am self-confident enough to believe that to plug away at the policies I have advocated since the end of the war will do it—but one thing seems to me as clear as day. That is that the one sure way to lose the cold war, is to lose Germany; and that the one sure way to lose Germany is to convince Germans that we are prepared to sacrifice German interests for an accord (or for what looks like an accord) with Russia.

This sort of talk has always frightened you off. You have excluded it from your generous approval of my 1962–63 series of articles and speeches. As Holmes said, "Deep seated principles cannot be argued about. You cannot argue a man into liking a glass of beer." I have made a much more careful attempt to explain my point of view in a paper for the September Cambridge Conference of the Institute of Strategic Studies. If your patience is equal to another assault upon it, you might want to have a try at the enclosure.

Aside from this return to a familiar theme—even though it is a pretty fundamental tenet in the doctrinal scheme—I accept the gospel according to St. John.

· · ·

Alice's love joins mine to you both.

As ever,

To **DONALD G. BROWNLOW**

October 24, 1963

Mr. Donald G. Brownlow
Department of History
The Haverford School
Haverford, Pa.

Dear Mr. Brownlow:

I have just returned from five weeks in Europe and hasten to reply to your letter of October 14 regarding the recent decision by our government to sell wheat to the Soviet Union.

I would support the decision to sell the grain, but not because our relations with the Soviet Union have changed in any substantial way or that this transaction can be expected to affect our relations in any substantial way. I would support it because it is a good business deal for the United States. We are selling surplus grain which we do not want for gold, which we do want. If we refrain from making this sale, we injure ourselves and do not do the Russians any material harm. The Russian people may have less to eat, but they will still have plenty, and the Russian government in the past has not been particularly worried whether they eat well or meagerly. I think that it is a mistake to try to inject political considerations into every transaction, because in many of them they simply do not exist. I am enclosing a speech which I recently made, in which I point out that I do not believe the test ban agreement marks any permanent or far-reaching change in Soviet policy. Therefore, it isn't a first step toward anything.

Finally, I do not believe that the wheat transaction bears any similarity whatever to the scrap iron sales to the Japanese before the last war, which I vigorously opposed.

Sincerely yours,

To **DAVID C. WHEELER**

Richard Rovere, referred to here, was author of Senator Joe McCarthy.

October 28, 1963

Mr. David C. Wheeler
2968 North 84th Street
Milwaukee 10, Wisconsin

Dear Mr. Wheeler:

You are quite right to be concerned at the thought that national interests might be subordinated to the whims of one man; i.e., in this case, the late Senator Joseph McCarthy. My views are set forth at some length in my book, *A Democrat Looks at His Party* (Harper & Brothers, 1955), which you may want to read for further discussion than I can give in this reply.

I shall not try to assess his effect on Congress or on the Eisenhower Administration. Essentially, my view is that, so far as the conduct of our government under President Truman is concerned, the policies of the government were made, submitted to Congress (which to a very great extent supported the policies by legislation*), and were carried out without glancing over our shoulders at the shadow of McCarthyism. There was, I believe, one exception to this, which I shall mention later. But, so far as our Far Eastern and European policies, about which you specifically ask, were concerned, they were not affected by the Senator.

However, the attacks upon the Administration launched by the Senator, had great effect throughout the country and upon the 1952 Presidential campaign. As I have written in my book (pp. 65–66), "In 1950–52 the ferocity of the Republican attack knew no limits. It went beyond the policies involved and the competence of leaders. It struck at the character and patiotism of those who devised and executed policies. It assaulted institutions of government and, as in the Bricker Amendment, even government itself. Nor did it stop at the water's edge. It involved the motives and character of nations and peoples associated with us. It is hardly too much to say that the whole conception of trust and confidence, including the confidence of the people in their own judgment, was brought into doubt. Officials and departments of government, the army civil servants, a whole political party, the labor movement, teachers and institutions, churches, writers and artists, all were cast into the limbo of doubt. The house of government was gutted. The new tenants found themselves the inheritors of suspicion."

I referred to one major exception to the imperviousness of the Truman Administration to the bludgeonings of McCarthyism. This was the administrative action under the President's Executive Order 9835 and the Act of August 26, 1950. Again in my book (pp. 123 et seq.) I discuss this subject, saying that I thought grave mistakes had been made and there was failure to foresee consequences which were inevitable. None of us involved in the Administration could escape responsibility. As I pointed out:

"There is no more vigorous and determined defender of the faith than President Truman.... The President believed that his Executive Order could and would be carried out with fairness and restraint.... But his expectations were not fulfilled by the multitudinous administrators of the loy-

---

* On pages 75–76 of *A Citizen Looks at Congress* (Harper & Brothers, 1957), I state: "... many of those [in Congress] who demanded the dismissal of the Secretary of State in 1950–52 joined in passing all the major legislation he laid before the Congress, including the Japanese and German treaties on the very eve of the campaign of 1952."

alty program, pressed, as they were, by the emotions generated by the reckless political attack on the Administration. . . . Experience proved again how soon good men become callous in the use of bad practices."

So, as you must see, I do not think Mr. Rovere has overstated his case. The consequences to the country and to individuals were incalculably detrimental, even though, as I have said, almost all constructive governmental policies were carried out without regards to the attacks—difficult as indeed it was at times to hold to the course.

Sincerely yours,

To J. MILLARD TAWES

October 28, 1963

His Excellency
J. Millard Tawes
Governor of Maryland
Annapolis, Maryland

My dear Governor:

It has been my experience that far more people write to a public official before a decision advising him how to decide than write to him afterward in support of his action, even when it was what they advocated. To help redress this balance, may I express my admiration of your action in commutating the sentences of the two Gileses and Johnson from the death penalty to imprisonment. Your decision was wise, just, and courageous.

Respectfully yours,

To MRS. MORTIMER SEABURY

Mortimer and Frida Seabury were friends of the Achesons from their vacations in Antigua, West Indies.

October 29, 1963

Dear Frida:

What a Public Relations Manager you are! I am impressed and grateful by and for your efforts and success in carrying my words to the great preoccupied public. Also I am warmed as always, by the glow of your friendship.

Alice and I had an absorbing, tiring, in some ways discouraging five weeks in Europe. I spoke perhaps a half dozen times, twice at large public occasions in the Hague and Bonn, and four times informally in England and Holland at unreported conferences and meetings. Britain, where I talked to mostly conservative, but some Labor MPs, I found moving swiftly to a Little

England, almost Swedish, position; France more and more to a nationalist, anti-American—and if we act wisely—isolated position; Italy, wholly self-concerned, prosperous and divided, is hardly an international force. Germany alone is subject—very much subject—to our influence (for good or bad, whether we know it or want it or not). The old Chancellor, bitter and mischievous, is encouraging the German Gaullists on the right. The new Chancellor, whom I like, does not have the mystique of a superman about him, and may face the ambitious challenge of an able junior, Schroeder. It was a most interesting visit, gratifying in that I found myself received, in a way, as the LaFayette of the new Germany; worrying, in that I have returned to tell a somewhat incredulous Administration that in being exasperated and irritated by the neurotic and irrational conduct of German officials—and often the German public—they are making the mistake of a busy parent annoyed by the pressing of a high-strung, insecure, but affectionate—almost too affectionate—child. It is a mistake to take what it says literally; and the worst thing to do is to shout at it or slap it. Keep it usefully employed, keep its confidence; and realize—please realize—that it is the only country in Europe (except Holland) which wants to do anything like what we want to do, or have done.

Sicily we thought very beautiful—wholly different from our preconceptions in the bigness and boldness of its physical beauty. Its Greek remains, many of them not ruins at all, are quite breath taking, and its twelfth and thirteenth century, Norman and Hohenstaufen buildings wholly unknown to me.

Then the lovely sound of Italian and the cheerful, picaresque, courtesy of all Italy delights me always. Perhaps, the most bizarre of our experiences was to hear in an hour of "son et lumière" in the Greek theatre in Taormina some Sophocles and Euripides recited in Italian. We agree that it sounded for all the world like Madame Butterfly.

We shall surely be in Antigua this winter; probably in February this year. Archie and Ada will be here in two weeks when we shall work it all out.

Our love to the Lord and Lady and all the company of Little Deep.

Affectionately,

To **SIR WILLIAM HALEY**

December 2, 1963

Sir William Haley
The Times
Printing House Square
London, E.C. 4, England

Dear Sir William:

When I told my wife of your kind note about sending me a copy of Noel Annan's book on Leslie Stephen, she purported to remember that we had the book in our library at the country and had both not only read it but discussed it with Noel when we stayed with him some years ago. This was such a shattering blow to what passes for my mind and memory that I, unwisely, made bold to doubt her. But a visit to the country today confirmed that we, indeed, have the book. I no longer dare to doubt further.

So I hastily write to thank you for your kind steps to find a copy for me and absolve you from further effort. This episode raises the gravest questions about the value of reading—or, perhaps, I don't mean that; but, rather, about putting any reliance on memory. One of my old instructors, long dead now, used to tell us that reading—so he hoped—in addition to giving pleasure, in some vague and general way improved one's judgment. At any rate, he added, it rarely did much harm.

Since we met, we have been through a horrible and shameful time. We may be thankful for one thing. I know no one in the country who is better fitted to pick up the dead President's burden than Mr. Johnson. For many years we have worked together. He has in him the stuff of command and a rare knowledge of government. Nonetheless, we have been badly hurt.

Our luncheon with FF was, as you wrote, a memorable and delightful one. Felix was better than I have seen him for many months.

Sincerely yours,

To **ARTHUR J. FREUND**

Freund was a personal friend who had written to DA shortly after the murder of President Kennedy.

December 3, 1963

Arthur J. Freund, Esquire
7 North Seventh Street
St. Louis 1, Missouri

Dear Arthur:

The last week of November will long be remembered as a week of horror and of shame. Tragedy was followed by the grossest ineptitude, incompetence, and sheer primitivism in Texas. To use a horrid word, the image of the United States as the world saw us was little, if any, better than that of the Congo. The police and bar of Texas have been a national disgrace.

I agree that the Chief Justice needs protection. As one who once was officially responsible for the Secret Service, there are limits to the scope of its effective service.

Sincerely,

To **JOHN FISCHER**

DA declined an invitation to write a periodical column for Harper's *Magazine.*

December 17, 1963

Mr. John Fischer
Harper's Magazine
49 East 33rd Street
New York 16, N.Y.

Dear John:

My small talk at dinner parties must be better than I thought; but, surely not up to Mr. Dooley or good enough for *Harper's*. Even where it is quotable, it is likely to run perilously close to slander and even closer to that undesirable social failing, "questionable taste." Usually it is stimulated by the stuffed shirts, the pompous and pretentious, who multiply in Washington like algae in a summer pond.

So you are most unwise to encourage me to write this stuff down, as, indeed, I would be to succumb to your blandishments. All I need to blow up my budding reputation as an "elder statesman," a sort of Barney Baruch, junior grade, is just a touch of Mr. Dooley.

Get thee behind me, Satan.

Sincerely,

To JOHN PATON DAVIES

John Paton Davies, a senior Foreign Service Officer and one of the so-called "Old China Hands" in the Department of State when DA was Secretary, had been dismissed from his post by John Foster Dulles on recommendation of a (Department) Loyalty Board, seemingly as a sop to the McCarthy fever. (He was exonerated and restored to his security clearance in 1968, but did not return to active duty.) DA here commented on an article which Davies had sent him.

March 12, 1964

The Honorable John Davies
Prescott 215
San Isidro
Lima, Peru

Dear John:
Your delightful piece on the troubles a colonial power has in pushing its fledglings out of the nest and keeping them out did, as you suspected, amuse me a lot. I passed it on to Roger Makins, who was in town on a visit after having retired from the service of HMG, and suspect that his amusement will not be as great as mine.

Why don't you do another on what a terrible time those well-meaning old codgers, John Bull and Uncle Sam, are having in maintaining a *pied-à-terre* around the world in these nice friendly new countries which are the hope of the future. The trouble all comes from the habit of the exuberant youngsters in burning the places down, or, if they are more moderate, just sacking them, whenever the poor arthritic old fellows don't move as fast or in the direction that our young friends think they should. It would not be anything to worry about except for the cost, because quite clearly we are only going through the cycle which Charles Lamb pointed out in the roasting of pigs. The delights of roast pig were first discovered by an accidental fire. For a while incendiarism became the accustomed method of roasting until the heat was more economically contained. Perhaps until these hopes of the future learn to read and write and use plumbing, we ought to have symbolic embassies, which they could burn down as a realistic protest. We might even learn from this that it wasn't necessary to have any embassies.

At any rate, the idea is yours.
With warmest greetings,

Sincerely,

To GARY A. CHILCOTT

Chilcott, a schoolteacher, had written asking DA his views on the value of classical languages.

March 17, 1964

Mr. Gary A. Chilcott
10785 Park Avenue
Clarence, New York

Dear Mr. Chilcott:

Replying to your letter of March 2, I derived great pleasure and knowledge of English from the study of Greek; some, but less, of both from Latin. Greek really teaches one style and precision in expression. I remember at school an exercise in putting the leading editorial in the *New York Times* into Greek each morning. Greek was so much more precise than English that the English words might have meant any of several things. Often, in picking a Greek translation, the suspicion grew that the writer himself was not too sure. Then the substance of our reading was unequalled. Caesar, Virgil, Cicero, I found heavy; the Latin poets better. But Homer, Xenophon, Thucydides, the New Testament, and especially the dramatists, have to be read in Greek to be appreciated.

Sincerely yours,

To MRS. ELMER MORSE

The early reference is to the Panic of 1893, the year of DA's birth and Mrs. Morse's. She had written DA about his published memoirs of Middletown, Connecticut and revealed that she was his contemporary there.

September 23, 1964

Dear Mrs. Morse:

So we were bottled in the same vineyard in the same year. What a vintage that was! The country was all upset about the financial panic [of 1893] that was going on at the time. But you and I rose above it, worked hard at our immediate responsibilities and soon had the country back on its feet— even before we were.

I am glad that you are writing some recollections for your grandchildren. They love these; and, if my own experience is any guide, remember that a recollection does not have to be an affidavit. My own grandchildren— and, indeed, in this respect, they were like their parents (or, at least, like half of them)—liked a good dash of poetical license in the narrative. Truth is so precious a commodity that it ought not to be expended in too lavish a manner. At any rate, this view I attribute to them and they have never denied it.

I am glad, too, that you survived both Pamecha Pond ice and Chrystal Lake water. Do you remember my father's clerical colleague in South Farms, the Reverend Mr. Gilbert, of the Episcopal chapel there? We possibly did him an injustice by regarding him as completely mad; but I rather think that we were right. At any rate it did him no harm, nor did his oddities do much harm to anyone, except my father who was continuously frustrated in refuting his errors by forgetting them.

I am at work on my major recollections up to my middle fifties which ought to be out soon, to be called "Morning and Noon." The earlier part might give you some further nostalgia. But it soon becomes serious and so dull.

With many thanks for your delightful letter.

Most sincerely,

To **ARCHIBALD MACLEISH**

Harewood
Sandy Spring, Maryland
September 25, 1964

Dear Archie:

I have just this minute read a sentence which I must share with you. It fills me with hope and joy.

William (Johnson) Cary in "Eton Reform," 1861:

"A certain amount of knowledge you can with average faculties acquire so as to retain; nor need you regret the hours you have spent on much that is forgotten, *for the shadow of lost knowledge at least protects you from many illusions.*"

I have for half a century clung to the belief that 9/10ths of my reading was not wholly wasted effort, better spent in sleeping in the shade. Now I know what keeps those damned illusions from getting into my dreams.

A pretty wise old guy, I says.

Cowles showed up at a meeting at the White House and a lunch thereafter given by Dean Rusk. He was in fine shape and asked good Cowlesian questions which Rusk couldn't answer—and admitted it. We are reveling in Sandy Spring.

Yours,

To **ELEANOR ACHESON**

"Eldie," daughter of David and Pat Acheson, was about to turn a birthday (Oct. 9). Here DA cast Eldie's father as the "heavy," the better to

garner credit for a gift. The reference to "Dave's knee injury" was to Eldie's brother, David Jr., who had, until that casualty, been a star quarterback in the 8th grade.

Harewood
Sandy Spring, Maryland
October 6, 1964

Dear Eldie:

This brings you much love for your birthday. I asked your genial father whether I might send your birthday present to you to blow on some depraved thought of your own; but he reproved me sternly and sequestered it to build you up, I hope to some greater and gayer extravagance when you are more on your own to enjoy it. But we can not put it off much longer. Spending deferred maketh the heart grow weary.

I am distressed about Dave's knee injury which takes him out of football this year. He seemed to me to be a sure bet for a hero, junior grade, before the season is over. What is the matter with you David Achesons that you get spavined like this? It must be some of that Castles blood undercutting us! But don't tell Pat that I said so, or I am in real trouble.

Alice sends her love. She has just sold one of her large, rather modern oils for a very satisfactory sum, and is feeling her oats. I have finished my book and am feeling mine. If you could hear what we say about you, you would be feeling yours.

Yours ever,
Grand Daddy

To JOHN COWLES

October 13, 1964

Dear John:

Many thanks for sending me your statement on Johnson-Humphrey. It was a most powerful and persuasive one, and should have an important effect. Also, it must have [sic] a difficult position for you to take—not on the merits of this particular election, but in the light of your traditions and activity over the years. I admire and respect your doing so.

I agree with a remark of Betty's in her recent letter to Alice that she will be glad when this election [1964, Johnson vs. Goldwater] is over as it makes her uneasy and unhappy. It has the same effect on me. I feel confident of the result. But the daily reminder that so many of our fellow citizens are fools or worse, and the knowledge that they are confirming each hour the doubts and suspicions which so many over so vast a part of the world have of this country is deeply depressing.

How good that you are getting away soon after the election with such delightful companions to so lovely a spot! We shall look forward to seeing you there in January.

As ever,

To **ELEANOR ACHESON**

DA here recalled the unusual distinction of Alice Acheson in her Wellesley College class.

Harewood
Sandy Spring, Maryland
October 31, 1964

Dear Eldie:

I can give you Alice's class at Wellesley since we were married just before her graduation, due to my powerful advocacy which made Alice the first Wellesley undergraduate to get married without getting fired. She was in the Class of 1917.

Concord from which we returned yesterday was strenuous but interesting. I did one hour of lecturing and three hours of classes each morning for three days. Alice had a show, and 2 hours of classes a day. Each evening something went on. . . .

We liked the School and the girls. We are distressed about your knee and hope that it is not last year's trouble again. What a fate—to be weak in the knees!

Love,

To **LADY PAMELA BERRY**

November 20, 1964

Lady Pamela Berry
18 Cowley Street
Westminster, S.W. 1
England

Dear Pam:

. . .

After recovering from the hangovers of election night and the vast relief of the next morning's news, Washington has taken a large dose of metaphorical barbiturates and is having a long slumber. After Thanksgiving we shall have to wake up, return to the problems of the day and Mr. Wilson's visit, and then plunge into the State of the Union and Budget Messages of early January, and the inaugural speech of three weeks later. The President has been away pretty steadily since the end of the campaign, which was the most protracted, depressing period since the events of just a year ago which made him President.

He has done, I think, an almost incredible job. I wrote him after the election to congratulate him, as I said, not primarily upon his majority, to which his opponent made a substantial contribution, but upon the achievement which was his alone of pulling together a shattered country and bringing us through grave troubles to a new unity. Like all powerful men, he has his faults; and some are not small, including his vanity. But I believe the election will do him far more good than harm. It will not, I think, feed his vanity, but will give him assurance, which he sometimes lacks, and bring home to him the vast responsibility which has been placed upon him. He has encouraged me to annoy him with advice, which I shall do with great moderation.

We send our warmest greetings to you and Michael and will hope to see you in England in 1965.

Yours ever,

To LUCIUS BATTLE

DA, in writing to his former executive assistant, now the U.S. Ambassador to Egypt, expressed surprise at being labeled a poor correspondent. The negotiating role he mentioned was as President Johnson's emissary to mediate the Greek-Turkish dispute over Cyprus.

December 7, 1964

His Excellency
Lucius D. Battle
The American Ambassador
Cairo, Egypt

Dear Mr. Ambassador:

How pleasant to so address you!

And how strange that I must begin by urging discretion on you—you, the very apotheosis of discretion. But when you write to me, "You are probably the world's worse correspondent," remember what eagle eye will catch it first and annotate it as this one was, "Where does he get that idea? He's no St. Paul himself!"

In fact I am not a bad correspondent, though I admit that I would hate being an ambassador. When I asked a member of David Bruce's staff why David immolated himself by staying at balls until five AM., the reply was that he was having the time of his life. Do you remember my shameless behavior in refusing to go to a ball in Paris with Vangy Bruce, Ellen McCloy, Diana Cooper and Princess Margaret? You are quite right; the social part of the ambassadorial role would drive me crazy.

But the negotiating role which I had in Geneva this summer was great fun. My Turkish and Greek colleagues became friends, if not of one another, at least of mine; and we came close to an understanding which might have cropped the Archbishop's whiskers and solved the idiotic problem of Cyprus to your Mr. Nasser's disappointment and chagrin. Our weakness was Papandreou's weakness, a garrulous, senile, windbag without power of decision or resolution. He gave away our plans at critical moments to Makarios, who undermined him with the Greek press and political left. A little money, which we had, the Greek 7th Division in Cyprus, which the Greeks had, and some sense of purpose in Athens, which did not exist, might have permitted a different result. The Turks could not have been more willing to cooperate.

. . .

We all send love to all of you and shall miss you at the Christmas Carol Party.

Affectionately,

PART

IV

To **NOEL GILROY, BARON ANNAN**

Noel Annan, at this time Provost of King's College, Cambridge, was a friend and correspondent of Felix Frankfurter as well as of DA. Annan had apparently planned a visit in February, failing which DA wrote to bring him current.

March 15, 1965

Dear Noel:

February has come and gone without any intimation of your presence on this side as you foresaw it in December. Perhaps Harvard and Columbia absorbed you altogether. Alice and I went off in January for six weeks in Antigua, a great success. . . .

I did a good deal of work. Some of which is now coming out. I enclose a few samples to show that one never knows what an article by me will turn out to be. This keeps the readers alert.

We returned just a week before Felix died, for which although [sic] I thought I was prepared—he had been so ill for so long—but found that I was not. Clearly he knew that the end was near for he had four of us to a luncheon over which he took infinite pains just a week before he died. At the end of it he said good-bye to each of us. We never saw him again. Whenever anything happens which I know would amuse him I find myself planning to dress it up to tell him as I have done for the last twenty-five years.

Houghton-Mifflin have in the hands of the typesetter another book of mine—autobiographical in nature though not an autobiography—about people and times long since gone. The small town in the Connecticut River Valley where I spent my childhood in a pre-automobile, golden age; our household in which my sister and I were the only American citizens and our views about affairs; the last frontier in Northern Ontario where I worked on the construction of the Grand Trunk Pacific Ry at eighteen; the old White Court with Holmes and Brandeis; Liberalism of the last days of Woodrow Wilson; my "brief encounter" with FDR; the "road back" to the State Dept.—and there it ends. Probably, too esoteric for the best seller lists, but not a bad book.

Whether H.M. & Co had talked with Jamie Hamilton (or anyone) about an English edition I don't know. His prior efforts for me have not been successes, I am sorry to say.

Things generally and broadly seem to be going badly. No government or country seems to escape. We have troubles at home and abroad and handle most of them like clumsy plumbers. Our neighbors, the Canadians, seem to be held together with string and safety pins and a flag to end all flags. Germany is in really bad shape. A good many of the cracks in Weimar are appearing in Bonn. My office has become a wailing wall for visiting German friends. Mon Général alone seems happy over the approaching troubles which will engulf him, too. Italy, Turkey, Greece, Britain—all are in the grip of painful circumstances. But I shall not become a one man wailing wall myself. Already some of us are at work to get LBJ out of his fixation on Alabama and Vietnam and back on to the even more—or, at least, equally important problem of leadership in Europe.

Our love to Gabriele and to you.

As ever,

To ERWIN N. GRISWOLD

Dean Griswold had written DA a moving letter of sympathy on the death of Felix Frankfurter.

March 22, 1965

Dean Erwin Griswold
Harvard Law School
Cambridge, Massachusetts

Dear Erwin:

You are very kind to write me as you did about my long friendship and relationship with Felix. Your words touched me deeply.

We have been close friends for half a century and very intimate ones for the last half of that time. Most of that time was sheer joy—perhaps the most joyous association of my life. Toward the end care and responsibility entered in too, but the joy still predominated. I find it hard to realize that it is all over. Almost every day something happens which I immediately remind myself to tell Felix about.

I appreciate your letter very deeply.

Sincerely yours,

To THE EARL OF AVON (ANTHONY EDEN)

Lyndon B. Johnson had been President for about a year when this was written.

[undated]

Dear Anthony:

Your article in the January 1965 issue of *Foreign Affairs* is wise and generous, qualities we have learned to expect from you. It also gently gives us some advice which will do us no harm. It will have a good effect here.

In the same issue I have some words which I wrote primarily for Mr. LBJ. Last year I said them to him in meeting preparatory to Harold Wilson's visit. Then he paid no attention. Instead he told Wilson and Erhard to go off and work out their differences together, which, of course, they were unable to do.

It is very hard to move from majority leader of a small body—a purely manipulative job—to a position of world leadership where one's personal position is the most important factor in the crystallization of decision. It takes all of our Presidents a good deal of time to learn about foreign affairs. Roosevelt took many years and never got a real grasp. Mr. Truman caught hold pretty quick, perhaps in 18 months. Ike never learned much of anything. Jack Kennedy was just catching on in 1963. LBJ tends to concentrate where the most noise is coming from. The way our system works instruction in foreign affairs does not play much of a part in the education of prospective presidents.

Houghton Mifflin has brought out a small book of mine, some parts of which may be of interest to you and Clarissa. I send it along to look at for relaxation.

Soon after the New Year and after bringing out a granddaughter—one who is happily both pretty and bright—Alice and I are off for our six weeks in Antigua. We look forward to it eagerly.

Alice joins me in warmest greetings as well as all the seasonable ones to Clarissa and to you.

As ever yours,

To WHOM IT MAY CONCERN

This testimonial to a spouse's character is a literary form not often seen.

May 3, 1965

My wife, Alice S. Acheson, is filing the necessary papers in support of her application to sponsor the immigration to this country of a domestic servant from Great Britain. I understand that a character reference is necessary and hope that one from her husband of forty-seven years will be appropriate and sufficient. While I may be accused of prejudice, I certainly know her character better than anyone else, and can in all truth and with enthusiasm state that it is of the highest caliber in every respect.

Very truly yours,

To THE GOODERHAM REUNION

DA's mother, Eleanor Gooderham Acheson, was one of twelve children of a leader of the Toronto business community. All remained in Toronto but DA's mother and by this date their living descendants were very numerous. DA sent this message to a clan reunion.

May 11, 1965

The Gooderham Reunion
Toronto, Ontario
Canada

Dear Cousins:

I salute you, assembled in your serried ranks! I wish that I could be with you. But I have long been committed to another reunion the very weekend of yours. Incredible as it seems to me, it was just half a century ago that, young beyond belief, I was graduated from Yale College. The sadly diminished remnant of that company is to gather and gaze at itself without recognition.

The last photograph I have of the Gooderham clan, before the turn of the century, shows some fifty or more of my generation. Not many of those are left. But most Gooderhams have heeded the biblical admonition and the early family example to multiply. We must be now about the dominant party in Ontario. I suspect that these reunions are merely a cover plan behind which to plot the Gooderham putsch. When the hour comes, let me know so that I can delay American intervention until we are firmly in the seats of power.

In the meantime, warmest greetings from the southern branch of the clan. It has not done too badly. Including captives by marriage, we can claim a total of about twenty-five.

May we ever increase and prosper! The Gooderhams forever!

Your faithful clansman,

To **ADA AND ARCHIBALD MACLEISH**

DA's thank-you note reflected a 50th Yale class reunion which was made a success, despite poor health and, as DA wryly observed, a rather random attrition of his classmates.

Harewood
Sandy Spring, Maryland
June 24, 1965

Dear Ada and Archie:

Tommy Corcoran is author of the apothegm that the greatest achievement is to turn a liability into an asset. This is what you did for me with this reunion. It could have been a horror and you turned it, if not into a delight, into a pleasure.

To our class Atropos, in the words of the general confession of sins, has done with shears those things which she ought not to have done and left undone those things which she ought to have done. This leaves the situation unbalanced, to say the least. But the Canfields' kindness and Archie's wise planning of our days brought home to me something of which I was vaguely conscious. We usually see one another in the company of pleasant friends, but nevertheless in company. The talk is sometimes amusing and sometimes purposeful—and some of this, perhaps a good deal of this, is desirable. But it leaves little room for the undirected, drifting, casual sort of talk which only comes with intimacy and quiet.

This to me was the priceless product of this reunion which even the battered and shabby frame could not spoiled [sic]. For this I am very grateful.

After another barium bout and a congeries of new drugs, I seem to be pulling out of the consequences of my misbegotten diet. It will teach me to leave myself—within limits—in the state to which it has pleased God to put me, belly, dewlap and all. My doctor told me that at a recent medical meeting, he had challenged the psychiatrists to give him a man selected as a thoroughly adjusted personality whom he would reduce in two months to a psychological wreck by acute and perpetual trots. I refused to be used as the subject of the experiment or to bet against him.

Our love to you both, dear friends, and please stick around!

Yours,

To **ERIK BOHEMAN**

Boheman had been Sweden's ambassador in Washington. He and his wife were particularly well-liked friends of DA. In this letter DA looked broadly, if ruefully, at the globe's problems. References are: "Mr. K"— Khrushchev; Jeff Parsons—U.S. Ambassador in Stockholm; "the Caribbean crisis"—revolution in the Dominican Republic.

July 7, 1965

The Honorable Erik Boheman
Stockholms Enskilda Bank
Stockholm 16, Sweden

Dear Erik:

If Jeff Parsons is a trustworthy Ambassador, he has informed you that I acknowledged my debt of a letter to you in answer to your most welcome one, and promised to pay. Here is promise fulfilled.

What we have been doing in May and June to be so busy is hard to recount. First, Alice had a very successful showing of her pictures in a Washington gallery and sold 34. This kept her busy. I made a series of speeches—one at a dinner in New York honoring President Truman, another at the launching of the nuclear submarine *George C. Marshall*—and wrote some magazine articles. Then came the 50th anniversary of my graduation at Yale and the 50th anniversary of the wedding of one of my roommates, which necessitated journeys and the inescapable acceptance that age was upon me. Finally, the State Department has drawn me—flatteringly but a little too persistently—into trying to penetrate the mists of the unfolding future and devise measures to help it unfold more advantageously than it otherwise might. I cannot point to any notable success; but that hasn't been for lack of trying. Whenever the spirits of my colleagues wilt, I encourage them by urging them to realize their blessings by contemplating the exchange of our allies, deplorable as they may be, for the bundle of horrors the Russians are punished with; or swapping the obstacle of the democratic political system with Walter Lippmann and the Teach-Ins for the one which bit Mr. K in the seat of his pants.

On the whole, the problems which absorb us and the press—those of Southeast Asia and the Caribbean—seem to me less difficult and baffling than those of which the White House and the press seem far less conscious—those which your continent and the British, who unhappily are not part of it yet, present so urgently.

The Washington scene, which is a way of saying the ambience of LBJ, is pretty well described in the fair, perceptive, and not unsympathetic piece by Joe Alsop, which I enclose.

The domestic political situation has been handled admirably. In this field LBJ is superior to FDR, though to say this is unfair to FDR since he beat into the heads of the economic Tories the understanding of the modern world which gives LBJ his starting point.

The Caribbean crisis was met sturdily and correctly, though brusquely. *Suaviter in modo* is not an indigenous Texan conception. However, it will turn out all right and has given the Lilliputians a healthy reminder that the threads with which they have been trying to bind Gulliver for twenty years don't even bother him when aroused. This realization upsets the liberals and intellectuals; but has brought considerable relief in Latin America.

The Vietnamese problem is delicate, often infuriating, very hard and puzzling for the soldiers and others on the spot, but not basically obscure. By that I mean that what needs to be done is not obscure. How to do it with the human material available, in the God-awful terrain given and against the foreign-directed and supplied obstacles is very hard indeed. The Vietnamese have no sense of territorial loyalty. Theirs is traditionally dynastic or religious. The former has gone; the latter is now a source of three-way division. Then there is the historic northern-southern dislike and distrust, with a million northern refugees in the south. As a result the essential need for a legitimate government which can engender consent has been so far impossible to supply.

Probably it can't be supplied until enough of a military success is achieved to convince the Vietcong and Hanoi that they can't win through insurgency and that to continue the war threatens them with a takeover by China. There are difficulties—though not insuperable ones—about a military success, but the greatest difficulty is political. If we take over the war, we defeat our purpose and merely take the place of the French.

Europe's challenge to reason and common sense seems to me much more baffling; the course to pursue much more obscure. First, there is England. The state of Britain is a most distressing one. Now that the precious years when the UK could have become a member of Europe have been wasted and de Gaulle has foreclosed the possibility, I can see no government, present or future, able to deal with Britain's disease and survive. Only the harsh reality of competition in the Common Market can do that. So disaster seems certain whatever likely course is followed, and a disaster which will surely involve others, especially the U.S.A., and greatly weaken the Western world. The state of the pound, present and future, certainly precludes carrying responsibilities for defense in Europe and east of Suez. Equally, to cast off international responsibilities, including those involved in the use of sterling as a reserve currency and in the support of former colonies, will cause almost as great a crash. Finally, any attempted rescue operation will just as surely be futile as a cure, and of little value as a respite.

Has England ever faced so bleak a future since the Roman legions withdrew and the long night closed in? I am naturally a sanguine, if not a cheerful, character, but I see no hope here. If you do, please share it with me!

My guess about the Continent is that by the turn of the year de Gaulle will move to dissolve NATO and edge us out of Europe. We should not wait for him, but begin to act after the German elections. It should not be aggressive anti-French action, which would frighten our allies; but should be in the interest of European gains already made and in agreement with Germany and Britain, if possible, to begin with. I would try for some agreement on political policy toward Central Europe and German unification, a quiet review of the relation of types of military power in Europe to political policy, planning for a step forward on international monetary arrangements and tariff agreements. These I would push so that de Gaulle will have to disclose a full policy of obstruction. He should not be permitted to choose the battle areas and win isolated (appearing) victories.

Although I preach this crusade, I have no royal converts and a Children's Crusade would be no crusade at all, not even a disaster. That would follow inaction.

Alice sends much love to Margaret and to you, as do I.

Yours ever,

To HARRY S TRUMAN

DA described here a meeting of some of LBJ's cabinet with some of Truman's and with LBJ himself. Vivian Truman, brother of Harry Truman, was recently deceased.

Harewood
Sandy Spring, Maryland
July 10, 1965

Dear Boss:

Just a line to say that my thoughts are very much with you these days. I know how close you and Vivian have always been and that his death has been a sad break with so much that you have dear. Alice and I want to send you a special message of love and devotion—a message which goes also to Bess.

On Thursday a few of us, whom LBJ calls his panel of advisers, met with him for three hours to talk about Europe, Latin America and S.E. Asia. We were all disturbed by a long complaint about how mean everything and everybody was to him—Fate, the Press, the Congress, the Intellectuals and so on. For a long time he fought the problem of Vietnam (every course of action was wrong; he had no support from anyone at home or abroad; it interfered with all his programs, etc., etc.). Lovett, Bradley, McCloy and John Cowles were there with McNamara, Rusk and Fowler. I got thinking about you and General Marshall and how we never wasted time "fighting the problem," or endlessly reconsidering decisions, or feeling sorry for ourselves.

Finally I blew my top and told him that he was wholly right in the Dominican Republic and Vietnam, that he had no choice except to press on, that explanations were not as important as successful action; and that the trouble in Europe (which was more important than either of the other spots) came about because under him and Kennedy there had been no American leadership at all. The idea that the Europeans could come to their own conclusion had led to an unchallenged de Gaulle.

With this lead my colleagues came thundering in like the charge of the Scots Greys at Waterloo. They were fine; old Bob Lovett, usually cautious, was all out, and, of course, Brad left no doubt that he was with me all the way. I think LBJ's press conference of yesterday showed that we scored.

I am reading the bound galleys of a biography of Roger B. Taney by Walker Lewis, a very fine book on a man whom I have always admired. Houghton Mifflin is publishing it this fall.

As ever yours,

To ALEXANDER M. BICKEL

DA was the impresario of a memorial symposium for Felix Frankfurter at the Supreme Court. This letter conveyed some suggestions to Professor Bickel about the latter's contribution.

September 13, 1965

Professor Alexander M. Bickel
Yale Law School
New Haven, Connecticut

Dear Alec:

Your letter delights me and fills me with gratitude.

It is not for one who asks a benefaction to submit specifications, but here is one who is bold enough to make suggestions. I do not ask a comprehensive essay on FF the jurist, the legal thinker, the teacher, but something more simple and, perhaps, more difficult, Felix on the Court. How, if at all, did he bend the twig and shape the growth of the tree? You will see how what I have written leads up to this. In 1939, old and once flaming issues were dead. Not even a glow lingered in the embers. The work of Holmes and

Brandeis had been finished by the War, the Depression, the New Deal and the Court Packing battle. The red portieres opened to admit FF on a new day, to a new Court for the decision of new issues. What did he do?

On memorial occasions too many people talk allegedly about the same subject and usually say very little. The happy introduction of Archie Mac-Leish on the program will insure one different point of view. Henry Friendly will do the usual review very well indeed. In the Court Room we must bear the S.G., A.G., and C.J. with such fortitude as God gives us. What I have tried to do is to write the movements leading up to your finale. The theme is the glorification of chance, insistence upon the living and upon the present as the only time of not wasting it in planning for a future which never comes. One only lives between breaths and heart beats.

If Philip of Macedon had employed Aristotle to prepare Felix to go on the Supreme Court, he would have made a mess of it. Instead, by following, as Professor Ames advised him to do, "the dominant impulses of his nature," without plan or forethought he absorbed the experiences, insights and wisdom which equipped him as nothing else could for his work on the bench.

Now then, what did he do on the bench? He talked a lot, and wrote voluminously—too voluminously for one. I never could read those endless pages—but what would a "strategic bombing survey" show was the result of all his sorties? From his talks with me, I think that he regarded his effect as educational, in two ways, and as important in operational management. I doubt whether he was a "swing man," as Roberts was; in that FF persuaded and was not persuaded. He created a majority, and did not merely make one by joining others.

By operational management I mean something which perhaps cannot be shown now, or until his papers have been studied as you have studied the Brandeis papers. He told me that the issue in *Brown v. School Board,* had come up several times before the Court actually heard it, and that only his strenuous efforts had prevented argument on the merits, which would, he thought, have produced a decision the other way.

But his work on the education of those of his colleagues who would receive it was great—at first Roberts and Jackson, later Harlan and perhaps to some extent Stewart and White. This I think was not only on great issues, but on the common decencies of not taking and reversing every FELA case decided for an employer.

The practice of appraising a judge by quoting from his opinions seems a fruitless bore. In a memorial piece on Cardozo (not printed in the U.S. Reports but in the memorial volume) I tabulated and discussed his position on every case in which he sat. If you want it I'll send it on, but I don't recommend it. The purpose was to give a better view of his position rather than a few glowing quotes.

FF also had some belief that he wrote for the long record, or to educate mankind. I would not waste much time on this. One's job on the Court is there and then, and must be judged that way.

I have written too much, and hope that it will not scare you off. There will be enough of Felix, the myth, in all that is said and written. He is good enough to warrant telling the story straight and true. Please, also, edit my pages ruthlessly.

Most sincerely,

To GENERAL EARLE G. WHEELER

DA exposed here some fundamental views on nuclear disarmament and the test ban treaties then under discussion.

November 1, 1965

General Earle G. Wheeler
Chairman
Joint Chiefs of Staff
Washington, D.C.   20301

Dear General Wheeler:

After pondering your letter of October 25, with its enclosed list of questions, it is clear to me that I do not know enough about the proposed Comprehensive Test Ban Treaty or the Threshold Test Ban Treaty or the Nonproliferation Agreement to go into the specific questions which you ask. I must, therefore, approach this matter from a much broader point of view.

I do not see any useful results coming out of the Eighteen Nation Disarmament Conference to which you refer. The difficulties which lie in the way of reaching either a test ban or a nonproliferation agreement are far greater than technical ones inherent in the subject matter. There seems to be a real possibility that to pursue these matters actively at the present time may endanger their future success and may also further the present disintegration of the North Atlantic Alliance.

First, in regard to nonproliferation, we are told that the grave and immediate danger is that India, under the stimulation of the Chinese nuclear explosion, will proceed to develop her own bomb; that this will stimulate the Japanese. Together that will stimulate the Germans, etc., etc. Therefore, the conclusion is that we must not only get a nonproliferation agreement but that we must in some manner guarantee the security of India from Chinese nuclear attack.

This reasoning seems to me wholly specious and misunderstands the Indian political problem. My guess would be that India has already completed the preparatory work to develop a nuclear weapon and will go forward to develop one. This, of course, is put on purely military reasons—defense against China. But, again, my guess would be that the real reasons would be largely prestige and political ones. Therefore, I doubt that there is any practicable possibility of stopping this development in India. I cannot believe that the Indians would sign a nonproliferation agreement, and I do not believe that they would wish to be the nuclear wards of the United States.

So far as the Soviet Union is concerned, it is hard to see any reason why they would wish to proliferate nuclear weapons, but it is not hard to see that they might wish to develop the kind of nonproliferation treaty which might prohibit our present system of stationing nuclear weapons in Europe and the further development of anything like the MLF or ANF. If we were misled into accepting such a treaty or misled into spending much time discussing it, the effect on the alliance and upon the Germans could be very harmful indeed. The danger from Germany is not that the German Government or people would wish to develop a national nuclear capability, but that, if they were blocked off from an equal participation in some NATO arrangement, they could not accept a permanent position of inferiority to Great Britain, France, China, and possibly India.

When it comes to test bans, it seems to me highly unlikely that those nations which are developing a nuclear capability, that is, France, China, and perhaps India, would accept them. Secondly, I doubt whether the Soviet Union would accept the inspections necessary to prevent tests in all environments.

The debate whether disarmament can precede or must go hand-in-hand with the solution of grave political differences is an ancient one. My own experience leads me to the conclusion that it cannot precede, and that extensive discussion of these matters at a time when the most vital national interests of some nations are at stake is likely gravely to disturb the alliance with them. My own preference, therefore, would be to emerge from the period of inertia which has come over our NATO alliance, face up with the Germans and the British, and perhaps the Italians, to the problems which General de Gaulle has posed, both of a military nature and in the economic and military fields.

We have already tried the policy of urging the British and Germans to solve these problems by themselves in the first instance. It should now be clear that they cannot do so without American leadership. There cannot be any American leadership until this Government makes up its mind what it wants. If the present drift continues, it will lead to dangers which are as grave as they are unnecessary. I would, therefore, leave the disarmament talks for others to worry about and concentrate our energies on reviving the alliance and our position of leadership within it.

Sincerely yours,

To **WALLACE CARROLL**

Carroll ventured into treacherous waters in suggesting historical errors in DA's book Morning and Noon. *DA dealt graciously but firmly with Carroll's friendly sortie.*

November 10, 1965

Mr. Wallace Carroll
Editor and Publisher
Winston-Salem Journal
416-20 North Marshall Street
Winston-Salem, North Carolina

Dear Wally:

I am indebted to you for both your delightful verses and for your warm words about *Morning and Noon*. Barbara kept this from me for a while until she came out of the state of shock, which all suggestions of error in *Morning and Noon* produce, and could recheck her original checking of these two points. Fortunately for her in this case, we think we are right on both points. It is definitely Richelieu who is the villain in *The Three Musketeers;* Mazarin became Cardinal—and, I believe, protector of Anne of Austria—after the period covered by the story. As to who was the Countess Gizycka, Eleanor Medill Patterson ("Cissy") married the Count Jospeh Gizycka on April14, 1904. He died somewhere along the line, and she remarried in 1925. At the time of which I wrote, to the best of my recollection and belief she was the Countess Gizycka. But, in any event, we are very grateful for your interest, and, if you think we are still wrong, let me know.

I was very sorry not to see you when you were here last week. Please let me know a little ahead of time the next time.

With warmest regards and many thanks.

As ever,

To G.L. CORNELL COMPANY

Straight commercial letters left DA esthetically unsatisfied, hence the fancy packaging.

March 14, 1966

G.L. Cornell Company
4715 Miller Avenue
Bethesda, Maryland   20014

Dear Sirs:

I have your form letter of March 9th in which you are far too self-critical, regretting that you have not been able to repair my "turf equipment." Self-criticism, as Mao Tse-tung tells the Chinese people, is good discipline. But in your case it is quite unnecessary because you have repaired my "turf equipment." The enclosed tags which came back with two power mowers ought to reassure you. It will be my own fault if you bill me, when you get over your unjustified guilt complex.

However, for two years now, although I have clearly written that I have three (3) pieces of equipment, you have taken and repaired only two (2). The Cinderella of the family, a hand-pushed rotary mower you consistently neglect. This, too, I understand, since I did not buy it from you and it is not much good. So I now suggest that I buy one of yours which in the future you may look upon with kindly eyes and treat as well as you do the other two.

Would you, therefore, sometime before grass-cutting begins deliver to me an 18-inch hand-pushed, rotary power mower and take my present one away on any basis you think best.

My house is clearly marked on Meeting House Road in Sandy Spring. The caretaker, Joseph Dorsey, 774-4659, lives on the place and will be authorized to receive the new mower and turn over the old one.

Yours truly,

To THE EARL OF AVON (ANTHONY EDEN)

DA had undertaken to review a recently published book by Eden, Full Circle, *about the period of Eden's public service, and here commented on the merit of the book, which he proposed to send to LBJ. The letter goes on to describe a colorful row with LBJ.*

June 29, 1966

Dear Anthony:

Your letter and the proofs of your book arrived about the same time. I am so glad that you wrote both. The first brought me pleasure; the second, knowledge and insight. Bill Bundy, who read the proofs before going off to the Far East, thought that you will do much good both by your helpful (because fair and accurate) account of the conflict and by your analysis of the built-in frustrations of the problem. Most discussions—certainly here—regard the whole matter as black and white and moralistic, or as a matter of "fighting to win." The echoes from Europe suggest an attitude of "you wouldn't do this if you really loved me."

Your suggestion of a possible way out seems to both Bill and me the best that the available material will permit. It presents some problems; but alternatives seem to present more. For instance, the precise Geneva format does not adequately recognize the interests established since then by Korea, Australia, and New Zealand, and, perhaps, overstresses that of France. Then there is the question of ICC membership. Both India and Canada are weaker brethren than they were in 1954. But who else is there?

You focus the reader's mind on the problem as it actually exists. He cannot differ with your statement of the case. If he differs with your solution of it, he will be hard pressed to improve on it. I shall say all of this and more in my review for the Washington *Post*—perhaps the best organ for reaching members of Congress and the USG—and will send a copy of your book with a note to LBJ.

That gentleman and I have been having a love-hate affair for the past few months. In acting as Chief of Staff for the France-NATO crisis, I have found myself in the middle of a whole series of intra-USG vendettas—Defense vs. State, White House vs. State, JCS vs. McNamara, Gaullists vs. European Integrationists, and LBJ-turn-the-other-cheekism vs. DA-let-the-chips-fall-where-they-mayism. This finally led to a press leak campaign, conducted out of the White House, directed against George Ball, Jack McCloy and me as anti–de Gaulle extremists. This all blew up at a White House meeting when, at some crack of LBJ's, I lost my temper and told him what I thought of his conduct and that I was not prepared to stand for any more of it. Rusk and McNamara dove for cover while Ball and I slugged it out with Mr. Big. Dave Bruce was a charmed witness.

It was exhilarating and did something to clear the air. Since then I have been inundated with action photographs of LBJ and me, and—more important—he has approved most of my recommendations. Whether anything will be *done* about them, is doubtful. I have not seen the Department so disorganized since the end of the Hull regime.

To prepare you for Canada I am sending you a book on that confused country by a group of Canadians and Americans to which I have contributed a brutal piece on Canadian foreign policy, entitled "Canada, Stern Daughter of the Voice of God." I should have added "Or How to Win a Nobel Peace Prize Without Trying."

What you say about *Morning and Noon* delights me. What stronger proof that you are a loyal and true friend than that you can read it and remain one.

Despite your complaints "Rose Bower, Broad Chalke" sounds enchanting. Alice joins in most affectionate greetings to Clarissa and to you.

As ever,

To BARON CASEY OF BERWICK (RICHARD G. CASEY)

DA had sent his Australian friend, Casey, the memorial symposium in honor of Felix Frankfurter. Casey, Governor General of Australia at this date, had been wartime Australian Minister in Washington.

August 15, 1966

Dear Dick:

I am so glad that you liked what all of us said about Felix. We tried to bring some warmth of affection into that formal occasion, as we were all pupils and long time friends. We miss "the little judge," as he was universally called, more than I can say.

Your news of Owen Dixon makes me very sad. His was a delightful mind, amusing and amused as well as scholarly and wise. A very fine judge, who belonged with the few great of the English-speaking bench. Felix was sure of this.

We hear great praises of you and Maie and of the work you are doing. I hope it brings you pleasure as well as the satisfaction of important work well done.

I have just finished a four months' stint of volunteer work in the State Department, taking the de Gaulle-NATO crisis work off Rusk and Ball and working directly with LBJ and Bob McNamara. It helped, I believe, but rarely have I been so frustrated. There must be an easier way of doing things than those presently in vogue in Washington.

Your new P.M., like your old one, is in high favor here.

Alice, who happily is well, joins me in affectionate greetings to you and Maie.

As ever,

To HARRY S TRUMAN

Truman had sent DA a warm note of sympathy upon the death of DA's brother, Edward Campion Acheson. In thanking Truman, DA limned a character sketch of President Lyndon Johnson, with whom DA had recently been working.

Harewood
Sandy Spring, Maryland
October 3, 1966

Dear Mr. President:

The message which you and Mrs. Truman sent me was most kind and thoughtful of you, as you have always been to me. My brother, who was ten years younger than I, died very suddenly, as he was reading at home. He had no history of heart trouble, though he had been in poor shape for some years from progressive emphysema. One of his proudest memories was of holding the title of your "Personal Representative" in late '47 or '48 when John Hilldring sent him off to Scandinavia to buy fish for the Germans to eat on Fridays. Now I am the only one left of my generation in the family, although I was the oldest.

We had hoped to go to an Army dinner in honor of you and were saddened to get word that the Boss had wisely decided to save your energy for other things. It is too long since we have seen you. I do hope that you are coming back strongly from your illness.

This year I put in five months of what Lincoln called "unrequited toil" in the State Department for LBJ and Dean Rusk on the de Gaulle–NATO crisis. I found it—between you and me—a most disillusioning experience in regard to both men. I recommended Rusk to Kennedy when he wanted to appoint, of all people, Fulbright, and had high hopes of him. He had been a good assistant to me, loyal and capable. But as number one he has been no good at all. For some reason, unknown to me, he will not disclose his mind to anyone. The Department is totally at a loss to know what he wants done or what he thinks. All sorts of channels spring up between various people in the Department and White House aides which result in conflicting policies getting rumored about.

LBJ is not much better. He, too, hates to decide matters, is a worse postponer of decisions than FDR. The phrase for that now is "to preserve all one's options." That means to drift and let decisions be made by default. It passes for statesmanship in our town to-day.

Two other things about LBJ. He can't carry on more than a few matters at once. Now-a-days his preoccupations are Vietnam and the balance of payments. So Europe is forgotten and a good deal that you, General Marshall and I did is unraveling fast. For the Chief of the world's greatest power and the only one capable of world responsibility, this is a disaster.

The other is that he is not only devious but would rather be devious than straightforward. While I was doing my best to advise him on NATO, and while he was writing messages and making speeches I wrote for him, he was circulating rumors in the press that my views were not his. If they were not a half hour's talk could have gotten us together. But it was not until I blew up that we had it and then I never did find out what he wanted done differently.

At any rate, I am now a free man, writing a book about my years in the State Department and about another President who used to do things very differently.

It is really too bad about LBJ. He could be so much better than he is. He creates distrust by being too smart. He is never quite candid. He is both mean and generous, but the meanness too often predominates. He yields to petty impulses such as the desire to surprise everyone with every appointment. It is too childish.

Well, I have gotten a lot off my chest.

Alice who is blooming (can you believe that we shall have been married 50 years next May!) sends her love to you and Bess, as do I.

As ever,

To **HARRY S TRUMAN**

DA had become seventy-four on April 11, a milestone noted by Truman, for which DA sent thanks and some somber reflections.

2805 P Street
Washington 7, D.C.
[undated]

Dear Boss:

The report about that birthday of mine was true and you were very kind to take note of it. My seventy-fifth year opened without noticeable pain. I am now getting accustomed to the idea, though it does run counter to an idea of myself which still hovers in my mind—that I am a promising lad and may get somewhere if I work hard and stay sober.

Poor old Adenauer is gone. Like Churchill he rather outlived his reputation and, as the British say, rather blotted his copy book in the last few years by the vindictive way he treated his less gifted successor. Both he and Churchill simply could not let go of power. Your predecessor had the same weakness but more reason for it. You were very wise and right in stepping down as you did. As I look back, I know that I was tired out when we all left office. We might have saved Europe from much that has gone wrong since, if we had stayed on, perhaps two years, or even one year more. But I could not have lasted through another four.

I see John Snyder who keeps me posted on you and seems well and cheerful himself, and occasionally Harry Vaughan and Clark Clifford. The latter I think is a wise and helpful advisor to LBJ. He is better than I am at surmounting the difficulties in personal relations which make helping LBJ so difficult and disagreeable. I have about stopped the effort and dodge whenever I can. The phrase, "he is his own worst enemy," was never as true of anyone as it is of him.

How very appropriate it was of the Greeks to give you that old helmet last month. I was struck with the changes in head sizes over two and a half millennia. After my experiences in 1964 with the old fool Papandreou over Cyprus, I began to wonder whether the Greeks were worth saving after all. The Turks certainly were.

You yourself will have a birthday coming up soon and Alice and I will soon have been married for half a century. Here's good luck to all of us, and to you and the boss much love from Alice and me.

Ever yours,

To WILLIAM R. TYLER

Tyler had commented upon the association of voter revolt with dissatisfaction, in political affairs, and got a Voltairean reply from DA. "Mildred" is the widow of Robert Woods Bliss. They had given Dumbarton Oaks, their Washington residence, to Harvard University.

May 17, 1967

The Honorable William R. Tyler
American Ambassador
The Hague, The Netherlands

Dear Bill:

Alice and I were sorry to miss you. We know you must have been busy in Washington and probably saddened, too, by poor Mildred's unhappy condition. She is a gallant old girl, but time is telling on her.

I am shocked at the cynicism of your question, "If people are getting fatter, hear more coins jingling in their pockets, and don't feel scared, why should they want basic changes in the order of things?" One might suggest a reason: Because even the intelligence of a super-simian should tell him that the order of things as it exists is too unstable to continue. Your answer, of course, will be that you are speaking of super-simians, and with that the debate closes.

Our love to Betsy.

As ever,

To LOUIS HALLE

Halle had been a member of the Policy Planning Staff in the State Department, and was (and is) a writer of perception and felicity. He and DA had exchanged views about DA's current writing project, DA's book Present at the Creation, *which was to be published in 1969. The de Gaulle matter was the support by de Gaulle for French separatism in Quebec.*

August 14, 1967

Mr. Louis Halle
Plan Proz
Les Granges s/Salvan
Valais Suisse
Switzerland

Dear Lou:

Your article seems to me much improved.

You greatly mistake my purpose in writing. I really am not concerned by "the verdict of history." As I have written elsewhere, there ain't no such thing (see enclosure); and, as for historians, they are only men or women whose unpredictable, and often unfounded and changeable, views will worry me less when I am dead than the little they have when living.

No, I am not wasting fleeting and precious hours of living upon a future which will not concern me. I write because I like to and I write about myself because my efforts at what might be called "pure" fiction have been, while amusing, slight. An autobiography is a good way to slip across observations and it gives a framework to a day not given over wholly to idle pleasures. Incursions into the world of affairs have left me disturbed, cross, and frustrated.

Mike Pearson writes me that de Gaulle has made problems in Canada by stirring up a matter which everyone, or almost everyone, had decided was bad medicine. Now like the press with McCarthy, comment and controversy have again become mutually stimulating. He would be better in the Invalides. What a wicked old fool! I find the Devil easier to believe in than God.

Yours ever,

To GENERAL MATTHEW B. RIDGWAY

DA admired and liked General Ridgway, who had succeeded General MacArthur as Supreme Allied Commander in Korea. DA commented here on MacArthur's performance in Korea.

October 17, 1967

General Matthew B. Ridgway
918 Waldheim Road
Pittsburgh, Pennsylvania   15215

Dear Matt:
    That book of yours is a very fine job. It tells the truth; it tells it clearly; and its views beyond narrative are wise. I was going to write that so few of our senior service officers have had the judgment and balance that you, General Collins, General Bradley, and the hero of all of us, General Marshall, have had. Then I said why say this of the military profession? It is as true of my own and all other professions.
    I am now dealing with the period you have written about and find immense help in your book. You are, I think, too kind to MacArthur. He was insubordinate; his insubordination did the country vast harm; and tended to involve us in wider warfare, which one can say he did not intend only if one repudiates the legal maxim that one must be taken to intend the ordinary and reasonable consequences of his acts. His advance after October 26 seems, and seemed to me at the time, unworthy of a plebe at West Point, unless he intended to spark something more.
    My warm congratulations on a splendid job.
    Letters that suggest a reply are usually a nuisance. If you can tolerate a mild one, you might care to give me a line or two on these questions.
    1. Where do you think the line was to which the JCS orders of September 27–30, 1950, told MacArthur to advance? I have always thought it was Pyongyang-Wonsan.
    2. When do you think he went off contrary to his instruction? October 19 or 26?
    3. When should the President's advisers (GCM and DA) have alerted him to incipient disaster? I should say after the fighting around Wonsan in late October?
    With warm greetings.

Yours ever,

To WILLIAM BRAITERMAN

The remainder of this letter is lost, but this portion conveys pretty well the major premises from which DA approached the animosity between Israel and the Arabs.

November 1, 1967

Mr. William Braiterman
Allied Merchants Credit Bureau
590 North Gay Street
Baltimore 2, Md.

Dear Mr. Braiterman:
    I do not wonder that you were surprised and puzzled by the outrageous article in *The Jewish News*. In this article you will find six lines of alleged quotation from me—which are reasonably accurate—and a whole column of abuse. Since you would like to hear what actually occurred, I shall be glad to tell you.
    During the course of one of my lectures to some five or six thousand students during the celebration of the 150th anniversary of the founding of the University of Michigan, I was asked what I thought were the chances for peace between Israel and the Arabs.
    I replied that I thought they were dim. Feelings were so deep and so bitter on both sides that I saw little chance of any accommodation being reached by discussions between them. The United Nations seemed to me impotent, since both the Afro-Asian majority and the Communist bloc were using the issue for anti-Western propaganda. I said further that if one examined the issues one could understand the depth of feeling if one had any objectivity whatever.
    To the Jews the conception of a homeland in Palestine was a matter of the most fundamental religious belief; to this was added the bitter psychology of a surrounded, beleaguered state. On the part of the Arabs there were equally deep emotions. Palestinian Arabs had lived on land now occupied by Jews for 2000 years, and there was some justification for their feeling that this was not too short a time for a political statute of limitations to quiet title.

To **SIR HOWARD BEALE**

Beale had been the Australian Ambassador in Washington and close friend of DA. Prime Minister Holt had recently disappeared while skin-diving near a reef on the Australian coast.

December 19, 1967

Dear Howard:
    What a nice letter came to us from you today. The best way of giving you my views on the current scene is to enclose excerpts from the transcript of a television interview, which the Washington *Post* printed a week ago. With you I find the current scene depressing almost everywhere I look.

In the last few days we have all been dismayed by the extraordinary development in your own country through the disappearance of Harold Holt. We, of course, remember him well and had dinner at his house in 1962. We were remarking at breakfast one morning that if we had read this in one of the current thrillers, it would have seemed overdrawn even for Ian Fleming. Who is likely to succeed him, and how, as you see it, does this affect the Australian scene?

My own fortunes have been moving in a way not altogether desirable. After a rather unpleasant four or five months of service in 1966 in connection with NATO affairs and a period of happy estrangement from the White House, I have now become a fair-haired boy again. This involves long hours of presence in boring meetings and so far as I can see a very delayed effect upon events, if any at all. It is true that NATO has now adopted the strategic theory that I have been urging since 1958 and upon which I have prepared endless memoranda for Presidents and Secretaries of Defense and State ever since. More recently I have been asked about the Middle East and Vietnam, with perhaps fifty-fifty results. Advice, not asked, has been proffered on relations with Portugal, Rhodesia, and South Africa. It has been treated with the neglect that it probably deserves.

Vietnam is a weary ordeal; Korea was the same. We had lots of trouble with the latter, but I think handled it more forthrightly and had the immense bad luck of MacArthur. However, the country got pretty sick of us and perhaps will have the same reaction to Lyndon Johnson. I do not think as yet this is true. Further, there is no charismatic leader like Eisenhower to head the opposition to him. All his opponents, Republican and Democratic, are silly asses and demonstrate this so clearly that few can doubt.

I do not think it is wholly old-age that makes me feel that this absence of leadership is symptomatic of our times. It is going on in Asia and in Europe. I predict that within eighteen months de Gaulle will announce his withdrawal from NATO and yet I know no one here who is thinking about the situation which his action will produce. And leadership in England, Germany, and Italy is even worse than ours.

I do not, however, go around being gloomy. I am having a good time writing my book. I stay in the country as much as possible. I try to read everything except the newspapers and have found this summer in Maryland extraordinarily beautiful. So for the time being, at least, I find compensations for the general oppressive environment.

Alice is well, working hard on an exhibition of oils which she is scheduled to have here next month. We have just come back from a visit to Expo '67 in Montreal with Mary and Bill Bundy. Mike Pearson most generously put the Prime Minister's apartment in Habitat, the new apartment house built on the exposition grounds, at our disposal. We all greatly enjoyed the visit.

With most affectionate greetings to you and Margery.

As ever,

To SIR HAROLD MACMILLAN

Macmillan had been Prime Minister of the United Kingdom and had written a detailed, multivolume book about his public career. DA was working at this date on Present at the Creation *and observed here their differing treatment of controversial personalities. DA noted the strong Greek-American sentiment in support of the conduct of Greece (versus Turkey) over Cyprus.*

January 4, 1968

Dear Harold:

We shall be sad to miss you; there is so much to talk about. Not the least of the topics is your book which I have just finished with great pleasure and admiration. It is absolutely first rate in style and content. You delight me with so much to say by saying it infinitely better than that silly old . . . who has nothing to say. But your generosity to de Gaulle is admirable beyond words after the shabby way he treated you. I have just finished my chapter on the removal of Douglas MacArthur and have not been able to equal you in Christian charity. Too many people have treated him with kid gloves—Mr. Truman, General Ridgway and so on. I have decided to tell the plain and simple truth and will be in great trouble.

In view of your months of anguish over Greece you may be amused over my efforts to make my romantic fellow countrymen think a little more about that difficult country. I enclose the correspondence.

We are having some trouble working out our annual West Indian rendezvous with Anthony and Clarissa who are being very social this year.

With warm greetings

Yours ever,

To JOHN COWLES

This letter to the publisher of the Minneapolis Star *and* Tribune *reflected a transition point in DA's thinking about Vietnam, from an earlier general support of the Johnson Administration's policies to a belief that they were based upon distorted judgments of the military realities and of the limits of patience in the United States.*

February 27, 1968

Mr. John Cowles
Mill Reef Club
Antigua, W.I.

Dear John:

The situation in VN is very bad—nearer to your appraisal than to mine. Important decisions will be made soon, perhaps this week. I may be consulted but I think more likely not.* A group under General Wheeler will be returning to report. Information here even at the top is very soft; probably what will be reported will be pretty soft, too. "The facts" are probably undiscoverable.

What one has to consider falls under two main heads:

1. The military situation.

2. The internal VN situation.

The U.S. political you can judge as well as I. On that, one item floats around the press rooms here to the effect that Rocky is in trouble over an amatory episode, which has attained rather wide private circulation and which threatened family trouble. It is not yet in print but has not improved his availability.

1. The Military Situation

This is very serious. Everyone concedes that present forces are inadequate to a military solution. (I avoid the meaningless word "victory.") The request anticipated is for about 100,000 more men. This contemplates holding the marine position in the northwest and undertaking a spring offensive to meet one anticipated by Giap. The enclosed piece by Douglas Pike is a good one on the factual side. The opinions stated need much salt. The marines are not "besieged" in the Vicksburg or Ladysmith sense, although surrounded. They can get out whenever this is desired. They are holding the place as an offensive take-off point. But if they stay too long, without additional forces, this could change, though not imminently.†

No one has faced up to the military situation in the light of attainable and desirable political objectives. There has been too much emotion— "They can't do this to us!" etc. LBJ tends to this. The realistic military choices are about as follows:

(a) A very great increase in forces (500,000 upward) and unified U.S. command of all forces, together with an intensified search and destroy cam-

---

* Today LBJ told me he wanted to see me.
† In the light of later info. I think they are in a precarious position.

paign and bombing in the north. This means heavy casualities, calling up reserves, increasing concentration on S.E. Asia to the neglect of all other questions, internal division, etc. It could succeed, though not surely. The end would likely be a SVN in a shambles and governed for some time by us. This would be the win-at-all-costs strategy, which is advocated by more people than would support it if the real requirements were known or imaginatively considered. They will be presented in driblets, each as one more push to victory.

So far as forcing the NVN to the "conference table" is concerned, we have had a direct and excellent contact with Hanoi for some months and obtained not the slightest sign of interest in negotiation. A negotiation for the purpose of selling out I should regard as despicable.

(b) Scuttle and run. This is not practicable and outside the lunatic fringe is not and should not be considered.

(c) A reappraisal and limitation of objectives and military, political and geographical responsibility. Our present objective is to end the NVN attack on SVN, through its own forces and those raised, armed, trained, and directed in the South. This, for practical purposes amounts to an attempt to maintain the present GVN (Government of Vietnam) in sovereign control of that country within its present boundaries. It is not now in control of the country, was not when we started our effort and will not be even if by arms we subdue every resisting element in the country. We will be in control. We do not want to be in control. How do we try, at least, to attain as much of our purpose as we can and not something quite different?

This is an extremely difficult and dangerous thing to do, or even try to do, since it could bring about the collapse of the GVN. It must be done with honesty toward our ally and the realization that very little in Washington, D.C., remains secret. Some approach to secrecy must, at least, be maintained while the USG makes up its mind on a new strategy and consults with the GVN. Tactically we may have to do some unsound things to adjust ourselves to a new course and extricate ourselves from difficult positions. But the essential requirement is to make the basic decisions and get on with them, election or no election.

Present U.S. strategy is to use our own forces for a war of attrition, search and destroy, so as to exhaust NVN and VC manpower and end the war by exhaustion. We have left protection of population centers to the GVN forces. The trouble is that neither is adequate to their task.

The U.S. forces are inadequate because for reasons which may or may not be valid, but which seem to be endemic in our military practice, only about one-fifth of our 400,000 ground forces are fighting troops. A large part of them are immobilized around Khesanh. The rest are support forces. This is a larger "tail" than we had in World War II or Korea, but may be necessary. It seems excessive. General Giap is under no such costly handicap. The fighting forces that face one another are not so unequal. Our firepower is vastly superior, but the terrain is a handicap. Last year the tons of explosives used by us was just a little less than the total of the largest year of WW II, plus the largest year of Korea. It plainly hurt the enemy but has not stopped him. He has his troubles which we do not know as well as our own, but he dealt us a nasty blow in January.

The GVN forces guarding the centers of population are inadequate for several reasons. Their venality and unwillingness to fight has probably been overplayed. They are outgunned by the VC and NVN, who have many more automatic weapons, while the GVN troops have largely surplus WW II and Korean War arms. Also the scattered protecting units lack the communications and mobile reserves to reinforce them when they are attacked by larger than purely local VC, as they were in a large number of places in January. They fought well but many were overrun and civilians suffered and lost confidence in them and the GVN. It is expected that Giap will press this advantage before May, so that the next six weeks may be decisive.

Giap, as Pike [Douglas] in the *Post* article correctly says, is playing for the population centers and to break up the U.S. airfields and communications. A phony negotiating play or rumor could be used also to arouse doubts about us

What to do? The course I can see is to block Giap's plans before we lose the Government, the people, and possibly the marines. This means reorganizing the defense of the people (most of the people are in the South), using most of our forces as highly mobile reserves strategically placed, and others for search and harass missions with vast air preparation and support, but based where they cannot be cut off and besieged. I would also want to know why within present number ceilings, or less, we cannot get more combat troops, both U.S. and GVN.

This requires delicate but tough dealings with the GVN, including demands for progress toward area pacification where an end of belligerency within perhaps shrunken areas might be foreseen. We must always be aware that we are there in the role of helpers of the GVN. If that collapses, we have no future there and must be able to extricate ourselves.

This is dark picture, but the way I see it.

Yours,

P.S. After further discussions this week and next I will perhaps have some further thoughts.

To **THE FILE**

DA's views about Vietnam, expressed here, were still in a state of tran-sition. Abbreviations here and later refer variously to Government of North Vietnam, North Vietnam, Government of Vietnam, South Vietnam, and Vietcong.

CONFIDENTIAL

Meeting with the President   March 14, 1968
Re
Vietnam
and
The Gold Crisis

The President asked me to lunch with him today to discuss Vietnam. He was delayed until two o'clock discussing the gold crisis with Treasury, FRB, and Economic Advisers. At two o'clock we went to lunch alone in the White House private dining room, where we stayed talking until he left to resume the gold discussions at three o'clock.

What he said about gold is noted in an appendix.

The hour we devoted to discussing Vietnam was divided approximately equally between us, the President giving me a summary of the situation; I giving him the ideas that I developed over the last couple of weeks. His re-port was substantially the same as what I had learned during my various briefings.

He was quite aware of the serious knock that we have taken during the Tet offensive. About a third of our airlift in Vietnam had been lost, about a third damaged, and about a third not touched. Our casualties had been about 3000. The cities had been hurt, the morale of the people badly shaken. If the GNV had expected a general uprising, or, indeed, specific ones, or the collapse of the government, they had miscalculated. However, they would doubtless continue. The situation disclosed was a serious one, which he did not discount.

I gathered that the soldiers took a more optimistic view than he did. Westmoreland thought that the NVN were massing for a major battle in the north, either around Khe Sanh or before Hue. He thought they had brought down 24 to 25,000 new troops and might be producing more or perhaps an equal number. He would not move until he was clearer as to where the bat-tle would be fought.

What Westmoreland had asked for was a series of patchwork additions and replacements, which might go as high as 50,000 within the next four months, or more hopefully might be kept to half that number. They con-sisted of a few more marines, considerable additions to the medical staff—

doctors, nurses, etc.—and other supply troops. Our remaining reserves in the United States were so low that, if trouble broke out elsewhere, we might be hard pushed. He would probably have to call up total reserves in the neighborhood of 80 to 90,000, although the army wanted 200,000. He would not do the latter, but he might have to do the former in order to get such people as ready air reserves to send to Korea and other types of reserve troops to build units for this country.

The President said that he was being pushed by several quarters on the Hill and elsewhere to set up a committee to review the situation and advise on ends and means in Vietnam. He asked me what I thought about the situation.

I said that I would be strongly opposed to the committee idea. I thought it would be of no use to him and that as a political mechanism it would only cause confusion, to which he added that it would give the impression that he had lost confidence in himself.

I went on to say that what was called for now was more basis for judgment; that is, more knowledge of what had happened and what was happening and less uninformed opinion. I did not believe, and I doubted whether he did, much that was reported, since it fluctuated greatly by reflecting optimism on some cases and pessimism on others. For instance, I doubted gravely a figure of Westmoreland's that the President had mentioned to the effect that he had killed or captured 60,000 Vietminh troops during the Tet offensive.

I said that since any reinforcements we might send to Vietnam in the next six months could not possibly affect what happened there, I urged him to restrict what we sent to the minimum necessary to plug existing holes, and to make no major decisions until he could get clearer information on the facts. He agreed with this and said that he thought Dean Rusk and Clark Clifford would agree also.

It was, I thought, possible to have information collected and projections made within the Government which would be of the greatest help in coming to an appraisal of ultimate, as well as immediate, possibilities and objectives. These projections would relate to what we could expect at various periods over the next few years as the result of improved effort by the GVN in performing its tasks and by the best that the U.S. forces could do with their present numbers. I took it that the purpose of both efforts was to enable the GVN to survive, to acquire public support, and to be able to stand alone, at least for a period of time, with only a fraction of the foreign military support it had now. If this could not be accomplished at all or only after a very protracted period with the best that present numbers could do, it seemed to me that the operation was hopeless and that a method of disengagement should be considered. If, however, some measure of success could be expected, strategy should be redirected to obtaining that, even though it was far less than we had originally hoped. Therefore, he should not for the present commit himself to absolute positions. (At this point he interrupted to say that he had not and would not.)

I added that I was convinced from what I had learned that Hanoi had no interest whatever in negotiations and under present circumstances would have no interest in any negotiation which left a government in SVN which they could not control. Therefore, while negotiations at some point might be the only choice, at the present time to engage in them could only do great harm to the standing of the GVN.

I said that there was a younger group within the Government who could prepare for their cabinet superiors over a period of time the information and projects which I had suggested and that I would be glad, if he wished, to work up some names.

At that point Walt Rostow came into the room. The President said that he was going off to a gold meeting and wanted me to summarize what I had said for Walt and give him some names. Walt listened to me with the bored patience of a visitor listening to a ten-year-old playing the piano.

APPENDIX

I talked with the President about gold at lunch on March 14. The President had asked me to read a memorandum by Walt Rostow, summarizing the reasons for and against closing the London gold market as of the close of business on March 14. Apparently we had lost almost $400,000,000 in gold the day before and were expected to lose another billion if the market opened on the 15th. The Treasury hoped to have a meeting with the sponsors of the market over the weekend. The principal reasons for closing the market were to save the gold loss and to take the initiative in the present gold crisis; the reason against, which seemed to have been supported solely by Bill Martin, was to accept the loss in order to impress the other sponsors that we would have consultation with them before taking a decision.

He asked my opinion, which was in favor of closing the market. I did not think the advantage, whatever that might be, of not doing so was worth the price. I asked the President whether he and his advisers had consulted the views put forward by Emile Despres and Charlie Kindleberger, which involved stopping the purchase of gold and considering whether to devote our efforts to maintaining parity of the dollar with other currencies and not bothering about its relation to gold, perhaps making some arrangement with the monetary fund about our existing stock. He was aware of the proposals but had not discussed them. He then dropped the gold question and turned to Vietnam.

To J.H.P. GOULD

*Gould had become a close friend of DA through a lengthy annual re-
union at Antigua in the West Indies. In this note and enclosure, it appeared
that DA's views were hardening in disagreement with the Administration's
evaluation of risks and opportunities in Vietnam.*

2805 P Street, N.W.
Washington 7, D.C.
March 29, 1968

Dear J:

My latest musings on the all pervading subject—

The diagnosis is much easier than the cure. This too, I have been
working on but have no ideas yet worth reporting.

I am not very popular at 1600 Penna. Ave., but no one else is either.
The boys who have been saying that victory is just around the corner have
begun to remember a guy named Herbert Hoover. . . .

If Charlie Wight would care to see my memo, please show it to him.

Love to Lee.

Yours,

CONFIDENTIAL
MEMORANDUM

DA's Views
Regarding Vietnam
as of March 26, 1968

Point 1. In the time the American people will allow this President or
any other President to continue operations in Vietnam the belligerency
there cannot be brought by the use of the present means or any other that
they will permit to a point where the GVN can handle it.

Point 2. This fact, together with our broader interests in SEA, Europe,
and in connection with the dollar crisis, requires a decision now to disengage within a limited time. In accordance with that decision actions from
now on should not be inconsistent with it. There should also be some evidence of a new policy by mid-summer.

Point 3. Reasons for Point 1. My investigations and briefings over the
past month have convinced me that two contemporaneous and interrelated
struggles are going on.

(a) That of the GVN to maintain itself and obtain popular support; and
(b) That of the U.S.A. to subdue the NVN forces in SVN so as to keep

them off the GVN's back while (a) is being accomplished and to break the will of the NVN to continue the attack upon the GVN thereafter.

My investigations also convince me that both of these efforts are failing and will fail within the time allowable, because:

(a) At the present time and within the future of a year or so NVN and VC forces can move freely about SVN, thus being able to disengage from conflict with U.S.A. forces and to attack the countryside and centers of population, destroying confidence in GVN;

(b) The pacification program has been badly disrupted and will take months to get going again and can continue to be disrupted by the attacks mentioned above.

(c) The attitude of the population toward the GVN is one of apathy. The Tet offensive has increased this. They are not attracted to the VC and they do not dare risk attaching themselves to GVN. In other words, what is lacking in SVN is a missing component, i.e., popular support, which the U.S.A. cannot supply.

I do not know how much time the country will allow the USG to continue its efforts in SVN. I should not think more than a year or so, and I should guess not so long unless during the summer a sign appears indicating a new policy aimed at ending the conflict. One thing seems sure. The old slogan that success is just around the corner won't work.

To **JANE ACHESON BROWN**

This thank-you note for a birthday present (April 11) of material for a jacket was combined with some news from the home front. The island of Antigua had civil disorders soon after DA had returned from there. Washington had experienced, just a few days before, major disorders and fires upon the news of the assassination of Martin Luther King, Jr. DA's views on Vietnam were now crystallized in opposition to LBJ's course of action. Present at the Creation was nearing completion. DA's friend, Phil Reed, a retired chairman of the General Electric Company, was something of a rival in matters of dress.

Harewood
Sandy Spring, Maryland
April 13, 1968

Dearest Jane:

What a lovely piece of material. Phil Reed will go out of his mind when this is sprung on Antigua. We are putting it in train and will show you the result when you come north with the late birds.

We have had great goings on since we came back. First Antigua had strikes and riots in the approved black revolt against mostly their own ineptitude. This as you can imagine, worries the hell out of the white, wealthy patrons of Antigua, who can't figure what they did wrong, but are sure that the trouble can't be the fault of God's children who have all got wings.

So we came home and I was given the big briefing on VN at LBJ's orders, to advise him. I got it and came to the conclusion that we had been wrong in believing that we could establish an independent, noncommunist state in SVN. It's too complicated to spell out. The heart of it is that militarily we cannot keep the NVN off the backs of the SVN while they deal with the VC and build a state. What to do about it—which adds up to not much—takes another couple of hours.

I went through it all with LBJ who for a while seemed convinced, then decided to step out, now while staying out has had an adrenalin infusion from the brass, and now has everyone so confused that no one knows the points of the compass. . . . I just keep flowin' along, confident that we are going to hell in a hack with Mr. Nixon as our inspiring leader.

The last weekend was one to raise one's faith in the American dream, with the whole damned town burning down around us, Europe in a mess and as big a mess in Washington as we have had since the British burned it. Both they and the blacks botched the job.

I had quite a birthday letter from LBJ—an extraordinary man. A real Centaur—part man part horse's ass. A rough appraisal, but curiously true. I shall try to remember to ask B.E. to enclose a copy of this *Top Secret* letter to you.

Pat and Dave had a very gay party for me. The curfew just lifted in time for a 6:30 to 10:30 swing-ding. Bob McNamara and Clark Clifford both came with their wives so that those who wanted the lowdown could try to get it. Both were in top health and form.

On Thursday Lady Bird is having Margaret Truman unveil her mother's portrait in and for the White House and I am to make the speech. I expect to have some fun—one of the perquisites of age.

My publisher comes tomorrow for a visit and some talk of the transformation of my script into a book, with pages, volumes, dates—at least so I hope—beginning to take form. I am now about to write Chap. 45—out of 52 or 53.

My love and deepest gratitude to you.

As ever,

To JANE ACHESON BROWN

The complex transaction dealt with here touched upon DA's secret life as Beau Brummell: His daughter Jane had offered him a choice of materials and colors for handmade resort shoes. DA's eyes were acting up for the reasons disclosed here. His granddaughter Eleanor had recently written a letter to The New York Times *taking Chester Bowles to task.* Present at the Creation *had become a popular success.*

2805 P Street
Washington, D.C.   20007
[undated]

Dearest Jane:

Thank you for your very clear and helpful letter. I am overwhelmed by the choice. With help from ASA I have picked out the green trimmed with honey [illegible] like this

Second choice highly touted by ASA is brown lizard. Is this a Hemingway or a honey brown? Though this question should be disregarded. No 10 will be lovely.

My mysterious eye has been solved at last, with rather shattering consequences. It comes from thyroid deficiencies due to treatment by radioactive iodine some years ago to reduce hyperthyroid. The eyeballs have swollen; I see double and something not absorbed causes the swelling. Tests still go on. Our trip to Africa has been canceled. Rats and damn! as old Judge Jenks used to say. The treatment is probably cortisone every 3 to 6 months.

. . .

Enclosed is a letter from the NYT of October 23. The writer is whom you readily suppose. She told no one, but wrote it the day after Chester Bowles stupidly appeared and sent it off. It might be the President of Wellesley ticking off a rather backward freshman. What a girl! She now lives around the corner from us with two other girls and has a very good job with the Urban Institute, a research organization for urban problems.

The book has taken the country by storm. Sales are about 75,000 and reprinting goes on apace. The Book of the Month Club which made it only an alternate has now ordered 25,000 and is sending out a special notice offering it to its members for gifts for Xmas. This is all very gratifying. Eric Swenson of Norton's says that they have never had such a book. He gets "all choked up" over the reviews. I am very happy about it and Barbara evidently doesn't quite believe it.

. . .

Much love to you and Dudley.

Ever yours,

To J.H.P. GOULD

DA spoke at the Phillips Exeter Academy graduation of a grandson, David Acheson, Jr. Robert F. Kennedy had been assassinated shortly before.

June 11, 1968

Dear J:

This past weekend we flew to Boston and on to Exeter for Dave Jr.'s graduation where I spoke. The enclosed was the advance copy, the beginning of which had to be redone to take account of the "Day of National Mourning." In fact, it seems to have been a national wake. . . . But Exeter was very good indeed. Dave graduated "With High Honors" which was very pleasing to the old folks. Mr. Day, the Yale Principal of the school, told me that some of the more excitable of the seniors had started a plan to walk out as one on the theory that I was a "hawk" on Vietnam. He very wisely asked them to document their statement which they, of course, could not do. Then Dave undertook to meet the ring leaders and give them a sketch of my views over the years which surprised them a good deal. The speech made a great hit with the parents. Perhaps the "malcontents" wished they had walked out after all.

Archie's view of the Texas-based conspiracy to assassinate liberals seems to me absurd. This has always been a violent society. My son Dave believes that this recent example was largely the interaction of television and Bobby Kennedy's peculiar ability to rouse the rabble and provoke violent support and violent dislike. When this is carried as far and wide as television does carry it, the number of unstable people who become aroused is vastly increased. Add his determination to establish an almost physical contact with great masses, and violent assault becomes almost inevitable. How many nuts, he asks, do we suppose got overwrought by Warren Harding's front porch campaign from Marion, Ohio, or had the opportunity to get near him? I do not think that a Commission is needed to tell us the obvious. The television from gangster movies for the teenager to battlefront murder in Vietnam to the political and sentimental frenzy of the Kennedy funeral keeps this country in an emotional frenzy.

. . .

Love to Lee.

Yours ever,

To LINCOLN MACVEAGH

MacVeagh, an old friend of DA, had been U.S. Ambassador to Portugal and at this date was living in retirement outside Lisbon, in sadly failing health. W. Tapley Bennett was U.S. Ambassador there at the time.

August 19, 1968

The Honorable Lincoln MacVeagh
Casa das Laranjeires
Estoril, Portugal

Dear Lincoln:

A note from Tap Bennett has quite shattered Alice and me with its report of all that you have been through. Our thoughts and warmest affection go to you with every hope that you are turning the corner toward a better day. We always think and speak of you, both of the days past which we enjoyed so much and with the hope of seeing you again here or in Lisbon. Your troubles make us both feel revoltingly healthy.

However, we do not feel so buoyant about the world around us at home or abroad. Here for the past couple of years I have come to depressing conclusions about the President. Starting with high hopes of him, I have found them sinking steadily, until it was with relief that I heard him take himself out of public life. A complicated and not a very nice specimen, he is clearly a self-destroying character, first unfortunately destroying a good deal around him. Our personal relations have been pretty tumultuous, but on the whole, good. I have not hesitated to say exactly what I thought—when asked—which he generally did not like, but accepted in fair temper and occasionally acted upon. His great trouble is being deflected by emotions from his principal purpose and losing his way. Tap knows all this very well.

But beyond him, I am depressed by the mediocrity of leadership everywhere—here, in England, on the Continent (even including the aging de Gaulle), the U.S.S.R., China, Asia, Latin America. No one rises above the level of what we used to expect of respectable mayors. I had a depressing talk with Schroeder two weeks ago, who agreed that nothing can be expected out of Germany as far as he can see ahead.

In our campaign I expect Hubert Humphrey to be nominated and elected. He is clearly the best offering we have and pretty good, though not so good as our difficult situation calls for. The columnists are all comparing 1968 with 1960 and giving the edge to Nixon, the challenger, as the counterpart of JFK. I do not agree, but would compare it to 1948 and give the edge to HHH as the counterpart of HST. The antiwar students and the antiliberal South and northern reactionaries make more noise than labor, but they don't have the votes. We shall see.

My book is entering the home stretch. I hope to finish the writing by Thanksgiving—an appropriate day—and then tackle the less interesting chore of checking, editing, and polishing. The publishers, W. W. Norton, are happily pleased with it.

Our warmest greetings.

As ever,

To JOHN COWLES

October 1, 1968

Mr. John Cowles
The Star and Tribune
Minneapolis, Minn.   55415

Dear John:

I too am pessimistic about Hubert's chances. I think he did himself some good last night, by which I mean that as a campaign speech I thought it was helpful. There was a residue of a few sensible ideas and a great many silly but appealing ones. From the point of view of his electoral effort I thought it was a plus. However, he has a long way to climb. The thought of four years of Nixon is just too depressing to dwell on. I cannot believe that it would be more. . . .

. . .

With affectionate greetings to you both.

As ever,

To THE EARL OF AVON (ANTHONY EDEN)

December 11, 1968

Lord Avon
Villa Nova
St. John
Barbados, W.I.

Dear Anthony:

This note covers two matters—plans for the winter and a request about the book.

Taking the second first, the main body of the book is finished and I am working now on a short part at the end with concluding thoughts. In my account of the visit which you and Mr. Churchill made to us in January, 1952, I would like to mention an aftermath of it that arose from *Newsweek*'s publishing a mischievous report of alleged difficulties between you and me. This led to a letter from me to you and to a heartwarming reply from you to me. I would like, if you see no objection, to include them in the book. So that you may see the whole setting, I enclose the text as it would appear if you approve.

We plan to go to Antigua on January 4 and have the house until February 7. We are trying, but may not succeed, to extend our escape from the northern cold for another week or so. We would love to have you and Clarissa with us at any time after the 20th of January, when some friends from New York will be leaving us, but I understand that this may put a strain or the possibility of a strain upon you which you may wish to avoid. How are you feeling and what do you think about a visit one way or the other? Would it be wise to take what a yachtsman might call a "lay-year"?

Today Mr. Nixon is to announce his Cabinet, which already has been announced in this morning's *New York Times*. I have never met one of them and have heard before the last few days of only two. This may prove that I am more of a recluse than I think or that they are an undistinguished lot. Understandably, I am inclined toward the latter view. The election proves that we have now joined the great mass of mankind in that our leadership is feeble and our people deeply divided. The latter, of course, is the result both of the difficulties of the problems first and the lack of help of any leadership in thinking about them. Perhaps it will not hurt the country too much to relax, if it is permitted to do so, from high endeavor. It may not hurt the Democratic party to let their opponents chew for a while on the problems we have not been able to solve. At best, the next four years are likely to be boring here in Washington. And next to worse, we may be scared to death.

Messages of deep affection go to Clarissa and you from both of us

As ever,

To J.H.P. GOULD

DA described here his first postelection meeting with President Nixon and his rather surprised impressions.

March 21, 1969

Dear "J":

I have just had an experience which will, perhaps, interest and amuse you. For the present at least it had better be kept confidential—which does not, of course, exclude Lee.

After the Gridiron dinner at which I sat with John and which we both thought was far too long for the material available, I went to the suite in the Statler where the Cowles publications were entertaining friends. There, to my mild surprise, I saw Mr. Nixon for the time surrounded. After talking with Tom Dewey and other friends, I saw Mr. Nixon alone. So, deciding to make the first overture to deescalate our ancient feud, I introduced myself and congratulated him on his ABM decision, which I thought right. He responded courteously and hoped that he would have another chance to see me. I replied that I would always be at his service, which ended the meeting which I thought we had both conducted correctly. Three days later Henry Kissinger called me to give me two messages from his boss. He would like to see me the next morning and he would like me to come to his dinner for the

NATO foreign ministers on Apr. 11th, for which I would receive a formal invitation in due course but which was not formally sent. This was surprising.

The day before yesterday I duly showed up at Henry's office—Mac Bundy's old one in the West Wing. We went up the back way through the Cabinet room and the secretary's room into the oval office. This secrecy amused me as the daily schedule of the President's appointments released to the press including mine had appeared and had brought me several calls asking what was going on. Since I had no idea, no one learned anything and no one called again nor had anything been said or printed about it.

The President was alone. We sat on sofas facing one another across an open fire, Henry beside RMN and remaining quiet throughout. I remarked the famous rocking chair used by JFK and LBJ had been banished. The President said their was nothing symbolic about that; he simply didn't like it and thought talk was easier when people faced one another. This led on to his talks with LBJ with their distractions and RMN's view that his predecessor would be treated more kindly in the future than at present.

Then we got down to serious business, first about Vietnam. The talk went on for a full hour without an interruption of any sort. In Johnson's day people were running in and out of the room, sometimes with notes which he answered, sometimes handing him a telephone—often he motioned a speaker to continue while he listened and spoke into the phone—sometimes people joined or left the meeting. Once he had three silent televisions going, one of a rocket blast-off. Nixon concentrated on the talk interjecting comments or questions, sometimes surprise as we went along.

At the end of the hour a secretary announced another appointment. He rose at once, said he had not allowed enough time and would ask me to come soon again. I got a feeling of orderliness and concentration rather than of Napoleonic drive and scattered attention.

As he began he said that he wanted to draw on my experience and advice without impairing my independence to do and say what I chose. It would be hard to do and I must be free to call it off whenever I chose. The only way to try it out was to begin and he would begin with Vietnam. He would state his views and ask me to criticize. They were not very different from my own except to expect that more might come out [of] the secret talks now beginning in Paris. To test out our views I went over the whole history of Vietnam since 1950 and picked out the departure from policy and great mistake as LBJ's decision in 1965 to get involved in a major way. However, I had supported it. The President added that he had, too.

Further analysis led to agreement that the object was to reverse this error; the means, to do less, to show that we meant to do less by the withdrawal of bodies, by increasing Vm capability and never being led to resume bombing the North. The South might be given a capability to rocket bomb Hanoi from the sea. This went on for some time analyzing difficulties.

Regarding negotiations I thought we might never get a North-South agreement—as we had not in Korea—so we should separate the political from the military—i.e., ceasefire—negotiations. Here our real negotiation was in the field, to show them they could not win as Ridgway had shown the Chinese on the Kansas line. Of course, they could always resume the war; but so could the Koreans and it would be another war. The point was to get our objective firmly in mind and pursue it relentlessly regardless of criticism. He seemed to agree; but one cannot tell until the crunch. I told him that LBJ's trouble was in flinching in a pinch.

We went on to a brief survey of NATO which he wishes to continue before the ministers arrive. Then a discussion of what and when to negotiate with the Russians. He thought they were worried on both fronts and this might be a good time. I thought not. Russians do not negotiate under pressure—only when the "correlation of forces" makes it seem to their advantage. Today there is nothing they need from us which we can afford to give. If we allow NATO to slide we will have given up the battle for nothing. He spoke of the Glasboro episode showing the hunger here for a settlement. So I said did the yearning for a heaven, but it proved nothing. We are to continue.

Then I said that I wanted to present an item and gave him a clipping from the morning *Post* saying that the State Dept would vote with the Afro-Asians to end the South African mandate over S.W. Africa although France and Britain would abstain. This was madness, I said, and I wanted to be heard. Henry agreed. RMN seemed to be receptive. HK was told to look into the report of which neither had heard.

As I walked away a guard of honor arrived to rehearse for Trudeau's reception. I thought I had spent a more useful hour than they would.

Alice has asked me whether I have in any way changed my opinion about Nixon. I said, Yes, it has been moved toward a more favorable one and in this process I am quite conscious that a change in his attitude from abusive hostility to respect with a dash of flattery has played a part. But why not? Both changes show that we are both practical men who on occasion, as Henry Ashurst of Arizona so wisely put it, can rise above principle.

Our affectionate greetings. Today is spring in Georgetown; crocuses everywhere; no coats; no hats.

To **WILLIAM R. TYLER**

Tyler was about to leave the Foreign Service and become Director of the Dumbarton Oaks Research Library and Collection of Harvard University. In this letter, DA appeared hopeful, but cautious, about President Nixon.

March 21, 1969

Dear Bill:

Alice and I are thrilled by your news. You should have a delightful and satisfying life at Dumbarton Oaks and we shall have you both back again and close by. It was a brilliant idea of Nathan Pusey's. We shall look forward to welcoming you back to Georgetown next September.

My book is finished—a statement not wholly true if it is taken to mean that I am finished with my book. The writing is done; the business of seeing it through the press has begun. W.W. Norton is publishing it. We hope for bound volumes in mid-August and publication in October. The months between are going to be pure hell and hard, boring labor. The book covers my years 1941–1953 in the Department focused on the Truman postwar policies set in a broad historical ambience. I think you will like it. At least, it is not dull—that is not often.

Two days ago to my surprise I was called to the White House and had a twin surprise. Mr. N impressed me favorably; and our talk was relaxed, serious and informative both ways. He told me his views on many matters frankly, and learned some inside history which he did not know. I thought him sensible and so far as we went on the right track. He seemed away ahead of his party and his public self. This raises problems of credibility which we shall have to wait and see about. But compared to what we have just had, it seemed like spring to me.

. . .

Our affectionate greetings to Betsy and you.

As ever,

To **HENRY KISSINGER**

DA here followed up his attempt to persuade the Nixon Administration to adopt a policy toward Southern Africa that allowed a greater margin for major premises which differed from those of the United States.

March 25, 1969

Dr. Henry Kissinger
The White House
Washington, D.C.

Dear Henry:

The other day, when the President was talking with us, he said very wisely apropos of Southern Africa that in our relations with other nations we should be more concerned with whether they follow foreign policies that are compatible with ours than with whether they follow domestic policies that some of us would prefer (though others might not). This pamphlet reports some developments in South African foreign policy highly beneficial to its black neighbors which we might well encourage rather than join in silly resolutions in the United Nations, which only annoy without accomplishment of any sort.

Yours,

To LAURENCE C. EKLUND

DA was made aware of objections to an honor that was proposed for him and defended himself in his patented style.

July 9, 1969

Mr. Laurence C. Eklund
Washington Correspondent
The Milwaukee Journal
Room 734
National Press Building
Washington, D.C.

Dear Mr. Eklund:

You ask me whether the comments about me by Mrs. J. Martin Klotsche, wife of the Chancellor of the University of Wisconsin, and Mr. Bruno V. Bitker, an attorney of your city, as published in your paper, affect my decision to come to Milwaukee on October 10. You kindly enclose a clipping.

Mrs. Klotsche is reported quoting her august husband that I am "an old hack." The Klotsches undoubtedly have a point in their adjective. I have passed the biblical span and must admit to seventy-six years, the age at which President Tyler was married for the second time. However I am still under the domination of my only wife, and although Methuselah would regard me as a stripling, I will not quibble about the accusation of age. "When the clock strikes sixty," writes Duff Cooper, "old age begins."

However, an old "hack" is another matter. Undoubtedly, what is meant is a drudge, although Webster has half a column of synonyms including a "short broken cough," a "carriage for hire," a "prostitute," and a "caboose," the tail end of a freight train. Clearly the Chancellor had in mind an undistinguished member of the older generation as against one of the brilliant young leaders who have helped him bring the University of Wisconsin to public attention in the recent past. His opinion is one that I can understand under the circumstances. That he should hold it does not hurt my feelings sufficiently to keep me away from Milwaukee.

Mr. Bitker's objection is directed against alleged conduct of mine which, he says, has contributed to world unrest by encouraging nations to "rely on armaments" to settle disputes. He wants me to be confronted by "someone of equal stature, so that he [i.e., Acheson] can support his position of brute power against someone supporting world peace through law."

Frankly, this charge surprises me. I had thought my record was pretty good. The Acheson-Lilienthal Report on the International Control of Atomic Energy furnished the basis of our proposals to the United Nations in 1946 which the Russians turned down. In 1951 I presented to the General Assembly the Anglo-French-American proposals for the Reduction and Control of Armaments. Mr. Vishinsky's response was that they kept him awake all night by the laughter they provoked. As a lawyer I have appeared twice at the Peace Palace in The Hague as counsel in cases to settle international disputes through adjudication. World peace through law would be fine if all aggressors would obey law—in other words, cease to be aggressors, as unhappy Czechoslovakia learned once from Hitler and now again from Brezhnev. From the earliest times in our history we have believed in God and kept our powder dry. "Praise the Lord and pass the ammunition!"

It is fashionable to deprecate power: hence, Mr. Bitker's pejorative phrase, *"brute"* power. Does the policeman's power or St. Michael's sword represent "brute" power? Without American power we might have peace—a Soviet peace through Soviet law supported by Soviet "brute" power. No, Mr. Bitker will not keep me away from Milwaukee.

I may well be unworthy of the honor your city proposes to confer upon me; but I am deeply grateful and propose to come there and say so.

Sincerely yours,

To SIR ROY WELENSKY

Welensky had twice been Prime Minister of Rhodesia. He and DA carried on a wide-ranging correspondence and DA was at this date planning a trip to Southern Africa which illness twice prevented.

August 28, 1969

His Excellency
Sir Roy Welensky
P.O. Box 804
Salisbury, Rhodesia

Dear Roy:

. . .

Broadly speaking, the country seems to me to be in a conservative mood. After the war and the long innovative Roosevelt period before it the country started a swing to the right. The Republicans took the Congress in 1946. In 1948 Mr. Truman retained the presidency, largely on his own personal performance and Mr. Dewey's lackadaisical one during the campaign. The trend to the right continued and culminated in the eight Eisenhower years. In 1960, as in the last campaign, neither candidate had much appeal, but unrest was growing and elements in the population that are now clearly evident were restless and reacting strongly against the dead hand of ultra-conservatism. The next eight years, chiefly the last five under LBJ, and the impact of the Warren Court brought about startling innovations that upset the South, the more conservative trade unions, businessmen, and the suburbanites. This reaction is still continuing; and if Nixon had more imagination and more energy, he could capitalize on it most successfully.

The present Washington scene is a puzzling one. The Administration is made up on the whole of pretty good men, intelligent, high-minded, conservative, but wholly inexperienced in government and—so it seems to me—naive beyond words. They apparently have not settled on any firm decisions. Action seems to go by starts, stops, and movements to either side. It is a series of indecisions and wobbles. If the Administration would focus its mind on three principal issues—Vietnam, internal order, and inflation—it could, I believe, easily expand its present minority position in the center by accretions from right and left into a majority position. What is required are quite simple actions aimed at fairly short-range objectives. The great trouble seems to be the absence of any objectives.

In the broader international view, I see problems and frustrations ahead for us, due to changes in the power situation that put obstacles in the way of either substantial agreement with the Soviet Union or successful opposition to its obvious policies. Take, for instance, two very difficult problems in the way of reaching agreement. One is the entrance of China into the list of nuclear powers; the other is Russia's predominance in intermediate ballistic missiles in Europe. It might be possible for the Russians and ourselves to so limit our nuclear capabilities that neither would have a first strike capability and both would have a second strike capability (both of which merely mean the same thing). But when each of us begins to add a capability to deal with China, it impresses the other as an attempt to unbalance such a result. Furthermore, even though some method is found for dealing with this, the problem of Russia's superiority vis-à-vis Europe remains and in the long run must surely impair American influence in Europe and increase Soviet capacity for blackmail. These are worrying questions. If one tries to find the answer to them, in the political or economic fields, one discovers sooner or later that agreements in these areas cannot produce an answer to a power superiority.

When I talk like this here, people call me a Metternich born out of time. And yet they have no satisfactory answers, except a rather evangelistic belief in the perfectibility of man, which I cannot share.

Put these thoughts in your pressure-cooker and cheer me up before or when we meet.

Alice joins me in warm regards to you both.

As ever,

To JOHN KENNETH GALBRAITH

Galbraith had reviewed Present at the Creation. *DA's letter thanks him, but a sharp edge is detectable.*

October 21, 1969

The Honorable Kenneth Galbraith
30 Francis Avenue
Cambridge, Mass.   02138

Dear Ken:

You are as good as your word; indeed, even better. "I must repudiate Acheson," you said, "but shall embrace his book." You gave the book a very warm embrace and me only a mild repudiation. The net was a good plus, for which I am grateful.

Many thanks also for your book, which Bill Bundy (who is temporarily with us) snatched from me. However, I read enough to know that I shall enjoy it and to gain an idea that it was better for both of us that our respective tenures did not overlap.

With warm regards.

Most sincerely,

To STANLEY ANDREWS

Andrews was a private consultant on agriculture and economic development about to visit Vietnam.

October 31, 1969

Mr. Stanley Andrews
Route 1, Box 52-AA
Alamo, Texas 78516

Dear Stanley:

Your letter of October 9 was a most welcome one. Please when you come back from Vietnam write me again and tell me your impressions. One hears here that things have improved, but—as you say—that has been said before with little justification, so one is inclined to doubt. In March '68, when LBJ asked me for an opinion, I refused the customary briefings and asked for what Mr. Charles Evans Hughes called "the papers," the operating officers' reports. They showed a very different state of affairs than one heard from Westmoreland or the Ambassador. It seemed to me that we had to reverse course without delay. LBJ could not make up his mind to do so wholeheartedly and destroyed both himself, HHH, and the Party. I think that Nixon is doing and will do much better.

Your firsthand views would be enormously helpful.

My book when it gets to Texas—as it surely will—will recall old days for you.

With warm greetings.

Sincerely yours,

To CLEMENT HAYNSWORTH

President Nixon had nominated Haynsworth, a reputable federal appeals judge in South Carolina, to the Supreme Court. His nomination having been rejected by the Senate, DA wrote to him to share the philosophy of one who had also undergone political attack without submitting to distress.

November 27, 1969

Dear Judge Haynsworth:

Almost twenty years ago when our country was facing disaster in Korea and I myself was under heavy attack, a wise colleague wrote me a private note. "In international, as in private life," it said, "what counts most is not really what happens to someone but how he bears what happens to him."

It is very true. I have read in the press that you are considering resigning from the bench. The inclination is a natural one but please do not follow it. Please go on with your work and continue to show the world the course of an honorable and just judge, which your colleagues and so much of the bar know you to be. This is the course followed by your distinguished predecessor Judge John J. Parker to universal esteem.

Forgive this intrusion into your personal affairs by a stranger but well wisher.

Sincerely yours,

To **PAUL E. ELLIS**

DA responded here to a previously unknown correspondent seeking expert advice.

April 15, 1970

Mr. Paul E. Ellis
Rt. 1, 322-A
Huntersville, North Carolina

Dear Mr. Ellis:

Yours is no trivial problem, as anyone must agree who has dealt with a mustache for half a century. I have tried all the aids to handling the wretched thing that I can find, with varying degrees of success and disaster, from some that gave me an acute skin rash to the one on which I have now settled for a great many years. This is a wax that comes in a tube with the following lines on one side of it:

> Pomade
> Hongroise
> Professional Use Only
> Paris Ed. Pinaud

I have bought it in many drug stores and do not find it hard to come by. For a long time I have been puzzled by the meaning of the line, "Professional Use Only." In the case of mustachioed gentlemen, how do you tell the amateurs from the professionals?

The mystic words I use in asking for it are "Ed. Pinaud's white mustache wax." It comes also in brown and red. I hope this may be of some help to you.

Sincerely yours,

To **JOHN COWLES**

DA's philosphy leaned strongly toward leaving the internal affairs of other countries alone, as a principle of U.S. foreign policy.

April 21, 1970

Dear John:

From all sides we hear glowing accounts of your cruise on the "Giriz" and of the magnificence of the yacht. Even "J" Gould with his cracked ribs is enthusiastic. He tells me that he is giving those cracked bones a chance to knit by laying off croquet for a while.

You kindly ask about my eyes. I think they are what the doctors quaintly call "stabilized"; that is, they are not getting any worse and they are not likely to get very much better. Some new prism glasses help me greatly with reading and more distant looking, but it is suggested that I do not get adventurous enough to drive, at least not in city traffic. I have been trying to get someone to do that for us.

As you will see from the enclosure, our battle over relations with Rhodesia goes on. In this current issue of *Rhodesian Viewpoint* I lead off and the Minneapolis *Tribune* is quoted along with other editors commended for their wisdom. How this matter is coming out I do not see. One effect of the sanctions is already becoming clear. In both Rhodesia and South Africa the pressure is moving the white communities toward the right. In Rhodesia Ian Smith won all the white seats in Parliament. The forecast for South Africa is that in their election this week Mr. Vorster's Nationalist Party will probably maintain its present large majority but that pressure thereafter will either move him to the right or weaken him in favor of the break-off rightist party. This seems to have been the history of splits in the Africaaner Party. So far the right has always profited. We are most unwise to encourage this result.

Our love to you and Betty.

As ever,

P.S. In December I ordered for you and Betty a copy of K. Clark's "Civilization." Our copy has just come. Harper & Row published it.

To **J.H.P. GOULD**

Apart from a bizarre anecdote, this letter put the Middle East tensions in a fair perspective and accurately forecast another outbreak of fighting, in which Israel took painful losses.

April 21, 1970

Mr. J.H.P. Gould
Tamarind
Mill Reef
Antigua, W.I.

Dear "J":
    What wretched luck to get your ribs cracked on your delightful cruise.
You must have been bucking into some pretty good seas to have been
thrown around so vigorously.

. . .

    Your quotation of the Sunday *New York Times* of April 12 about my
speech in Independence is very amusing. On arriving at the airport at Kansas City, I met two old friends from the press, who told me that they would
not be present at the exercises but would like to have an advance account of
my speech so that they could file their reports in advance. I told them that I
did not expect to make a speech. They said that I certainly would; and, in
any event if I did make a speech, what would I say? To please them I made
up a speech. This they duly reported and added for verisimilitude that I received prolonged applause. In fact I made no speech whatever.

. . .

    I very much fear that John Leslie's views on the Middle Eastern situa-
tion have no very firm foundation. I presume that when he talks of Israelis
and the Palestinians he means by the latter the Palestinian Arabs now in the
conquered part west of the Jordan and their fellow countrymen on the other
side. The differences between these two parties are among the most difficult, but in some respects the least [sic: most] important of all the problems
in this troubled area. They involve the dreadful problems of Israel if it aban-
dons its Jewish religious theory of a state in favor of incorporating almost as
many Arabs as Jews in a secular state to which none of its citizens would
owe much loyalty. But the real trouble is the unresolvable hostility to a Jewish state of the other Arabs, driven on by Nasser, and the unwillingness of
the Jews to sacrifice any element of their present strategic situation for
promises of future good behavior by their enemies. Underlying all of this is
the desire of the Russians to keep all the animosities aflame so that the
Arabs will nationalize our oil interests and let the Russians act as manager
and exploiter of this vast oil reserve.
    Finally, I see a grave difficulty in the way of any American policy that
would appeal to the Arabs arising from the fact that we in this country have
the world's largest Jewish population, which owns a great deal of our press
and electronic media, whereas there are few, if any, Arabs living here. The

idea that the Russians, British, and French would ever agree with us upon a policy to be imposed on the Middle East situation seems minuscule and the possibility of our being able to impose it rather less than that.

As I think I said to you this winter, it seems to me that another bout in the Middle East war is inevitable, but this one may be more prolonged than those that preceded it and more costly for the Israelis, and that possibly mutual exhaustion may put a new aspect on affairs. I see little else that is likely to do so.

As ever,

To JOHN COWLES

DA's views on Southeast Asia were invited by Cowles's specific questions.

May 5, 1970

Mr. John Cowles
The Star and Tribune
Minneapolis, Minnesota

Dear John:

I am glad to do the best I can with your questions:

1. Nixon was, I think, most unwise to send our troops into Cambodia. This new version of the search-and-destroy strategy, I think, is bound to lead us a chase around Cambodia. The chances of cornering any substantial number of enemy forces seems small. The whole oratory of the Presidential broadcast seemed to bear little relation to the importance of the mission. Meanwhile the university population is getting more and more upset, the market is declining, and the Nixon Administration is getting into more and more trouble. I fear that his judgment is very bad.

2. I am not seeing the President regularly. In fact I declined to attend a meeting at the White House with him tomorrow, making it clear that, since I disagree strongly with the policy, I could not be of any help.

3. The CIA did not play any role in the overturn of the Cambodian government. They did not have anyone in Cambodia at all.

4. I think that it would be very hard to catch up with any substantial group of enemy troops in Cambodia. The country is very large and is a very difficult area in which to operate. I am told that the President does not intend to keep our troops there; and unquestionably, if that is the case, the enemy is likely to come back when the troops leave. My worry would be that it is easier to send our troops in than it is to get them out.

5. I doubt whether the President is very much moved by clichés like "saving face." The dialectics are quite likely to be wholly different from the real motivation. My guess is that he is being pressured in very much the same way that LBJ was.

6. Again, and for much the same reason as given above, the word "Vietnamization" causes far more confusion than anything else. The purpose that I had understood was being followed for the last year was to withdraw our own troops steadily and to build up the equipment, training, and morale of the South Vietnamese, to bring home to them that we were in truth withdrawing and that they would have to be on their own very shortly. It was also to make clear to them and to our own people that we were giving the South Vietnamese the best chance we could to take care of themselves; that, having done that, we could and would not do any more. It was not and should not be our purpose to force the Vietnamese into a compromise of any sort. Whether they could survive or not was to be left to them, and we were not to make any compromises for them. We were, I thought, perfectly clear that we were going to withdraw and that no Vietnamese were going to control our policies in Asia.

7. I assumed that for a short time we would maintain a few, say thirty to forty thousand troops, in a strong base on the coast. If these were not attacked, they would contribute to the maintenance of morale for a time. If the war continued, they could be withdrawn with strong naval and air pro)ection. It seemed that this was the best choice available and might just possibly work. The worst course would be to wobble without clearly expecting to leave and devoting all our energies to achieving that purpose.

As ever,

To SIR ROY WELENSKY

DA expanded in this letter upon President Nixon's decision to mount a military expedition in Cambodia and touched upon other puzzles.

June 30, 1970

The Right Honorable
Sir Roy Welensky
P.O. Box 804
Salisbury, Rhodesia

Dear Roy:

I have not written you for some time since I have had the misfortune of being ill this spring. Through a series of mischances—undertaking too much, minor illnesses, etc.,—I got pretty tired out and run down, resulting in a slight stroke that put me in the hospital for a couple of weeks and will take me out of circulation for somewhat longer. The physicians have canceled my trip to Africa and have rusticated me until the autumn. This I am trying to take in a fatalistic way, enjoying what good weather we have and not getting too depressed at the direction that affairs are taking in the world at large.

. . .

Since I wrote you last, our government has taken a new dive into Southeast Asia's quagmire. When I came back from Antigua, I was assured by what the press call authoritative sources—indeed, the most authoritative of all—that we would continue with the policy of withdrawal and would not be drawn into any adventures in Cambodia. Then Sihanouk very foolishly left his own country and opened the possibility of a *coup d'état*. My own information is that almost all advisers within our government, except unfortunately the Ambassador and the General in the field, shared this view. However, Bunker and Abrams thought that the short-run military advantage exceeded the very serious internal division that deeper intervention would produce. The President's judgment was, I think, wholly wrong in this respect. I doubt that he can resume the policy of withdrawal, which was going forward pretty well; that is, I doubt that we can make up what we have lost by extending the war forty miles or so to the west, thereby saddling the unfortunate South Vietnamese with still greater responsibilities. The so-called sanctuaries have been there for years and are no more serious now than they were some time ago. The President seems to suffer from the malady of a farmer in South Carolina who was a client of Jimmy Byrnes's when the latter was a young man at the bar. The farmer kept buying land to the point where Mr. Byrnes warned him that he would soon become hopelessly financially involved. The man voiced surprise at the warning and said that he had no mania for land; that all he wished to acquire was the property that adjoined him. This seems to me Mr. Nixon's weakness.

What I find hardest to do is to remain calm and cool when decisions on all sides seem to be wrong and getting us into increasingly more complicated and more frustrating predicaments. The country desperately needs what the Constitution defines as one of our primary domestic needs—domestic tranquility. Instead, each new adventure stirs up the youth, the blacks, the women, and inflation. I am enclosing, as you requested, and as I meant to do some time ago, the final version of my Air University speech in May. From this you will see that I am not so far from you as you might imagine in your view of the large and disturbing contribution that women are making to change in American society.

The purport of my speech, as you will see, in its final revision, is that the cumulative changes over the last half century have had major effects. These are colossal in magnitude and bewildering in extent and speed. Nobody really knows where they stand, especially our politicians, in trying to adjust themselves to them.

With warmest regards.

As ever,

To SIR HOWARD BEALE

Beale had recently reviewed Present at the Creation *in Australia.*

August 17, 1970

The Right Honorable Sir Howard Beale
P.O. Box 4516
G.P.O. Sydney, Australia 2001

Dear Howard·

Thank you very much for the interesting account of your travels and your far more than generous review of my book. I was deeply touched by what you said about it and about me. It is a great comfort to have so loyal a friend who will perjure himself like a gentleman to help me out. I am glad to say that the book continues to do well. It is now being put out in paperback and the publisher is also doing several sections of it in small paperback volumes for school and college use. The Korea war is already in the works and I think the Marshall Plan and NATO will follow.

You are quite right. I think that the world not only seems to be going to hell in a hack but is actually going there. Somehow or other we will get out of Southeast Asia without leaving too many of our tail feathers in the door jamb. My real worries center about Willi Brandt's foolish flirtations with the Russians and Rogers' even more foolish ones with them in regard to the Middle East. These two escapades will, I fear, cost us dearly. The Russians are hell-bent on supplanting the British and ourselves in the Middle East, gaining control over the management of Arab oil and thereby getting a hold on the economic life of Europe, and reopening the Suez Canal to gain a position in the Indian Ocean. Some day a good many people will be looking around for someone to blame. Arthur Balfour and the British are hardly worthwhile blaming and I fear their eye will fall on Mr. Truman and the establishment of Israel. They really ought to blame themselves. It is the American passion for keeping the peace. I am not in favor of involving ourselves in Middle East fighting, but I would not be averse to supplying the means by which others were involved. It seems a little foolish to help the

Russians get control of the situation by doing in the Israelis.

Last week we had the pleasure of seeing Bob and Pattie Menzies, who were resting up for a day on their way, via Honolulu, to Melbourne. Bob, I regret to say, was not looking well—greatly overweight and with only a portion of his old verve. To see one's friends get old brings one's own condition home to one even more acutely than the mirror.

Our love to you and Margery,

As ever,

To **SIR ROY WELENSKY**

President Nixon's role in the Congressional election of 1970 had dashed the hope which DA had briefly entertained, that Nixon had outgrown his partisanship. DA gave Welensky a stark view of U.S. and world leadership.

November 16, 1970

Dear Roy:

This past month has been a most bothersome and disillusioning time, out of which has come only one encouraging aspect, the demonstration that widely scattered parts of our people can spot the worst sort of political nonsense and repudiate it. I am enclosing three pretty keen bits of postelection analysis, which seem to bear this out. The worst part of the election, however, has been to destroy the illusion that the President and his advisers were maturing and gaining the ability to identify our real and growing problems and to pull us together in dealing with them. Mr. Nixon under election pressure ceased to be a national leader and reverted to his earlier tendency to become an unlovely political adventurer of rather poor judgment. This is disturbing in the face of puzzling and adverse developments at home and abroad.

We are going to face the need here—as Heath will in Britain—of dealing with the economy, and especially the labor side of it, to check the continuing inflation and provide for continuing military and civil needs despite the SALT talks and the slowing of military needs in Southeast Asia. I see no signs that the Administration sees any such need, or, indeed, any need equal to that of its continued hold on the White House two years from now. My own party is disorganized, bankrupt, and without first-class leadership. . . .

In the overseas world developments are eroding our power and position. Russian energy, time, and development of nuclear physics will move us to very considerable effort and expense to maintain a standoff, infinitely less favorable than our position in the fifties and sixties, which by a breakthrough on the other side could leave us dangerously weakened. Latin America is drifting toward alignment against us—Cuba, Chile, Guatemala—when aid and confiscation have been exhausted. Russia's position of interior lines to Europe, Africa, and Asia will be hastened and strengthened by success in the eastern Mediterranean and control of Arab oil. Europe is already moving eastward after the pied piper led by France, Germany, and Italy. The Sixth Fleet and the army in Germany could become hostages rather than outposts.

This is not inevitable; but it is the direction of drift, and of feckless leadership. It will take better leadership than any I see here to make up for the total absence of any in Europe. Furthermore only rarely is the ability of democracies to concentrate great enough to permit of dealing with more than one great foreign problem at a time. Europe has the very difficult one of fitting Britain into the Common Market; we have that of getting out of Vietnam. Neither of us can really focus on our mutual relations in less than two years. We can drift far in that time.

. . .

With these cheerful thoughts and warm greetings, I leave you for a time.

Yours ever,

To T.C. BRYANT

DA stated his thumbnail appraisal of General de Gaulle.

December 1, 1970

Mr. T.C. Bryant
1811 Rusk
Houston, Texas 77003

Dear Mr. Bryant:

Thank you for sending me the clipping of Joseph Alsop's column on General de Gaulle. I share the opinion that he was a great man and brought about a near miracle for France, but I deeply regret and deplore the havoc he wreaked on European unity.

With kind regards.

Sincerely yours,

To J.H.P. GOULD

DA's wry mood touched both personal and public matters in this note.

December 3, 1970

Mr. J.H.P. Gould
Mahkeenac Farm
Lenox, Massachusetts 02140

Dear "J":

I was delighted to get your news from Antigua. We are looking forward keenly to our visit there next year. Your remark about . . .'s demise reminds me of an observation of Judge Holmes's some time in the twenties, when we were talking about a report out of Chicago that two gangsters had shot and killed one another. Holmes observed that reports such as this always led him to believe that society was well served.

I am being drawn back without enthusiasm into Presidential consultations. Last week I met with Jack McCloy's committee, which advises the President on disarmament and similar questions, to discuss our lack of policy toward Europe. On Monday McCloy, Tom Dewey, Lucius Clay, and I will meet with the President on the same matters. I do not expect very much to come out of it. The photostat of Jack McCloy's letter to me will show you with what levity the views of this elder statesman are received.

Our love to you and Lee.

As ever,

To COUNTESS DÖNHOFF

DA was highly critical of Chancellor Willi Brandt's "Ostpolitik" policy, that of seeking separate political accommodations with the Soviet Union.

December 16, 1970

Countess Marion Dönhoff
Editor-in-Chief
Die Zeit
2000 Hamburg 1
Pressehaus, Germany

Dear Countess Dönhoff:

Thank you very much for your note of December 8 and for your touching "Lament for East Prussia." Hardly had you written your note than I repeated at a luncheon given for me by some journalists a few of the views I had discussed with you. It caused more of a flurry than I had expected. Indeed, your Ambassador called on me to express his pain and to try to correct my errors.

My disagreement with what the German Government is doing is based on the positive harm I think it is causing to interests that the United States and its allies in Europe, including Germany, have held for twenty years, and pursued with varying degrees of determination. Our common interest is in the development of a united Europe with the strength that comes from common interests, carried out by common means and common policies, including common political purposes vis-à-vis the Soviet Union. These have been gravely prejudiced by the separatist policies of France. The attempt of Germany to ease the lot of East Germans by separate recognition of the *status quo* is not only an exercise in futility but divisive of united policies both within Europe and between Europe and North America. Germany, as the manager of the alliance in negotiating a settlement with the Russians will not be followed. I see no more likelihood now than in earlier periods for any improvement in access or other recognition of interests except Russian or East German ones. Discussions with the Soviet Union have to have a solid base of European-American unity or they can only divide the countries of Europe and Europe from America. Therefore, the Chancellor's efforts, in giving sanction to Russian demands for the division of Europe, seem to me to be harmful. To regard his efforts as primarily a matter of German politics is wrong.

My best wishes for the Christmas Season and the New Year.

Yours ever,

To **JOHN COWLES**

Cowles was too ill to make his usual winter visit to Antigua. DA sought to cheer him up and give him an appraisal of the Nixon Administration.

Mill Reef Club

Antigua, West Indies

January 12, 1971

Dear John:

This is a saddened place as the result of the report from you on the state of your health. Antigua without you is even more forlorn than Hamlet without the Prince. The purpose of our days is gone. No more "perfect positions" are called for. No more conversations are managed. Very little Scotch is drunk. The sparkle has gone out of our days.

. . .

My sad, current conclusion is that the present Administration is the most incompetent and undirected group I have seen in charge of the U.S. government since the closing years of the Wilson Administration. No one is evil, whatever some may think of Agnew, just plain ignorant and incompetent.

My main point, however, is to tell you how much you are missed by devoted friends and to wish you well.

Yours ever,

To J.H.P. GOULD

DA's last winter vacation turned out badly and led him to doubt that he would repeat his visits to Antigua, annual since 1953.

Caneel Bay Plantation
February 25, 1971

Dear J:

To all my friends and companions at Antigua a fond farewell for 1971. This part of it ended in a collapse of the flesh on the part of us both. Alice led off with a bad cold caught on the way here which over the weekend she passed on to me. We both took the message hard and have put in bad and boring days.

A cold in the Caribbean makes life a burden. We are now ready and glad to go home to the land of ice and snow from which only the vanity of man led him to try to escape his fate. We hope you succeed.

Our love to you all. What we shall do another winter must await the renewal of hope and faith in a better world.

Yours ever,

To J.H.P. GOULD

DA had completed a television interview for the British Broadcasting Corporation, dealing with the 1962 Cuban missile crisis, among other things.

2805 P Street
Washington, D.C. 20007
April 15, 1971

Dear J:

. . .

Here is my BBC broadcast interview which has been well received. One friend, Jock Balfour, writes of its recalling to him the chill of the missile crisis and the limerick which ran:

There was an old man who cried, "Run!
The end of the world has begun!
The one I fear most,
Is that Holy Ghost.
I can cope with the Father and Son."

Spring is creeping in with many a backward glance and icy blast of farewell from winter.

Love to Lee,

To **THE EARL OF AVON (ANTHONY EDEN)**

DA reflected here upon the Nixon Administration's opening to the People's Republic of China.

May 8, 1971

Dear Anthony:

Your television remarks were very good and very sensible. The television discussion here has been, as so much of our public discussion is, most volatile. One day China is Public Enemy No. 1; the next, our dearest friend. Bernard Lewis of London Univ. made the wise observation before Sen. Jackson's Committee that one of the first requirements in a stated foreign policy was to be able to distinguish your friends from your enemies.

General Marshall regarded Chou En-lai as one of the ablest men he had ever dealt with. Away ahead of Chiang. The ping pong gambit is already being used by him to draw a line between the friendly American people and the unfriendly American government. I doubt whether he cares anything about the U.N. except as a stick to beat us with—and a good one it is. Our State Dept. has filed a brief in the World Court describing South Africa as "in belligerent occupation of S. W. Africa" in defiance of the U.N.

If China is represented in the U.N. by Mao, then Chiang is in belligerent occupation of Taiwan and we are in defiance of the U.N. Years ago when Foster Dulles was foolish enough to get us into a treaty with Chiang I urged that while we could still control the U.N. Assembly we get it to recognize Chiang's government as the government of Taiwan and admit it to the U.N. without prejudice to claims to the status re China. Now that seems to be impossible.

The other day I pointed out to a group that the two-China policy did not solve practical problems any more than did acceptance of plural marriages. Moslems and Christians agreed on the latter; but Moslems believed in them simultaneously, while Christians believed that they must be engaged in successively.

. . .

To **SENATOR BARRY GOLDWATER**

At Goldwater's invitation DA stated here his views upon executive and legislative prerogatives in military action, a subject with which Congress was much preoccupied at that time.

May 18, 1971

The Honorable Barry Goldwater
The United States Senate
Washington, D.C.

My dear Senator:

You flatter me in your letter of May 8 by saying that my views will be helpful to you in thinking about the problem so much discussed on the floor of Congress these days as to the proper rights and powers of the executive and legislative branches of the government in taking military action to protect the interests of the nation. The predominant desire in the Congress seems to be for legislation, whereas you tell me that you are thinking that perhaps a constitutional amendment might be the better course.

As you requested, I read your thoughtful memorandum and also the longer and more formal statement that you made before the Senate Foreign Relations Committee. Somewhere in one or the other of these documents I think you said that personally you were satisfied with the situation as provided for by the Constitution. May I say that I, myself, heartily agree with this view and would be very sorry to see the present constitutional provisions altered by either legislation or constitutional amendment. Let me say why I am of this opinion.

More than a hundred years ago Alexis de Tocqueville commented that, because we had a written constitution and because so many members of Congress were lawyers, sooner or later every political question in the United States was turned into a constitutional question. This is preeminently true of the question that the Congress is spending so much time discussing at present.

You are entirely right that over the life of the nation Presidents have exercised the powers now being exercised, most often without opposition in the Congress and very often with judicial sanction. There can be little doubt that, if the Congress wished to stop any use of military power, it could do so by legislation or the lack of legislation, by which I mean either refusing funds or limiting the numbers of troops or certain dispositions of them. This is not done either because the Congress does not wish to undertake the responsibility or because a deadlock between the two branches of government concerned with the execution of foreign policy would bear most unfavorably upon the interests of the nation.

Instead, Americans like to argue about what they call legal machinery to deal with situations that have to be dealt with, ultimately, by human wisdom. There is a story told about former President Taft, after a talk with President Hoover, reporting that he had just come from a discussion of what Hoover called "legal machinery," adding, "And, you know, Hoover thinks it really is machinery." Today computers make us all the more likely to believe that some intricate procedural arrangements can take the place of good judgment. The Founding Fathers did not think so. They did not need the experience of Uruguay to teach them that to put executive power into committee is a way of paralyzing action. The executive power of the United States *is* vested in the President of the United States. He *is* the commander in chief, and in him is vested—and rightly vested—the power to conduct our relations with foreign states and, when necessary, to use force to protect the interest of the nation.

Very often Presidents will consult the Congress and obtain legislative approval of what they have done or are about to do. Sometimes the exigencies of the moment do not permit this. President Johnson did it when the Tonkin Gulf resolution was passed, and I see no reason to believe that Congress would have acted any more wisely if it had postponed its decision for thirty days, as some are now proposing. On the other hand, President Truman exercised his executive power at the time of the invasion of South Korea. It was his judgment, in which I heartily concurred, that, at a time when the South Koreans and our own troops were fighting desperately to maintain a foothold on the peninsula, he had no alternative but to act. To have debated the propriety of the fighting either when it began or thirty days later, when it was even more desperate around Pusan, would not have been in the national interest.

Any attempt to spell out procedural requirements and limitations on executive power will tend to make rigid that which must be flexible. If the President and the Congress are to assume attitudes of hostility, the nation in this modern world will be subject to grave perils. The separation of powers is not based upon the premise of their fundamental hostility. Criticism and restraint are contemplated in the workings of the system, and can be accomplished. The present legislative proposals do not seem to me to provide for this, but, instead, by setting up a series of rigid rules, to limit the powers of the President beyond safety and to give the Congress, by inaction, what the Constitution never contemplated, a veto upon executive action.

I think this about expresses my views. If I can be of any further help to you, please do not hesitate to call upon me.

Most sincerely yours,

To JOHN COWLES

In this letter and the next, DA reported his successful effort to organize influential men of both parties to defeat the Mansfield Amendment. That legislation would have required reductions in U.S. commitment of troops to NATO.

2805 P Street
Washington, D.C. 20007
May 21, 1971

Dear John:

. . .

We have had a fine old ding-dong fight down here in which those of us who rallied to the President's side have been subjected to a degree of vilification unequaled since the McCarthy days. It has been great fun and resulted in a most satisfying victory. I got a charming note from RMN in which he said that I could now justly claim to have been present both at the creation and the resurrection. The liberals will excommunicate me for good when they learn that I have lunched with Mr. Agnew.

This period is reckless and bitter as the first thirty years or so of the Republic.

Yours,

To SIR ROY WELENSKY

888 16th Street, N.W.
Washington, D.C. 20006
June 2, 1971

The Right Honorable Sir Roy Welensky
P.O. Box 804
Salisbury, Rhodesia

My dear Roy:

. . .

The appearance of both of us old crocks on a far more controversial stage than my last appearance with my NATO comrades to support the President and oppose my mad Democratic friends in the Senate should stir up quite a tempest in a teapot. This came about by Senator Mansfield, the majority leader, calling up his long-dormant resolution to reduce our NATO forces by half and trying to tack it onto the draft extension act. The White House was ambushed and panicked. Talk of compromise flew about; I was called on for suggestions and urged a battle royal with no quarter asked or given, starting off with a meeting at the White House of all the old NATO guard, soldiers and civilians from Truman days on, to support a short statement by the President, which at his request I drafted.

It went off well, led by the two former Presidents, Secretaries of State, Supreme Commanders, and so on, plus an assist from Brezhnev's statement about negotiations for mutual force withdrawals from Europe. The liberal press attacked us as antediluvian cold warriors. Mansfield was defeated 63 to 22. Afterward the President wrote me a note saying that, while I was the only one of the group "Present at the Creation," we all might claim to have been present at the Resurrection. I replied that the suggestion was a reassurance since the Press seemed to have cast me for the role of both thieves at the Crucifixion for whom there was no such sequel.

. . .

My guess at this point on the 1972 election here is that minimum good sense and luck on the President's part would bring him in going away almost by default.

I hope your travels refreshed you.

Warmest welcome back to our correspondence.

Yours,

To JOHN COWLES

DA regarded as shoddy and unprincipled the conduct of The New York Times *and the* Washington Post *in publishing the "Pentagon Papers," known to have been filched from government custody.*

July 30, 1971

Mr. John Cowles
The Star and Tribune
Minneapolis, Minn. 55415

Dear John:

Thank you very much indeed for your letter giving me your views on the fascinating *Case of the Purloined Papers*. As I wrote you at the time, I did not expect you to agree with me and so was not surprised when you did not. Furthermore, your views have been brought home to all of us pretty thoroughly in all the editorial pages that come my way.

I thought the other day and wrote to my friend, Anthony Avon, that I have spent my life among professional men who were deeply convinced by a sense of mission. My father's profession retained the imprint made by the laying-on of St. Peter's hands. My own profession believes that it is the guardian of law, which they regard as quite as important as religion. Indeed, they talk of world peace through world law. And my friends of the Fourth Estate, who are many, believe that their crusade is to protect suffering humanity from all governments everywhere, even if in so doing they usher all of us into a well-intentioned state of anarchy.

However, my views, I am told by your former employee, Carl Rowan, are anachronistic; indeed, he compares them to those of former slaveholders and quite rightly thinks that I have no message for what he calls the "common man." I would add the "uncommon man" also, a description of most of my friends, at the forefront of whom I place you.

I continue to keep busy. Two books are coming out next month, which I shall send to you and I have a few more papers destined for the *New York Times* OpEd page.

We have been having so far a quite bearable summer, as I hope you have had too. We think and speak of both you and Betty often. Please give her our love.

As ever,

To **MICHAEL DIGIACOMO**

DA described here his expanded definition of education.

August 5, 1971

Mr. Michael DiGiacomo
152 Pondfield Road West
Bronxville, N.Y. 10708

Dear Mr. DiGiacomo:

Perhaps the best way to answer your question about the best schooling and prior experience to be helpful to a future President would be to recount something of an interview I had with former President Sachar of Brandeis University, who is now giving some lectures over educational TV on contemporary history. He read me an introductory statement he was making about President Truman in which he expressed astonishment that a man who had never been formally educated beyond high school should have been such an outstanding success in the White House.

I told Mr. Sachar that I found his view totally wrong. I thought President Truman's earlier education excellent and, instead of stopping after he was through high school, it continued on through his later life. Mr. Truman's eyesight was so bad that games which required seeing at any distance were precluded. When he was not working on the farm, he told me, he read all the books in the little library in Independence. This included three entire encyclopaedias. He became deeply interested in geography, history, and biography. His experience as the County Administrator in the important county seat of Kansas City was the presidency in miniature, with foreign affairs reduced to dealings with the sovereign state of Missouri. He learned how complicated was government and how different from the thoughts of it that are usually brought to government positions by lawyers and businessmen. He understood the difficulties of administration, which are more judicial in their nature than most people realize. He understood the frustrations of the governmental process. Here the elements of command and authority are greatly diluted both by conceptions of the operation of power and those of democracy itself. He had training in decisiveness. He did not, in General Marshall's phrase, "fight the problem," but solved it.

Well, I think you begin to get my idea. One can float through four years at the most distinguished university listening to lectures by scholars whose experience was largely limited to learning how to be scholars and lecture to students, and learn very little.

Here endeth the first lesson.

Sincerely yours,

To **PHILIP C. JESSUP**

In this note DA recalled one of the milestones in the long gamesmanship series between Justice Frankfurter and Wilmarth Lewis.

August 11, 1971

The Honorable Philip C. Jessup
Council on Foreign Relations
The Harold Pratt House
58 East 68th Street
New York, New York

Dear Phil:

The quip about the NYT is delightful and new to me.

Your note on The Crillon pad reminds me of a long game between Felix and Lefty Lewis. On a visit to FF's chambers Lefty purloined a Supreme Court memo pad and thereafter wrote FF notes on its paper. FF told me about it and said he would test Lefty's self-restraint by making no reference to the paper in answering the notes. Lefty saw the challenge and continued blandly using the pad. Of course, in time it was used up. When this became clear FF and I conferred with the result that FF sent without note or comment another pad in a Supreme Court envelope. This broke Lefty. Thus do great jurists and scholars amuse themselves.

. . .

Love to Lois.

As ever,

To **ARCHIBALD MACLEISH**

DA referred here to his original view that opposed Under Secretary Joseph Grew's wish to retain in office the Emperor of Japan. In Present at the Creation *DA stated that he was quite wrong and Grew right. After reading part of David Bergamini's book* The Imperial Conspiracy, *DA feared that his "recantation" might not be as solidly founded as he had thought.*

August 15, 1971

The Honorable Archibald MacLeish
Uphill Farm
Conway, Massachusetts 01341

Dear Archie:

My recantation is noted at the bottom of page 112 and at the top of 113 in "Present At the Creation." It was based largely on the fact that the occupation of Japan went so smoothly that I concluded, I think rightly, this was because the emperor system was left intact and MacArthur was largely put on top of it. As you read Bergamini's book (I have finished Volume I) I think you will conclude that this was in part due to the fact that he did not bring about any fundamental change in Japan, although he did bring about a good many useful changes. I wonder whether it would have been possible for anyone to have brought about basic changes if one had destroyed the system and started over again. Another wonder is whether if a fundamental change did occur, it would have been in the direction of communism rather than the imperial system. I am not defending my recantation but merely admitting that I am not as sure about it as I was before reading the book.

I remember in 1950, before advising President Truman to go ahead with the kind of treaty we actually wrote and to terminate the occupation, I got John Allison to take the views of all of the Far Eastern experts and let me know the general opinion as to what the chances of keeping Japan allied to us would be. He reported that the consensus was not better than 50%. In Germany, where we tried the opposite tactic and destroyed both the Nazi regime and the German state itself, I am not sure that we have accomplished any more lasting result.

. . .

This is enough for one day.

Love to you both,

To **WALLACE CARROLL**

The reference here is to the journalist James (Scotty) Reston's hospitalization in China, while Henry Kissinger slipped in and out of Peking concealed by his hosts from Reston's reporter's eye.

August 17, 1971

Mr. Wallace Carroll
P.O. Box 3157
Winston-Salem, North Carolina 27102

Dear Wally:

We would love to go with you to the concert of Moravian music at the Kennedy Center on Sunday afternoon, September 12. We would be even happier if you and Peggy would stay with us at Harewood while you are here.

MacLeish writes me: "I've been reading Scotty-in-China with delight—particularly the acupuncture scene. There is a man dogged with luck: no thing more fortunate could have happened to him on arrival than that appendix. It put him really *inside* in 24 hours."

However, I find another aspect of Scotty-in-China even more amusing. On what you journalists call unimpeachable authority I learn that Scotty's plans to travel from Canton to Peking ran into an unexpected mix-up and delay. While all this was being cleared up amid profuse apologies to so august a member of the American establishment, another traveling more obscurely slipped in and out of Peking. When Scotty got there only what Archie calls the "acupuncture scene" awaited him behind the chrysanthemum curtain. Which proves a profound and disturbing truth: even a Scotsman is no match for a Chinaman in ways that are dark and tricks that are vain. Back to the forage, presbyterianism and fencing stolen property for those denizens of the barren wastes of the north.

Our love to Peggy.

Yours ever,

To **ERIC SWENSON**

Eric Swenson was DA's editor at W.W. Norton, publisher of Present at the Creation.

August 25, 1971

Mr. Eric Swenson
W.W. Norton & Company
55 Fifth Avenue
New York, N.Y. 10003

Dear Eric:

Thank you for *Eleanor and Franklin*. I have read some and will read more, but Eleanor was such a do-gooder that I found her very hard to take. Curiously enough after FDR's death, when she was on her own and not intriguing behind the scenes, I liked her much better. In 1951 she went to Paris on the delegation to the U.N. meeting. There she was a good trooper. When Warren Austin had a stroke and I had to go to Rome for a NATO meeting I left her in charge of the delegation. There were several items in our instructions with which she disagreed, such as keeping the Chinese Communists out and Chiang's crowd in, but she loyally carried out the official line. I was amused to read her note to FDR saying that the State Department with Clayton, me, and Stettinius was as bad as Dewey would have been. She lived to know better when Eisenhower put Dulles in.

· · ·

Yours,

To MATTHEW H. FOX

DA, as former public servant and currently active private researcher, gave his views here on security classification of government papers.

September 1, 1971

Mr. Matthew H. Fox
Research Associate
The Twentieth Century Fund
41 East 70th Street
New York, N.Y. 10021

Dear Mr. Fox:

· · ·

You ask my views of the security classification system, which you have been "researching" since January. Too often research means turning over the documentary manure in departmental barnyards rather than preparing the seeds of thought one wishes to fertilize. The issue often is made to be between the bureaucrats' desire for protective secrecy and the public's and scholar's need and right to know. Neither, I think, are valid interests in a broad sense, but I shall return to them as well as to the preference given to former officials in preparing memoirs. These are all of secondary importance.

Government officers in nearly all fields need protection from publicity and outside (public) interference in studying, discussing, and making decisions on most matters, certainly at early stages. This is clear in diplomacy and defense. It is also true in NIH decisions on priorities in medical research and the same in Agriculture on the study of pests. Indeed, in most work—governmental, business, and professional—the importance of privacy outweighs the contribution of over-the-shoulder kibitzing. . . .

So I would say to the researcher, get your values straight before you start and, in doing so, don't believe all you read, hear, and see about need for a democratic system to know all, see all, and have a cloud of witnesses participate in all to report it daily. I would reverse most folk beliefs in this field.

Furthermore, the incredible multiplicity and fecundity of record communication devices make person-to-person communication nearly impossible. The XYZ papers nearly involved the United States in war with France and they were handwritten and published by the government. Today the *New York Times* would have had them before they were dispatched. When in 1949 we negotiated the end of the blockade of Berlin only five persons in the United States knew the matter was under discussion and, as I recall, no written record was made until agreement was ready for release. It is hard for me to believe that arrangements for Mr. Kissinger's journey to Peking could have been made through any agency in the United States.

There are thus some matters regarding which privacy, often amounting to complete secrecy, is desirable or essential. For these, high classifications and stiff official-secrets-act penalties are necessary, though some I would not trust to paper at all and would share with very few people. Some of these papers—or, at least, their substance—need remain secret only for a fairly short time, until, for instance, the Berlin agreement and Council of Foreign Ministers Meeting of 1949 was announced.

Other papers require to remain closed for varying lengths of time and to have varying security classifications. Generally speaking I would reach some gentleman's agreement on a closed period for communications between foreign statesmen to encourage candid discussion. Twenty-five years does not seem excessive unless earlier consent is given. Where it seemed necessary to get out a White Paper that might be harmful to foreign diplomatic personnel, editing might be necessary.

As I look back over my own experience in public office, I am impressed by two factors bearing on the time the general run of papers should be closed to public examination. One is the period after which there is little danger the disclosure of these papers would impair the public interest. The other is the longer period when the sensation monger—politician, journalist, or self-styled scholar—would be tempted to embarrass a public official by something he had written under different circumstances. The former I would put at about ten years; the latter at, say, fifteen. I don't mind particularly people being embarrassed in later life; but I should regret their being cagey and over-cautious when young. The classification of the highest secrets should be reviewed after fifteen years.

In sum, this is a hard problem and not as important as articulate liberals would make it appear. The scholarly victims of the "publish or perish" doctrine don't warrant much concern. It is easier to modify the system that pinches them. . . . As for former officials as memoir writers, they have something special to offer, as many historians have told me. The why of many events, the decisive why, is apt to survive only in their memory. The use of documents to me was most important more as a corrective to memory than as a supplement. My memory, I find, is often very clear and at the same time mixed up, sometimes putting people at places and meetings at which they were not present or as taking positions taken by others. The memoranda taken at the time straightens out a sometimes involved sequence. Furthermore, an active imagination or twice-told tale often creates the equivalent of Sam Morison's "Flyaway Islands," which bedeviled the early cartographers. If it isn't in the record, the memoir-writer should doubt it.

To JOHN COWLES

DA here expounded his view (by 1979 rather orthodox) that inflation's causes and cures (if any) are political rather than strictly economic.

September 1, 1971

Mr. John Cowles
The Star and Tribune
Minneapolis, Minn. 55415

Dear John:

In order to get you some of my views on Mr. Nixon's latest performances, I am sending you a xerox of a letter to Roy Welensky in which I have set them out.

I quite agreed with you that the present temporary wage-price freeze is not going to stop inflation. To do that will require more prolonged controls, which I am not sure we are capable of instituting. If we should be capable of doing so and did it, I, like you, cannot imagine the ultimate consequences. Some time ago Phil Reed sent to me, and I think also to you, some material on how to stop inflation, including, I believe, some excerpts from the *Wall Street Journal*. They seemed to me pretty sound and also very difficult to accomplish.

The question really gets back to what elements in the population are in control of the country, what they wish to accomplish, and whether what they do will accomplish what they wish. Salazar in Portugal was employed by and represented the officer class of the Portuguese army. He conducted the economy of the country in the interests of the middle class and possibly the upper middle class. His support came from the army. He never forgot it and the army never forgot that only he could accomplish what they wanted.

In this country we have gradually extended the franchise so that it is complete universal suffrage over the age of eighteen, with no requirements of any sort, except that a prospective voter must not have been convicted of a felony.

Beginning with the New Deal, the law, both as enacted by Congress and interpreted by the Supreme Court, has given increasing power to organized labor and has increasingly advanced the standards and demands of the lower economic groups, while the progress of technology has decreased the opportunities for employment. The control of industry is not in the hands of those who own it, but of those who manage it. The result is that the economic controls are in the hands of people hired on the one hand by labor and on the other hand by stockholders. Collective bargaining between the two groups of hired managers results in steadily and rapidly increasing wages, followed by increasing prices. This, as I see it, is the heart of the inflationary process. There is no mechanistic, fiscal, or monetary formula that can correct this. It is a question of power within the society and what group or combination of groups is exercising the dominating power.

To control inflation, the middle class should become conscious of its interests, articulate and sophisticated enough in the use of power to restrict and manipulate our almost total democracy, elect people who will serve its interests, and will not cheat on them by buying support of outside groups. This, as you can see, will introduce greater authority into government than the various formulators of opinion are willing to accept or than the present interpreters of the Constitution will enforce. This, I think, is the problem in a nutshell and a very tough one it is.

Yours ever,

To CARL B. SPAETH

Here, DA's thanks for reading material and criticism of the product are mixed.

September 10, 1971

Professor Carl B. Spaeth
Director, Center for Research in International Studies
Stanford University
Stanford, California 94305

Dearl Carl:

My thanks go to you and Mr. George. I must confess that I fell at the first jump on page 2. There I was told that the NSC system "reduced some of the dysfunctional consequences associated with the freer play of 'bureaucratic politics,' " although "sub-units of the Executive Branch tend to engage in 'quasi-resolution of conflict' and to avoid uncertainty in relation with each other by means of 'negotiating the internal environment' within the organization." This brought to mind a remark of the late President Vincent of the Rockefeller Foundation that much academic discussion could be summed up by one colleague saying to another, "You hold the sieve while I milk the barren heifer." Seeing 66 more pages to follow, I pled a dwindling life expectancy and quit.

. . .

With warm greetings.

Yours ever,

To **WALLACE CARROLL**

Wallace Carroll was at this time Editor-Publisher of The Winston-Salem (N.C.) Journal and Sentinel.

September 23, 1971

Mr. Wallace Carroll
Piedmont Publishing Company
Post Office Box 3159
Winston-Salem, North Carolina 27102

Dear Wally:

Thank you so much for going to the immense trouble of sending me all the papers in the school cases. Either because I read them in the evening or because they were pretty jumbled up, I did not get a clear impression of them. It was sufficient, however, to let me say that I agree with you that the Chief Justice stirred up a lot of unnecessary trouble.

I find the whole idea of judicial government repulsive and also the idea that by busing thousands of children back and forth for several hours a day one does much to help education or to bring about integration over a long time. I would think this has to be dealt with by enlisting the aid of legislatures, both federal and state, to deal with both living patterns and school construction, rather than by forcing one or the other into the present procrustean bed.

We loved seeing you.

As ever,

To ARCHIBALD MACLEISH

In answer to MacLeish's questions, DA stated here the basics of the U.S. Government's abrupt financial measures relating to the "trading partners" of the U.S.

October 1971

Dear Archie:

You flatter me by your questions. My views, derived from talks with wiser men in a suburb of Sandy Spring, are about as follows:

Question one—August 15th. Due to a mixture of our own mismanagement (about three-quarters of the total cause) and unhelpful contributions from Europe and Japan (about one quarter) drastic action was called for. RMN took this without consultation with what are called our "trading partners." This is the first point of controversy. The phrase is a deceptive color phrase. They—Western Europe, Canada and Japan are not trading partners but more competitors, like fellow poker players. To have discussed the moves with them would have frustrated them. Japan, France do not discuss their proposed courses with us except when they are to be purely negative. The Japanese are indeed today as positively deceitful about doing nothing as they were about planning positive action in 1941. So I approve RMN's tactic of surprise and secrecy.

The action consisted of "floating" the dollar (i.e. refusing to redeem it in gold or attempt otherwise to maintain an exchange rate with other currencies), imposing a 10 per cent additional import tax on dutiable items, and ordering (under Democratic legislation) a price, wage and dividend freeze. The last was for 90 days only; the first two were said to be "temporary" until our trading partners agreed on monetary arrangements which would bring about a $13 billion reversal in our balance of payments. This was a shocker, too much and a David Harum bargaining opener to impress the other players that this was a game for and by professionals. It has been said that the float and the tax should have been alternative and not cumulative measures. I thought so at first but have since been convinced that the floating of the dollar could have been largely circumvented—as the Japanese have done by exchange transactions. The 10 per cent import tax was a linebacker of formidable proportions.

These actions could if maintained too long without a bargain produce retaliation, trade wars, etc. They could be habit-forming like liquor—a danger which does not deter many of us. So far Connally's handling of the performance has impressed me as very skillful and effective. I am not worried that he will overplay his hand. He is as rough, tough and ruthless as the Japanese, Germans and French (the British are scared into not alienating the last two until Common Market decisions are behind them).

. . .

Yours ever,

INDEX